Ius Gentium: Comparative Perspectives on Law and Justice

Volume 52

More information about this series at http://www.springer.com/series/7888

Rainer Arnold
Editor

The Convergence of the Fundamental Rights Protection in Europe

Springer

Editor
Rainer Arnold
Faculty of Law
University of Regensburg
Regensburg, Germany

ISSN 1534-6781 ISSN 2214-9902 (electronic)
Ius Gentium: Comparative Perspectives on Law and Justice
ISBN 978-94-017-7463-5 ISBN 978-94-017-7465-9 (eBook)
DOI 10.1007/978-94-017-7465-9

Library of Congress Control Number: 2016935508

Printed on acid-free paper

This Springer imprint is published by Springer Nature
The registered company is Springer Science+Business Media B.V. Dordrecht

Preface

The protection of the individual by Fundamental Rights is the main subject of modern constitutional law. In Europe, various protection instruments exist, national constitutions, the European Convention of Human Rights (ECHR) and, for the Member States of the European Union, the EU Fundamental Rights Charter. These guarantees are legally autonomous but functionally interdependent and even interactive. The strongest influence seems to be exercised by the jurisprudence of the European Court of Human Rights on the interpretation of the national constitutional texts as well as on the EU Charter. The accession of the EU to the ECHR will strengthen this process.

It is a noteworthy phenomenon that the protection of the individual is progressively intensified and courts interpret the scope of civil rights in a broad sense. Substantive and functional efficiency is a requirement that flows from the anthropocentric approach of modern European constitutionalism. Fundamental rights constitute a comprehensive order of values to be interpreted in a way which gives efficient protection to the individual. Even if there is no explicit right, the judges, in particular the constitutional judges, have the obligation to complement the text by interpretation. Functional effectiveness means in particular that the legislator is prevented from restricting fundamental rights without limitation. Modern constitutionalism requires the legislator to observe the principle of proportionality as well as to respect the very essence of the right.

A further important phenomenon of European constitutionalism is that fundamental rights become increasingly convergent. Jurisprudence on the various levels of protection take notice of the understandings of other courts and compare the own approach to them. The Strasbourg Court takes a leading role in this convergence process.

This book tries to analyse various aspects of this process. The first contribution (*Rainer Arnold/Eva Feldbaum*) reflects on the phenomenon of convergence of fundamental rights in Europe and makes reference in this context to Germany, United Kingdom and France.

The second contribution considers human dignity as the ideological and legal basis of all fundamental rights (*Antonio-Carlos Pereira Menaut/Maria Carolina Pereira-Sáez*).

The Spanish Constitution expressly requires that the interpretation of the national fundamental rights has to adapt to the international jurisprudence, in particular to that of the Strasbourg Court. Thus the Constitution opens itself towards an Europeanization of their own provisions which is significantly reflected by the constitutional jurisprudence. Europeanization implies fundamental rights convergence to an important extent (*Pedro Julio Tenorio Sánchez*).

The Italian jurisprudence on Fundamental Rights is also particularly significant for the multilevel context in which rights are interpreted. *Luca Mezzetti* presents a comprehensive analysis of this phenomenon.

How the principle of equality and non-discrimination has been functionally enlarged by influences of supranational concepts is examined in the study of *María Cristina Hermida del Llano.*

The Nordic countries' approach to Fundamental Rights under the influence of the ECHR is subject of the contribution of *Joakim Nergelius.*

The Constitutions of the New Democracies take fundamental rights seriously. Manifest expression is the Europe-oriented constitutional jurisprudence analysed for Poland by *Bogusław Banaszak* and for Romania by *Bianca Selejan-Guţan.*

Turkey's Fundamental Rights approach is largely examined *by Selin Esen* and *Merih Öden.*

The international influences on the Fundamental Rights provisions of the new Constitution of Kosovo and the instruments of protection before the Constitutional Court are intensely studied by *Arbëresha Raça Shala.*

The rights protection on the level of the European Union itself is the concluding subject which is treated generally in a contribution by *Viktor Muraviov* and *Olena Sviatun*, and in a specific study on Article 36 of the EU Fundamental Rights Charter by *Jiří Zemánek.*

Regensburg, Germany
May 2015

Rainer Arnold

Acknowledgments

I would like to thank for their efficient help my collaborators Jessica Pham, Stephanie Lodola, Bethany McGhee, Stefan Nigam from Cambridge University, Lisa Poth and Samuel Cross from Oxford University, Nevila Saja from Albania, Timothy Wojewódka from Poland and from Germany Sebastian Seefried.

I also want to thank the Springer Publishing House, in particular Diana Nijenhuijzen, for continuous support of this project.

Contents

About the Authors

Rainer Arnold Dr. Dres.h.c. Professor at the University of Regensburg, in 1979 appointed holder of the Chair of Public Law, in 1999 nominated holder of the Jean Monnet Chair of EU Law and in 2008 holder of the Jean Monnet Chair ad personam "Legal Relations of the EU with Central, Eastern and Southeastern Europe". Nominated in 2000 hostujíci professor at the Charles University Prague. Corresponding Member of the Academy of Sciences of Bologna, Membre titulaire de l'Académie international de droit comparé, Fellow of the European Law Institute, in 2008 Fernand Braudel Fellow at the European University Institute, Fiesole/ Florence, former Visiting Professor at the University Paris I (Panthéon-Sorbonne), Paris II (Panthéon-Assas), Strasbourg, Toulouse, Rome La Sapienza, Bologna and others.

Bogusław Banaszak Prof. Dr. Dr. h.c. mult. Bogusław Banaszak, Dean of the Faculty of Law and Administration at the University at Zielona Góra. Holder of the Chair of Constitutional Law at this University, former (2006–2010) President of the Legislative Council of Poland, Professor at the University Viadrina/Frankfurt/Oder (1998–2008) and at University of Wrocław (1977–2014), International Awards, Author of numerous publications, such as *Konstytucja Rzeczypospolitej Polskiej – Komentarz (Constitution of Republic of Poland-Commentary).*

Selin Esen Professor of Constitutional Law in the Ankara University, Law Faculty. She was an academic consultant in the Constitutional Reconciliation Committee that was formed by the Turkish Parliament to draft a new constitution during 2012–2013. She is the member of the executive committee of the International Association of Constitutional Law and the vice president of the Asociación Mundial de Justicia Constitucional. Her research area includes judicial review, fundamental rights and freedoms and comparative constitutional law. She has several publications on secularism, political parties, constitutional complaint, Internet freedom, freedom of movement and emergency regimes.

Eva Feldbaum Dr., studied law at the University of Bayreuth with an additional qualification in economic science and a mediation certificate. From 2010 to 2013 Eva Feldbaum acted as a lawyer in Nuremberg; since then for Steinbeis School of International Business and Entrepreneurship where she has become Director of the SIBE Law School in 2014 with the key areas of International Law, esp. negotiation and mediation. In the same year, Dr. Eva Feldbaum obtained her doctorate at the University of Regensburg with a thesis on the British Law and the European Convention of Human Rights.

María Cristina Hermida del Llano Tenured Professor of Philosophy of Law at the Rey Juan Carlos University, Madrid (Spain). Alexander von Humboldt Foundation Fellow. Decoration of Honour in Gold for Services to the Republic of Austria. Prof. Jean Monnet. Leader of the European Module entitled "Integration and Fundamental Rights in the European Union". Corresponding Academic of the Royal Academy of Jurisprudence and Legislation of Madrid.

Luca Mezzetti Ph.D. in Constitutional Law, Full Professor of Constitutional Law at the Faculty of Law of the University of Bologna (Italy). President of the Italian Section of the Iberoamerican Institute of Constitutional Law. Director of the High School of Legal Studies at the University of Bologna. Professor of Constitutional Law at the University "L. Bocconi" of Milan. Visiting professor at several foreign universities. Member of the scientific committee of several Italian and foreign law reviews. Member of the Italian Agency for Anticorruption.

Viktor Muraviov Prof. dr hab., Chair of Comparative and European Law, Institute of International Relations, Kyiv Taras Shevchenko National University.

Joakim Nergelius Professor of Law at the University of Örebro, as well as Assistant Professor of Comparative and European Law at the Abo Academy, Turku (Finland) since 2003. He has also worked at the EU Court of Justice and the Committee of Regions and has published extensively in matters of European Constitutional Law.

Merih Öden Professor of Constitutional Law in the Ankara University, Law Faculty. He worked as rapporteur-judge in the Council of State during 1977–1981. In 1996, he conducted a research project in the USA under the Fulbright Program. His research area includes judicial review, fundamental rights and freedoms, comparative constitutional law and constitutional theory. He has several publications concerning the principle of equality, judicial process, political parties, parliamentary elections, women's rights and emergency regimes in Turkey.

Antonio-Carlos Pereira-Menaut Jean Monnet Chairholder of EU Constitutional Law, U. of Santiago de Compostela. Co-author, with C. Cancela, of *Re-setting the EU Constitutional Engine* (Regensburg, 2012).

María-Carolina Pereira-Sáez teaches Philosophy of Law and EU Law (University of A Coruña, Spain). She has lectured/given papers/made research in Britain, Portugal, Germany, US, Brasil, Perú, and Argentina. She has authored ***La autoridad del derecho. Un diálogo con J. Finnis***, (Granada, 2008), co-authored ***Teoría General del Derecho*** (Bogotá, 2013) and written a number of book chapters and review articles.

Arbëresha Raça Shala Dr., State Prosecutor at the Basic Prosecution Office in Prishtina from September 2014 to current. Meanwhile she is also engaged at lecturing at the ISPE College in Prishtina and in the Public University "Hasan Prishtina", Faculty of Economics. Before becoming Public Prosecutor, she has been working as a Secretary General of the Constitutional Court of the Republic of Kosovo from September 2009 until September 2015.

Bianca Selejan-Guţan PhD (Bucharest), LL.M. (Nottingham), is a Professor of Constitutional Law and Human Rights Law at the Law Faculty of the Lucian Blaga University of Sibiu, Romania. Her main areas of research are judicial review, comparative constitutional systems, and European law of human rights.

Olena Sviatun Ph.D., Associate Professor of the Chair of Comparative and European Law, Institute of International Relations, Kyiv Taras Shevchenko National University.

Pedro Julio Tenorio Sánchez Professor of Constitutional Law at the UNED; Legal advisor of the Constitutional Court of Spain (2001–2011); 14 books published (authored or coauthored); more than 50 articles published in legal journals; over 110 lectures at Harvard, Brussels, Salzburg, Miami, San Francisco, Reykjavik, Regensburg, Bologna and Rome, Houston, Albuquerque, Los Angeles, among other places; Doctorate by University of Bologna; Visiting Scholar at Stanford University.

Jiří Zemánek JUDr. Ing, CSc., Judge at the Constitutional Court of the Czech Republic; Jean Monnet Chair of European Law at the Law Faculty of Charles University, Prague; former Vice-Dean for External Relations, Managing Director of teaching programs "Czech Legal System in European Context" (Erasmus) and "Introduction to German Law"; former member of the Council for legislation of the Czech Government; member of the academic forum "European Constitutional Law Network" and of the Board of Advisors of European Constitutional Law Review; former president of the Czech Branch of ILA and Czech-ECSA.

Aspects of Fundamental Rights Convergence in Europe with Some Comparative References to the Developments in Germany, United Kingdom and France

Rainer Arnold and Eva Feldbaum

Abstract In the field of Fundamental Rights a process of convergence is going on in Europe. There are three protection levels which are autonomous but functionally interconnected: the national constitutions, the European Convention of Human Rights (ECHR) and, for the member states of the European Union, the EU Fundamental Rights Charter. A total convergence comes into effect when the EU Charter applies in the member states, alternatively to the national Constitution. The impact of the ECHR on the signatory states' orders leads to a *relative convergence* by conceptual transfer. In Germany, the national fundamental rights have to be interpreted in the light of the ECHR independently from its internal rank equivalent to ordinary federal law. In UK the Human Rights Act has established a mechanism which effects the adaptation of legislation to the jurisprudence of the Strasbourg Human Rights Court. In France, Article 55 of the Constitution gives the ECHR primacy over internal legislation. The accession of the EU to the ECHR is not yet been realized but the influences of the Strasbourg jurisprudence are significant. The EU Charter has to be interpreted, in important parts, in the light of the ECHR. It seems justified to state that fundamental rights in Europe undergo a significant convergence process.

R. Arnold (✉)
Faculty of Law, University of Regensburg, Universitätsstr. 31, 93053 Regensburg, Germany
e-mail: jean.monnet@gmx.de

E. Feldbaum
Steinbeis University, SIBE Law School, Albrecht-Dürer-Platz 4, 90403 Nürnberg, Germany
e-mail: feldbaum@steinbeis-sibe.de

R. Arnold (ed.), *The Convergence of the Fundamental Rights Protection in Europe*, Ius Gentium: Comparative Perspectives on Law and Justice 52,
DOI 10.1007/978-94-017-7465-9_1

On Convergence Processes

Convergence of Law in Various Forms

The transnational convergence of law is a phenomenon with various appearances. Convergence can be effectuated through the transfer of a different order by direct reception which leads to total convergence or by a functional transfer of principles and concepts.

aa) *Total convergence* is exceptional and is connected with the direct applicability of norms stemming from a different legal order. An example may be the application of the European Union Fundamental Rights Charter (EU FRCh) into the national legal order in case of implementation of EU law by the member states. The Charter applies directly, as is provided by its article 51.1, instead of the national Constitution. The relationship between the Charter and the member states' Constitutions is alternative and not cumulative as is the case with regard to the European Convention of Human Rights (ECHR). This form of total convergence of the fundamental rights protection results from the fact that it is a convergence by substitution, the Charter replaces national fundamental rights.

The fact that the exact border between the field of application of the Charter and that of the national Constitution is not yet completely clarified[1] does not hinder the statement that the application of the Charter is an example for first mentioned form of convergence in the field of fundamental rights.

In this context, beyond the question of the Charter's application, an obstacle to total convergence might result from the recent tendency of EU member states constitutional courts to limit the primacy of supranational law over the national constitutional order by declaring national "constitutional identity" to be sacrosanct (FCC 2009, para. 208, 218–219, 226, 239, 240–242, 331–332, 339–340 etc., Arnold 2014a). Supranational law shall not have the power to override the identifying core elements of the national Constitution.

As the identity barrier has been erected against a too far-reaching impact of EU law on the national Constitution it could be used as a means for keeping the Charter concepts outside in order to conserve the "home made" constitutional basics. In such case convergence in the field of fundamental rights would not be total but limited.

We can state that total convergence in form of a direct normative reception of the fundamental rights protection from a different autonomous legal order as the supranational order takes place in strongly integrated units but is subject to conflicts to a greater degree than the other convergence processes connected in particular to the impact of the ECHR.

---

[1] See the allegedly opposite positions of the Court of Justice of the EU (CJEU) particularly in the case Åkerberg Fransson (2013, para. 19–31) on the one hand and the German Federal Constitutional Court (FCC) in the case Antiterrordatei (FCC 2013, para. 88) on the other hand. See Burgorgue-Larsen 2013.

It is not yet foreseeable whether relativizing processes will also take place in the supranational order, such as the recognition of national margins of appreciation which we see in the development of the less strongly integrated relationship between the ECHR and its signatory states. The Omega decision of the ECJ (ECJ 2004) could be understood as a first step in this direction. Total convergence would then be transformed into a form of functional convergence.

bb) The European Union complements the fundamental rights protection by the Charter with general principles of EU law, as article 6.3 TEU says. These principles stem both from the ECHR, which is not yet internationally binding on the EU but gives it a normative orientation, and the common constitutional tradition of the member states. The harmonizing potential of these references to the Convention and to the member states' Constitutions is evident. This functional connection between the supranational, conventional and national levels (Arnold 2009) is an important form of convergence building. The European Union is the receiving part insofar as it receives inspiration from the national orders and from the Convention while it actively creates convergence through the effect of its general principles on the member states orders.

The general principles of Union law (Grabenwarter and Pabel 2013, art. 6, para. 86–93) have binding force, in a complementary way to the Charter, on the EU institutions as well as on the member states when they implement EU law. In this respect, the general principles also substitute the national fundamental rights protection. By this, convergence effectuated by the general principles has the same origin and structure as convergence effectuated by the Charter.

Both, Charter and general principles have both an active, convergence – constituting function and a passive, receiving dimension which consists adopting conceptual impulses from other legal orders. Both aspects contribute to the formation of convergence.

General principles are based on the transfer of national and conventional concepts into the supranational order, a transfer which ends up in a selection process for making them fitting into the structure and finality of the EU. This comparative-selective adaptation creates autonomous EU law convergent with the main sources of constitutional law in Europe.

A similar statement can be made for the Charter which is autonomous primary law of the EU, although inspired by a whole range of European protection systems, the Convention, the national constitutions, the European Social Charter and EU law itself. It can therefore be regarded as a European Charter by convergence.

The Charter as well as the general principles are, by their functional origins, products of constitutional law convergence and do affect themselves, convergence by substitution, with high functional power, in the spheres of the member states.

Convergence is created by a plurifunctional process with adaptations, modifications and transformations. The process of adopting concepts from a different order and integrating them into the EU fundamental rights, the Charter or the general principles through interpretation, does not lead to a re-transfer of identical concepts to the member states in the moment when they are applied to them. This is a transfer of Europeanized concepts to the member states. The adaptation of the original concepts to the EU structure and finality when transformed into EU law principles has originated new, autonomous concepts although they bear similarities to the transferred ones since they stem from a common constitutional culture and tradition.

The Charter has however been created as an autonomous source of EU law, through the inspiration from a spectrum of the various important fundamental rights protection systems in Europe. In this context the double dimension of the convergence process is equally manifest: different concepts melted together and transformed into supranational law which substitutes, when applied, different constitutional protection systems. This creates convergence by establishing one European text from various inspiration sources and thereby replacing various national fundamental right systems with this text.

Despite the autonomous character of the Charter it upholds the link to its inspiration sources through interpretation. Convergence with the ECHR is ensured by of for example chapter "Fundamental Freedoms and Rights in Contemporary Europe" of the Charter which is drawn from Art. 6 and 7 of the Convention in the light of the Strasbourg jurisprudence. Convergence by interpretation on the basis of the constitutional tradition common to the member states necessarily means Europeanization of the relevant fundamental rights of the Charter. The interpreter has to select on which concepts in which of their forms the interpretation should be based. A selective-critical perspective as to the various approaches to constitutional jurisprudence of the member states has to be applied in a similar way as has been done for the determination of general principles (ECJ 1970, para. 3, 4). It can therefore be stated that the field of fundamental rights is particularly relevant for convergence processes.

cc) A further article should be taken into consideration: art. 2 TEU. This provision enumerates the values on which the European Union is founded and which are common to EU and member states: human dignity, freedom, democracy, equality, the rule of law and the respect for human rights, including minority rights. These values are regarded as being interconnected with a society characterized by pluralism, non-discrimination, tolerance, justice, solidarity and equality between men and women. The very basis of fundamental rights is thereby recognized, human dignity, the principle of freedom and equality, values which also constitute the basis for rule of law and democracy.

Article 2 TEU has a dual character: it constitutes the EU value order, therefore is one of the pillars of the EU constitutional structure, and it obliges the member states to be based on the same values, an obligation to be ensured by the Union. This provision is therefore simultaneously constituent element and a control criterion for the member states.

It is evident that the obligation to have common values which are importantly individual–related is of high significance for the convergence of constitutional values in the EU and its member states. As far as reference is made by this provision to fundamental rights, they are relevant in the form in which they are specified in the Charter.

The other values expressed by Art. 2 TEU have to be understood in their contents in accordance with the concepts developed in the member states as belonging to a common European tradition. However, it must be admitted that there is no strict correspondence between the meanings of the national and supranational values. The constitutional basics are common but divergences in details or specific understandings must be admitted to each particular order.

Convergence in this context is not total convergence which operates by substitution as in the cases of the application of the Charter and of general principles with the function of fundamental rights as it has been pointed out above.

Convergence in the context of Article 2 TEU (and in the important context of the ECHR which will be examined later) is limited to the principles and does not extend to details. What must be convergent is the functional dimension of the value, not necessarily the institution. Democracy can be realized in its genuine function by a system of representative democracy or in system which combines representative with direct democracy. With regard to fundamental rights the efficient protection of the individual is relevant, not the detailed dimensions of the written guarantees. Art. 2 TEU can only demand that the functions of fundamental rights, democracy or rule of law are the same, that the finalities of these values are adequately fulfilled at the national and supranational level regardless of the institutional structure in which these values appear.

For the main convergence processes this functional approach seems to be decisive.

The Role of the ECHR in the Convergence Process

Regarding the convergence process connected to the ECHR there are two dimensions to be taken into consideration: the fulfilment of the international obligation of each of the signatory states to avoid interference with the conventional rights and the adaption of an internal order to meet the requirements of the Convention, in particular to make internal laws conform to these requirements. The second dimension is the degree of acceptance the signatory state offers to the Convention in its internal constitutional system. This means the position which is attributed to the Convention in the internal legal order and how national jurisprudence deals with it.

In general it can be said that convergence effectuated by the Convention is a process than convergence by the EU Charter because it covers 47 Council of Europe member states. However, the modalities how convergence is created and the degree of intensity of convergence are different.

In contrast to the supranational EU system of fundamental rights protection this type of convergence is not a convergence by substitution. It is a *functional convergence* as explained above, mainly concentrated on compatibility in principle.

This functional convergence approach is based on the recognition of the anthropocentric perspective of constitutional law that is on the constitutional foundations which consist of the respect of human dignity, the principle of human freedom and the autonomy of the person (Arnold 2014b). These three pillars of contemporary democratic constitutionalism are interconnected and are the basis for the constitutional philosophy of the legal order. The principle of freedom dictates that freedom of the individual is primordial, a direct expression of its dignity, and public power intervention for a legitimate common interest must remain exceptional and needs justification. This relationship between the principle of freedom and the exception of public intervention must be adequately equilibrated in correspondence with the principle of proportionality (Arnold et al. 2012). The principle of freedom, furthermore, requires acknowledging that the fundamental rights protection of the individual is not limited by the written text but has to correspond to the basic concept of *substantive and functional efficiency* (Arnold 2015) of this protection inherent in each democratic Constitution of today.

This principle requires that fundamental rights protection has to be extended to all dangers which exist at present and will emerge in the future without any exception. Substantive efficiency excludes the existence of gaps within the protection system. The protection texts reflect the time period in which they have been created but have functionally to be operative during all the time the text is in force. As constitutions as well as constitutional texts even if they have the form of international treaties as the ECHR are "living instruments" (ECtHR 1995, para. 71), their protective function has to be adapted to the changes which are going on in politics, the economy and in particular in technology. Newly emerging dangers for the individual have to be covered by the existing protection system which has to be complemented either by constitutional reform or by interpretation. The judges, in particular the constitutional judges have power and even the obligation to complement the written text by developing the law through interpretation. Regularly, interpretation is the adequate means. The written fundamental rights text is normally rather indefinite and contains general clauses which can be seen as the written expression of the general principle of freedom, usable as sources of new aspects of freedom formulated by the judge as additional specific rights. As the German Basic Law (BL) established in 1949 mentions no data protection right the constitutional jurisprudence (FCC 1983, p. 44 et seq.) has worked it out with reference to human dignity (article 1.1 BL) and the general right to deploy one's personality as expressed in article 2.1 BL (a right which has been extended to generally protecting freedom, expression of the above-mentioned general principle of freedom). The judges can refer, for the purpose of developing new aspects of fundamental rights or even rights as such, to written provisions whose contents are close to the new protection aspects and extend their protection range by a large, dynamic or evolutionary interpretation or specifically by analogous application. It would be even possible for judges to find a new fundamental right without any reference to the written text, deriving it from the basic idea of the efficient protection of the individual as expression of its dignity and freedom, idea inherent in the Constitution.

Functional efficiency of fundamental rights means ensuring the function of fundamental rights by preventing the legislator from affecting the core elements, the very essence of fundamental rights (Hufen 2011), when restricting them on the basis of a constitutional authorization. The principle of proportionality is the main instrument for keeping up functional efficiency permitting interventions into the freedom of the individual only if they are necessary for a legitimate public interest and adequately weighed against the private interest (Arnold 2010).

Functional convergence in the above sense means that the basic values are accepted, in particular dignity and the principle of freedom, which necessarily imply substantive and functional efficiency. Which solution is found in a concrete case is not the direct object of convergence. The *principles* that are applied when resolving the concrete problem are important for convergence. The details can vary, the specific solution depends on the particular circumstances of the case. The question of convergence does not refer to them. What is important in this context are principles and functions.

Convergence and Constitutional Impact: Some Considerations on Germany, United Kingdom and France

The Constitutional Basis

Convergence of fundamental rights is regularly accompanied by considerable impact on the existing constitutional structures in a country. For analysis of the intensity and reach of these impacts the constitutional basis for the convergence shall be briefly considered.

It seems appropriate to concentrate on the two main sources of fundamental rights convergence, the EU FRCh and the ECHR ("Charter" and "Convention" in the following text). In *Germany* article 23 (formerly 24) BL permits a transfer of "sovereign rights" ("*Hoheitsrechte*") to multinational organizations such as the European Union. According to the understanding of the constitutional jurisprudence, Germany "opens" (FCC 1974, p. 280) its sovereignty giving supranational law direct entrance into the internal legal order. By that, the normative validity of EU law, together with that of national law, within the German order is accepted. In case of conflict primacy of EU law over national law is ensured.

An important characteristic of the European Union institutional system is that most of the EU secondary law is executed by the member states administration. This gives rise to the question which fundamental rights are applicable if supranational law is carried out through national administrative actions, the national or the supranational fundamental rights. This question has already been the issue of the famous *Solange I* (FCC 1974, p. 271, 280) and *Solange II* (FCC 1986, p. 339, 387) decisions of the German FCC, finally in favour of the European Community/EU. The fundamental rights protection was considered as "identifying" the German constitutional order and being of such importance that its existence was indispensable, no matter whether on the national or on the supranational side. Since at the time of the *Solange I* decision no fundamental rights protection at the community level existed at all, the Court's solution was to apply in cases of the execution of supranational law by German authorities – in "mixed" cases of both sides' participation – the fundamental rights of the German BL. When unwritten fundamental rights were developed by the Community judges, this form of jurisprudential charter was considered sufficient as protection, which was from now on to be exercised by the supranational side. However, the guardianship of whether the protection by supranational rights remains sufficient was reserved by the German court (FCC 2010, p. 155 et seq.).

Primacy of EU law including supranational fundamental rights (if they satisfy the requirement of sufficient protection) has been accepted by the FCC. This also implies the acceptance of article 51.1 of the Charter which determines its fields of application. However, as underlined above, the discussion as to the exact interpretation of this provision is yet ongoing.

Primacy of supranational law is not accepted by the FCC if it affects constitutional identity (FCC 2009). In some contrast to EU concepts the Court claims to be the exclusive holder of the power of defining what identity is. This position is the same as for deciding whether a supranational act is *ultra vires* or not (FCC 2010, p. 155, 188). The identity barrier is also applicable for fundamental rights. The definition of what constitutes constitutional identity in German constitutional law is based, in the view of the FCC, on the so-called eternity clause of article 79.3 BL. This clause enumerates the matters which cannot be subject to a formal constitutional reform (Art. 1 and 20 BL) and therefore constitute the core elements of the Constitution thereby forming its identity. Conflicts are possible in particular with reference to article 1 BL which guarantees human dignity and is seen as the fundament of the specific fundamental rights.

In the United Kingdom, the application of the Charter is in dispute. The protocol no. 30 to the Treaty of Lisbon is sibylline insofar as it states, in its article 1, that the "ability" of the UK courts and tribunals will not be "extended" to "find that the laws, regulations or administrative provisions, practices or action of the UK are inconsistent with the fundamental rights, freedoms and principles" of the Charter. As the Charter reaffirms and makes evident the general principles of EU law protecting fundamental rights having been developed by jurisprudence; these latter principles as well as the Charter reaffirming these principles have binding effect on the UK and are criteria of examining internal laws on their consistency with them. The judgment of the CJEU in case C-411/10 and the opinion of the Advocate General (CJEU 2011, para, 99, 119) put forward this view which is shared by important *dicta* from within UK. Whether article 1.2 of Protocol no.3 exempts UK judiciary from applying social rights according to Title IV of the Charter is not yet clear at all.

On the assumption that the Charter is in general applicable to the UK, the introduction of it into the internal UK law has been effectuated, in correspondence to the requirements of the UK parliamentary sovereignty doctrine, on the basis of the concept of the European Communities Act 1972. EU law is given internal normative effect within the UK by s. 2 of this Act which is therefore the legal basis for the permanent introduction of supranational law into the internal order. This model differs from other continental systems of EU law reception and stands in contrast with the concept of direct validity and applicability as developed by the ECJ jurisprudence (ECJ 1964). This basic concept has not been modified by some later European

Union Acts 2008[2] and 2011[3] and will remain untouched even if the UK Parliament (Sovereignty) Bill[4] would be realized in the next legislative period.

The existence of a formal Constitution in France which contains, in its new Title XV, specific rules on the European Union even permitting a transfer of sovereignty instead of a mere sovereignty limitation, makes it possible that EU primary law including the Charter is directly incorporated into the French legal order. Article 55 of the Constitution is the basis for this form of reception, following the monist introduction model. EU primary law therefore enters the internal legal order and enjoys, according to article 55, primacy over ordinary legislation. However, Title XV of the Constitution goes further and makes possible the direct validity of EU law and its primacy not only over ordinary but also over constitutional law. However, it seems that also France's "constitutional identity" is a limit of primacy, a similar barrier as in Germany. In a certain contrast to the German position, the system of fundamental rights protection in France is to some extent dogmatically less consolidated, developed in its basis more by jurisprudence than in Germany and probably not strictly seen as an element of constitutional identity.

Article 51 of the EU Charter does not encounter any constitutional obstacles to acceptance and can lead to convergence by substitution, in its result in the same way as in Germany.

The ECHR, an International Treaty with Constitution-Reforming Power

As has already been pointed out, the ECHR is the basis of a functional convergence of fundamental rights protection in Europe. There are two aspects to be taken into consideration: the effect of the Convention itself and the reactions of the signatory states as concerns the introduction of the Convention into internal law as well as the consequences national jurisprudence attributes to it.

According to the transformation system as provided for by the BL, the Convention is formally accorded the rank of ordinary federal law but undergoes a process of constitutionalizing which corresponds to its importance for the protection of the individual. This process does not consist in attributing it a constitutional rank but by interpreting the Constitution in the light of the Convention. As fundamental rights are regularly formulated in general words, interpretation can have a considerable impact on the meaning of the rights. By interpretation they can be made compatible with the standards of the Convention, a process of convergence. Interpretation in

---

[2] See the text of the European Union Act 2008: http://www.legislation.gov.uk/ukpga/2008/7/contents.

[3] See the text of the European Union Act 2011: http://www.legislation.gov.uk/ukpga/2011/12/contents.

[4] https://www.gov.uk/government/news/eu-bill-to-include-parliamentary-sovereignty-clause.

the field of fundamental rights seems to be a flexible, efficient instrument of giving the rights the appropriate position in a way in which formal normative categorization is not able to do. The way to achieve convergence is not formal reform of the Constitution (which is politically difficult to realize) but an approximation by interpretation. The FCC has declared it an obligation to apply German fundamental rights only in a way that corresponds to the high standards of the Convention. This adaptation is seen as an implicit requirement of the national Constitution. Failing to comply with would be a violation of the national fundamental rights. This could be invoked by means of an individual constitutional complaint. Rule of law is considered to comprise not only national but also international law (Silkenat et al. 2014). This is a functional not a formal adaptation of the Constitution.

In France, the constitutional jurisprudence of the *Conseil constitutionnel* is formally not linked with the Convention because the *Conseil* only applies constitutional law as such. However, the Convention is implicitly taken into consideration when legislation is reviewed for avoiding later critics from Strasbourg. As Art. 55 of the Constitution makes a conformity control possible for the ordinary and administrative judges, an adaptation by interpretation is an instrument for settling a conflict in advance. The impact of the Convention is more significant at the level of ordinary than of constitutional law. The preventive effect of the Convention can be clearly stated for the process of legislation drafting.

The Human Rights Act in the United Kingdom has established a mechanism which combines judicial and political intervention for making laws compatible with the Convention. The declaration of incompatibility by judges of higher courts initiates a process which further involves Government and Parliament. It seems that sovereignty of Parliament, the fundament of English constitutional law, is only formally respected by this system. The main intervention is that of the Minister responsible for the legislation in question who adopts an order with modifying effect while Parliament gives its consent, beforehand, in urgent cases also subsequently.

The Convention is made part of the internal law, however, it is not transformed as in Germany but introduced as an appendix to the HRA which upholds the legal nature of the Convention. The introduction mechanism is therefore on the one hand in line with the dualistic concept the English doctrine adheres to and on the other hand able to make the Convention as such, and in particular as shaped by the Strasbourg jurisprudence, a direct criterion for the compatibility control.

This control has to duly consider the whether national margins of appreciation are to be respected in order to comply with the idea of value subsidiarity, an idea strongly promoted by English politics.

German, French and English approaches on the role of the Convention contribute considerably to the growing functional convergence of the fundamental rights protection in Europe.

Bibliography

Arnold, Rainer. 2009. The concept of European constitutional law. In *The emergence of European constitutional law*, XVIIth congress of the international association of comparative law, Utrecht 2006, National reports, ed. Arnold Rainer, 15–23. Sakkoulas: Athens. Bruylant: Brussels.

Arnold, Rainer. 2015. Substanzielle und funktionelle Effizienz des Grundrechtsschutzes im europäischen Konstitutionalismus. In *Von der Kultur der Verfassung, Festschrift für Friedhelm Hufen zum 70. Geburtstag*, ed. Christian Bickenbach, Max-Emanuel Geis, and Markus Winkler, 3–10. München: C.H. Beck.

Arnold, Rainer. 2010. *Le juge constitutionnel et la proportionnalité*, Annuaire internationale de justice constitutionnelle, Institut Louis Favoreu, vol. XXV. 2009, 115–122. Paris: Economica, Presses universitaires d'Aix-Marseille.

Arnold, Rainer. 2014a. La Cour de Justice de l'Union Européenne comme gardienne de l'identité constitutionnelle des États membres. In *Longcours, Mélanges en l'honneur de Pierre Bon*, 49–56. Paris: Dalloz.

Arnold, Rainer. 2014b. L'État de droit comme fondement du constitutionnalisme européen. *Revue Française de Droit Constitutionnel*. Numéro spécial, 25 ans de droit constitutionnel, no 100: 769–776.

Arnold, Rainer, J. I. Martínez Estay, and F. Zuniga Urbina. 2012. El principio de proporcionalidad en la jurisprudencia del Tribunal Constitucional. *Estudios Constitucionales*, Santiago de Chile, 10: 65–116.

Burgorgue-Larsen, Laurence. 2013. Chronique de jurisprudence européenne comparée (2013). *Revue du Droit Public et de la science politique en France et à l'étranger*. L.G.D.J. Paris. No. 4–2014.1077–1113, 1078 et sequ.

Grabenwarter, Christoph, and Katharina Pabel. 2013. Commentary Art. 6 TEU. In *The Treaty on European Union (TEU). A commentary*, ed. Hermann-Josef Blanke and Stelio Mangiameli. Berlin: Springer. Para 86–93.

Hufen, Friedhelm. 2011. *Staatsrecht II Grundrechte*, 3rd ed, 124–125. München: C.H.Beck.

Silkenat, James R., James E. Hickey Jr., and Peter D. Barenboim (eds.). 2014. *The legal doctrines of the rule of law and the legal state (Rechtsstaat)*. Dordrecht/Heidelberg/New York/London: Springer.

Decisions

CJEU. 2011. Case C-411/10, N.S. (C-411/10) v Secretary of State for the Home Department and M. E. and Others (C-493/10) v Refugee Applications Commissioner and Minister for Justice, Equality and Law Reform. Judgment (Grand Chamber) of 21 December 2011. ECLI:EU:C:2011:865.

CJEU. 2013. Case C-617/10, Åklagaren v Åkerberg Fransson, Judgment (Grand Chamber) of February 26, 2013, ECLI:EU:C:2013:105.

ECJ. 1964. Case C-6/64, Flaminio Costa v E.N.E.L. Judgment of Juli 15, 1964. Reports of Cases 1964 01141, ECLI:EU:C:1964:66.

ECJ. 2004. Case C-36/02, Omega Spielhallen- und Automatenaufstellungs-GmbH v Oberbürgermeisterin der Bundesstadt Bonn, Judgment (First Chamber) of December 14, 2004, Reports of Cases 2004 I-09609, ECLI:EU:C:2004:614.

ECJ. 1970. Case-11/70, Internationale Handelsgesellschaft mbH v Einfuhr- und Vorratsstelle für Getreide und Futtermittel, Judgment of Dezember 17, 1970, Reports of Cases 1970 01125, ECLI:EU:C:1970:114.

ECtHR. 1995. Loizidou v. Turkey (preliminary objections), Judgment of 23 March 1995, Application no. 15318/89.
FCC. 1974. Decision of May 29, 1974, vol. 37, 271 et seq. – 2 BvL 52/71, Solange I.
FCC. 1983. Decision of December 15, 1983, vol. 65, 1 et seq. – 1 BvR 209/83, Volkszählung.
FCC. 1986. Order of October 22, 1986, vol. 73, 339 et seq. – 2 BvR 197/83, Solange II.
FCC. 1987. Decision of April 10, 1987, 2 BvR 1236/86, NJW 1987, 3077, Melchers.
FCC. 2009. Order of June 30, 2009-2 BvE 2/08. ECLI:DE:BVerfG:2009:es20090630.2bve000208.
FCC. 2010. Order of July 06, 2010, vol. 89, 155 et seq. – 2 BvR 2661/06, Mangold decision. ECLI:DE:BVerfG:2010:rs20100706. http://www.bundesverfassungsgericht.de/SharedDocs/Entscheidungen/EN/2010/07/rs20100706_2bvr266106en.
FCC. 2013. Decision of April 24, 2013–1 BvR 1215/07, Antiterrordatei. https://www.bundesverfassungsgericht.de/entscheidungen/rs20130424_1bvr121507.html.

Convergence of the Protection of Fundamental Rights Between the Spanish Constitutional Court and the European Court of Human Rights

Pedro Julio Tenorio Sánchez

Abstract To make ECtHR rulings prevail over final Spanish judgments is a matter for the legislator, not for an extreme or exaggerated interpretation of a law that has not been promulgated for that purpose.

Within the context of the doctrine introduced by the Administrative Bench of the TS, the current or subsisting character of the violation of the fundamental right turns out to be a key issue. However, from the examination of the Constitutional Court's jurisprudence on this point, in order to assess the extent of the above-mentioned doctrine of our Supreme Court, we conclude that this concept is difficult to pin down.

Obviously, the Draft for the reform of the Organic Law of the Judicial Branch (LOPJ) we have discussed above renders the Supreme Court's interpretation meaningless. Indeed, the aforementioned reform draft of the LOPJ proposes the appeal as a way to implement the ECtHR judgments; on the other hand, a return to pre-2007 wording regarding the nullity suit; the approval of this proposal, for both reasons, would put an end to the practical relevance of the doctrine of the Supreme Court on the motion for dismissal of actions as a way of enforcement of ECtHR's judgments.

The Rules of International Law as Ratio Decidendi of the Judgments of the TC

Formulation, Genesis, Relevance and Content of Art. 10.2 of the Spanish Constitution

1.1. If one were to sum up the Spanish Constitution (hereinafter *CE*) in one article, it would be art. 10. It is true that, within it, the first section is more important than the second but the latter has great relevance.

P.J. Tenorio Sánchez (✉)
Universidad Nacional de Educación a Distancia (UNED), Madrid, Spain
e-mail: pedrojuliotenorio@gmail.com

R. Arnold (ed.), *The Convergence of the Fundamental Rights Protection in Europe*, Ius Gentium: Comparative Perspectives on Law and Justice 52,
DOI 10.1007/978-94-017-7465-9_2

Art. 10.1 CE stipulates that "The dignity of the person, the inviolable rights which are inherent, the free development of the personality, respect for the law and the rights of others, are the foundation of political order and social peace".

More interesting for our purpose here today is art. 10.2 EC, which states that "The norms relative to basic rights and liberties which are recognized by the Constitution shall be interpreted in conformity with the *Universal Declaration of Human Rights* and the international treaties and agreements on those matters ratified by Spain".[1]

1.2. In order to understand why our constitutional fathers included this provision, we should take into account that the Spanish democratic transition was essentially led by a government part of which had been in power before the advent of democracy. It is easy to understand why our constitutional fathers, when writing the Constitution, included provisions to prove that they were establishing fully constitutional rules, a system of freedoms comparable to those of the most important Western democracies.

Therefore, they not only drew inspiration from well established constitutions, when they acknowledged the different rights, but also wanted to make sure that these texts would be interpreted in accordance with the prevailing trends in Western democracies.

This provision was incorporated to the constitutional text despite substantial opposition. The decisive point seemed to be securing the guarantee of some rights the Constitution had not explicitly recognized, particularly the right to education, closing the debate about this controversial right.

1.3. We cannot say that art. 10.2 CE is an original Spanish contribution to comparative constitutionalism, since our precept was preceded by art. 16.2 of the Portuguese Constitution of 1976. But it does seem to join a tradition that later inspired other constitutions, such as the Romanian (art. 20) or the Colombian (art. 93.2).

1.4. Since its creation, our Constitutional Court case law has fully implemented that provision, and has stressed its importance. To clarify the meaning of art. 10.2 CE in our system, we should take into account how it has been interpreted and applied by the Spanish Constitutional Court:

1.4.1. This provision does not add to the fundamental rights recognized by the Spanish Constitution. The fundamental rights recognized in Spain are, as our Constitutional Court has established, just those recognized in the Constitution. So, if a claimant invokes a right contained in an international treaty, the action before the Court shall not prosper. Whoever invokes legal rights or positions explicitly recognized in an international treaty (but not in the Constitution) has to prove that they are also recognized in the Constitution. In this regard, we must recall that the right to appeal of any person convicted of a criminal act, recognized in art. 14.5 of the *International Covenant on Civil and Political Rights* (hereinafter *ICCPR*), has

[1] Sáiz Arnáiz has exhaustively analyzed CE, Art. 10.2; that this synthesis is based on his work is acknowledged. Vid. reference section of the present article.

been recognized by the Constitutional Court in line with either the right to effective judicial protection (art. 24.1 CE) or the right to the due process of law (art. 24.2 CE).

1.4.2. Article 10.2 establishes a requirement of 'consistent interpretation' of fundamental rights according to international human rights treaties ratified by Spain, a requirement that somehow has initiated a new kind of interpretative argument.

From its first judgment, our *Constitutional Court* has systematically implemented and emphasized the importance of this provision. Specifically, it has underlined the interpretative value of the *European Convention on Human Rights* (hereinafter ECHR) and the judgments which, pursuant thereto, are issued by the *European Court of Human Rights* (hereinafter ECtHR). One example is the Judgment of the Constitutional Court (hereinafter STC) 91/2000, Legal Ground 7 –'legal ground' hereinafter LG-: "To clarify, specifically, what are these rights and contents the CE proclaims in an absolute way and therefore projects universally [...] particularly relevant are [...] *the Universal Declaration of Human Rights* and other international treaties and agreements relating to the same matters ratified by Spain, which art. 10.2 CE refers to as an interpretative criterion of fundamental rights. Therefore, from its earliest rulings, the Court has recognized the important hermeneutic role that the international human rights treaties ratified by Spain have in the determination of fundamental rights [...] and, most uniquely, the *European Convention for the Protection of Human Rights and Public Freedoms* [...]".

This gives this type of treaties an unusual scope. In the Spanish legal system, international treaties become part of domestic law through the provisions of art. 96.1 CE. Under that provision, "1. Validly concluded international treaties, once officially published in Spain, shall form part of domestic law. Their provisions may be repealed, amended or suspended in the manner provided for in the treaties themselves or in accordance with the general rules of international law". This applies to all international treaties, not only those that recognize rights but also those on different subjects. This transposition turns treaties into domestic law, in principle subject to the Constitution (without prejudice to the international responsibility to be incurred by the State as a result of the breach of this type of agreement).

Art. 10.2 CE provides international treaties containing fundamental rights with a new and different scope to that of art. 96.1 CE. Pursuant to art. 10.2 CE, international treaties are an interpretative standard for the rights recognized in the Constitution. It should be specified that they are criterion for interpretation, not only in the version they had at the time of the adoption of the Constitution, but also in its future versions.

Virtually all fundamental rights are affected by this: both procedural rights (effective judicial protection and due process of law) and substantive rights (equality, religious freedom and freedom of expression, to name but three of them).

International legislation has exercised a remarkable influence on many sectors, not only in areas such as extradition or immigration, but in others that, at first glance, may seem more remote, such as military and juvenile justice or penal correction law.

The Concept of "Fundamental Rights"

Art. 10.2, in order to determine the circle of rights affected by the interpretation construed in accordance to international treaties, refers literally to "fundamental rights and freedoms recognized by the Constitution".

This has raised a controversy in Spain about what should be considered 'fundamental rights and freedoms'. Indeed, the Constitution's Title I is under the heading "Basic rights and duties" (Articles 11–55). Title I is divided into three chapters: the first one is entitled "Spaniards and aliens" (Articles 11–13). The second, "Rights and Freedoms" (Articles 14–38). The third, "Guiding principles for social and economic policy" (Articles 39–55). In Chapter II, in turn, there are two sections. The first is entitled "Fundamental rights and freedoms" and comprises Articles 15–29; the second, "Rights and Duties of Citizens" and comprises articles 30–38. This raises the question whether the fundamental rights and public freedoms referred to in art. 10.2 CE are only those of Section 1, Chapter II, Title I, entitled "Fundamental rights and freedoms", or whether a less literal interpretation (that includes Chapter II entirely or Chapters II and III) is in order.

Let us consider the position of the Constitutional Court in this regard. Its jurisprudence seems to suggest that it considers 'fundamental rights' those included in Chapter II of Title I. Indeed, it is clear that rights protected by the amparo before the Constitutional Court, i.e., the right to equality (art. 14 CE) and Section 1, Chapter II, Title I rights, entitled 'Basic Rights, Public Liberties' including articles 15–29, are included. In addition, the Court has explicitly established the applicability of art. 10.2 to the rights recognized in articles 30–38 CE (i.e., Chapter II of Title I. In this sense, for example, the STC 36/1991, LG 5, says that "[the Constitution] does not give constitutional status to international rights and freedoms that are not also included in our own Constitution, but requires the interpretation of our constitutional provisions in accordance with the content of such Treaties or Conventions [...]") (STC 199/1996, LG 3).

It should be noted that the Court is emphatic in that fundamental rights are only those defined as such in the Constitution, so that if you invoke a right contained only in an international treaty, the action will not succeed. However, an attempt at protecting rights or defending juridical positions explicitly included in an international treaty (though absent from the Constitution) is possible by bringing them in line with a fundamental right that is included in the Constitution. In this respect, Sáiz Arnáiz has suggested that the right to appeal of any person convicted of a criminal act, included in art 14.5 of the *International Covenant on Civil and Political Rights* (hereinafter ICCPR) has been recognized by the Constitutional Court by linking it to either the right to effective judicial protection (art. 24.1 CE) or to the right to a procedure that meets all the standards of the rule of law (art. 24.2 CE).

Treaties and International Agreements on Fundamental Rights

As we have seen, the Constitution recognizes the interpretative value of treaties "on the same matters". However, how is this expression supposed to be interpreted? Is it to be understood in a formal sense, inclusive only of treaties *stricto sensu*, that, moreover, by their title and purpose are clearly intended to regulate fundamental rights? Or are we supposed to understand it in a material sense, including any rule of international law that has any reference to fundamental rights?

The Spanish Constitutional Court has opted for a 'material' orientation. Thus, for example, in its resolutions, it has used not only Conventions by the UN (such as the Convention against torture – STC 120/1990, LG 9 – or on the elimination of discrimination against women – STC 12/2008 LG – or on the rights of the child – STC 36/1991, LG6) but also it has referred to Resolutions adopted by the General Assembly, which, in principle, have no binding force, but rather have a limited value: STC 36/1991, LG 5 and STC 215/1994, LG 2. Similarly, within the Council of Europe, a distinction must be made between Conventions (which States ratify, such as the ECHR), Resolutions and Recommendations. The Council of Europe's legislation has had considerable significance in some cases, such as the integration of art. 18.4. a from the *Convention for the Protection of Individuals With Regard to Automatic Processing of Personal Data* (STC 254/1993) or the configuration of the right to conscientious objection (Constitutional Court rulings – hereinafter SSTC – 15/1982, LG 6 and 7, 160/1987, LG 5, and 161/1987, LG 5).

Moreover, and not least, it must be considered that the Spanish Constitutional Court has employed primary and secondary Union law in the interpretation of rights.

The Spanish Constitutional Court's anti-formalism has led it to apply international treaties before they had been ratified by Spain. In this regard, the reference to the *Charter of Fundamental Rights of the European Union* before it was binding should be recalled at this point: STC 292/2000, LG 8, and 138/2005, LG 4.

In some cases, the Spanish Constitutional Court, on the grounds that fundamental rights are basic fundamental decisions that have to inform the entire judicial order, has interpreted a basic right in the light of a treaty, considering a reservation formulated by the State as not having been made: STC 21/1981, LG 10 and 44/1983, LG 1.

Obviously, under art. 10.2 CE, the fundamental rights of the Spanish Constitution have been interpreted in accordance with the *Universal Declaration of Human Rights* (hereinafter UDHR) and with the international agreements to which Spain is a party. Sáiz Arnaiz points at the UDHR, the ICCPR (the *International Covenant on Economic, Social and Cultural Rights*), the ECHR and EU law, as the main sources of international legislation used by the Spanish Constitutional Court and stresses that the most frequently cited international text is the ECHR. In the period 1999–2004, 75 % of the Constitutional Court's rulings on amparo contained references to the ECHR. Surely, the prestige of the ECtHR is a reason for this, but what technically justifies the significant presence of the jurisprudence of the ECHR in the Spanish Constitutional Court's rulings is not just the fact that the Spanish Constitution refers to the European Convention of Human Rights, but also the reference of the European Convention on Human Rights to the European Court of Human Rights regarding its application and interpretation (art. 32.1 ECHR).

This does not mean that there is no discrepancy between these two Courts. Whenever the ECtHR condemns Spain, it is often against the Spanish Constitutional Court's criterion, which would normally be involved in the matter, since all judicial remedies in Spain must first have been exhausted in order to be able to appeal to the

ECtHR. Moreover, the Constitutional Court does not consider itself a mere executor of the ECtHR's criteria, as explicitly stated in STC 245/1991, LG 2: "From the perspective of international law and its binding force (Article 96 CE), the Convention neither introduced in the domestic legal order a higher supranational instance, in the technical sense, that reviews or directly controls the internal judicial or administrative decisions, nor does it impose on Member States specific procedural measures of annulling or rescissory character, to ensure repair of the violation of the Convention found by the ECtHR (or, where applicable, by the Committee of Ministers of the Council of Europe, in accordance with art. 32 of the Convention). The Convention does not oblige Member States to eliminate the consequences of the act that has been found contrary to international legal obligations assumed by the State, restoring, as far as possible, the situation prior to the act; on the contrary, art. 50 allows for a replacement of the restoration (that would question the final and executive character of the internal judicial decision) by a just satisfaction [...]". The interpretation of ECtHR doctrine is a matter for the Constitutional Court, as stated in STC 119/2001, LG 6, regarding the case of López Ostra.

The Constitutional Court does not consider the judgment of the Committee of Ministers of the Council of Europe relevant, from the perspective of Article 10.2 CE, on the grounds of the diplomatic, non-jurisdictional, nature of that body: STC 114/1984, LG 3.

On the contrary, the Spanish Constitutional Court (hereinafter TCe) does take into account decisions by the *European Commission on Human Rights* (which was suppressed by Protocol XI, which entered into force in 1998), in some cases giving them large effect on the outcome of the case. For example, STC 2/1987, LG 2–4, but overall it used to do it in the absence of a ECtHR ruling: STC 53/1985, LG 11.

Undoubtedly, the TCe, from its earliest rulings, has taken the jurisprudence of the ECtHR into consideration as a highly relevant one, under the provisions of art. 10.2 CE (STC 22/1981, LG 3), without acknowledging the need for additional theoretical justifications. Actually, Strasbourg jurisprudence is so important for the TCe that sometimes the Court notes its inexistence on a particular issue, thus making quite clear its decisive value (STC 53/1985, LG 6).

The primary law of the European Union is not oriented, in its origins, to the recognition and guarantee of fundamental rights, and secondary law is not agreed on. Therefore, fundamental rights could only be interpreted in primary and secondary law through a broad interpretation of art. 10.2 CE. Indeed, the TCe started doing so purely for dialectical purposes, as in STC 132/1989, LG 12. However, from 1991, Union Law is recognized as interpretative criteria of fundamental rights, under art. 10.2 CE, as in SSTC 28/1991, LG 5 and 64/1991, LG 4: "Community law, whose rules, besides specific means of enforcement [...] could come to have, where appropriate, the interpretative value assigned to International Treaties, under art. 10.2 CE."

As with the law of the Convention, the TCe recognizes this interpretative value to the Union law, accepting the interpretation provided by the ECJ. For example, EU law and its interpretation by the ECJ have been instrumental for the configuration of sex discrimination, prohibited by art. 14 CE. Reference should be made in this matter to the Constitutional Court's Opinion 1/2004, LG 6. The Spanish

Constitution provides that the Government may request an opinion from the TCe on the compatibility with the Constitution of an International Treaty prior to ratification. During the term of the present Constitution of 1978, the Government has availed itself of this possibility only twice: First, to inquire about the constitutionality of certain aspects of the Maastricht Treaty. At that time, we had to proceed to a small amendment to the Constitution, prior to the ratification of said treaty, to dispel the contradiction that the Constitutional Court had found. The second time the Government consulted the Constitutional Court was on the constitutionality of the Treaty establishing a Constitution for Europe. The Court, on this occasion, did not identify any unconstitutional issues. Although the aforementioned Treaty has not come into force by reason of the refusal of other countries, the doctrine of the Constitutional Court's opinion is fully valid and very valuable to understand the Court's position on the relationship between EU law and Rights of domestic origin and more specifically the value of the Charter of Fundamental Rights of the European Union and even of the jurisprudence of the Strasbourg Court. On this occasion, the TCe was consulted if there was a contradiction between the Spanish Constitution and Articles II-111 (scope of the Charter) and II-112 (criteria for its interpretation). The TCe replied stating the interpretative value of the Charter of Fundamental Rights of the European Union and added that this should not pose any particular problems, since Article II-112 assumed the validity of the ECHR and of the Strasbourg jurisprudence. The validity of the *European Convention on Human Rights* had been affirmed by the Court, because nothing could prevent that "as a convention ratified by Spain, through the procedure established in art. 93 CE, its interpretative effectiveness about the rights and freedoms proclaimed in the Constitution would reach as far as provided for in art. 10.2 CE".

As regards the Strasbourg jurisprudence, the opinion reads as follows: "The interpretative value that the Charter on Fundamental Rights would have in our legal system, within this scope, would not cause greater difficulties than those which currently exist as a result of the Rome Convention of 1950, simply because both our own constitutional doctrine (on the basis of art. 10.2 CE) and article II-112 (as shown in the 'explanations' that, as an interpretation, are incorporated into the Treaty by paragraph 7 of the same article) operate with a set of references to the European Convention that eventually turn the jurisprudence of the Strasbourg Court into the common denominator for the establishment of a minimum set of shared interpretative elements […]".

This reduction of the complexity inherent to the concurrency of criteria for interpretation says nothing new on the subject of the value that the jurisprudence of the EU Courts should have for the definition of each right. In other words, it means no qualitative change to the relevance of that doctrine in the final configuration of fundamental rights by the Spanish Constitutional Court. It simply means that the Treaty appropriates the jurisprudence of a court, doctrine of which is already built into our legislation by virtue of art. 10.2 CE, so that no new or more substantial difficulties are to be expected in the orderly articulation of our system of rights. And those that are, as stated above, can only be apprehended and solved on the occasion of the constitutional processes that we may come across" (DTC 1/2004, LG 6).

Binding Nature of the Requirement in Art. 10.2 CE and Its Guarantee

Art. 10.2 CE is not confined solely to allow recourse to international treaties in order to interpret fundamental rights, but also obliges to do so. It is not directed only to the Constitutional Court, but to all legal operators and it does not only refer to the constitutional rules, but to all the rules governing fundamental rights. Let us consider these three characteristics of the content of Article 10.2 CE.

As for references to the mandatory character of the content of art. 10.2 CE in the constitutional doctrine, just toned down claims are to be found. In this regard, the STC 36/1984, LG 3, suggests that article 10.2 CE "authorizes and even recommends" to refer to the treaties. However, what these statements mean is that the interpretative value cannot turn these treaties into an autonomous source of Constitutional Law and that art. 10.2 is not a norm violation of which can be remedied by an appeal before the Constitutional Court. Let me stress this point: the treaties cannot add fundamental rights to those already guaranteed by the Constitution. If we consider that a provision of an international treaty on fundamental rights has been violated and we want to remedy the harm done, we will have to justify the simultaneous infringement of a fundamental right in the Constitution.

Secondly, we said that the mandatory character of art. 10.2 CE is addressed to all public authorities and particularly to the legislator. This was stated by the TCe in its STC 236/2007, LG 5: "Like any other public authority, the legislator too is required to interpret the relevant constitutional provisions in accordance with the content of such treaties or conventions, which thus become 'constitutionally declared content' of the rights and freedoms set forth in chapter two of title I of our Constitution". Indeed, it is a common thing that the Explanatory Memorandum of Bills on fundamental rights invokes international law: Organic laws 7/1988, 2/2002, 13/2003 and 6/2007 are examples of this.

Thirdly, the treaty compliant interpretation not only concerns the rules contained in the Constitution, but all norms relating to fundamental rights and public freedoms that are set forth in the constitution. The TCe reminded this in STC 78/1982, LG 4.

Negative or Positive Link of Interpretation and the International Text

In an attempt to be more precise, one is right in questioning, as the legal doctrine did, if the interpreter of the fundamental right can afford all those interpretations that do not contradict the international treaty (i.e., if it is negatively linked by the latter), or, on the contrary, if he or she should only produce interpretations implementing the provisions of the treaty, that is, interpretations that derive from it (positive relationship). Some statements in the doctrine of the Constitutional Court which would suggest a positive link can also be found. Indeed, STC 236/2007, LG 5, said that the content of the agreements to which we have been referring becomes, under art. 10.2 CE, "the constitutionally declared content of the rights and freedoms set forth in chapter two of title I of our Constitution"; but it seems that the connection, unless from the nature of the regulated domain requires otherwise, will be a negative one. This follows from some statements by the TCe, such as STC 113/1995, LG 7, which says that the rights "should not be interpreted in conflict" with the ECHR.

On the other hand, as for the ECtHR, let us remember that it has stated that it cannot be used to reduce or lower the level of the rights recognized in the various States: Art. 53 ECHR.

The Rules of International Law as Ratio Decidendi of the Judgments of the TCe

It may well be asked whether our Constitutional Court, when it invokes international treaties on fundamental rights and in particular the ECHR – or the jurisprudence of the ECtHR – does so as a supplementary argument or if such an reference is integrated into the *ratio decidendi* of the case. The answer is that examples of both types can be found.

Undoubtedly, there are cases in which the ECtHR jurisprudence is *ratio decidendi*: among others, in the SSTC 51/1982, 37/1988 and 70/2002 the TCe has recognized every criminally convicted individual the right to appeal to a higher court, on the grounds of both art. 14.5 of the *International Covenant on Civil and Political Rights* and art. 2 ECHR Protocol, though rerouting them through the right to effective judicial protection or the right to the due process of law. The STC 254/1993 recognized the right of *habeas data* after the *Council of Europe Convention for the Protection of Individuals* with regard to automatic processing of personal data by linking it to art. 18.4 CE. The STC 5/1984 recognized the right to an interpreter for every accused person who does not understand the language used in court, after articles 14.3 f of the *International Covenant on Civil and Political Rights* and 6.3.e of the ECHR, rerouting it to art. 24.2 CE.

Therefore, we must conclude that the Constitutional Court has used the jurisprudence of the Court of Justice of the European Union and the European Court of Human Rights as *ratio decidendi*. The jurisprudence of the ECJ has been used regarding the prohibition of discrimination on grounds of sex, which is set out in art. 14 of the Spanish Constitution. Many rights included in Chapter II of Title I of the Spanish Constitution, and specifically in the first section, have been interpreted in accordance with the jurisprudence of the ECtHR. The following is a non-exhaustive list:

On the one hand, conceptual categories created or assumed by the ECHR have been incorporated by the Constitutional Court. In this regard, we note that, in deciding whether there has been undue delay or not (forbidden under art. 24.2 CE), the TCe has decided to use the same "test" used by the ECtHR to decide whether the right to a 'process within a reasonable period' under art. 6.1 ECHR (e.g. STC

223/1988) has been violated. Another example is provided by the use of the ECtHR interpretation of art. 3 of the ECHR to prohibit inhuman or degrading treatment and tell it apart from torture, when interpreting art. 15 of the Spanish Constitution, as in STC 120/1990, LG 9. ECHR criteria are also used to realize the fundamental right to fair trial (STC 69/2001, FF JJ 14–22) or the right to legal assistance free of charge (STC 37/1988, LG 6).

In other cases, we have to acknowledge the incorporation of new content. For example, the STC 49/1999 incorporates certain aspects of the jurisprudence of the ECtHR to the content of the right to privacy of communications. The STC 167/2002 – requiring a review of the standard of proof in criminal appeal through immediacy and contradiction – perfects the due process of law as established in the jurisprudence of the ECtHR. Moreover, at this point, the STC 167/2002 opens up a whole jurisprudencial line that carefully monitors the evolution of the ECtHR's case law in this regard. The STC 119/2001 initiates protection against noise following on the jurisprudence of the ECtHR, reshaping it to the right to personal integrity and privacy of home and family life. Finally, the STC/2003 acknowledges the principle *non bis in idem*, which our constituents did not explicitly considered subject to amparo appeal before the Constitutional Court.

Effectiveness of the Rulings of the European Court of Human Rights in Spain

7.1. On the question of the execution of the ECHR rulings in domestic law, there have been two recent developments: on the one hand, a Supreme Court ruling holding that an appeal for annulment is suitable for the enforcement of a judgment of the ECtHR. On the other hand, the proposed reform of the Organic Law of the Judiciary, which is suggesting the revision of the final judgment.[2]

---

[2] On the influence of the latter on the execution of ECtHR's rulings, see the excellent contribution by De Miguel Canuto, E. 2013. "Eficacia interna de las sentencias del Tribunal Europeo de Derechos Humanos", *Revista Quincena Fiscal*, p. 1 and ff. See also Díez-Picazo, L. M. 2005. *Sistema de Derechos Fundamentales*, 2ª ed., Madrid: Civitas; García de Enterría, E., Linde Paniagua, E., Ortega Álvarez, L., Sánchez Morón, M. 1983. *El sistema europeo de protección de los derechos humanos*, 2ª ed., Madrid: Civitas; García Jiménez, M.E. 1988. *El Convenio de Derechos Humanos en el umbral del Siglo XXI*, Valencia: University of Valencia; García Roca, F. J. and Santaolaya Machetti, P., (coord.) 2005. *La Europa de los Derechos. El Convenio Europeo de Derechos Humanos*, Madrid: Centro de Estudios Políticos y Constitucionales; Martín Retortillo Baquer, L. 1998. *La Europa de los Derechos*, Madrid: Marcial Pons; Martín Retortillo Baquer, L. 2006. *Vías concurrentes para la protección de los derechos humanos*, Madrid: Dykinson; Ripol Carulla, S. 2007. *El sistema europeo de protección de los derechos humanos y el Derecho español*, Barcelona: Atelier; Ruiz Miguel, C. 1997. *La ejecución de las sentencias del Tribunal Europeo de Derechos Humanos: un estudio de la relación entre el derecho nacional e internacional*, Madrid: Tecnos; Salinas Alcega, S. 2009. *El sistema europeo de protección de los derechos humanos en el siglo XXI: el proceso de reforma para asegurar su eficacia a largo plazo*, Madrid, Iustel; Shelton, D. 2005. *Remedies in International Human Right Law*, 2nd ed., Oxford: Oxford University Press.

7.2. The jurisprudence of the last two decades indicated that ECtHR's rulings did not have an annulling effect in Spain, that is, do not deprive the domestic act causing the violation of the Convention of its own validity, and that those sentences are declarative in nature, lacking the executive effectiveness of a genuine sentence.

The amparo resolved by STC 245/1991, of December 16, on the Bultó case, began the debate about the effectiveness of the ECHR judgments. According to our Court, the European Convention neither obliges Spain to recognize in our legal system, the direct enforceability of decisions of the ECtHR, nor to introduce legal reforms to allow judicial review of final judgments as a result of the declaration, by the ECtHR, of a violation of a right guaranteed by the ECHR; however, this does not mean, in terms of our constitutional system of fundamental rights protection, that public authorities are to remain indifferent to the statement of violation of the rights recognized in the Convention (STC 245/1991 of December 16, on the Bultó case, LG 2). In this case, the Constitutional Court argues the permanence or timeliness of the fundamental right infringement and upheld the appeal. Pursuant to this legal theory, a negative position with regard to ECtHR's judgments against the defendant has been gradually taking root. However, periodically, both the legislator and the courts, including the Constitutional Court, are considering how to resolve this contradiction, this shortcoming. What procedure should be followed to enforce the annulment, when appropriate, however exceptional these cases may be? The motion for execution,[3] the extraordinary appeal for review,[4] the motion to void proceedings,[5] and the amparo itself[6] have all been attempted but all of them have failed.

However, Recommendation (2000) 2 of the Committee of Ministers on January 19, 2009, requested of the signatory states of the Convention legislative measures which would permit and regulate formulas for the reopening of domestic proceedings in cases of judgment against a defendant, especially when they are the only way to alter the negative consequences for the injured party resulting from the internal decision.

---

[3] The problems encountered in the motion for execution this attempt may be found in the case *Fuentes Bobo*, refused when decided upon (STC 197/2006, July 3, on a termination of employment procedure).

[4] Exponent of this attempt is the Castillo Algar case, resolved by ATC 96/2001, of April 24, which did not work out either.

[5] Amparo 114/2003, promoted by Juan Alberto Perote Pellón against the Supreme Court ruling that denied the annulment of acts of a court martial, because he had been convicted of a crime of disclosure of information relating to the national security and defense. The declaration of invalidity was based on the alleged infringement of the rights to fair trial and effective remedy. The issue at stake was the impartiality of the Court resolving a motion for dismissal of actions, denied in a criminal case, after Judgment of the European Court of Human Rights for lack of injury or actual breach. The Constitutional Court upheld the judgment of the Supreme Court and denied the amparo.

[6] This attempt was also unsuccessful: see the *Fuente Ariza* case, decided by ATC 119/2010, of October 4.

In this context,[7] the thesis of the Administrative Bench of the Supreme Court (hereinafter TS)[8] has joined the debate: under current regulation, the motion to void proceedings – established by Organic Law 6/2007[9] – makes it a suitable to fit the claim for reconsideration of actions when this is necessary to carry out the enforcement of a judgment by the ECHR, according to a recently published resolution. The aforementioned Supreme Court ruling of May 13, 2013 resolves a motion for dismissal of proceedings in which the appellant seeks the annulment of the judgment of the Supreme Court, taking back actions to the time of sentencing, based on a ruling by the ECtHR for violation of the right to a court. The Supreme Court summarizes the doctrine of the Constitutional Court and argues that the policy change[10] experienced in regulating the motion for dismissal of actions by the LO 6/2007 makes the Constitutional Court competent to enforce an ECtHR judgment.[11]

[7] In the doctrine, the delivery of this power to the Constitutional Court has been suggested, interpreting, in a very broad way, one of the reasons that, according to STC 155/2009, provides an appeal with 'special constitutional significance' (one which provides the same constitutional Court with the opportunity to clarify or change its doctrine, as a result [...] of a change in the doctrine of legal guarantee bodies, responsible for the interpretation of treaties and international agreements referred to in art. 10.2 CE, so that it not only includes rulings decided after the change of doctrine by the ECHR, but also the resolution itself that has led to declare infringement of the right by the Spanish State). This will configure the constitutional protection as a procedural mechanism through which to proceed to the reopening of domestic proceedings following a violation found by the ECtHR. This solution is inspired in STC 245/1991, of December 16, in the Barberá, Messeguer and Jabardo (Bultó) case, a view that has been gradually abandoned by the Court, though it has never been expressly rejected. See García Couso, S. 2010. "El nuevo modelo de protección de los derechos fundamentales tras la aprobación de la L.O. 6/2007: la objetivación del amparo constitucional y la tutela subjetiva de los derechos por la jurisdicción ordinaria y el TEDH". *Revista Europea de Derechos Fundamentales, 15, p. 161 & ff.*

[8] Supreme Court ruling of May 13, 2013, appeal no. 4386/1998, Oro-Pulido López speaker. An analysis of this ruling and of its consequences is included in Miguel Canuto, E. 2013, p. 9–14.

[9] The key is in the grounds for revocation. Faced with the previous regulation where the motives were based on formal grounds resulting in the absence of legal uncertainty and inconsistency of the correct form of helplessness, and, finally, inconsistency of a court decision, the L.O. 6/2007 expands the reasons to "any violation of a fundamental right under Article 53.2 of the constitution."

[10] As noted by the Court's ruling regarding the unfeasibility of the motion for dismissal of actions to channel a claim of this kind, the ruling itself—Third Chamber of the Supreme Court of April 27, 2005, appeal no. 2419/1997—reads: "but -and this is important- in relation to the former wording of Article 240 of the Organic Law of the Judiciary [...]".

[11] For the Supreme Court, in the legislation now in force, we find that Article 241 of the LOPJ states that the motion for dismissal of actions "founded on any breach of a fundamental right referred to in Article 53.2 of the Constitution" may be admissible and this new legal characterization of the incident, given the breadth of the reference containing the violation of fundamental rights, opens the door to the possibility of including in it, as grounds for invalidity, breaches of such rights as detected and declared by a Judgment of the European Court of Human rights (LG 3).

How do we view this initiative of the Supreme Court?

1. To make ECtHR rulings prevail over final Spanish judgments is a matter for the legislator, not for an extreme or exaggerated interpretation of a law that has not been promulgated for that purpose.[12]
2. Within the context of the doctrine introduced by the Administrative Bench of the TS, the current or subsisting character of the violation of the fundamental right turns out to be a key issue.[13] However, from the examination of the Constitutional Court's jurisprudence on this point,[14] in order to assess the extent of the above-

---

[12] The Supreme Court is aware of this, because it says it takes that stand "while waiting for the legislator to address this issue once and for all, through a reform of procedural laws".

[13] The Supreme Court believes to have found a legal way to implement the judgments of the ECtHR (although limited to the rights that are both in the ECHR and also in art. 53.2 of the CE). However, it adds a condition derived from the constitutional doctrine: the intended annulling effect with respect to a previous ruling by a domestic court, specifically by the Supreme Court, can only be obtained if the impairment of the right or the actuality of the breach persists and continues demanding reparations (LG 3 *in fine*, of the STC 197/2006). The Supreme Court further explains that: "Moreover, this nuance or exception to the general rule, expressly qualified by the TC itself in its recent resolutions as 'most exceptional', has only been applied on matters of criminal nature, although we can not rule out the possibility of extending such casuistry to other fundamental rights' violations appreciated and declared by the ECtHR, not strictly related to criminal matters, as long as they are violations of rights that may be considered current or persistent compensation of which necessarily requires a procedural action in the form of taking the proceedings back to the time when the violation was committed."

[14] Undoubtedly, the starting point is the doctrine developed in STC 245/1991, of December 16, Bultó case. "[...] The problem then is not the lack of enforceability of that judgment (the ECHR's) but [that] once verified the actual infringement of Art. 24.2 CE (which implies the simultaneous violation of Art. 17.1 CE), it is up to this Court, to the extent that the actors have not received adequate compensation for the infringement of that right, to declare the alleged infringement of the right to due process, and correct and repair the violation of fundamental rights, taking into account the characteristics of the sentence" (LG 5).

In the ATC 96/2001, of April 24, Castillo Algar case, that equitable satisfaction is enough to consider the breach repaired and therefore ineffectual.

In the STC 197/2006, of 3 July, Fuentes Bobo case concerning a process for dismissal, it was understood that there remained no injury, which, besides the just satisfaction, supposed the full repair of the said injury: "That claim cannot be accepted, since, on one hand, the breach of the fundamental right to freedom of expression of the appellant, when he was dismissed from his post in TVE (Spanish public television) effective April 15, 1994, no longer exists at present (unlike what we have seen when it came to custodial sentences still being served), [...] and, on the other, because, in any case, the damage was no longer present, given that it was the European Court of Human Rights in its judgment of February 29, 2000, ... that, having declared the violation of freedom of expression, had awarded compensation to the plaintiff because of economic and moral damage caused by the dismissal [...]" (LG 4, IV).

However, the absence of subsistence of the injury is not an issue without controversy, but thoroughly discussed in a separate opinion of Judge Pérez Tremps, revealing it is a difficult notion to grasp.

In the ATC 129/2008, of May 26, Puig Panella case, it is considered that the injury is not present but past because equitable compensation involves repair. This is in harmony with the solution given to the Castillo Algar case.

In the STC 119/2010, of October 4, Case Source Ariza, actuality of the injury is refused, because the ECtHR had already rejected the baseless grounds he now seeks to assert in this (his

mentioned doctrine of our Supreme Court, we conclude that this concept is difficult to pin down.

3. Obviously, the Draft for the reform of the Organic Law of the Judicial Branch (LOPJ) we have discussed above renders the Supreme Court's interpretation meaningless.[15] Indeed, the aforementioned reform draft of the LOPJ proposes the appeal as a way to implement the ECtHR judgments; on the other hand, a return to pre-2007 wording regarding the nullity suit; the approval of this proposal, for both reasons, would put an end to the practical relevance of the doctrine of the Supreme Court on the motion for dismissal of actions as a way of enforcement of ECtHR's judgments.
4. The Proposed Reform of the Judicial Power includes the following provision: "1. The provisions of the preceding Articles shall not preclude recognition of the jurisdiction of those supranational and international courts established by international treaties to which Spain is a party. 2. In particular, the judgments of the European Court of Human Rights, in cases in which Spain has been the defendant and the violation of a right has been declared, will be ground for review of the final judgment of the Spanish Court in its *a quo* process, at the request of those who would have been the claimants before that particular Court" (Article 5).

The following comment may be made, at this point: The upholding of the appeal will bring the annulment of the judgment under review. But it is unclear whether the following confirmatory judgment of the domestic Court may be object of further review. However, this proposed rule, part of the new LOPJ, does not affect the Constitutional Court, which is not integrated into the judiciary, and whose rulings are not subject to review. When the Constitutional Court is the author of the violation, the problem remains unsolved. The solution to this problem would require the reform of the Organic Law of the Constitutional Court (LOTC). Moreover, the Constitutional Court will normally either have caused or, at least, confirmed the violation, so that the Court in charge of enforcing the sentence of the ECtHR will somehow make the latter's interpretation prevail over that of the Constitutional Court, unless we admit that the resulting ruling of the domestic court is in turn subject to appeal before the Constitutional Court.

---

second) amparo appeal. What the ECtHR had declared contrary to the Convention was the rejection of the first amparo.

[15] The explanation given by the Explanatory Memorandum to the Proposal for a reform of the Judiciary Act is relevant in this respect: "beginning with the judicial power itself, the only new relief is given by the expectation that the judgments of the European Court of Human Rights declare the impairment of a right shall be grounds for review of the judgment handed down in the process *a quo*. This will, in line with what other European countries do, strengthen the influence of the institution that is entrusted with the creation of a *ius commune* of human rights at a continental level and—what is even more important—to provide satisfactory remedies to people whose rights the ECtHR has declared violated, but cannot see them re-established to the previous juridical situation. Note too that it takes a much needed precaution: the review is open only to the final judgment in the case which was then considered by the Strasbourg Court, however similar the case would be. In other words, the review of final judgments for real or alleged infringement of the jurisprudence of the ECtHR is not allowed".

Bibliography

Bustos Gisbert, R. 2006. La función jurisdiccional en escenarios de pluralismo constitucional. In *Integración Europea y Poder judicial*, dir. A Sáiz Arnáiz: 211 et seqs. Oñate: IVAP.

De Miguel Canuto, E. 2013. Eficacia interna de las sentencias del Tribunal Europeo de Derechos Humanos. *Revista Quincena Fiscal* 19: 61–83.

Ferreres Comella, V. 2006. El juez nacional ante los derechos fundamentales europeos. Algunas reflexiones en torno a la idea de diálogo. In *Integración Europea y Poder judicial*, dir. A. Sáiz Arnáiz: 231 et seqs. Oñate: IVAP.

López Castillo, A., A. Sáiz Arnáiz, and V. Ferreres Comella. 2005. *Constitución Española y Constitución Europea*. Madrid: CEPC.

Revenga Sánchez, M. 2004. En torno a la eficacia de las sentencias del TEDH: ¿Amparo de ejecución o afianzamiento de doctrina? *Revista Española de Derecho Europeo* 12: 521–538.

Rey Martínez, F. 1989. El criterio interpretativo de los derechos fundamentales conforme a normas internacionales. *Revista General de Derecho* 537: 3625–3631.

Ripol Carulla, S. 2007. *El sistema europeo de protección de los derechos humanos y el Derecho Español*. Barcelona: Atelier.

Rubio Llorente, F. 1997. Los derechos fundamentales. Evolución, fuentes y titulares en España. *Claves* 75: 2–10.

Sáiz Arnáiz, A. 1999. *La apertura constitucional al derecho internacional y europeo de los derechos humanos. El art. 10.2 de la Constitución Española*. Madrid: CGPJ.

Sáiz Arnáiz, A. 2003. El derecho fundamental al recurso en el orden penal y la interpretación del arte 24.1 de la Constitución de conformidad con el Derecho Internacional y Europeo de los derechos humanos (especial referencia a la situación de los aforados y a los supuestos de conexidad): un ejemplo de desafortunada jurisprudencia constitucional. *Revista Española de Derecho Europeo* 5: 123–157.

Human Rights, Between Supreme Court, Constitutional Court and Supranational Courts: The Italian Experience

Luca Mezzetti

Abstract This essay analyses the role of the Italian Constitutional Court and of the Supreme Court of Cassation in recognizing and protecting human rights. These courts, indeed, have deeply contributed to the implementation and to the promotion of that part of the substantial Constitution that can be identified in the recognition and protection of human rights. In particular this work analyses the role of the constitutional principles about human rights (as human dignity, personalistic and solidarity principles, equality principle) and the emersion of new rights (as privacy, life, personal identity, oblivion, ...) in the constitutional framework.

This essay adopt a multilevel approach because it analyses also, how both at the regional level and at the supranational level, human rights are protected.

Moreover it is considered the process of integration between the Italian Constitutional Order and Supranational Legal Orders, in particular looking at the role and at the case law of Supranational Courts (ECJ and ECHR).

Introduction

The Italian Constitution belongs to the first wave of constitutions that started the process of constitutional transition and democratic consolidation after the end of World War II and was reported at the time of its entry into force for the innovation, breadth and articulation of the content of the first part, dedicated to the recognition and protection of human rights, providing a good example for successive constitutions. If compared with the constitutions of the second wave which occurred during the second half of the 1970s (particularly Greece, Portugal, and Spain) and the third wave of constitutional transitions that affected the legal systems of Central and Eastern Europe after 1989 (the Constitution of Poland, 1997, appears in this respect of peculiar importance and interest) (Mezzetti 2003, 115; Vergottini 1998), the structure of the rights covered by the *formal* Constitution appears outdated and

L. Mezzetti (✉)
School of Law, University of Bologna, via Belmeloro 12, 40126 Bologna, Italy
e-mail: luca.mezzetti@unibo.it

R. Arnold (ed.), *The Convergence of the Fundamental Rights Protection in Europe*, Ius Gentium: Comparative Perspectives on Law and Justice 52,
DOI 10.1007/978-94-017-7465-9_3

overwhelmed by the economic, social, cultural and technological progress. This phenomenon has remedied case law of the Constitutional Court and the Supreme Court of Cassation who have significantly contributed to the development of the *substantial* Constitution, both exploiting the potential of contents inherent in the formal Constitution and maintaining a constant dialogue with the Court of Justice of the European Union and the European Court of Human Rights.

The Italian Constitutional System for the Recognition and Protection of Human Rights

The Italian system of protection of rights and liberties adheres to the multilevel scheme and is based firstly upon a core of principles and constitutional dispositions contained in the Constitution of 1948: articles 1–11 enunciate various principles pertaining in direct or indirect ways to the protection of human rights and fundamental liberties, the whole part I of the Constitution, articulated in four chapters (chapter I – civil relationships, chapter II – ethical-social relationships, chapter III – economic relationships, chapter IV – political relationships) is devoted to the recognition and the guarantee of classical *fundamental rights* (habeas corpus, inviolability of the domicile, freedom and secretiveness of the correspondence, freedom of circulation and stay, freedom of reunion, freedom of association, religious freedom, freedom of expression, right of defence, freedom of art and science), of *social rights* (among others, right to health, right to education, welfare rights), of *economic rights* (among others, the worker's rights, freedom of labour association, right to strike, freedom of private economic initiative, property right), of *political rights* (right to vote, right to associate in political parties, right of petition, right to have access to public offices and public positions) (Mezzetti 2013b, 1).

The system of recognition of rights and freedoms is completed by the individualization of incumbent duties on the citizens or on all the members of the society (among others, duty of defence of the Country, duty to contribute to public expenses, duty of fidelity to the Republic, duty to carry out public functions with discipline and honour) (Polacchini 2013, 596). The development and the updating of such system is due to the jurisprudence of the Constitutional Court (CC) and the Supreme Court of Cassation (SC), that have contributed in a decisive way to the integration and the development of the rights originally recognized in the text of the fundamental Charter. Such work has been developed and is carried out in constant and profitable dialogue with the Court of Justice of the European Union and with the European Court of Human Rights.

The recognition and protection offered by the ordinary legislator are added to the constitutional level through the predisposition of various *codes* (for example the code for the protection of personal data, the consumers' code), as well as the recognition of principles and rights within the Statutes of ordinary Regions. The legal status of aliens is regulated by the Constitution and by ordinary legislation.

The Constitutional Principles About Human Rights

Within the fundamental constitutional principles, which represent the essential values and – following the Constitutional Court's words (CC 1146/1988) – "*belong to the supreme values essence over which the Italian Constitution is founded*", different principles that are directly related to human rights and fundamental freedoms are included. These principles are *human dignity* (the "most fundamental" principle), the *personalistic principle*, the *solidarity principle*, *equality*, the *international principle*, the principle of *jurisdictional protection*; and also the *republican principle*, the *democratic principle*, *popular sovereignty*, *separation of powers*, *rule of law*, the *labor principle*, *autonomy and decentralization*, *protection of minorities*, the *secular principle*, and the *principle of cultural State* (Mezzetti 2011, 1).

The Principle or Value of Human Dignity

Human dignity is a principle or a supreme value that the Italian Constitution does not qualify explicitly. The Constitutional foundation of the principle may be found in the combination of articles 2 and 3 of the Constitution. The Constitutional Court recognizes a connection between the value of dignity and the primacy of human beings as persons (Drigo 2011, 177).

In the CC decision 74/1968 – where the Court was asked to decide over the constitutionality of madhouses' law – the value of human beings as persons already arose in our constitutional system as a principle of central importance concerning the idea of dignity. In fact, the constitutional judges assumed that "*the act of the authority for the public security*" should have been taken "*respectfully towards the human person*" (art. 2 and 32 of the Constitution), and that the same authority "*cannot act without consideration of the disabled person, while it is stated in article 32 that the treatment of a disabled must be inspired by maximum concern*". Furthermore, there are several decisions which refer not only to "*equal social dignity*" as stated in art. 3 Const., but also to the wider concept of "*equal personal dignity*". These decisions take into consideration "*the primacy of human persons and the rights with which they are endowed*" as a founding element of the constitutional system (CC 26/1999, 390/1999, 159/2001, 448/2002, 341/2006, 561/1987). The Court recognizes the endowment with inviolable rights to the people as long as they are intended as "human beings" and not because "they take part in some specific political community" (CC 249/2010, 105/2001). The concept of dignity has been positively anchored by the Court to the constitutional principles included in articles 2 and 3 Const. and it has been particularly underlined in the motivations of the decision 78/2007. In that case, the constitutional judges, who were asked to decide over the constitutionality of some acts regarding the penitentiary system, stated that the determination of the balance between the different exigencies involved by the infliction of a punishment is a legislator's competence and not a Court's one. Nevertheless, the judges found the implementation of a law intended to diversify criminal punishment on the basis of the citizenship of illegal immigrants as unconstitutional. The Court held that "*the general and absolute prohibition to get the benefit of an alternative punishment rather than prison [...] is against the principles inspiring the penitentiary law which, on the basis of the constitutional principles of equal personal dignity and re-educative purpose of punishment (art. 2, 3 and 27 Const.), prevents any discrimination about criminal treatment on the basis of the respect of migration law*".

There are many other decisions that put the concept of human dignity only in relation to the principles of art. 2 Const. For example, the decision 479/1987 (regarding the law about workplace health conditions) underlined "*the absolute value of the human being as a person stated in art. 2 Const.*". In a later decision (CC 217/1988), the Court held that among "*the tasks the Government can never reject*" there is that imposing "*to take care of people's life in order to make it reflect the universal representation of human dignity every day and under every single aspect*". Other interesting cases where the concept of human dignity comes up just from the provisions of article 2 Const. are also represented by the decisions 167/1991, 368/1992, 81/1993, 224/1996. Moreover, the reasoning of the Court in the decision 364/1988 appears to be particularly convincing. In that case, the constitutional judges defined with clarity the importance the Constitution gives to the value of human person and, as a consequence, to human dignity. It has been stated that the constitutional system "*put the human person at the top of the values' hierarchy*" (so, it cannot be restrained even for purposes of general prevention) and that "*the Constitution requires all the individuals to endeavor maximally and constantly in order to respect other persons' interests...if the absolute irrelevance of the criminal law ignorance is accepted, the protection of juridical goods will prevail unconditionally in spite of the liberty and dignity of the people*". This interpretation would entail a violation of "*the whole spirit of the fundamental Charter and the essential principles which inspired it*" or, in other words, "*it would dismantle the fundamental warranties a democratic Government recognizes to the citizen and it would manipulate the concept of human being as a person, letting it degrade from the priority position it fills, and that it must fill, in the constitutional protected values hierarchy*".

Many decisions about the right to health included in article 32 Const. refer to the concept of human dignity (CC 40/2011, 61/2011, 148/2008, 432/2005, 509/2000, 309/1999, 267/1998, 252/2001). There is a reference to the inviolable dignity of human persons in the decision 304/1994 regarding the "right to health treatment". In some cases the Constitutional Court recalled the concept of dignity in order to strengthen other constitutional values, but there is no lack of other cases where it represents an independent reference as an autonomous relevant value. In this sense the decision 37/1985 can be cited because it sets a connection between the concept of human dignity and the recognition of a right to alimony. When statutes explicitly provide for it, the provision of the duty to pay alimony is functional for the protection of essential values such as life and human dignity. That protection is due "*to solidarity reasons towards members of the family community which are in a state of need*". It is possible to find another reference in the decision 10/2010 (recalled by the later decision 61/2011) where the Constitutional Court justified a central governmental invasion of regional competences when it's necessary "*to guarantee effective protection to subjects which are in a state of need and are endowed with a fundamental right so connected with the protection of the unrestrainable core of dignity and of human person that it must be respected all over the Nation in a uniform, appropriate and timely way by a coherent regulation for that purpose*". Moreover, another reference is found in the decision 561/1987 where the judges recognized a constitutional protection to a new right (the right to sexual liberty) without referring to another constitutional right or recalling the general article 2 Const. as an open clause, but reasoning on the base of human dignity concept. In fact, it has been held that "*the sexual liberty*" represents "*a form of expression of the human person*" and that "*the right to have it at one's disposal is, without any doubt, an absolute subjective right which must be included among the subjective positions directly protected by the Constitution as an inviolable right of the human person*". The Constitutional Court often recalled the notion of dignity as related to the concepts of freedom and equality. In this sense there are many decisions of the Court where the judges made an attempt to build such a relationship among the three different values. So far, freedoms come up to be thought as having a correlation with human dignity through a "*conscious passage among the dignity, the rights and the freedoms, where the first one will represent the foundation for many of the second ones, and these, in their complex, will let freedoms to be effective for each man, demonstrating the natural inclination of dignity towards freedom*" (Pirozzoli 2007). In this way the value of dignity, once it gained more importance in its unchanging consistency, can be seen as an essential element (founding or strengthening) for most of the rights whose protection will guarantee the freedom of every man. For example, the CC decision 334/1996 about the freedom of religion and the CC decision 112/1993 about the right of information can be cited. The analysis of the connection between dignity and equality seems to be much more complicated under a taxonomic point of view. It's worth to notice that the Court, in this context, uses two expressions which are similar in form but different in content. These two expressions are "equal dignity" and "equal social dignity" (Pirozzoli 2007, 17).

"Equal dignity", when it's not used referring generally to a human person, can be found frequently associated with the proper meanings of equality, especially when it is used referring to subjects belonging to specific categories (e.g. members of the parliament – CC 417/1999 – or taxpayers – CC 287/2000 – or believers of a recognized church – CC 329/1997). Notwithstanding this, there isn't a perfect coincidence between equality and dignity for, at least, two reasons. Firstly, under a linguistic point of view, the junction between the word "equality" and the expression "equal dignity" evokes a relationship of coordination and not of coincidence because, otherwise, it would be redundant. Secondly, under a logical point of view, if the Court intends the concept of equal dignity to be perfectly coincident with the concept of equality, there would be no reason to use the first expression (Pirozzoli 2007, 23).

The expression "equal social dignity" seems to be founded on an external factor represented by the perception we have of other people's opinion, acknowledgment or feedback within the social community and by the actual consideration we have of that community. Even in this context we have lots of examples in constitutional jurisprudence, mostly about positive actions (CC 109/1993) or about substantive equality (CC 48/1991, 15/1996, 422/1995 and 494/2002). Beyond the cases where the notion of dignity emerges from the constitutional frame as an autonomous value which sometimes amounts to a real principle, there is no lack of decisions where it comes out with a substantial meaning involving positive law. In fact, many Constitutional Court's decisions conceived the connection between dignity and liberty under a limitative prospective so that the first one is intended as a real limitation of the second one. The concept of dignity becomes a parameter for balancing the application of constitutional rights by the legislator or by the constitutional judge. In this sense, the value of dignity works as a limitation for the governmental action that won't be free to cause "*an infringement or a deterioration of the person's dignity or honor so severe to be considered like a subdual to someone else's power, and, so far, constituting a violation of the habeas corpus principle*" (CC 68/1964).

Moreover there are several decisions inhering the connection between the freedom of economic initiative and the value of dignity intended, again, as a general limitation. For example, it's useful to recall the decision 270/2010 about the freedom of economic initiative and market competition. In that case (article 41 Const. establishes that "*the private economic initiative cannot be exerted contrary to the social utility or in a way that jeopardizes the security, the freedom and the human dignity*") the Court affirmed that "*every economic activity, public or private, can be directed and coordinated in order to implement social purposes*". So far, it's not surprising the Court reached the conclusion that "*the constitutional provision allows regulations which can guarantee the protection of interests having nothing to do with the protection of a competitive market*".

Two other decisions (CC 111/1974 and 12/1970) pointed out a different but coherent perspective. In those cases the constitutional judges consented to a limitation of the economic initiative freedom in order to protect the value of human dignity. The Court held that "*human activities may be carried on in many different ways and a regulation intended to protect dignity and human personality cannot rule human activities without taking into consideration the different way of living*" (CC 345/2005, 161/2005, 419/2000, 427/1995, 479/1987, 125/1963).

Concluding the analysis of the connections between dignity and fundamental liberties, an influential doctrine observed that the constitutional jurisprudence has delineated a concept of human dignity apt to work as a "*border aim for the constitutionally protected freedoms, just because it represents the only aim they always must respect and follow*". Under this prospective, "*human dignity ends up to constitute a***super constitutional***value compared with other liberties protected (art. 13 and subsequent) and with inviolable human rights*". It has to be underlined that "*the expression just used, in the context of constitutional values hierarchy, has the function of substantial "completing rule" or founding and abstracting value/principle at the base of the teleologically personalistic nature of our legal system*" (Ruggeri, Spadaro 1992, 228).

The Personalistic Principle: The Solidarity Principle

The first part of article 2 Const. includes the provision that follows: "*the Republic recognizes and guarantees the inviolable human rights individually and towards social communities where the individuals realize their personality*". With such a provision the Founders acknowledged that the establishment of powers has not created fundamental human rights but they are logically antecedent. This acknowledgment assumed a priority of values which entails "*the full development of a human person*" as the main aim of the social organization (personalistic principle) (Vedaschi 2011, 274).

The personalistic principle postulates the existence of a range of individual autonomy which cannot be infringed by government powers, even in presence of public purposes or, generally, of specific goals that the social majority thinks deserve protection. This principle represents an expression of a peculiar conception of human dignity intended, first of all, as an inviolable right to physical and moral integrity of the person. The same right is protected by other constitutional provisions involving more specific aspects (under this point of view, art. 13^{3} Const. is interesting because it provides that "*every physical or moral violence on people, however restricted in their liberty, must be punished*" and, so providing, it recognizes and confirms the inviolability of the essential/minimal core of the human person idea which, being a value by itself, cannot be used just to achieve different social purposes). Other constitutional provisions regarding this point of view are art. 3^{1} Const., art. 27^{3-4} Const., art. 32^{2} Const.: "*the law can* ***never*** *violate the limitation imposed by the respect of the human person*". The protection of human dignity, as a value included in the personalistic principle, does not just entail the duty of self-restraint from unduly interfering with the range of individual autonomy (negative duty) for the Government, it also entails the relative duty to protect that range of individual autonomy from unduly interferences of other private subjects (positive duty). This conclusion derives from two factors. Firstly, it comes from a natural "*horizontal efficacy*" of the human dignity clause and of some fundamental liberties that carry out its significance. Both the Founders and the international declarations about human rights accepted this idea in different ways (CC 122/1970). Secondly, the above illustrated corollary comes from the development beyond the static concept of fundamental freedoms on the basis that "one of the Republic's main tasks is to modify or to remove the economic or social conditions which hinder the full development of the human person" (art. 3^{2} Const.).

The personalistic principle is strictly connected with the pluralist principle because the concept of a human person does not include only the individual profile as characterized by decisional and moral autonomy and by the capacity to be endowed with "fundamental rights". The human person is also intended as a centre of multiple relationships that give shape to autonomous organizations ("intermediate bodies") endowed with some rights. The provision included in art. 2 Const., in fact, recognizes inviolable human rights not only to individuals but also to people gathered in "*social formations where they can realize their personality*". The social formations the Constitution refers to are the organizations ruled by law and, in a manner more or less detailed, by constitutional provisions, as much as free aggregations born in the exertion of the right to assembly (art. 18 Const.). For the purpose of this analysis, every real human person is intended as a centre of complex relationships that can find realization through different unlimited fundamental expressive functions. The primary value recognized to human persons, so intended, strengthens the opinion under which the rights that are made explicit in the Constitution (articles 13, 14, 15, 24 Const.) or that are granted to all the people without distinction (articles 19, 21, 22, 25 Const.) are not the only ones considered inviolable, because some liberties expressly reserved for citizens must also be recognized inviolable as well. This reasoning brings to the conclusion that, beyond what is explicitly written in the Constitution, all people – and not only citizens – should have been endowed with all the guarantees that are necessary for the exertion of fundamental rights. In this sense the guarantee of formal equality (art. 3^1 Const.) is a peculiar example (CC 46/1977, 54/1979).

The tendency to extend the range of application of constitutional provisions that guarantee the endowment with fundamental liberties derives from a peculiar technique of interpreting the Constitution intended to emphasize the unchanging profile that characterizes that kind of law provisions (*value oriented interpretation* or *rationale continuum interpretation*). So far, the opinion to share is that under which art. 2 Const. would have the function to protect and guarantee all the "freedom claims" that, even if not yet codified in constitutional provisions, are already defined by social life. This approach is frequently experienced in the international practice of recognizing new liberties (CC 404/1988, 388/1999, 135/2002). Therefore the provision of art. 2 Const. represents an "*open formula*" because it constitutes the framework for constitutional codified rights, for "*new rights*" – added because of the jurisprudence or the legislator's intervention – and for incoming rights. This opinion generally prevailed and it brought to the recognition of the *right to sexual liberty* (CC 561/1987), the *right to a dwelling* (CC 404/1988, 252/1989, 419/1991 and 119/1999), the *right to privacy* (CC 139/1990), and also the *rights to decency, to honor, to respectability, to intimacy and to reputation* (CC 38/1973), *to a healthy environment* (CC 210/1987, 641/1987), the *rights to personal identity* (CC 13/1994), *to life* (CC 223/1996), *to sexual identity* (CC 161/1985), the *right to leave the Country* (CC 278/1992), the *right of the minor to take part in a family* (CC 183/1988) and the *right of the disabled to be accompanied* (CC 346/1989). For the same reasoning it seems possible to consider as "fundamental" some other rights like abortion, free sexual orientation, divorce and, generally, all new claims of liberty that are already an essential part of public opinion, especially when they are endorsed by international or national consent (Mezzetti 2013a, 489).

A tight connection between rights and compulsory duties of political, economic and social solidarity exists, which the Republic requires to be fulfilled (art. 2 Const., second paragraph, CC 77/1983). From this idea derives the idea that individual rights are not unlimited because the legislator can reasonably restrict them for purposes of general interest (CC 29/1977, CC 252/1983) without violating human dignity. Another perspective contemplates the existence of duties as an expression of the principle of human solidarity/responsibility. On the base of that principle, individual and collective liberties cannot be expected as granted by the Government if there is no will to take part in the realization of others, in the development of social life (CC 75/1992), in the responsible preservation of human species and in the recognition of the dignity of the future existence of humanity (CC 259/1996, where the Court held that the use of water intended as a limited resource must take into consideration "solidarity as a parameter and the fundamental right to preserve human species and future generations"). *Duties* are usually divided in *two categories*. For the first category of duties prevails the *political profile* [faithfulness to the Republic (art. 54 Const.) and election participation (art. 48 Const.). For the second category of duties prevails the *social and economic profile* (duty to defend the Country (art. 52 Const.), right-duty to work (art. 4 Const.) and duty to pay taxes (art. 53 Const.)).

The Equality Principle

The principle of formal equality included in art. 3[1] Const. provides that "all citizens (...) are equal before law without distinction of sex, race, language, religion, political opinions, personal and social conditions" (Polacchini 2011, 251). The constitutional doctrine agrees on the idea that the concept of formal equality defines, first of all, the strength and the general efficacy of law (CC 206/2004), because it implies that law must apply to members of the Government as much as to the governed people (articles 97 and 101 Const.). The provisions of art. 3[1] Const. imply also a presumed prohibition of individual or personal legislation (CC 70/1960, 134/1978, 461/2000). Notwithstanding the "hard core" of the provision, the principle of formal equality does not entail an absolute prohibition to make any distinction between different subjects categories, because "a system which doesn't distinguish a circumstance from another one (...) is not even thinkable, also for the reason that it would end up not to put any rule at all" (CC 64/1961). The constitutional jurisprudence has shared the opinion under which the formal equality is not constituted simply by the prohibitions mentioned in the provisions of art. 3[1] Const. and it must be considered as included among the highest general principles pervading the whole system of law. The same jurisprudence observed that from the aforesaid constitutional principle derives "*a general canon of coherence for the system of law*" (CC n. 204/1982, n. 25/1966) which can be modulated on the basis of the different law realities. Then the principle of formal equality allowed the development of a general principle of non-discrimination among the different egalitarian articulations that were possible. This general principle came out because no other classification criterion was explicitly included in art. 3[1] Const. and "*the principle of equality would have been, however, violated if the law, without a reasonable justification, applied a different treatment to citizens that were in the same situation*" (CC 15/1960). This approach does not require that a correct application of the equality principle results in an absolute obligation to adopt law differentiations, but it demands the adoption of reasonable differentiation criteria. So far, a *principle of reasonableness* inspires this interpretation and it bounds the legislator to treat in the same way what is objectively the same and to treat in a different manner what is objectively different, respecting characteristics and diversities (CC 21/1961, 5/1980) (Morrone 2002).

The reasonableness appreciation of an act which distinguishes similar contexts or assimilates different circumstances needs an assessment of the general purposes of the law, or of the specific aims which inspired the act. After that assessment, the coherence and the finalization of the provision must be verified in connection with the assessed legitimate purpose that has to be followed (CC 91/1973, 89/1996, 223/2004, 27/2005). The correct application of the principle of reasonableness influences the content of the law as long as it is required to "limit unjustified derogations and arbitrary exceptions within the borders of established rules or of general principles of law" (CC 314/1983, 28/1957, 9/1975). It should be noticed that the provisions of art. 3^1 Const. include an explicit *antidiscrimination clause* which prevents making any difference on the basis of some factors expressly indicated (i.e. sex, race, language, religion, political opinion, social and personal conditions). This clause hides a presumption of unconstitutionality for law treatments based on these "suspected factors" (CC 56/1958). This presumption is characterized by a relative nature and cannot be assumed as a presumption *iuris et de jure.* If it were otherwise, the opportunity (allowed by art. 3^2 Const.) to legislate in favor of vulnerable categories would entail a judgment of unconstitutionality. Eventually the mere suspected distinction is not enough to jeopardize equality, because it needs to be unreasonable and unjustified. This approach, based on a rule of reason, brings to allow distinctions apparently prohibited and, on the other side, it tends to extend the prohibition out of a reasonableness judgment. Beyond the national boundaries there is a tendency to interpret equality (especially the antidiscrimination clauses) in the light of the human dignity value. It seems reasonable and, in some way, plausible that the Italian constitutional jurisprudence assessed the lack of justification and so the unconstitutionality of law classifications which, even if not involving suspected factors, have the unique purpose to hinder an unpopular minority, so violating the right to human dignity.

The provisions of art. 3^2 Const. state also the *principle of substantive equality* for which "*it's a Republic's task to remove economic and social obstacles that, limiting in fact the liberty and the equality of citizens, prevent the full development of the human person and the effective participation of all workers in the political, economic and social organization of the Country*". This principle can be intended as a guarantee for the effective application of formal equality because the latter cannot prevent the substantial inequality due to social and economic difficulties. So far, the formal equality provides a universal endowment of fundamental rights, while the substantial equality provides the equal opportunity to exert these rights in fact, charging the Republic with the duty to remove all social and economic hinders. The aforesaid article promotes the full development of individuals' personality on the basis that there can be no effective human dignity without the universal guarantee of the essential capacity to exert fundamental rights. In this sense, art. 3^2 Const. justifies pieces of legislation "*apparently discriminating towards categories or groups of citizens but that, eventually, recover the condition of equality for these categories or groups*" (CC 106/1962). This kind of legislation is generally called "positive actions" and is intended to promote, through combination of incentives, the same original condition between man and woman, for example, about work (CC 109/1993). On the other side, art. 3^2 Const. does now allow justification for the legislation limiting the opportunity for both sexes to be represented in electoral lists beyond a specific proportion ("*pink share*"). In that case, the purpose to promote women access to elective positions was not enough to save the law because it infringed art. 51 Const., which establishes that "*all citizens of both sexes can have access to public offices and to elective positions with equal conditions, respecting the requirements imposed by law*". Sex cannot be intended as a requirement of eligibility because it's not a prejudicial and necessary condition to be elected and so it doesn't constitute an essential factor to exert the political passive right (CC 422/1995). Regions with special statutes tried to avoid the effects of the Court decision implementing ad hoc "*pink amendments*" [e.g. art. 15 St. Valle d'Aosta has been approved as constitutional (CC 49/2003) for the occurrence of the constitutional reform (Const. reform act n. 2/2001 and the new art. 117[7] Const.)]. The constitutional reform act No. 1/2003 represented an attempt of the Republic to implement new measures for equal opportunity between men and women to have access to public offices and elective positions (new art. 51 Const.). A relevant application of this reform is represented by the provision of art. 3 (act No. 90/2004) where it's provided that, for European Parliament elections, "*both sexes must not be represented in electoral lists in a proportion that is superior to the two thirds of the number of candidates*".

New Rights

The birth of a new rights' category represents a *third generation* of rights that is distinguished from the *first generation*, civil and political rights – *negative liberties* – and from the *second generation*, social and economic rights – *positive liberties* (Ferrari 2011, 1). The new generation of rights derives from the protection progressively accorded by the legislator or by the jurisprudence (even in European or in other international contexts) to particular situations deserving formal consideration for the public opinion and previously not considered. These rights are "new", in other words, because they are not explicitly included in the Constitutional Charter, but derive their importance from the people's experience and consideration. They are characterized as heterogeneous because they can be reserved for individuals or for social groups. The extension of these rights, along with the reasoning that affords full constitutional protection, changes also on the basis of the approach thought to be followed. In particular, it's of crucial importance the interpretation given to art. 2 Const. as a "closed or open formula". In the first instance, in fact, the new rights can be interpreted as a development of the "implicit potentialities" encompassed within the constitutional provision that can have place through an extensive and evolutive interpretation. Instead, in the second instance, art. 2 Const. can already guarantee constitutional protection to new rights as long as they are generally advocated by the people and the legislator, by the jurisprudence, or if international declarations recognize them. The Constitutional Court has adopted the second approach and, through this way, it has afforded constitutional protection to some new personality rights among which there are the *right to life* (CC 223/1996), the *right of the minor to take part in a family* (CC 183/1988), the *right to privacy* (CC 39/1990), the *right to social liberty* (CC 50/1998). The application of this approach started with the decision 561/1987 where the Court stated that "the *right to sexual liberty* is, without any doubt, an absolute right of the individuals because it represents an essential way to express the human person. It has to be included among the subjective positions directly protected by the Constitution and, so far, it must be considered an inviolable right of the human person under the guarantee of art. 2 Const."

Furthermore, an influential doctrine defines some "new rights" as a consequence of the constitutional jurisprudence analysis. First of all, the *right to personal identity* or "the right to be yourself" is intended as the respect of the subject representation as participating in the social life. This right ends up to interest the shared experiences and ideas, the ideological, religious, moral and social opinions, that distinguish and characterize individuals. The Constitutional Court decision n. 13/1994 recognized this right as "*unforsaking asset of the human person*" under the protection of art. 2 Const. (CC 297/1996, 120/2001, 494/2002).

Moreover, the *right to sexual identity*, the *right to honor*, the *right to a dwelling*, the *right to have access to administrative documents*, the *right to procreate* (CC 151/2009, 97/2010), the *unborn rights to life and health*, the *right to peace and to the preservation of the universal heritage of humanity*, the *right to social, economic, cultural and political development* are some of the new rights the doctrine defined.

It's worth to spend some words about a recent doctrinal debate around the definition of a new right like the *right to security*. The debate increased after the recent law reforms enacted as a consequence of the international terrorism phenomenon's worsening. The general interest protected by this right is the prevention of any behavior that can put in jeopardy the security of the people or that can ingenerate a feeling of "insecurity". In this sense, the last law reforms enacted and well known as "2008/09 Security Package" (including act No. 125/2008 converting the decree No. 92/2008 "*Urgent measures about public security*", act No. 38/2009 converting decree No. 11/2009 "*Urgent measures about public security, sexual violence and persecution behaviors*", act No. 94/2009 "*Provisions about public security*") must be taken into consideration.

The Right to a Healthy Environment

The right to a healthy place of living isn't explicitly provided in the Constitution and it has been developed by the constitutional jurisprudence along with the doctrine. The constitutional law reform of Title V, second part (const. reform act No. 3/2001) introduced the concepts of "environment" and "ecosystem" in the Italian Constitutional Charter through new art. 117. Before this law reform, the jurisprudence of the Constitutional and of the Supreme Court recognized a specific *right to the environment protection* reasoning on the base of articles 2, 9 (regarding the landscapes protection), 32, 41 and 42 Const. Some decisions of the Supreme Court must be mentioned like, for example, SC 1463/1979 and, particularly, SC 5172/1979, stating that the right to health includes a *right to a healthy environment*. Constitutional Court decisions like CC 88/1979, 101/1989, 391/1989 took into consideration the right to a healthy environment as given.

In the constitutional jurisprudence evolution, two decisions dating 1987 represented the cornerstone. With the first decision, the Constitutional Court confirmed the legitimacy of the powers recognized to the Minister of the Environment for coordinating and directing purposes regarding decisions about the impact on environment. The Court held that the extension of such powers is justified on the basis of the European obligations the Republic bears and of the necessity to safeguard national interests and primary constitutional values like environment and health (articles 9, 32 Const.). This development entails a new conception of the environment safeguard as a fundamental right of the people and as a general interest of the community (CC 210/1987).

With the second decision (CC 641/1987), the Court recognized the environment as "unique immaterial good" and as "primary and absolute value" recalling past decisions (CC 247/1974, 184/1986) where the claim under art. 2043 of the civil code was admitted in front of ordinary judges in order to recover damages for the violation of the aforesaid rights. The later evolution of the Court's decisions, instead, qualified the environment just as a *constitutional value*, rejecting the prospective of environment protection as a subjective claim and reconnecting it with other constitutional values (CC 407/2002). Despite the last approach the Court adopted, the constitutional judges started abandoning this interpretation dating from 2007. More recently they have qualified environment as a theme technically intended, specifically regarding new art. 117 Const.

The Right to Privacy

The right to privacy is not explicitly provided in the Constitution, but it is constitutionally founded on the liberty of domicile included in art. 14 Const. and on the liberty and secrecy of every form of communication included in art. 15 Const. (CC 135/2002).

This right has been recently reformed by the parliament. Firstly, the act No. 675/1996 (Privacy Act) established the *Authority for personal data protection,* implementing the Strasburg Convention of 1981 and the European directive No. 95/46. More recently, the act No. 196/2003 (Personal Data Protection Act) abrogated and replaced the older Privacy Act and enacted the new European directive No. 2002/58 about the treatment of personal data and the protection of private life in the context of electronic communications. The Supreme Court decisions recognized the *right to privacy* as an inviolable human right that is founded and granted in the fundamental Charter because it interests the right to representation, the right to a name, the right to honor and reputation, which are all aspects about the importance the Constitution gives to human personality as one (SC 25157/2008, 26972/2008).

The Contribution of the Supreme Court in Enucleating Human Rights

A key area in which the Italian Supreme Court of Cassation has contributed to the implementation and promotion of the substantial Constitution could be identified in the recognition and protection of human rights.

The Court of Cassation's case-law has been crucial not only in enucleating and developing a wide catalogue of "new rights" (personal identity, healthy environment, privacy, oblivion), but also in the elaboration, implementation and realization of the content of new rights already established by the Constitutional Court case law (life, sexual freedom, sexual identity) (Fanotto 2012).

The Right to Life

The *right to life* has not been expressly declared by the Constitution but it was recognized as inviolable according to Article 2 of the Constitution by the case-law of the Constitutional Court (CC 54/1979; 132/1985; 223/1996). Furthermore, with its decision No. 27/1975 the Constitutional Court argued that the protection of an unborn child has constitutional bases as "art. 2 of the Constitution recognizes and guarantees inviolable human rights, including the legal status of the unborn child".

With its decision No. 26 of February 10, 1981, the Constitutional Court has decided on the constitutionality of abortion, stating that "the safeguarding of the *nasciturus*, which is not still a person, cannot prevail over the right to life and the right to health of the mother which is already person".

More recently, in its decision of February 10, 1997, No. 35, the Constitutional Court, judging the admissibility of a referendum on abortion, considered that the right to life is inscribed among fundamental rights protected by Article 2 of the Constitution. More precisely, the Court argued that the right to life has to be included "among those rights that occupy in the constitutional order a privileged position, as they belong to […] the essence of supreme values on which the Constitution is found".

The Constitutional Court in another decision (CC 223/1996), originated from the well known case of an Italian citizen of which the United States of America asked for extradition because of a crime punishable in the USA by death, noted that the right to life as the primary inviolable right protected by the article 2 of the Constitution imposes an absolute guarantee.

The case-law of the Supreme Court has contributed to the clarification of certain issues related to the protection of the unborn child. In our legal system art. 1, paragraph 2 of the Civil Code provides that fundamental rights recognized by law in favour of the unborn child are subordinated to the birth event. This legislative provision introduces two principles: (a) the rights of the unborn child must be provided by law; (b) in any case, these rights are subordinated on the event of the birth. Thus, the unborn child has the legal capacity to be recognized by a natural parent (art. 254, paragraph 1 of the Civil Code), to succeed due to death (art. 462, paragraph 1of the Civil Code), to acquire by donation (art. 784 of the Civil Code).

The Supreme Court has not yet completely clarified the legal status of the *nasciturus*; notwithstanding that in its decision No. 14488 of July 29, 2004, it reminds us that the sacrifice of the *nasciturus* cannot be configurable as a right of the mother and is allowed only because the physical and the mental health of the mother is considered as a preeminent interest. The case originated from a complaint proposed by parents who, after the birth of their daughter that suffered from *thalassemia major*, have requested a compensation for damage against the obstetrician who didn't inform them of the risks for the *nasciturus*, denying thus the existence of a right to be born healthy and consequently the existence of the right to be not born malformed. The Court of Cassation also noted: "the legal system is protecting the unborn children and the pregnancy only to the birth, and not also to the "no-birth", configuring in this way a "right to be born" and a "right to be born healthy", which must be understood, however, only in its positive sense".

More recently, with the decision No. 10741 of 2009, concerning a similar case, the Supreme Court stated that the legal subjectivity has to be recognized to unborn children although this recognition is limited to the ownership of certain personal and protected interests.

In this case we can identify profiles of continuity and discontinuity with the previous case law. On the one hand the decision endorses the conclusions reached by the previous case law (SC 11503/1993; 14488/2004) about the existence of the right of unborn children to be born healthy as the explanation of the right to health under art. 32 of the Constitution. On the other hand the decision moves away from the previous case law in which the Supreme Court didn't recognize the legal subjectivity of the unborn children. Indeed, the Supreme Court affirmed that "no one can recognize to the person-*nasciturus* the ownership of a protected interest without attributing them the subjectivity". Consequently, starting from the existence of a right to be born healthy, the Court of Cassation states that the *nasciturus* has the right to compensation for damage for failure to fulfil the duty to provide information to parents and for administration of teratogenic drugs despite the dutiful awareness of the existing and scientifically documented risk.

The Right to Die

Recently, the Supreme Court was called to decide on the *right to refuse medical treatments* which represents not only the negative aspects of the right to health, but also the right to live with dignity, understanding the latter as a freedom to choose matters of the highest privacy and the most personal nature without influences imposed coercively by third parties.

With the decision No. 21748 of October 16, 2007, concerning the well-known case of Eluana Englaro, the Supreme Court has addressed the problem of the existence, the extension and the definition of the right to life, entering in this way in the bioethical debate that has assumed "global" dimensions whereas the most effective legal solutions are offered by supranational Courts and States' Higher Courts.

Indeed, the Supreme Court has had a full awareness of the international phenomenon on the topic, having identifying in the Oviedo Convention on Human Rights and Biomedicine, implemented in Italy by act No. 145 of March 28, 2001, although not yet ratified, one of the main interpretative parameters to use in order to give a proper solution to the case. Similarly, the decision contains many references to the solutions offered by other Courts, especially the German Constitutional Court and the House of Lords, and to the principles developed by the European Court of Human Rights in the right to life field in connection with the right to self-determination in choosing medical treatments.

The Supreme Court identified in the right to self-determination and in the right to life two subjective situations in potential conflict and established some key principles. According to the Court, if a patient is in a state of irreversible coma, cannot relate in any way to the outside world and is hydrated and fed by nose-gastric tube, the Court may authorize the disabling of medical treatments only when the vegetative state is, according to a rigorous clinical appreciation, irreversible, and there is no chance of recovery according to internationally accepted scientific standards. Furthermore, the Court may authorize the disabling of medical treatments only if this request expresses the idea that the patient had acquired about the dignity of life, to be inferred from its previous pronouncements or personality or from the style of life adopted until the loss of capacity.

The Court of Cassation excluded that artificial hydration and nutrition with nose-gastric tube constitutes a form of aggressive medical treatment and considered that in the Italian legal system there doesn't exist a duty of the individual to health which involves a duty of the patient not to deny cures and therapies that helps to keep him/her alive.

The solution adopted by the Court of Cassation in its decision No. 21748/2007 didn't find a confirmation under the Constitutional Court case law. Indeed, in its ordinance No. 334/2008 the Constitutional Court was called to decide on the constitutional conflict promoted by the Chamber of Deputies and the Senate due to the decision of the Court of Cassation but the Constitutional Court decided not to express itself on merits of the case.

The Right to Personal Identity

The rights that emerge from the *right to personal identity*, such as a name and likeness, can be expressed as the interest that everybody has to be represented with his/her real identity, i.e. with the identity that appears in concrete and unequivocal circumstances of social life. In other words, it is the claim that one's cultural, professional, religious, political, social experiences should not be distorted, misrepresented, falsified, confused, contested, or the like, by means of the ascription of false (even if not necessarily defamatory) statements or acts.

In terms of case law, the *right to personal identity* appeared for the first time in a decision given by the District Court of Rome of May 6, 1974, in which was stated that the law protects one's right to the acknowledgement of one's own acts, and, conversely, the right to repudiate acts that one has never done; in other words, the right to personal identity.

However, only with the decision of the Supreme Court No. 3769 of June 22, 1985, so called *Veronesi case*, the right to personal identity was definitely recognized in the Italian constitutional order. In particular, the Supreme Court, overturning the approach of lower courts, argued that each person has to be represented with his/her real identity. The Court also noted that the Parliament didn't provide expressly for a protection of personal identity despite the intangibility of social projection has to be considered as an important moment of the individual personality. The hallmarks of the name and of the pseudonym identify the subject only on the material plane of existence and of the civil and legal status, while the image evokes only the person's physical appearance. The identity is otherwise a synthetic formula to describe subjects from a global profile, in its many special features and events.

The Supreme Court explicitly recognized in its decision the autonomy of this right, and rooted its normative foundation directly in art. 2 of the Constitution, accepting the "open clause" conception of the latter. The Court of Cassation observes that "the right to personal identity aims to ensure the accurate and complete representation of the individual personality of the subject within the community in which that personality was held, expressed itself and developed. It is an essential, fundamental interest that qualifies the person. The purpose of Article 2 of the Constitution is to protect the human person in its entirety and in its ways to be essential. Article 2 does not simply summarize the rights expressly protected in the Constitution and even those inherent to the human person in the Civil Code, but it places in the centre of the entire constitutional system and takes as its point of reference the human being in the complexity and unity of its values and needs, both material and spiritual".

Ten years later the Constitutional Court has followed the same line of argumentation recognizing the autonomy of the right to personal identity.

In this terms, the Constitutional Court in its decision No. 13/1994 (see also CC 297/ 1996; 120/2001; 494/2002) has affirmed that personal identity constitutes a good in itself, independently of the personal and social condition of the subject, whose constitutional basis are to be found in Art. 2 of the Constitution.

Later the Court of Cassation in its decision No. 978/1996 partially corrected its approach of 1985, affirming that the normative foundation of the right to personal identity can be found directly in Art. 2 of the Constitution, in conjunction with Art. 3, paragraph 2 of the Constitution.

The Right to Sexual Identity

Before the entry into force of act No. 164/1982, the case law of the Supreme Court, not always followed by lower courts, was exclusively oriented in the sense that "the correction of the indication of the sex in contrast with physiological element and psychological attitude of the subject cannot be legitimate for the surgical intervention that artificially altered the original sexual apparatus" (SC 3948/1974).

This approach of the Supreme Court was due to the literal interpretation of the provisions then in force, and was related to a more general qualification of sexual identity, tending to give priority to somatic-exterior aspects rather than to implications of a psychological nature (SC 1236/1975; 1847/1972).

In its decision No. 1236 of April 7, 1975, the Supreme Court noted how the reference to cultural values existing in the community can be seen as fundamental in defining the expressed guidelines, for which the difference of sex is essential for the determination of relationships that take place at a certain level of intimacy, emphasizing that "the common conscience funds meeting between people of different sex on the bases on natural and not artificial recognition".

The Constitutional Court expressed a similar view to that expressed by the Supreme Court in the decision No. 98/1979. The Constitutional Court argued that the right to recognize and register a different sex doesn't form a part of the inviolable rights acquired with a surgical transformation and does not form a part of inviolable rights. According to the Court, the possible solutions of the problem can evoke in Italy, as in other countries, the attention of the Parliament, but cannot be solved in terms of constitutionality of the contested provisions.

In a second phase, the Court of Cassation, in its decision No. 2161 of April 3, 1980, reaffirmed and explained that the "phenomenon of transsexualism cannot constitute a sufficient ground for holding that the person must be qualified according to its sexual characteristics".

The Legislative, prompted in part by the case law of the Supreme Court and of the Constitutional Court and by critiques of many scholars, adopted the Act No. 164/1982.

The changing of the legal framework led the Constitutional Court to recognize, in its decision No. 161/1985, both the right to sex change in case of natural evolution of situations originally not well defined and in the case where, on the basis of a psycho-declared sexuality in contrast with the presence of other sex organs, has occurred the sex change surgery, enabling the subject belonging to the opposite sex, under Articles 2 and 32 of the Constitution.

The Right to Sexual Freedom

The freedom of sexual behaviour can be understood as the right of self-determination of the subject in full autonomy and as the freedom in the implementation of sexual relations.

The protection of freedom of sexual behaviour can be found in the criminal case law that, while not directly addressing the issue of sexual freedom, however recognizes its existence. In particular, the Supreme Court stated in a decision of October 19, 1987, that the parent, pursuant to Art. 147 of the Civil Code, is also the guarantor of the moral integrity and of the sexual freedom of the children. According to the Court, from this provision derives a legal obligation for parents to prevent, whenever possible, any event that threatens personal rights of children.

Following the decisions of the Supreme Court, the Constitutional Court has argued in its decision No. 561/1987 that "sexuality is one of the essential ways of expression of the human person whereby the right to dispose freely of sexuality is certainly an absolute individual right". The Court recognized the autonomy of this right and rooted its normative foundation in art. 2 of the Constitution. This approach allowed the Court to clarify that any violations of the right to sexual freedom involves non-pecuniary damages because the "sexual violence implies [...] the infringement of fundamental values of freedom and human dignity and may also result in prejudices in social life. These infringements have an independent significant respect to the suffering and to the psychological disturbances that sexual violence involves and respect to any financial loss resulting from this: and their repair is unavoidable, since those values are, in fact, subject to direct constitutional protection".

More recently, the Supreme Court (SC 16417/2007) concluded that homosexuality should be recognized as a "condition that must be protected in conformity with constitutional provisions"; from this approach derives that sexual freedom should be understood "also as the freedom to live without interference and restrictions to the sexual preferences which are an expression of the right to the implementation of one's personality, protected by art. 2 of the Constitution".

Following the recognition of the right to sexual freedom pronounced by the Constitutional Court, the Supreme Court through its case law has further implemented the protection of sexual freedom.

The Right to Health as a Right of Personal Integrity

The *right to health* is the only right that the Constitution defines as *fundamental*. It is also defined by the Constitutional Court as *primary and fundamental* (CC 103/1977; 88/1979; 184/1986; 559/1987; 992/1988; 1011/1988; 298/1990; 455/1990).

In addition, the right to health is not only fundamental but also protean, due to the multiplicity and heterogeneity of subjective situations that it constitutionally guarantees. In fact it is covered by at least three different subjective legal situations: (a) the right to personal integrity; (b) the right to medical treatments; (c) the right to healthy environment.

Under the first profile, concerning the *right to personal integrity*, the Constitutional Court has specified that the object of protection under the Constitution can be identified in a psycho-physical integrity and not only in physical integrity (CC 161/1985, 215/1987, 167/1999, 282/2002).

Following the argumentation of the Constitutional Court, the Supreme Court has also recently argued that health should no longer be understood "as the mere absence of illness but as a state of complete physical and mental welfare that involves also the interior aspects of life as perceived and lived by the subject in his experience" (SC 21748/2007).

The Supreme Court has further defined the *right to health*, especially in his sense of a right to personal integrity, as a primary and absolute right, valid *erga omnes* which is directly actionable in front of Courts, without the need of a legislative intervention (SC 796/1973; 999/1973; 3164/1975; 1463/1979; 5172/1979; 3675/1981; 9389/2000; see also CC 167/1986; 184/1986; 559/1987; 307/1990; 445/1990; 202/1991; 356/1991; 218/1994; 118/1996; 399/1996).

An important aspect related to health protection can be found in recognizing by the case law of the right to the refund ability of biological damages. With its decision No. 88/1979 the Constitutional Court argued that the Constitution gives to the right to health a primarily protection. From this provision derives that the indemnity of the damage "is not limited to the consequences from violations that affect on the attitude to produce income", but also includes effects produced by the infringement of the right (see also CC 184/1986; 559/1987; 561/1987; 87/1991; 356/1991; 37/1994 and SC 233/1981; 2258/1981; 3675/1981; 2396/1983; 2422/1984).

The Right to Privacy

With the decision of September 14, 1953, the Court of Rome decided on the limits of the freedom of artistic expression affirming on the basis of the interpretation of Art. 10 and Art. 93–97 of the Copyright Act that in the Italian legal system exists the right to privacy involving the prohibition of any interference by third parties in the personal life of the person. However, 3 years later, the Supreme Court, with the decision No. 4487 of December 22, 1956, concerning the case of the film on Caruso's life, has denied the existence of an absolute right to respect the intimacy of private life. The Court noted that "no express provision of law allows to conclude that the absolute respect of the intimacy of private life is recognized as a general principle and as a limit to the freedom of art".

In a second time, with its decision No. 3199 of December 7, 1960, the Supreme Court mitigated the rigidity of its approach, specifying the limits within which the private sphere of the person can be engraved.

In a third moment, with its decision No. 990 of April 20, 1963, the Supreme Court recognized the configurability of a right to privacy, affirming that "the existence in our legal system of an absolute right to self-determination in the development of personality can be considered implicit. This right can be considered violated when information of a private life of a person is disclosed without his/her consent".

In 1973, the Constitutional Court with the decision No. 38/1973 placed incidentally the right to privacy among the inviolable human rights protected by the Constitution, referring to Art. 12 of the Universal Declaration of Human Rights and to Art. 8 of the European Convention on Human Rights.

Finally, the Supreme Court, in its decision No. 2129 of May 27, 1975, both exceeded the previous approach and conformed itself to the orientation given by the Constitutional Court, and established definitively the existence of an autonomous *right to privacy* and made a first attempt in order to limit the content of this right by introducing the concept of "social interest to information" as a principal limitation of the right to privacy.

It has to be stressed also the decision of the Supreme Court No. 10690/2008 concerning the particular case of the publication of an article considered detrimental. The publication of the article was followed by a partial correction and by a proposition of an action for damages. The newspaper, however, published a letter in which the victim had asked for compensation, giving the name and the surname of the person whose privacy was violated.

The decision is of particular interest because it summarized that "freedom of the press and criticism, which has its basis in the constitutionally guaranteed freedom of the press (Art. 21, second paragraph of the Constitution) due to fundamental public interest to be informed, is liable to result in prejudicial activities to the personal identity, understood as a social image, even if the publication does not offend the honour or the reputation".

Based on this premise, the decision stated that: (a) the right to privacy, which protects the needs of the person that the events of his private life are not publicly disclosed, has merged into the right to protection of personal data pursuant to the provisions contained in the Act of December 31, 1996, no. 675 [...] (b) it is different from the right to moral integrity because the prohibition of the diffusion of private facts of life is independent of their shameful attitude; it relates to a core value of the person and is within the inviolable rights of the individual proclaimed by Art. 2 of the Constitution; (c) the infringement of a absolute right to privacy implies the civil obligation for compensation for pecuniary and non-pecuniary damage; (d) the freedom of the press prevails over the right to privacy and the right to honour, as long as the publication is justified by the function of the information and conforms itself to the standards of professional integrity. In particular, it is justified by the function of the information, whereas there is a considerable public interest in the knowledge of private facts in light of cultural or educational purposes, and more in general, the social significance of such equipment.

Decisions in which the Supreme Court dealt with the *right to image*, understood as a "classic" right of personality as well as a manifestation of the right to privacy, are also of particular interest. A first case to note is the decision No. 7261 of 2008, on the delicate issue of the publication of a private person's image in the newspapers. In similar cases several fundamental rights are opposed to each other: the right to privacy, understood as the right of the person, through the protection of the image, to keep unpublished a photo in which is deducible the detention and the freedom of the press protected by art. 21 of the Constitution. In this specific case, the Italian Data Protection Authority had prohibited the further diffusion of a photo which represented the subject in a state of detention, already published in the newspaper. The decision of the Supreme Court contained an important assertion, affirming that "the inessentiality of the publication of a photo in relation to a case that involved the freedom of the press is not reflected in any normative acts. On the contrary, the legality of this publication is expressly confirmed in art. 114 of the Criminal Procedure Code [...] that states that "it is forbidden to publish the image of a person deprived of personal freedom taken while the person was handcuffed or was subjected to other means of physical coercion, without the permission of the interested person. The Court recognizes both the primary importance of the right to information (of which the image publication represents a legitimate explication) and argued that the publication is essential respect to the information. Furthermore, the Court affirmed that is not "the detention highlighted by handcuffs or other forms of coercion that makes the image unpublishable but the representation of the detention in manner predicted by the published image. In other words, the image of the person under arrest with handcuffs on his wrists, if represents the subject in a pose where the handcuffs are not visible, does not meet any normative prohibition of publication".

As it can be seen, the sensitivity of the matter and the importance of the conflicting interests makes a choice necessary, so a right will result recessive to the other.

In a decision No. 12433 of 2008, concerning the case of an actor against a publisher for damages resulting from the unauthorized publication of two photos that represented him "in an article that advertised a new Kodak film", the Supreme Court reaffirmed that the right to image "falls within the rights of personality that integrate the inviolable rights of the person". The violation of these rights determinate the right to compensation for non-pecuniary damage. However, since "each person has the exclusive right to its image and the exclusive right to exploit it economically, it follows that with the unauthorized publication the offender misappropriates the economic benefits accruing to the victim. The benefit compensation consists in the re-transfer those benefits from the offender to the victim".

The Right to Oblivion

A few months after the decision No. 978/1996 on personal identity, the Supreme Court has recognized the existence of a constitutional *right to oblivion*, whose constitutional basis derives from art. 2 of the Constitution.

The Court of Rome in its decision of November 20, 1996 affirmed that the claim to regain the exclusive possession of the information of one's own life which, although publicized, has lost its relevance, rooted its normative foundation in art. 2 of the Constitution, intended as a general clause which may provide constitutional cover to the emerging values of the person.

In its decision of April 9, 1998, No. 3679, the Supreme Court confirmed this approach stating that it is not permissible to divulge again, after a substantial time, news that had been lawfully published, as it comes to "consider a new view of the right to privacy – recently described as a right to oblivion – understood as an interest of every person not to remain indefinitely exposed to the further damage of his/her honour and reputation from the repeated publication of a notice legitimately published in the past. In other words, the right to oblivion is understood as the right to silence on past events in life that are no longer occurring". This approach was confirmed more recently by the Supreme Court in the decision No. 5525 of April 5, 2012.

The Reasonable Duration of the Trial

Only with the reform of art. 111 of the Constitution in 1999, the Italian constitutional order has implemented the principle of the reasonable duration of the proceedings which falls within the system of values ensuring a fair trial.

However, compared to the international level, where the reasonable duration of the trial is enucleated in terms of subjective rights, the violation of which leads to the injured party to give a "fair satisfaction" (art. 41 ECHR), into the domestic law the principle is referred to the legislator which must adopt normative acts on trials and organization of justice in order to ensure the reasonable duration of the proceedings. In other words, as stated by the Supreme Court, "the principle of procedural economy [...] is clearly incompatible with any unnecessary repetition of procedural activities and any waste of energy in the performance of the Courts" (SC 11228/2003).

More specifically, from the explicit introduction of the principle of reasonable duration of the process in art. 111, paragraph 2 of the Constitution derives a dual obligation on the legislative: (a) to give to the trial a structural setting that can ensure the rapidity of the trial without compressing other fundamental guarantees (CC 204/2001, 78/2002, 317/2009); (b) to provide the whole "system of justice" with adequate instruments in order to ensure the reasonable duration of the proceedings.

In fact, all the latest reforms in procedural matters appear to be inspired by the need to give effect to this constitutional principle. For example, we can consider the act of November 26, 1990, No. 353, which amended a large part of book II of the Civil Procedure Code; the decree of February 19, 1998, No. 51; the decree of March, 14, 2005, No. 35, converted into the act of May 14, 2005, No. 80 and amended by the act of December 28, 2005, No. 263; the act of May 26, 2009, No. 69.

The so-called Pinto act, that enables claimants to obtain a equitable remedy for damage due to the violation of the reasonable term of the process, has allowed a growth of a phenomenon of interaction and integration between European and domestic case law in the matter of protection of fundamental rights.

In this regard, the Supreme Court in the last 10 years stated that the constitutionalization of the principle of the reasonable duration of proceedings requires a new sensitivity and a new interpretative approach. Any solution concerning provisions that regulate trials must be verified both in terms of logical and conceptual coherence and for its operational impact in order to achieve the principle of reasonable duration of the trial (SC 20604/2008).

The Protection of Rights

As for the constitutional tools to safeguard the fundamental rights against the possible interferences coming from the public powers or the privates, it is necessary to make reference, besides to the *saving law clause* and the *saving jurisdiction clause*, conceived by the Constituent framers to the guardianship of some fundamental liberties [the saving law clause has in such cases absolute character, since it is up only to parliamentary statutes, being excluded, therefore, the normative sources of secondary rank – to establish the hypotheses ("cases") in which and the procedures ("ways") through which restrictions of the liberty will be admitted; the saving jurisdiction clause allows only judges to determine with a motivated act an intervention limiting the personal liberty] – to the jurisdictional and administrative guarantees (Fanotto 2012, 498).

They belong to the group of *jurisdictional guarantees* of the rights:

- The principle according to which everyone can act in judgment for the protection of his/her own rights (Art. 24, paragraph 1, Const., that recognizes the *right to access to justice*)
- The proclamation of the *defence* as "inviolable right in every state and degree of the proceedings", to be assured also to the not well-to-do, through the predisposition to their advantage of special institutes to act and to defend themselves before every jurisdiction (Art. 24, paragraphs 2 and 3)
- The provision of the *reparation of the judicial errors* (Art. 24, paragraph 4 Const.). On this matter, the Constitutional Court has affirmed that "the last paragraph of Art. 24 of the Constitution enunciates a principle of highest ethical and social value, that must be interpreted – under the juridical point of view – as a coherent development of the most general principle of protection of the inviolable human rights (Art. 2), assumed in Constitution among those that are at the base of the whole republican order and specifying itself in the guarantees constitutionally prepared to the single individual rights of liberty, with stronger accentuation to those among them that are an immediate and direct expression of the human personality" (CC 1/1969)
- The principles according to which "nobody can be removed from the natural judge instituted by a statute" (Art. 25, paragraph 1 Const.), neither "to be punished if not according with a statute entered into force before the committed fact" (Art. 25, paragraph 2 Const.). The first principle – to which is added the rule according to which "extraordinary or special judges cannot be instituted" (Art. 102, paragraph 2, Const.) – aims evidently to assure to the citizen the fairness and, therefore, the impartiality of the judge. The second one enacts, to the citizen's guarantee against the repressive action of the State, the principle of the non-retroactivity of criminal law, as well as of the peremptoriness and exactness of crime provisions
- The provision of specific "organs of administrative justice" (the regional administrative courts and the State Council) to which is attributed the jurisdiction for the protection of rights towards the public administration (Art. 103, paragraph 1

Const.). Such disposition is completed by the following art. 113 Const., according to which "against the actions of the public administration the jurisdictional protection of the rights is always admitted in front of the organs of ordinary or administrative jurisdiction" (paragraph 1); "such jurisdictional protection cannot be excluded or limited to particular means of remedy or for determined categories of acts" (paragraph 2) and it is up to statutes to establish "what organs of jurisdiction can annul the actions of the public administration in the cases and with the effects provided by law" (paragraph 3)

– The principles of the fair trial, introduced in Art. 111 Const. by the constitutional reform act No. 2/1999, finalized to guarantee: the contradictory among parties, under conditions of parity, in front of a third and impartial judge (to which is added, in the criminal trial, the principle of the contradictory in the formation of the evidence); the reasonable duration of trials; in the criminal trial, the accused person's right to be informed, reservedly and in the briefest possible time, of the nature and of the reasons for the accusation (as well as the correlated right to have the time and the conditions necessary to prepare his/her defence)

It must be underlined, particularly, the choice of the Framers to confirm the "dualistic" system of the jurisdiction that had been delineated by the ordinary legislator, in which the distribution of jurisdiction between ordinary judge and administrative judge essentially is based on the juridical situation (subjective right or legitimate interest) whose protection is claimed.

The fulcrum of the *administrative guarantees* of rights, that the citizens can use against the powers of the public administration, is represented by the principles concerning the organization of public offices (Art. 95 and 97 Const.), by the principle of legality of administrative action (Art. 23 and 97 Const.), by the principles of good practice and impartiality of administrative action (art. 97 Const.), by the principles of inexpensiveness, transparency, slenderness of administrative action (act No. 241/1990), as well as by Art. 28 Const., according to which servants and employees of the State and the public entities are directly responsible, according to criminal, civil and administrative laws, of actions made in violation of rights "and in such cases the civil responsibility extends to the State and the public entities".

The Legal Status of Aliens

According to article 10, paragraph 2 of the Constitution, "*the legal status of aliens is ruled by law in accordance with international law and treaties*". Such constitutional provision, requiring the Italian lawmakers to abide by international law, is an example of the so-called *strengthened saving clause*, meaning that the legislator is not entirely free to act when exercising his power, but rather is bound to respect principles and provisions of international law (Martelli 2013, 545).

Article 10, paragraph 3, grants the *right to asylum* to foreign citizens who, in their own Country, are forbidden to effectively enjoy the democratic freedoms guaranteed by the Italian Constitution.

Article 10 paragraph 4, subsequently, affirms the prohibition to extradite aliens for political crimes.

The refugee law in Italy only sets forth the legal requirements for an asylum seeker to be recognized the status of refugee. The main national law sources concerning the refugee status are the legislative decree of November 19th 2007, No. 251 and the legislative decree January 28th 2008, No. 25.

According to Italian legislation, a "refugee" is "a foreign citizen" (or a stateless person) who, for fear of persecution, stays outside the territory of his own country, and cannot or do not want to ask for protection in that country". As a complementary status, the Italian State may grant the so-called "subsidiary protection" in favour of a foreign citizen (or a stateless person) who, even though not fulfilling the requirements to obtain the refugee status, would anyway face serious risks of being harmed if returns to his country of origin.

The Supreme Court (SC 18353/2006) affirmed that Article 10, paragraph 3 of the Constitution, is of full and immediate applicability. Hence, while there currently exist no specific law to actualize such constitutional provision, the Supreme Court upheld the right of everyone to claim the application of the Constitution. More precisely, the Court's position implies the right for any alien to enter the Italian territory and obtain a temporary residence permission; however, as long as there is no law to actualize the Court's verdict, aliens can only refer to the application of refugee law.

According to some scholars, the right to asylum adopted by the Italian Constitution would entail a wider concept than the mere one of refugee status or of "subsidiary protection"; in fact, this would imply just an objective absence of civil liberties in the Country of origin, although there was no serious risk for the person.

Thus, the right to asylum would in reality be a *genus*, while the refugee status or the right to "subsidiary protection" two minor *species* only. Indeed, refugee status has to be based on a well-founded fear of being victim of a concrete persecution for reasons of race, religion, nationality, political opinions or membership of a particular social group in the country of origin.

Additionally, scholars believe that article 32, paragraph 3, of the legislative decree No. 25/2008 actually grants another right: the right of protection for serious humanitarian reasons, a right that should be considered subsidiary to both the refugee status and the right to "subsidiary protection". Also this right can be directly claimed in courts, in accordance with the above legal framework: in line with this consideration, public administrations are not allowed to exercise their discretional powers.

It shall be added that, according to Article 117 paragraph 2 of the Constitutional Charter, the Parliament has the duty to regulate the right to asylum, as well as the legal status of non EU-citizens and immigration rules.

Furthermore, the Italian Constitutional Court, in interpreting Articles 2, 3 and 10 paragraph 2, of the Constitution, has extended to aliens the fundamental rights granted to Italian citizens, assuming that those rights are of any person's concern, every human being, conceived as "free living being" (CC 120/1967, 21/1968, 144/1970, 244/1974, 62/1994, 219/1995, 105/2001, 231/2001, 198/2003, 432/2005).

It shall be noted, furthermore, that the Constitutional Charter expressly qualifies some fundamental rights as belonging to "everyone" (hence, to both citizens and aliens) (Articles 13, 14, 15, 19, 21, 24, 32); whereas, in other cases, it explicitly circumscribes its application only to "citizens" (Articles 3, 4, 16, 17, 18).

According to some scholars, equality of treatment for aliens constitutes a *principle* but not an imperative rule. On that view, in fact, "the lawmaker is not forbidden to impose special legal burdens on aliens, as long as their establishment is grounded on reasonable motivations due to the peculiar status of foreign citizens" (Bin-Pitruzzella 2015, 476).

This position is sustained by the Constitutional Court too.

The Court's jurisprudence, in fact, confirmed on one hand that foreign citizens are to "enjoy all the Constitution's fundamental rights", and on the other hand that, because of the specific condition of "aliens", they inevitably fall within a separate legal framework for matters such as entry, circulation and residence. In line with this view, aliens are subject to special bindings and primarily the Parliament has to determine them on account of "several public interests such as, for instance, national security, public health, international law, and the national immigration policy". The legislator, then, holds a wide discretion in ruling this area of law, the only imperative guideline being the reasonableness of the decisions taken (CC 148/2008). In this decision, for example, the Court found itself legitimate to uphold the law qualifying drug-smuggling related convictions as a motive to reject renewals of a permit to stay, when those convictions are based on plea bargains not providing the dangerousness' evaluation of the convicted; on that, the Court noted how it does not appear manifestly unreasonable to make the alien's entry and stay conditional to the non-committance of serious crimes.

In the decision No. 306/2008, the Court instead declared unconstitutional the law according to which aliens (non EU-citizens) were to be excluded from the disability allowances if not meeting the income-requirements set for the long-residence permit (legislative decree January, 8 2007, No. 3, incorporating the EU directive 2003/109). The Court deemed manifestly unreasonable to tie the grant of social allowances to criteria concerning the issue of permits of stay which, in addition, demand the subsistence of regular incomes. Such provision was found in breach of Articles 32 and 38 of the Constitution.

Among other decisions, of particular relevance is that issued by the Supreme Court, September, 9 2009, n. 19393, according to which "the legal condition of aliens applying for a residence permit grounded on humanitarian reasons configures a subjective right pertaining the category of fundamental human rights". Following the Court's reasoning, the established general rule is that the jurisdiction to rule over such matters belongs to ordinary civil courts, and not to administrative tribunals. In addition, the general protection framework, set forth by Article 2 with regard to fundamental rights, fully guarantees the right of everyone to appeal rejections of humanitarian residence permits' applications. Consequently, only the Parliament owns the power to define what balance is to be struck among all the different involved interests (the humanitarian reasons of the applicant, the national security of the host State, etc.), whereas public administrations can only verify, case by case, the effective subsistence of the legal requirements.

According to the EU treaty law, EU-citizens benefit of a different and more favourable treatment, if compared to Third-Countries nationals.

Generally speaking, the law tends to jointly administer the legal status of aliens together with the rules concerning immigration. The main source is the legislative decree No. 286/1998, a legal text which has been often modified and revised, notably by two acts: the Act No. 189/2002, concerning the deportation of immigrants (several times the Constitutional Court was asked to scrutinize the legitimacy of this act: CC 222, 223/2004), and the Act No. 94/2009.

Evidently, the immigration law field is characterized for presenting an high level of fragmentation and uncertainty. Most likely, the reasons for that are to be found in parliamentary political and ideological divisions, which make it extremely hard to build consensus on the matter.

Additionally, the legal discipline of aliens embraces at least three sectors: the immigration law, the legal status of regular migrants, and the legal status of illegal migrants.

The Protection of Rights at the Regional Level

According to articles 123 and 116 of the Constitution – particularly after the amendments that reformed Title V of the Part II of the Constitution (Const. reform act No. 1/1999 and Const. reform act. No. 3/2001) – each Region has to adopt a Statute. The debate concerning the inclusion of fundamental rights in regional Statutes has gained momentum especially after three landmark decisions issued by the Constitutional Court (CC 372, 378 and 379/2004.) (Belletti 2012).

Regional Statutes do not constitute an homogeneous category, neither for their structure nor for their contents: some of those Statutes have a preamble (Marche, Emilia-Romagna and Piedmont), others don't. Every statute, either in the preamble or in the firsts articles, provides principles, objectives and purposes that should guide the political and legislative activity of each Regional government. Among others, some of the most relevant principles to be recalled are: peace, refusal of violence and war, democracy, respect for human dignity, and the values of the social community.

More specifically, regional Statutes include both classical fundamental rights (political, social and civil rights) and "new rights". Within this last category, we can find references to: rights of vulnerable categories such as children, elderly people, and disadvantaged people; rights connected to bioethics, peace, and environmental protection; rights of future generations; rights of the "family" (conceiving family as something wider than the one founded on marriage); specific rights for immigrants (as the right to vote in administrative elections).

The fact that Regional governments have started to enforce provisions setting forth rights, additional to those already established at the constitutional level, has triggered debates among scholars: for some of them, this "new course" is to be seen favourably, while for others Regions are simply not legitimated to contemplate additional rights to those protected by the Constitution.

The Constitutional Court expressed its position on this topic with some important decisions (CC 372, 378, 397/2004). These decisions dealt with the provisions of some regional Statutes: the Statute of Umbria and Tuscany were criticized by the national Government because of some provisions that envisaged the recognition of the rights of unmarried people who lived together as a couple; while the Statutes of Emilia-Romagna and Tuscany were criticized as including provisions aimed to promoting the right to vote for immigrants.

Although regional Statutes' provisions have been contested for several reasons, the Court deemed the questions "clearly inadmissible", and refused to decide on the merits of the cases. Indeed, the Court affirmed that "the role of general representation of the interests of local communities would justify some "extra-contents" in the Statutes and that those "extra contents" could be expressed by general provisions".

Nevertheless, the Court also highlighted that all regional Statutes provisions establishing new rights, even if part of a formal source of law, "do not have any practical legal effect, because they express only the political sensibility of the regional community of people at the moment of the approval of the Statute".

In its decisions, the Constitutional Court referred to regional Statutes as a source of "reserved and specialized competence", meaning that at any event these source of law shall respect every constitutional principle and provision (CC 196/2003).

The Constitutional Court also added that the Regional Statutes shall not be considered as regional constitutions (CC 372/2004).

Consequently, the provisions of the Statutes, even if general or setting forth principles, do not function as interpretive instruments for other legal sources.

Analysing the mentioned cases more specifically, it appears evident how the main issue is not the nature of the contested provisions, but rather the fact that the Region, enforcing such provisions, exceeded the limits of regional legislative competence.

More specifically, those provisions stated that "the Region, in accordance with the constitutional principles, promote the right to vote for immigrants"; the Region pursues "the recognition of forms of relationship different from the traditional marriage"; the Region pursues "the respect of ecology, environmental protection and cultural heritage, the protection of biodiversity, the promotion of a culture of respect for animals" as well as "the protection and valorisation of historical, artistic and landscape patrimony".

Additionally, the Region pursues "the promotion of economic development, free competition in business, innovation, research and education, in respect of the principles of social cohesion and environmental sustainability".

Finally, the Region pursues "the valorisation of free enterprise and public enterprise, the role and the social liability in business" as well as "the promotion of cooperation as instrument of economical democracy and social development".

The deep meaning of those decisions can be understood if we consider the fears and doubts expressed by the Government in contesting the legitimacy of provisions of regional Statutes.

The first concern and worry was that, with those provisions, Regions could ignore or elude constitutional provisions (article 117, paragraph 2 of the Constitution) on exclusive State's legislative competence (for example in the field of the protection of environment, vote-rights, commercial laws, etc.).

For these reasons the Constitutional Court stated that the regional provisions being contested had only a political or cultural influence and not a legal effectiveness.

Hence those provisions have only the meaning to permeate, culturally and politically, regional policies and actions: they can not state any regional power in contrast to constitutional provisions.

Conversely, there are also some other Statutes provisions that did not exceed the regional legislative competence: those statutory provisions can relate to the very foundation of the regional legislative activity (for example in the healthcare field, health organization, scholastic organization, social services, etc.), or also to fields strictly related to the protection of fundamental rights.

The fact that Regions are competent also to regulate some rights, follows, *a contrario*, on article 117, paragraph 2 – lit. *m*), of the Constitution, that is to say that it follows on the existence of the national exclusive legislative competence to "determine the essential level services". It means that national legislation has to pick out the essential level in the right's protection that must be granted in the whole national territory, while Regions, according to article 117, paragraph 4, can intervene with legislative acts approved on the base of statutory provisions.

Regional rights, indeed, have the purpose to expand the minimal (or essential) protection level set forth by the national legislator in fields such as healthcare, social protection or education.

Some other regional provisions concerning rights have the purpose to actualize national provisions, especially with regard to vulnerable categories, such as immigrants, returned migrants, gypsies, detainees, people discriminated because of sexual choices, poor and mobbed people.

Regions seem to be very careful about the enforcement (or denial of enforcement) of rights (rights of consumers or security rights) as shown by the actions taken by their administrative offices: there are in fact provisions specifically dedicated to the implementation of communications and the sharing of public information.

The Statutes contain provisions on several typology of rights: the so called "*rights for objectives*" and the so called "*policies rights*".

By the first expression we mean all the outcomes that Regions generically identify, such as the valorisation of human personality, the respect of human dignity and of human rights, the improvement of rights (specially voters rights) of regional people who reside abroad.

With the second expression we intend to pick out some new rights and policies – such as health care and assistance, environment and territory, infrastructures, labour and economic development, culture and instruction – in relation to which Regions are primarily involved.

Moreover, recurring provisions of regional Statutes on rights concern the all-inclusive protection of gender equality (for example on the access to public offices) and the removal of any discrimination. Those provisions, according both to administrative judges and the Constitutional Court, are directly applicable to every person, and hence every citizen can claim them (Regional Administrative Court of Campania, No. 1985, April 7, 2011; State Council, No. 4502, July 27, 2011; Regional Administrative Court of Sardinia, No. 864, August 2, 2011; CC 81/ 2012).

The Integration Between the Italian Constitutional Order and Supranational Legal Orders

Three main levels of protection of fundamental rights can be identified (apart from the regional one) with: (a) the Council of Europe and the European Convention for the protection of human rights and fundamental freedoms – (ECHR, signed in Rome in 1950 and ratified in Italy by Act. No. 848/1955); (b) the European Union (EU); and (c) the Italian Constitution. This means that a "multilevel system" of protection of rights in Europe is characterized by the coexistence of different sources, each of which recognizes and protects fundamental rights in different ways with varying levels of efficiency.

From these interconnections can arise conflicts between the different systems (the European Court of Justice at the EU level; the European Court of Human Rights at the Convention level; and the Italian Constitutional Court at the national level) (de Vergottini 2010).

In the Italian legal order it may be considered acquired the principle of the immediate applicability of ECHR provisions, but this outcome was not automatic: it was the result of a long process of integration (Mezzetti 2012, 56).

Recently, the Supreme Court (SC, No. 32678/2006, *Somogyi*) has reconstructed the evolutionary process of the national jurisprudence for the implementation of the progress of integration (Pietropolli 2013, 279). The first case in which the Court recognized the direct applicability of ECHR's provisions (as legislative source of law) was affirmed by a decision which dates back 1967 (SC, No. 2762/1967), and this outcome was uphold also by subsequent decisions (SC, No. 6978/1982 – *Iaglietti*; SC, November 23, 1988 – *Polo Castro*, and – more significantly – SC, May, 5, 1993 – *Medrano*. In this last case there was the direct application of article 8 of the European Convention, as interpreted by the Strasbourg Court, and the judges recognized to conventional provisions a relevant binding force over conflicting national legal sources).

This aptitude of conventional provisions is derived from provisions of article 2 of the Constitution and this clause would implicitly recognize to those provisions the nature of general principle of the Italian legal order. This implies that conventional rules have a particular binding force over national legal sources, even adopted subsequently. Scholars justify this particular force either in the principle *lex generalis non derogat priori speciali*, or in the principle *pacta recepta sunt servanda*. In any case, beyond formalistic and positivistic approaches, the binding force of conventional provisions is due to its nature of general principle in the legal order, upheld by the jurisprudence for years, before the constitutional reform of 2001.

This interpretive solution was echoed also by the jurisprudence of the European Court of Justice (ECJ May 14, 1974, *Nold*; ECJ December 13, 1979, *Hauer*).

The Luxemburg Court, indeed, affirmed both to have the duty to consider also the general principle of law set by the European convention (although the European Community and the European Union weren't Parties of it) and that also the action of national judges should be guided by the respect of those principles (even thought there weren't the conditions to appeal the European Court of Strasbourg yet).

The crucial relevance of fundamental rights has found express recognition in EU Treaty law. The Treaty of Maastricht (1992), Article 6, provided that "the Union must respect fundamental rights as guaranteed by the ECHR and as they result from constitutional traditions common to Member States, as general principles of Community law". This provision was subsequently amended by the Amsterdam Treaty in 1997 and now, after the Lisbon Treaty, it states that the Union is founded on the principles of "liberty, democracy, respect for human rights and fundamental freedoms, and the rule of law, principles which are common to Member States". This rule has also provided a procedure to check serious breaches of human and fundamental rights committed by a Member State, which could lead to the suspension of the right to vote for the government's representative of that Member State in the Council (Article 7 EU Treaty Law, as modified by the Lisbon Treaty).

Furthermore, the Charter of Fundamental Rights of the European Union, proclaimed in Nice in December 2000 and now part of the Lisbon Treaty, represents another step towards the protection of human rights and, as set forth by article 52 paragraph 3 of the Charter, "the meaning and scope of those rights shall be the same as those laid down by the said Convention" (ECHR).

Looking at the national contest, a fundamental step in the ECHR integration process was due to the jurisprudence. Indeed the Supreme Court judges recognized the ECHR as an atypical legal source and therefore a source that could not be annulled by an ordinary act. Furthermore, the Supreme Court's judges stated that a national law could not be applied if in contrast with conventional provisions.

In *Dorigo* – SC, December 1, 2006 – the Supreme Court affirmed that, under Art. 670 of the Penal Code, judges are bound to suspend the execution of any sentence on which the European Court of Human Rights ascertained that the verdict was reached in breach of Art. 6 ECHR on the right to fair trial, and that, consequently, the condemned has got the right to call for a new trial, *even though the lawmakers still have not established the rules to do so*.

The recognition of ECHR as an atypical legal source, and therefore a source that cannot be annulled by an ordinary level's source of law, was also affirmed by the Constitutional Court (CC 10/1993). The Court, more recently, also specified the "juridical force" to be recognized to international provisions on human rights (CC 393/2006).

Additionally, it was observed that those rights are expressed also in the Constitution (CC 399/1998): not only by the general provision of article 2 – which provides rights strictly connected to the protection of human dignity (CC 167/1999) – but also because, beyond the textual coincidence of formal catalogues of rights, it can be highlighted a continuous process of integration and reciprocal influence between legal orders (national and supranational), which reciprocally integrate themselves because of Courts' interpretation (CC 388/1999).

Those principles were also affirmed by the Supreme Court jurisprudence.

In 2005 the Supreme Court stated that the "Act No. 648/1955, in ratifying and making executive the European Convention on Human Rights, has introduced in the national legal order fundamental rights mostly coincident with those set forth by article 2 of the Constitution. Referring to those rights, conventional rights would have a confirmatory nature". The Court also added that "conventional provisions would have a particular force that implies the impossibility to apply national law in contrast with conventional provisions of direct applicability" (SC, No. 28507/2005. See also SC, No. 1338, 1339, 1340, 1341/2004).

Additionally, the same decision affirmed that "ECHR provisions, as ratified in Italy, imply the duty upon national judges to abide by the jurisprudence of the European Court of Strasbourg, even though this entails, through the review of past criminal proceedings, challenging the principle of final sentences' non-alterability".

It seems important to indicate some other cases – the decisions of the Supreme Court No. 10542/2002 No. 28507/2005 – with which the judges expressly recognized that, in case of contrast between national laws and ECHR provisions, the conventional provisions have to prevail, in reason of an objective of substantial justice.

The relevant value of ECHR provisions in national legal orders is due also to the binding force (as they were sources of law) of the decisions of the European Court of Strasbourg which establish a State violation of conventional provisions.

The nature of source of law recognized to the decisions of the Strasbourg's Court has been confirmed after the amendment of article 46, consequent to the approval of ECHR Protocol No. 14 approved on May 13, 2004 and ratified in Italy by the Act No. 280/2005.

In the same perspective we shall interpret the Act No. 12/2006 ("Execution of the European Court of Human Rights decisions"). This act establishes that the Prime Minister has to assure that the Government activity shall be consistent with European Court's decisions. Additionally, The Prime Minister has to communicate any new European decision to parliamentary commissions, so that they could be examined. He also to present to the Parliament an annual report on the state of execution of those decisions.

The position of Italian Courts, to regularly incorporate Strasbourg's decisions, is confirmed by the decree No. 289/2005. Under its provisions, each decision due to review an Italian sentence is to be published in conjunction with and as a completion of the original Italian verdict.

The verdicts of the Court of Strasbourg that state the violation of any conventional provisions charge the Parties of duties and rights.

Consequently, the State which has been condemned has the duty to remove the prejudicial effects of its violation of conventional rules; the citizen has either the right to be compensated for the damages he received, or the right to obtain the so-called "*restitutio in integrum*" (for example being put on trial again if, according to article 6 ECHR, the State was condemned for the violation of the right to a "*procès èquitable*").

Recently, a confirm of the interpretative results exposed above is offered by the text of the Act No. 69/2005, according to which Italy executed the Council framework decision 2002/584/JHA of June 13, 2002.

According to article 2, paragraph 1, Italy "shall execute the European arrest warrant, in respect of those rights and principles established by international Treaties and the Constitution: (a) fundamental rights assured by the ECHR, as ratified by the Act No. 848/1955 (specifically articles 5 and 6 ECHR) and its Protocols".

According to this principle, article 18, lit. *g)*, imposes the refusal of the handover of detainees if "people have not been judged in the respect of the rights granted by article 6 ECHR".

The provisions of articles 2 and 18, Act No. 69/2005 – even expressing principles on extradition (Art. 720 paragraph 4 of the criminal procedural code; Art. 705 paragraph 2, lit. *a)* of the criminal procedural code) and principles on the recognition of foreign judgments on criminal law (Art. 733 paragraph 1, lit. *b))* and *c)* of the criminal procedural code) already existent in the domestic legal order – in referring to articles 5 and 6 ECHR, make clear the privileged role recognized to all ECHR rights, whose guarantees are risen to the level of general principles of the legal order.

In the *Somogyi* case the Supreme Court stated that a final judgment of a national court can not be considered an obstacle for the claim of a *restitutio in integrum* when the trial has been celebrated *in absentia*.

It means that it is always possible, for someone who claims that the national trial violated article 6 ECHR, to obtain the condemn of the State by the Strasbourg Court and be put on trial again.

Subsequently, in the *Dorigo* Case, the Supreme Court, in interpreting article 670 of the procedural criminal law code, stated that the domestic judgment of condemn could not be executed.

Indeed, if the Strasbourg Court states the violation of article 6 ECHR, this verdict origins the right to be put on trial again and consequently the first final sentence can not be executed.

After all, it has been observed that the overcoming of the national final judgment is implied by ECHR system: the fact that the Strasbourg Court may only deal with the matter after all domestic remedies have been exhausted, implies that it decides on national final decisions (Article 26 ECHR).

By interpreting the national law in accordance with the Strasbourg's pronouncements, the Italian Supreme Court contributed not only to the evolution of domestic criminal law, but also attests how the European Court is to be considered an undisputable reference for the correctness of the law.

The reasoning of the Supreme Court stresses the binding force both of ECHR and of the Strasbourg's Court. The two profiles are strictly connected by article 46 paragraph 1 of the Convention, according to which "Any of the High Contracting Parties may at any time declare that it recognizes as compulsory 'ipso facto' and without special agreement the jurisdiction of the Court in all matters concerning the interpretation and application of the present Convention".

Moreover, the Supreme Court recognizes the binding force of ECHR because its provisions would be of immediate applicability. Those rules would have an higher level than ordinary legal sources and the judges would avoid to apply internal rules in contrast with conventional provisions.

To individuate a binding force also for Strasbourg's decisions, the Italian Supreme Court highlights the link between the monopoly of the European Court in the interpretation of conventional rules (Art. 19 ECHR) and the obligation for the States Parties of the Convention, to execute the decisions of the Strasbourg's Court (Art. 46 ECHR).

The valorisation of this link is consistent with the consciousness that the Conventional norms are something more than the written text. These norms shall be individuated in the interpretation of conventional provisions given by the Strasbourg's Court.

Consequently, it must be excluded the possibility of the national jurisprudence to give an autonomous interpretation of conventional provisions. According to this, the States are free to execute Strasbourg's decisions (Art. 46, paragraph 2, ECHR), but their action must be consistent with European jurisprudence.

Lastly, in *Drassich* (Drassich v Italia, December 11, 2007) the ECHR ruled against the Italian Court's decision because deemed in breach of Art. 6. The ECHR found, in fact, that in such proceedings Italian judges applied an *ex officio* requalification of the facts which resulted in the worsening of original charges, without any confrontation. Because of the *ex officio* requalification, it became impossible for those charges to be extinguishable by prescription (the prescription terms always refer to the original *nomen iuris*). On top of that, the requalification was made without informing the defendant and, hence, without allowing him any legal reaction.

The Supreme Court, by interpreting Art. 521 of the Criminal Code, acknowledged the obligation lying on each judge to duly pre-inform the defendant and his counsel of any possible modification on the original ascribed charges. Such provision, read in conjunction with Art. 625-*bis* of the Criminal Code, led the Court to confirm that, whenever a requalification happens, there's no need to set a new trial, but rather that the same can be resumed in consideration of the new accusations.

More recently, the Constitutional Court, with the decision No. 113 of 2011, declared unconstitutional the provisions of Article 630 of procedural criminal law code because its provisions were not consistent with provisions of Article 46 paragraph 1 of the European Convention on fundamental rights.

Additionally, the administrative jurisprudence, by virtue of Article 6 of the European Union Treaty Law (as modified by the Lisbon Treaty), stated the direct applicability of ECHR provisions.

The State Council (the Supreme Court of administrative jurisdiction), deciding on an expropriation case, affirmed the necessity to apply "the principles on effectiveness of judicial protection stated by article 24 of the Constitution and by articles 6 and 13 of ECHR" and specified that the latter are "of immediate applicability further to articles 6 TUE provisions" (dec. No. 1220/2010).

Additionally, the Regional Administrative Tribunal of Lazio highlighted the great importance of Article 6 paragraphs 2 and 3, TFUE in the definition of the connection between the ECHR legal order and the Italian legal order (dec. No. 11984 May 18, 2010). According to administrative judges, "*the fact of the immediate applicability of conventional provisions among member countries of EU [...] opens new scenarios for the conformative interpretation or for the non-application of national laws in contrast with ECHR provisions, [...] specially when the Strasbourg Court has already stated on the question. [...]. This will be valid for all conventional rights and not only for the rights that could have a particular relevance in the European Union legal order*".

According to the reasoning of administrative judges, "*the recognition of ECHR fundamental rights as internal principles of the UE [...] has some immediate consequences because it leads to the immediate applicability of conventional provisions in European Countries members of EU, and consequently, also in Italy by Article 11*" and, now, Article 117 paragraph 1 of the Constitution.

As known, the extent of the integration between ECHR and the Italian legal system has been lacking for years and the ECHR's integration was based exclusively on Italian execution of ordinary legislation and mostly due to the interpretive action of the jurisprudence. But according to Article 6 paragraph 3 of the European Union Treaty Law, as modified by the Lisbon Treaty, the European Court of Justice upholds ECHR rules since they were general principles of EU law. This implies that the implemented rights of the ECHR, similarly to EU law principles, become binding under the Italian legal system *ex* Article 11 Cost and *ex* article 117 paragraph 1 Const.

The Constitutional Court followed paths not exactly coincident with those followed by the jurisprudence of the Supreme Court. The jurisprudence of the Supreme Court has often recognized conventional provisions as an atypical legal source and therefore a source that cannot be annulled by an ordinary level's act. However, this was not at the level of constitutional law.

The clearest dividing line was represented by the 2001 constitutional reform that amended Article 117 Const., whose first paragraph provides that "Legislative powers shall be vested in the State and the Regions in compliance with the Constitution and with the obligations deriving from EU legislation and international obligations".

The Constitutional Court considered this provision as the constitutional parameter by virtue of which ECHR's rules specify and integrate the duty of the legislator to respect international obligations. Additionally, the high value of conventional provisions makes them privileged instruments for the interpretation of domestic law. All of this represents the *humus* of a new approach to the problem of ECHR's integration in the Italian legal order. In this context the Italian Constitutional Court's decisions No. 348/2007 and 349/2007 constitute a new paradigm.

The Court, in both cases, decided around the provision of Article 117 according to which State and Regions should exert their legislative power in compliance with the constraints deriving from EU legislation and international obligations.

It is important to stress that international obligations bind the State not only in its external profile, as a subject of international law, but also in its constitutional profile, since their respect is a requirement for the valid exertion of legislative power.

In this context, ECHR's provisions are considered "interposed rules" and consequently the Court can exercise the "conventional control": so it can verify and decide on the contrast between internal rules and conventional provisions.

According to that, ECHR's rules integrate the constitutional parameter of interpretation and should be considered as "sub-constitutional" norms.

Additionally, in case of contrast between a domestic rule with a conventional one, the national judge shall not simply aside the domestic provision, but it shall ask to the Constitutional Court to exercise the power of judicial review to verify the constitutional legitimacy of it.

More recently, the position of the Constitutional Court on the relationships between the Italian legal order, ECHR's legal order and EU's legal order has been resumed in the case No. 80/2011. The Court highlighted two aspects. Firstly, the domestic judge shall interpret internal rules in compliance with conventional provisions. Here it is evident the purpose of interpretive conciliation.

Secondly, in case of impossibility for an interpretive conciliation, the judges have to appeal the Constitutional Court. This means that there will be not recognized any space for an immediate applicability of ECHR's provisions (although some scholars thought differently and some ordinary judges did it).

Moreover, according to the Constitutional Court's position: (a) only the Court of Strasbourg can interpret conventional rules, and (b) in case of contrast between ECHR and the Constitution, conventional rules (that are considered sub-constitutional legal sources) do not integrate the constitutional parameter.

Three main consequences emerge from this assumption.

Firstly, the impossibility to diverge, even marginally, from the Strasbourg's interpretation. Secondly, the peremptory confirmation of the hierarchy of sources existing between constitutional and conventional norms. Thirdly, whenever contrasts arise between ECHR and the Italian Constitution, the former is to be considered inadequate to integrate the latter's text. Such a position shall be interpreted not as requiring a conventional norm's total annulment, but rather as only implying that the norm is to be set aside just for the case at hand.

After having resumed his conceptualisation of conventional provisions in the Italian legal order, the Court analyses the possible consequences of the Lisbon Treaty.

Has ECHR become part of the European Treaty (with the obvious consequences on the structure of the legal sources of law)? The Constitutional Court has excluded it, also because EU has not yet acceded to the Convention.

The Constitutional Court, with this decision, finds a precise duty of the ordinary judge: indeed, the bound of an interpretation consistent with the conventional rules means that the judge has the duty to find any possible interpretation that could be in compliance with ECHR. Only if this interpretation is vain, the judge can ask the intervention of the Constitutional Court.

The valorisation of the interpretive power of judges is really significant.

Significantly, with the decision No. 239/2009, the Constitutional Court considers that the previous tentative to interpret internal rules in compliance with conventional provisions is a kind of a "*pre-condition*" to activate a judicial review's judgement.

In this sense, the Constitutional Court can consider admissible only the question on the constitutionality of a norm that could not have been interpreted in compliance with conventional provisions (in the meaning given them by the Court of Strasbourg).

It shall be added that this technique of interpretation (so-called *adapting interpretation*) was already used by ordinary judges (SC, No. 1339 to 1341 of 2004, with which it was imposed to the judge to follow the interpretation of conventional rules given by the Strasbourg's Court), but significantly, only in consequence of the decision of the Constitutional Court, this technique has become a real bond for the ordinary judge.

The Constitutional Court upholds that ECHR's provisions *live* in the interpretation of the Strasbourg Court (decisions No. 348 and 349 of 2007) and their main characteristic is the fact that in national orders they are "interposed norms", which shall be interpreted exactly as the Strasbourg's Court did (dec. No. 39/2008).

Consequently, the domestic jurisprudence, both constitutional and ordinary, is unconditionally bound by the interpretation of conventional rules given by Strasbourg's jurisprudence, and the fundamental steps of this process are the decisions of the Constitutional Court No. 348 and 349/2007; 39/2008; 311 and 317/2008; 187 and 196/2010.

From the decisions No. 348 and 349 of 2007 emerged an "*eminent interpretative function*" of the Strasbourg's Court and the Constitutional Court restates that ECHR's rules and their interpretation are under the jurisprudence of the Court of Strasbourg. Therefore, it is the sub-constitutional disposition that enters the Italian order and becomes the norm, as the product of interpretation, and not the ECHR's provision.

However the Court, emphasizing the role of the ECHR, also affirms, in relation to the control over the constitutional legitimacy of domestic legislation, that ECHR's decisions are not unconditionally binding. It means that "the judicial review of legislation has always to be informed to a reasonable balance between the international bounds *ex* Art. 117 paragraph 1 Const. and the protection of other constitutional interests".

So with the cited decisions, the Constitutional Court did not expressly recognized an interpretive exclusive monopoly of the Strasbourg's Court in the determination of the exact meaning of conventional provisions.

Later, in the decision No. 38/2008, the Constitutional Court better spelled out its position to clarify what in the previous 2007s decisions seemed to have remained untold. The Court there affirmed that, as – in its view – already stated in the 2007s decisions, the special status of the ECHR provisions lies in the fact that, with regard to their interpretation, all State Parties are bound to abide by the ECHR jurisprudence (except for cases involving constitutionality matters).

It was, thereof, confirmed, the absolute interpretative bound of the conventional jurisprudence in the determination of the exact meaning of the ECHR's provisions.

This bound did not clearly emerged from decisions of 2007 but it has been confirmed by the decisions No. 311 and 317 of 2009. With those cases the Constitutional Court affirmed that, unless the ECHR's provision are in contrast with the

Constitution, "it can not interpret conventional rules in a way divergent from that of the Strasbourg's Court".

The interpretive function of the Court of Strasbourg is now so deep and eminent to exclude the possibility for national – and even constitutional – judges to integrate the meaning of conventional provisions that had been already interpreted by the European Court.

In any case, it still exist the possibility that the same Court of Strasbourg accords to the States the power to upheld an autonomous interpretation of the conventional provisions. This, as well specified by the Italian Constitutional Court with the decision No. 311/2009, can occur when, "*in case of reasons of relevant public interest*", the legislator can avoid the ban to interfere with the administration of justice, stated by Article 6 ECHR.

From above examined decisions emerges the consciousness of the national jurisprudence – both of the Constitutional Court and of the Supreme Court – that the text of the ECHR lives through the decisions of the Strasbourg Court, which makes it meaningful.

This is confirmed by the national ordinary jurisprudence. Indeed it is rare that any national decision – if it is asked to the Constitutional Court the exercise the judicial review or is valued the coherence of national legal sources with conventional provisions – in referring to an article of ECHR, does not refer also to the position expressed by the Court of Strasbourg.

The necessity, for the national judge, to conform its jurisprudence to the interpretation of conventional rules stated by the Court of Strasbourg has been recently highlighted by the Constitutional Court with the decisions no. 187 and 196 of 2010.

In the first case the Court, deciding a case about welfare rights and after having recalled the evolution of Strasbourg's jurisprudence, affirmed that "*the judicial review of national legislation has to be done considering interpretive results of Strasbourg's jurisprudence about the principle of non discrimination stated by Article 14 of the Convention*".

In the decision No. 196/2010, the Constitutional Court affirms that "*from the jurisprudence of the Court of Strasbourg, in particular on interpretation of Articles 6 and 7 of the Convention, it can be derived the principle according to which every kind of punitive measures adopted by the State have to respect the limits and regulation the State grant to offences*".

The cited decisions clearly show as the role of the Court of Strasbourg has been changed in the last years.

The procedure of decisions and the effect of the judgements have not been formally changed, but it is the meaning and the influence of the interpretive activity of this Court on national jurisprudence that has deeply changed.

The above cited decisions confirm the position of those scholars who had asserted – years ago – that the decisions of the Court of Strasbourg, even in absence of any formal provision or rule in this sense, will have an universally recognized binding force. Consequently they could both determine the illegitimacy of national provisions in contrast with ECHR ones and orient and influence the interpretation of national legal sources.

Conclusions

The globalization of human rights and in particular the protection of the principle of human dignity also implies in Italy a close synergy between the international and domestic order to protect the rights and promote the human dignity, making it untouchable in any place and at any latitude, and even before to create the pre-requisites (peace, prosperity, equality, solidarity) needed for making them acceptable everywhere the degree of their effectiveness. The criterion to distinguish between *absolute constitutional principles* and *relative constitutional principles* is based on the refractoriness – typical of the first one, and usability – feature of the seconds, to become the subject of weighting – balancing in case of conflict: in this sense, in the Italian constitutional system there are two absolute principles, an instrumental one and a material one. The absolute constitutional material principle nature is the human dignity and the constitutional absolute instrumental/procedural is represented by the proposition contained in the provision (Article 11 of the Constitution) that conveys within the constitutional fundamental principles of the domestic block of constitutionality the international and regional blocks of constitutionality, and in particular the principle that is at the top of both blocks, the human dignity, drawing it from the assets of principles and values expressed by the international and regional community.

The international block of constitutionality is formed by the Universal Declaration of Human Rights, its essential core, the Charter of the United Nations, the International Bill of Rights (New York Covenants on Economic, Social and Cultural Rights and on Civil and Political Rights, both of 1966, accompanied by the optional Protocols thereto), as well as the core treaties of international law of human rights.

In Europe, as recognized by the Court of Justice in its Opinion No. 1 of 14 December 1991 in relation to the nature of the European Community, the Treaty on the European Union and the Treaty on the Functioning of the European Union, although concluded in the form of international agreements, are the first two elements of the Constitutional Charter of the community of law that is the European Union. The third element of the constitutional charter of polycentric nature must be identified with the Charter of Fundamental Rights of the European Union, to which the Treaty of Lisbon has accorded the same legal value as the Treaties (art. 6 TEU). The block of constitutionality is complemented by the European Social Charter, by the European Convention for the Protection of Human Rights and Fundamental Freedoms, to which the Union is party pursuant to art. 6 TEU as amended in Lisbon, by case law of the European Court of Human Rights and by the constitutional traditions common to the Member States, showing complex the typical elements of a formal constitution and the structural components characterizing a substantial Constitution.

The axiological dimension of the international and regional legal systems permeates and pervades the structure of the fundamental principles enshrined in the national Constitution, the fundamental principles within the international block of constitutionality and within the regional blocks of constitutionality operate in a relationship of mutual complementarity and harmony with the fundamental principles of the national constitutional system. Three large sets constitutional, animated by a movement of mutual convergence, are destined to merge into a single pool of legal culture: it is, beyond hesitation and indecision, skepticism, doubts, an irreversible phenomenon, that the constitutional Court, the Supreme Court of Cassation and supranational courts are called to govern in order to reach a common identity and to achieve a reconciliation of the right to justice.

Bibliography

Belletti, M. 2012. *Percorsi di ricentralizzazione del regionalismo italiano nella giurisprudenza costituzionale*. Rome: Aracne.

Bin, R., and G. Pitruzzella. 2015. *Diritto costituzionale*. Turin: Giappichelli.

de Vergottini, G. 1998. *Le transizioni costituzionali*. Bologna: Società editrice il Mulino.

de Vergottini, G. 2010. *Oltre il dialogo tra le Corti*. Bologna: Società editrice il Mulino.

Drigo, C. 2011. La dignità umana quale valore (super)costituzionale. In *Principi costituzionali*, ed. L. Mezzetti. Turin: Giappichelli Editore.

Fanotto, L. 2012. *Corte di cassazione, corte costituzionale, costituzione sostanziale*. Bologna: Longitudini.

Ferrari, G.F. 2011. *Le libertà. Profili comparatistica*. Turin: Giappichelli.

Martelli, A. 2013. La condizione giuridica dello straniero. In *Diritto costituzionale*, ed. L. Mezzetti. Milan: Giuffré.

Mezzetti, L. 2003. *Teoria e prassi delle transizioni costituzionali e del consolidamento democratico*. Padua: Cedam.

Mezzetti, L. 2011. Valori, principi, regole. In *Principi costituzionali*, ed. L. Mezzetti. Turin: Giappichelli Editore.

Mezzetti, L. 2012. Primazia del diritto sopranazionale e supremazia della Costituzione nella giurisprudenza costituzionale degli ordinamenti dell'Europa occidentale (Italia, Germania, Francia, Spagna). In *Diritto costituzionale transnazionale*, ed. L. Mezzetti and C. Pizzolo. Bologna: Maggioli Editore.

Mezzetti, L. 2013a. I nuovi diritti. In *Diritto costituzionale. Casebook*, ed. L. Mezzetti. Rimini: Maggioli.

Mezzetti, L. 2013b. Storia dei diritti umani. In *Diritti e doveri*, ed. L. Mezzetti. Turin: Giappichelli.

Morrone, A. 2002. *Il custode della ragionevolezza*. Milan: Giuffré.

Pietropolli, M. 2013. L'impatto delle sentenze della Corte europea dei diritti dell'uomo sul sistema italiano. In *Diritto processuale dei diritti umani*, ed. L. Mezzetti. Rimini: Maggioli.

Pirozzoli, A. 2007. *Il valore costituzionale della dignità*. Rome: Diritti e dignità umana.

Polacchini, F. 2011. Il principio di eguaglianza. In *Principi costituzionali*, ed. L. Mezzetti. Turin: Giappichelli Editore.

Polacchini, F. 2013. I doveri inderogabili di solidarietà. In *Diritti e doveri*, ed. L. Mezzetti. Turin: Giappichelli.

Ruggeri, A., and A. Spadaro. 1992. Dignità dell'uomo e giurisprudenza costituzionale. In *Libertà e giurisprudenza costituzionale*, ed. V. Angiolini. Turin: Giappichelli.

Vedaschi, A. 2011. Il principio personalista. In *Principi costituzionali*, ed. L. Mezzetti. Turin: Giappichelli Editore.

Discrimination and Equality: Affirmative Action in Spain and in the European Union

María Cristina Hermida del Llano

This article has been elaborated in the framework of the research Project "Principio de no discriminación y nuevos derechos" (DER2011-26903).

Abstract Many different versions of equality have been proposed and defended, but they can be grouped according to the emphasis that they give to three different perspectives: historical, economic, and remedial. The remedial perspective expands on the historical perspective to consider the continuing effects of past discrimination. This perspective is most frequently invoked to justify programs of affirmative action. Here we focus on the programs of affirmative action in Spain in the previous years within the legal framework of the European Union. It is examined in this study whether affirmative action measures, particularly quotas, violate the principle of equality. This article aims to contribute to the Europe-wide debate on the converging concepts of equality.

The concept of equality has been considered from different perspectives that serve to build different constructions of a theory of Justice, which corresponds to distinct ideologies. Classically, one divides the perspectives of equality with regard to employment discrimination law into historical, economic, and remedial categories (Rutherglen 2010).

The historical perspective focuses on the immediate past. From this perspective, discrimination is a historical condition for which appropriate legal remedies have already been enacted. Usually the historical perspective is termed "equality as color blindness": any particular use of race, gender or creed is stigmatizing or stereotyping. This perspective presumes, based on past experience, that any use of race is undesirable (Rutherglen 2010, 17–18).

M.C.H. del Llano (✉)
Universidad Rey Juan Carlos, Madrid, Spain
e-mail: cristina.hermida@urjc.es

R. Arnold (ed.), *The Convergence of the Fundamental Rights Protection in Europe*, Ius Gentium: Comparative Perspectives on Law and Justice 52,
DOI 10.1007/978-94-017-7465-9_4

While the historical perspective looks to the immediate past, the economic perspective focuses on the near future, examining the consequences of enforcing prohibitions against discrimination. The crucial question from this perspective is whether the gains from eliminating discrimination outweigh the costs of legal enforcement, and, in particular, whether a legal prohibition is superior to deterring discrimination through the competitive pressure of the market. This approach is associated with a neoliberal or libertarian position, one that limits legal intervention in order to foster free market competition. In terms of equality, it rests on a view of merit as "careers open to talents," assuring individuals the right to compete based on their existing abilities as determined by their natural endowments and augmented by education and experience. As Sandel has said about market societies: "They open careers to those with the requisite talents and provide equality before the law. Citizens are assured equal basic liberties, and the distribution of income and wealth is determined by the free market. This system – a free market with formal equality of opportunity – corresponds to the libertarian theory of justice. It represents an improvement over feudal and caste societies, since it rejects fixed hierarchies of birth. Legally, it allows everyone to strive and to compete. In practice, however, opportunities may be far from equal" (Sandel 2009, 153).

This conception of equality as merit[1] does not guarantee the results of competition, nor indeed even the opportunity to gain the talents necessary to prevail in the competition. Individuals must compete based solely on the qualifications that they bring to the labor market. Nevertheless, this is a positive conception of equality because, in contrast to the negative conception of the historical perspective, it tells employers what to consider, not just what to avoid. Equality as merit in the economic perspective tells employers to consider the productivity of individual employees within the firm. The distinctive institutional commitment of the economic perspective tends to confer greater discretion upon employers than the alternative perspectives, with their emphasis on the legal system as the institutional means of achieving equality. Unlike the alternative perspectives, the economic view prefers a system of private decision-making over legally enforced rules.

Thirdly, the remedial perspective emphasizes the degree to which the consequences of past discrimination are likely to persist in the absence of broad and vigorous remedial measures. This perspective takes the historical perspective and enlarges it to consider the continuing effects of past discrimination. The remedial perspective looks back to consider all of the effects resulting from past discrimination and looks forward to determine whether these effects are likely to persist despite the abolition of past discriminatory practices. From this perspective, the central inquiry is whether present practices, even if they do not repeat the precise forms of

[1] Of course, it is possible to have different views of merit and of the related positive conception of equality, and to endorse different institutional arrangements to ensure that employees are selected according to merit. Merit might be interpreted more broadly, as it has been, for instance, by John Rawls, who would require "full equality of opportunity": providing individuals not only with "careers open to talents", but also with the same opportunity to develop their talents, regardless of differences in social and class background (Rawls 1971).

past discrimination, continue to perpetuate their unjust effects[2]: "This perspective adds to the historical perspective by going beyond a narrow examination of legal enactments and engaging in a deeper inquiry into the social consequences of past discrimination. It adds to the economic perspective a greater weight attached to the cost of discrimination in any form. Its focus is upon the continuing vestiges of past subordination and upon the steps that can be taken to eliminate them" (Rutherglen 2010, 16). To quote a famous school desegregation decision in the USA, past discrimination and its effects must be "eliminated root and branch" (Green v. County).

This perspective is most frequently invoked to justify programs of affirmative action that seek, in a variety of different ways, to compensate for present disadvantages attributable to past discrimination. In this context, it might be useful to remember a rights-oriented legal philosopher, R. Dworkin, who argues that the use of race in affirmative action policies does not violate anybody's right (Sandel 2009, 153). Segregation-era racial exclusion depended on "the despicable idea that one may be inherently more worthy than another", whereas affirmative action involves no such prejudice. It simply asserts that, given the importance of promoting diversity in key professions, being black or Hispanic "may be a socially useful trait" (Dworkin 1977).

The legitimacy arguments that are most commonly put forward in favor of affirmative action measures include the following: they attempt to put right or redress historic injustices; they are aimed at redressing social/structural discrimination; they are of great social use; they tend to create diversity or a proportional representation of racial groups; they help prevent social disturbances; they are a way to build the nation and an effective way to guarantee equality, in its numerous forms: equality before the law, equal treatment and equal opportunities.

The remedial perspective also figures prominently in the justification for imposing liability upon employers for neutral practices with discriminatory effects. Both affirmative action and liability for discriminatory effects are characteristically dworkinian positions and so is the remedial perspective. This perspective would extend the laws against employment discrimination to intervene in labor markets to foster a broad conception of equality: one that ensured the opportunity of previously excluded groups not only to compete for jobs, but to compete free of the debilitating effects of past discrimination. Unlike the economic perspective, the remedial goes beyond a concern solely with equal competition according to present qualifications; it supports a conception of equality that ensures a greater degree of fairness in acquiring the relevant qualifications.

This conception of equality, although broader than merit in the economic sense, does not guarantee "groups right" or "equality of results"; instead, only a right to compete, not a right to succeed. As President Lyndon Johnson said in a famous speech arguing for the passage of civil rights legislation: "You don't take a person who, for years, has been hobbled by chains and liberate him, bring him up to the starting line of a race and then say '[Y]ou are free to compete with all the others,' and still justly believe you have been completely fair" (Johnson 1965).

[2] I have treated this question in previous published articles. Vid. Hermida del Llano (2011), 151–172, Hermida del Llano (2012), 105–116.

Despite abundant and successful international implementation, affirmative action measures tend to be criticized. The main barrier to affirmative action measures is put forward by those who are still reluctant to accept the validity of the basic principles of human rights, in particular the principles of equality and non-discrimination. "The principle objection claims that, however worthy the goal of a more diverse classroom or a more equal society, and however successful affirmative action policies may be in achieving it, using race or ethnicity as a factor in admissions is unfair.... They are Kantian or Rawlsian liberals who believe that even desirable ends must not override individual rights" (Sandel 2009, 173).

To this can be added the conceptual confusion that has arisen here from using the term *positive discrimination*. Committee for the Elimination of Racial Discrimination (CERD) doctrine states that it is a contradiction to use this term, and that it should, therefore, be avoided. In the opinion of Mr. Marc Bossuyt, "If it is discrimination it cannot be positive, and if it is positive it cannot be viewed as discrimination" (Bossuyt 2002).

Increasing doubts are being voiced about affirmative action as a remedy for past discrimination: "As opponents of affirmative action note, those who benefit are not necessarily those who have suffered, and those who pay the compensation are seldom those who are responsible for the wrongs being rectified. (...) Even if it can be argued that compensation should not be understood as a specific remedy for particular acts of discrimination, the compensatory rationale is too narrow to justify the range of programs advanced in the name of affirmative action" (Sandel 2006, 102).

Nevertheless, the remedial perspective has been extended in surprising ways, and, in particular, to justify compensation of natural disadvantages or, more accurately, disadvantages not resulting from past discrimination. Both with respect to sex discrimination and discrimination on the basis of disability, the law has required employers to accommodate conditions, such as pregnancy and physical or mental impairments, that do not in any way result from past discriminatory practices. To be sure, these laws still speak in terms of prohibiting discrimination, seemingly in the negative sense of not taking account of an individual's sex or disability, yet the obligations imposed upon employers are just the opposite: to consider these characteristics, and to some degree, to compensate for them.

The remedial perspective does not explain existing law so much as assume a critical attitude towards it. A remedial conception of equality must offer an independent baseline for determining what constitutes past discrimination and its continuing effects that must now be remedied. Legal theorists from a variety of movements have offered different elaborations of the baseline from which the adequacy of different remedial measures can be assessed. These movements tend, at least in recent years, to be focused on specific groups so that, for instance, critical race theorists, feminists, and disability rights advocates offer different accounts of the disadvantages that the law should remedy. Critical race theorists, on the one hand, emphasize the continuing effects of centuries of slavery and segregation and persistent patterns of racism established in earlier eras, especially, in the USA. Feminists, on the other hand, emphasize the variety of social traditions that have confined women to the domestic sphere of home and children under the overall control and authority of men. These differences are multiplied when we look at the differences within these groups themselves. Not all ethnic groups identify the same wrongs and consequences that need to be remedied, and not all women identify the same traditions as sexist. And some members of these groups do not endorse the remedial perspective in any form. As Rutherglen said: "The value of the remedial perspective is that it brings these issues out into the open, and in doing so, reveals the gap between what the law seeks to achieve and what it has, in fact, accomplished" (Rutherglen 2010, 28).

As I said before, this remedial perspective is most frequently invoked to justify programs of affirmative action. The most important step in evaluating affirmative action is to understand what it is. In the European Union (EU), the term for affirmative action is "positive action" or "positive discrimination". Although the EU has made no official definition of affirmative action, Council Directive 76/207,[3] amended by Directive 2002/73 CE,[4] gives the general definition that the concept of positive action embraces all measures which aim to counter the effects of past discrimination, to eliminate existing discrimination and to promote equality of opportunity. This is because the EU places an emphasis on equality of opportunity. Arguments in favor of compulsory measures in the European Union are based on the premise that *slow changes perpetuate barriers*. In other words, quotas seek to achieve a gender balance rather than reserve jobs.

For many years, the European Member States have worked towards achieving a high level of employment and social protection, increased standards of living and quality of life, and economic and social cohesion and solidarity. They have also endeavored to create an area of freedom, security and justice. In EU countries, where social programs have a strong history and enjoy wide support, the concept of affirmative action is fundamentally in line with the tenets of society. Although societal issues are an important factor in determining whether or not affirmative action will be effective, it is also important to examine how affirmative action is placed in the political system. The EU has made an effort to incorporate affirmative action into law and has made the policy a more natural and, therefore, more accepted program.

---

[3]Council Directive 76/207/EEC of 9 February 1976 on the implementation of the principle of equal treatment for men and women as regards access to employment, vocational training and promotion, and working conditions.

Art. 1:

1. The purpose of this Directive is to put into effect in the Member States the principle of equal treatment for men and women as regards access to employment, including promotion, and to vocational training and as regards working conditions and, on the conditions referred to in paragraph 2, social security. This principle is hereinafter referred to as "the principle of equal treatment."
2. With a view to ensuring the progressive implementation of the principle of equal treatment in matters of social security, the Council, acting on a proposal from the Commission, will adopt provisions defining its substance, its scope and the arrangements for its application.

[4]Directive 2002/73/EC of the European Parliament and of the Council of 23 September 2002 amending Council Directive 76/207/EEC on the implementation of the principle of equal treatment for men and women as regards access to employment, vocational training and promotion, and working conditions. Vid. *Official Journal* L 269, 05/10/2002, pp. 0015–0020.

Affirmative action measures enjoy worldwide support in relevant international instruments like the International Convention on the Elimination of Racial Discrimination (ICERD), in which Article 1.4, reads as follows: "Special measures taken for the sole purpose of securing adequate advancement of certain racial or ethnic groups or individuals requiring such protection as may be necessary in order to ensure such groups or individuals equal enjoyment or exercise of human rights and fundamental freedoms shall not be deemed racial discrimination, provided, however, that such measures do not, as a consequence, lead to the maintenance of separate rights for different racial groups and that they shall not be continued after the objectives for which they were taken have been achieved".[5] Furthermore, the Convention not only allows affirmative action but, in Article 2.2,[6] clearly imposes a burden on states to adopt positive action measures if there is evidence that such are needed in order to ensure equality of outcome. It refers to *special and concrete measures*. For CERD, this expression is the functional equivalent of special measures.[7]

---

[5] International Convention on the Elimination of All Forms of Racial Discrimination. Adopted and opened for signature and ratification by General Assembly resolution 2106 (XX) of 21 December 1965 entry into force 4 January 1969, in accordance with Article 19.

[6] Article 2.2: "States Parties shall, when the circumstances so warrant, take, in the social, economic, cultural and other fields, special and concrete measures to ensure the adequate development and protection of certain racial groups or individuals belonging to them, for the purpose of guaranteeing them the full and equal enjoyment of human rights and fundamental freedoms. These measures shall in no case entail as a consequence the maintenance of unequal or separate rights for different racial groups after the objectives for which they were taken have been achieved".

[7] According to Committee for the Elimination of Racial Discrimination (CERD) doctrine, the special measures or affirmative action measures concept is based on the principle that laws, policies and practices that are adopted and applied for meeting the obligations established in the Convention should be complemented, when circumstances so dictate, by the adoption of temporary special measures aimed at guaranteeing that underprivileged groups can fully and equally enjoy their human rights and fundamental liberties. Special measures form part of the set of provisions established in the Convention that seek to eliminate racial discrimination.

In General Recommendation No. XXXII, CERD expressed its concern at the fact that affirmative action measures often tend to get confused with the constitutional rights of groups that are traditionally discriminated against, and it pointed out that the obligation to adopt special measures differs from the general positive obligation that states party to the Convention have of guaranteeing the human rights and fundamental liberties of persons and groups under their jurisdiction in a non-discriminatory manner; this is a general obligation which derives from the provisions established in the Convention taken as a whole, and is one they all have, the Committee stated.

In line with international case law and doctrine, CERD stresses the temporary nature of special measures, and clearly states that this means there is a need for a continuous follow-up system on application and results which uses quantitative or qualitative evaluation methods, as the case might be. The Committee thus tells states party to the Convention that they should provide information in their periodic reports about the following matters: the terminology applied to the special measures, as understood in the Convention; the justification for the special measures being adopted, including relevant data and statistics and information about the general situation the beneficiaries find themselves in; a brief description of how the disparities that need remedying arose and the expected results of applying the measures; who the beneficiaries of the affirmative action will be; the series of consultations which led to the measures being adopted, including those with the beneficiaries and civilian society in general; the nature of the measures and how they promote

Likewise, Article 4 in the Convention on the Elimination of Discrimination against Women[8] reads as follows: "1. Adoption by State Parties of temporary special measures aimed at accelerating de facto equality between men and women shall not be considered discrimination as defined in the present Convention, but shall in no way entail as a consequence the maintenance of unequal or separate standards; these measures shall be discontinued when the objectives of equality of opportunity and treatment have been achieved. 2. Adoption by States Parties of special measures, including those measures contained in the present Convention, aimed at protecting maternity shall not be considered discriminatory".

The scope and extent of this provision have been determined by CEDAW in General Recommendation XXV. Also worthy of mention is International Civil and Political Rights Pact Committee General Recommendation No. XVIII.

Likewise, the Framework Convention for the Protection of National Minorities[9] also includes language that highlights the need for affirmative action saying, in article 4:

1. The Parties undertake to guarantee to persons belonging to national minorities the right of equality before the law and of equal protection of the law. In this respect, any discrimination based on belonging to a national minority shall be prohibited.
2. The Parties undertake to adopt, where necessary, adequate measures in order to promote, in all areas of economic, social, political and cultural life, full and effective equality between persons belonging to a national minority and those belonging to the majority. In this respect, they shall take due account of the specific conditions of the persons belonging to national minorities.
3. The measures adopted in accordance with paragraph 2 shall not be considered to be an act of discrimination.[10]

---

progress, development and protection for the groups and individuals they apply to; areas of action or sectors where the special measures have been adopted, and the institutions responsible for applying the measures; the mechanisms that exist for carrying out follow-up on and evaluation of the measures and the reasons why these mechanisms are considered adequate, together with involvement of the beneficiaries in the institutions applying the measures; and provisional results of application, plans for adopting new measures and the justification therefore, and information about the reasons why measures have not been adopted in view of the situations which seemed to justify their being adopted.

[8] On 18 December 1979, the Convention on the Elimination of All Forms of Discrimination against Women was adopted by the United Nations General Assembly. It entered into force as an international treaty on 3 September 1981 after the twentieth country had ratified it. By the tenth anniversary of the Convention in 1989, almost one hundred nations have agreed to be bound by its provisions.

[9] The Framework Convention for the Protection of National Minorities, drawn up within the Council of Europe by Ad Hoc Committee for the Protection of National Minorities (CAHMIN) under the authority of the Committee of Ministers, was adopted by the Committee of Ministers of the Council of Europe on 10 November 1994 and opened for signature by the member States of the Council of Europe on 1 February 1995. Non-member States may also be invited by the Committee of Ministers to become Party to this instrument.

[10] In my opinion, it could be useful to recall the Resolution CM/ResCMN(2013)4 on the implementation of the Framework Convention for the Protection of National Minorities by Spain, adopted

These Conventions are further strengthened by the Racial Equality Directive and the Employment Framework Directive, which contain definitions of direct and indirect discrimination, harassment, and victimization, and also allow for affirmative action measures to be taken.

Of course, approving affirmative action in international legal instruments is not enough. Instead affirmative action must also seem normal on a level much closer to home, and the EU states have made great strides in bringing this idea back to each individual country. Unlike in the United States, European court cases have recently been expanding the powers of affirmative action programs. In the well known case of *Marschall v. Land Nordrhein-Westfalen*, a German law giving priority to women for promotions, barring special circumstances, affirmative action was upheld (Marschall v Land Nordrhein-Westfalen). And in 2000, it was ruled in *Connors v.*

---

by the Committee of Ministers on 10 July 2013 at the 1176th meeting of the Ministers' Deputies. The Committee of Ministers, under the terms of Articles 24–26 of the Framework Convention for the Protection of National Minorities (hereinafter referred to as "the Framework Convention") adopted the following conclusions with respect to Spain: "Spain has taken important steps to develop its legal and institutional framework against discrimination. A comprehensive Bill on Equal Treatment and Non-Discrimination has been elaborated, in consultation with civil society organisations which, if adopted, would widen protection against discrimination and remedy current shortcomings of the legislation in force.

The Council for the Promotion of Equal Treatment of all Persons without Discrimination on grounds of Racial or Ethnic Origin was established in 2009 as an independent body in charge of monitoring the situation in the field of discrimination and raising awareness of these issues in society as a whole. The Council established a Network of assistance to victims of discrimination, operating at the local level with the support of various NGOs.

A Comprehensive Strategy against Racism, Racial Discrimination, Xenophobia and other Related Forms of Intolerance was adopted at the end of 2011. Special Prosecutors against discrimination and hate crime have been appointed at regional and State levels. The Spanish Observatory of Racism and Xenophobia continues to carry out research and actions to raise public awareness of these problems. The authorities have undertaken substantial work to improve the management of the various challenges arising out of cultural and religious diversity, notably through the "Observatory of Religious Pluralism". Policies to support the integration of immigrants in society and promote tolerance and intercultural dialogue continue to be implemented....

1. Adopts the following recommendations in respect of Spain:

   The authorities are invited to take the following measures to improve further the implementation of the Framework Convention:

   - Take more resolute measures to implement effectively the policies aimed at improving the situation and the integration of the Roma, in close co-operation with Roma representatives; ensure that these policies are adequately resourced and are not disproportionately affected by budgetary restrictions
   - Eliminate the practice of "ethnic profiling" by the police which targets persons belonging to some minority groups; increase training of the police to combat racism and discrimination, on the basis of existing good practices
   - Consult with representatives of the Berber community regarding ways and means of improving the situation of the Berber community in keeping with the spirit of the Framework Convention (...)"

UK that "there is a positive obligation imposed on the Contracting States by virtue of Article 8 to facilitate the gypsy way of life" (Connors v. the United Kingdom).[11]

I would like to refer now to the decision of the Luxembourg Court of 22 November, 2012, on the case C-385/11, Isabel Elbal Moreno v. Instituto Nacional de la Seguridad Social (INSS), Tesorería General de la Seguridad Social (TGSS).[12] The plaintiff, Ms Elbal Moreno, was denied a pension in Spain despite having

---

[11] The applicant complained that he and his family had been evicted from a local authority gypsy caravan site, invoking Articles 6, 8, 13 and 14 of the Convention and Article 1 of Protocol No. 1.

[12] Judgment of the Court (Eighth Chamber) 22 November 2012. (Article 157 TFEU – Directive 79/7/EEC – Directive 97/81/EC – Framework Agreement on part-time work – Directive 2006/54/EC – Contributory retirement pension – Equal treatment for male and female workers – Indirect discrimination on grounds of sex). Case C-385/11, Isabel Elbal Moreno v Instituto Nacional de la Seguridad Social (INSS), Tesorería General de la Seguridad Social (TGSS).

"9 On 8 October 2009, aged 66 years, Ms Elbal Moreno – the applicant in the main proceedings – applied to the INSS for a retirement pension. Previously, she had worked exclusively as a cleaner for a Residents' Association part-time for 4 h a week (10 % of the 40-h statutory working week in Spain) for 18 years.

10 By the decision of 13 October 2009, Ms Elbal Moreno's application for a pension was refused on the ground that she had not completed the minimum contribution period of 15 years, required for entitlement to a retirement pension, as provided under Article 161(1)(b) of the LGSS.

11 A complaint lodged by Ms Elbal Moreno on 30 November 2009 was dismissed by decision of the INSS on 9 December 2009. Whereas, in Ms Elbal Moreno's case, proof was required of a minimum contribution period of 4931 days, the decision recognized that she had completed a contribution period of 1362 days.

12 Following the dismissal of her complaint, Ms Elbal Moreno brought an action before the Juzgado de lo Social de Barcelona (Social Court of Barcelona) in which she submitted that the Seventh Additional Provision of the LGSS, under which her application for a pension had been refused, entailed a breach of the principle of equality. That provision requires a part-time worker to pay contributions for a longer period than a full-time worker, even with the correcting factor represented by the 1.5 multiplier, in order to obtain a pension which is already proportionately lower. Ms Elbal Moreno also submitted that that rule entails indirect discrimination, since it is an indisputable statistical fact that women workers are the principal users of this type of contract (approximately 80 %).

(…)

29 In that respect, it should be noted that, according to the settled case-law of the Court, indirect discrimination for the purposes of Article 4 of Directive 79/7 arises where a national measure, albeit formulated in neutral terms, works to the disadvantage of far more women than men (see, inter alia, *Brachner*, paragraph 56).

(…)

32 It follows that such legislation is contrary to Article 4(1) of Directive 79/7, unless it is justified by objective factors unrelated to any discrimination on grounds of sex. That will be the case where the measures chosen reflect a legitimate social-policy objective of the Member State whose legislation is at issue, they are appropriate to achieve that aim and they are necessary in order to do so (see, to that effect, *Brachner*, paragraph 70).

(…)

38 Consequently, the answer to Question 4 is that Article 4 of Directive 79/7 must be interpreted as precluding, in circumstances such as those of the case before the referring court, legislation of a Member State which requires a proportionally greater contribution period from part-time workers, the vast majority of whom are women, than from full-time workers for the former to qualify, if appropriate, for a contributory retirement pension in an amount reduced in proportion to the part-time nature of their work".

worked as a part-time cleaner for 18 years because she had not completed the minimum contribution period of 15 years required for entitlement to a retirement pension in Spain. Ms Elbal Moreno argued that the rule entails indirect discrimination, since it is an indisputable statistical fact that women workers are the principal users of this type of contract (approximately 80 % in Spain). The Court ruled: "Article 4 of Council Directive 79/7/EEC of 19 December 1978 on the progressive implementation of the principle of equal treatment for men and women in matters of social security must be interpreted as precluding, in circumstances such as those of the case before the referring court, legislation of a Member State which requires a proportionally greater contribution period from part-time workers, the vast majority of whom are women, than from full-time workers for the former to qualify, if appropriate, for a contributory retirement pension in an amount reduced in proportion to the part-time nature of their work".

With this decision, the European Court of Justice has dealt a hard blow to the politics of pensions in Spain. The Court of Justice of the EU used a gender argument to find discriminatory treatment. As women hold most of the part-time jobs, the obstacles that the law creates for them to obtain a pension imply gender discrimination, although indirect. In fact, the plaintiff would have had to work 100 years to obtain the right to a pension.

In this context, I would like to mention the Spanish Law 3/2007, of 22 March 2007, for the effective equality of women and men (LOIE) (Merino and Franch 2007, 15–50),[13] that incorporates into Spanish Law the Council Directive 2002/73,[14] the Council Directive 2004/113/EC[15] and the Council Directive 97/80/EC.[16] Implicitly this law also addresses the main aspects of Council Directive 75/117/ECC,[17] representing an important step for gender equality in Spain.

The aim of Article 1 of the Law is to implement the principle of equal opportunities between women and men in matters of employment and occupation. Article 5

[13] This Law is in force but is being appealed before the Constitucional Court by the Partido Popular. The appeal focuses mainly on the articles which regulate the parity conditions for the electoral lists for candidates to political office in Spain.

[14] To amend the Directive 76/207/CEE about equal treatment for men and women as regards access to employment, vocational training and promotion, and working conditions.

[15] Vid. Council Directive 2004/113/EC of 13 December 2004, implementing the principle of equal treatment between men and women in the access to and supply of goods and services.

[16] The Law also follows the recommendations of the Committee of CEDAW. *Cfr. Observaciones finales del Comité para la Eliminación de la Discriminación contra la Mujer*: Spain. A/54/38; 30°. y 31° Session Periods, 12–30 January and 6–23 July, 2004: paragraph "Principales esferas de preocupación y recomendaciones".

[17] Although Law 3/2007 does not make direct reference to Directive 2006/54/EC, the Spanish Government considers that with Law 3/2007 for equality, the Recast Directive has already been transposed in Spain. Regarding Directive 86/378/CEE, regulation in Spain has no changed with Law 3/2007 of equality, except the matter related to collective insurance that is one of the instruments that can be used to guarantee the managerial obligations as for pensions. On this point, the Government is allowed to elaborate a Royal Decree in order to introduce some proportionate differences using the possibility of Article 5.2 of Directive 2004/113/EC.

indicates that this principle of equal opportunities will be guaranteed in the access to employment in the private sector, to employment in the public sector and also in self-employment, in vocational training, in professional promotion and in work conditions.

Law 3/2007 establishes a general frame for the adoption of measures of positive action, including any action that aims to correct situations of inequality of women with respect to men. Positive actions may be taken by the public authorities, but also by individual persons, and moreover it is specifically allowed to introduce measures of positive action by means of collective labor agreements to facilitate the effective implementation of the principle of equality of treatment and non-discrimination in working conditions between women and men. In Spain the occupational pension schemes are usually established through a collective labor agreement and from this point of view it could also be possible to take positive action in this field.

The law envisions and justifies a general framework for the adoption of affirmative action to achieve the effective real equality between men and women, measures that the Spanish Constitutional Court has supported in its jurisprudence.[18] The Spanish law transmits to all public institutions a mandate to correct the situations of relevant factual inequality that are not properly amended by the principle of juridical or formal equality. The law contemplates a special consideration to the case of double discrimination and refers to the particular difficulties that women suffer in a situation of special vulnerability because they belong to minorities, are immigrant women, or women with disabilities, a situation that has worsened with the economic crisis in Spain.

The law addresses special attention to correct inequality in the area of laboral relations. According to several measures, the right to reconcile personal, family and work life is recognized. For this purpose the law promotes a greater joint responsibility shared between women and men regarding family obligations.

It is remarkable that the Spanish jurisprudence of the Constitutional Court reaffirms the traditional roles of men and women: the mothers should take care of the children and the fathers must dedicate themselves to their work outside of the home.

[18]There are several decisions by the Spanish Constitutional Court to which I would like to refer because they are inspired by the goal of promoting the reconciliation between family life and the careers of mothers in the workforce. The first one is the decision 128/1987, of July 16, which has a special significance for the Spanish Constitutional jurisprudence on affirmative actions. The second one is the decision 109/1993, March 25. This case concerned the demand of a male worker against a rule that allowed as a worker's right time off for mothers to nurse their children. This case provoked a great debate that led to amending the Law 3/1989, March 3. This Law extended maternity leave and established special measures to promote the equal treatment of women in the work force, saying as follows: "This leave can be taken equally by the father or by the mother when both of them work". Despite this amendment, the decision of the Spanish Constitutional Court STC 109/1993, March 25, FJ 5°, affirmed that the rule was not discriminatory to men that work. This decision was based on the biological reality and in the necessity to adopt special measures in favor of disadvantaged groups, such as women in the work force. *Ibid.* FJS 4° and 6°.

This point of view has been criticized as a sexist position that does not help in achieving the real effective equality between men and women (Ollero 1999, 56).[19]

In the specific decision 128/1987, the Spanish Constitutional Court used sexist criteria to recognize that a social reality exists that is the result of a long cultural tradition in which the women fulfill the majority of the family obligations, in particular the care of children. Therefore, the Court found that the special measures that try to incorporate into the workforce socially disadvantaged groups are not discriminatory.

Even though the distinction is not completely clear between the affirmative actions that do not genuinely protect women and affirmative actions that are constitutionally legitimized, what is true is that "the principle which regulates the existing social relations between the two sexes – the legal subordination of one sex to the other – is wrong itself, and now one of the chief hindrances to human improvement; and that it ought to be replaced by a principle of perfect equality, admitting no power or privilege on the one side, nor disability on the other", in words written by John Stuart Mill (1869) more than a century ago, today is still a pending task in Spain, which according to the law 3/2007, requires new legal instruments.[20]

Bibliography

Bossuyt, Marc. 2002. The concept and practice of affirmative action. Final report in Accordance with United Nations Sub-Commission on the Promotion and Protection of Human Rights Resolution 1998/5. UN Doc. E/CN.4/Sub.2/2002/21.

Connors v. the United Kingdom. 2004. Application no. 66746/01.

Dworkin, Ronald. 1977. Why Bakke has no case. *New York Review of Books* 24: 11–15.

Green v. County Sch. 1968.

Hermida del Llano, Cristina. 2011. Desafíos jurídico-políticos en aras de una mayor integración del inmigrante latinoamericano en la Unión Europea: una apuesta por la igualdad y el concepto de ciudadanía cívica. *Revista de Derechos Humanos de la Universidad de Piura* 2: 151–172.

Hermida del Llano, Cristina. 2012. Equal opportunity as the basis for social-economic integration of immigrants in the European Union. *Annales Universitatis Apulensis, Series Jurisprudentia* 15: 105–116.

Johnson, Lyndon B. 1965. Commencement address at Howard University: "To Fulfill These Rights". June 4, 1965. http://www.presidency.ucsb.edu/ws/index.php?pid=27021&st=&st1=.

Marschall v Land Nordrhein-Westfalen, Case C-409/95 [1997] ECR I-6363. Available via http://eur-lex.europa.eu/smartapi/cgi/sga_doc?smartapi!celexplus!prod!CELEXnumdoc&lg=en&numdoc=695J0409.

[19] In this sense, Ollero affirms: "the principal disadvantages of the female citizens, as the discriminated gender, can lead to them being put in a box, with the apparent intention to protect them, as though they were in need of tutelage; in reality this will perpetuate a vicious circle of dependency".

[20] Some of the most important and specific legal norms in the scope of the equality of opportunity between men and women in Spain are the following: L.O. 39/1999, para promover la Conciliación de la Vida Familiar y Laboral de las personas trabajadoras; L.O. 1/2004, de Medidas de Protección Integral contra la Violencia de Género; L.O. 3/2007, para la Igualdad Efectiva de Mujeres y Hombres; L.O. 13/2007, de Prevención y Protección Integral contra la Violencia de Género.

Mill, John Stuart, and Harriet Taylor Mill. 2001. *Ensayos sobre la igualdad sexual.* Madrid: Cátedra.
Ollero, Andrés. 1999. *Discriminación por razón de sexo. Valores, principios y normas en la jurisprudencia constitucional española.* Madrid: Centro de Estudios Políticos y Constitucionales.
Rawls, John. 1971. *A theory of justice.* Cambridge, MA/London: The Belknap Press of Harvard University Press Cambridge.
Rutherglen, George. 2010. *Employment discrimination law. Visions of equality in theory and doctrine.* New York: Foundation Press.
Sandel, Michael J. 2006. *Public philosophy. Essays on morality in politics.* Cambridge/London: Harvard University Press.
Sandel, Michael J. 2009. *Justice. What is the right thing to do?* New York: Farrar, Straus and Giroux.
Sevilla Merino, J., and Franch A. Ventura. 2007. Fundamento Constitucional de la Ley Orgánica 3/2007, de 22 de marzo, para la igualdad efectiva de mujeres y hombres. Especial referencia a la participación política. *Revista del Ministerio de Trabajo e Inmigración* n VII: 15–50.
Stuart Mill, John. 1869. *The subjection of women.* London: Longmans, Green, Reader, and Dyer.

The Nordic States and the European Convention on Human Rights

Joakim Nergelius

Abstract When Denmark, Iceland, Norway and Sweden in 1953 became parties to the European Convention on Human Rights (ECHR) there was no need for any kind of "rights revolution", i.e. a reassessment of the role that the idea and concept of human rights had in the domestic, legal and political life of the Nordic states. The method used to implement the ECHR was *passive transformation*, that is an assessment that there was full normative harmony between the Convention and the domestic systems of law. The approach to the ECHR was characterised by a certain *Nordic arrogance*, a presumption that the countries of Southern or Central Europe had nothing to teach to the Nordic countries, known as champions in securing all aspects of the well-being of their inhabitants. It was of no importance that in the Nordic countries the individual is protected *in another way* than in countries that have a strong tradition of *rights-based* protection. In the Nordic tradition emphasis is put on protecting, in a rational and just way, the *interests* of human beings, through a political process and without giving individual rights any priority among various competing interests.

Introduction

When Denmark, Iceland, Norway and Sweden in 1953 became parties to the European Convention on Human Rights (ECHR) there was no need for any kind of "rights revolution", i.e. a reassessment of the role that the idea and concept of human rights had in the domestic, legal and political life of the Nordic states. The method used to implement the ECHR was *passive transformation*, that is an assessment that there was full normative harmony between the Convention and the domestic systems of law.[1] The approach to the ECHR was characterised by a certain *Nordic arrogance*, a presumption that the countries of Southern or Central Europe

[1] On different methods to implement international treaties and on the application of these methods in the Nordic countries, see Martin Scheinin, "General Introduction" in Martin Scheinin (ed.),

J. Nergelius (✉)
University of Örebro, Örebro, Sweden
e-mail: joakim.nergelius@oru.se

R. Arnold (ed.), *The Convergence of the Fundamental Rights Protection in Europe*, Ius Gentium: Comparative Perspectives on Law and Justice 52,
DOI 10.1007/978-94-017-7465-9_5

had nothing to teach to the Nordic countries, known as champions in securing all aspects of the well-being of their inhabitants. It was of no importance that in the Nordic countries the individual is protected *in another way* than in countries that have a strong tradition of *rights-based* protection. In the Nordic tradition emphasis is put on protecting, in a rational and just way, the *interests* of human beings, through a political process and without giving individual rights any priority among various competing interests.

Another background factor that can be identified is the fact that in the Nordic countries, with a certain exception for Norway, there has never developed any strong tradition of judicial review over the constitutionality of legislation (Nergelius 1996, 167–174, 182–188, 686, 697). Such arrangements constitute in many countries the fundament for an entrenched position for fundamental rights within the legal system. Though the legal doctrine in Denmark and Sweden has traditionally recognised the possibility of courts to set aside a law that is manifestly unconstitutional, only in Norway has the application of the institution gained practical significance. Even in Norway, though, the use of the institution is primarily related to a certain limited period of time which, in relation to latter decades, further emphasizes the exceptional nature of the institution (Eckhoff 1976; Smith 1990). In Finland, the old Constitution Act was understood to prohibit the judicial review of the constitutionality of laws passed by Parliament (Finnish Constitution Act 1919, 92.2; Nergelius 1996, 194). Only the new Constitution that entered into force in March 2000 takes a modest step in the direction shown by the other Nordic countries through a constitutional provision on the jurisdiction of courts to give the Constitution priority in relation to such an application of an ordinary law that would be in manifest contradiction with the Constitution (Constitution of Finland 1999, (Act No. 731) Section 106).

It is possible to distinguish three separate processes through which the Nordic countries have in the last 20 years undergone a process of "Europeanization" within their legal ideology and approach to individual rights.

First, during the 1990s, it was recognised in all of the Nordic countries that international human rights treaties, in particular the European Convention on Human Rights (ECHR), influence the application of the law, including the operation of courts. Although the ratification of the ECHR in the 1950s by the Scandinavian countries was characterised by a certain Nordic arrogance referred to above, it was realised only in the 1980s or in the beginning of the 1990s that the provisions of the ECHR must be taken into account in administrative and judicial decision-making. One factor contributing to this process was that the European Court of Human Rights found violations of the ECHR in several cases against Sweden. This sequence of judgments was initiated in 1982 by the case of *Sporrong and Lönnroth* (ECtHR 1982, s. A 52; ECHR 1986, s. A 125-A; 125-B; ECtHR 1989, s. 159). Although Denmark, Iceland and Norway were not quite as often subject to judgments by the European Court of Human Rights (ECtHR 1989, s. A 154; UfR 1990, 181–187), the Swedish cases were important for public discussion and legal thinking in these coun-

---

International Human Rights Norms in the Nordic and Baltic Countries, The Hague–Boston–London 1996.

tries. For Finland that was not a party to the ECHR before 1990, two Human Rights Committee cases establishing in 1989 and 1990 violations of the Covenant on Civil and Political Rights had a similar role (HRC 1989, 265/1987; HRC 1990, 291/1988).

Today it is easy to identify, in all five Nordic countries, cases in which the highest judicial bodies have applied the ECHR.[2] And in Finland, who ratified the ECHR as late as 1990, it did not take 30 or 40 years before courts started to apply the treaty. This can in part be explained by the fact that in Finland international treaties generally are incorporated into domestic law through an Act of Parliament. When Finnish judges in 1988 or 1990 started to cite international human rights treaties (Supreme Administrative Court 1988 A 48–49; Supreme Court 1990:93), they did not need to refer to something that formally was outside the domestic legal system. The other Nordic countries have traditionally followed a more orthodox version of the theory of dualism according to which the obligations of a State in international law and the domestic legal order form two separate legal systems. In the absence of formal incorporation in the Scandinavian countries, it took a long time for the judges to develop the paths of argumentation needed for applying the ECHR. In the 1970s, certain Swedish courts gave several rulings denying the judicial applicability of treaties that formally are outside the Swedish legal system (Arbetsdomstolens domar 1972, 75; NJA 1973, 423; Regeringsrättens årsbok 1974, 121). In later times, the position of judges has developed. Also in Sweden, where the theory of dualism was applied in its most extreme form, courts recognised in the 1980s that international human rights treaties can be made use of in the application of Swedish laws, even when the treaties are formally outside the Swedish legal system (Supreme Court 1984:170, 1988:108).

Constitutionally proclaimed individual rights are still taken for granted, but at the same time not as having a particularly strong status. When needed, the democratic legislature can legitimately establish the limits of such rights, usually through simple majority decisions. Denmark and Norway have so far not gone through major constitutional amendments, although Norway has introduced certain amendments in the details that have contributed to a growing importance of constitutionally guaranteed fundamental rights. A further, ambitious human rights reform is likely to occur in Norway in 2012.

In the constitutional amendments made in the 1990s in Norway, Finland and Sweden one can see an effort to make the Constitution reflect the ongoing rights revolution described above. In 1994 a new Article 110c was inserted in the Norwegian Constitution, expressing a general obligation of public authorities to secure internationally recognised human rights. This constitutional clause can be understood as the legitimation of the competence of Norwegian courts to apply the ECHR and other human rights treaties even if they formally were outside the

[2]Denmark: U 1990.12 HK, U 1990.181 H, U 1994.988 H; Finland: Supreme Administrative Court 1993 A 26–29, Supreme Court 1992:73, 1993:19, 1993:58; Iceland: Supreme Court 1990:2, 1990:92 and 1992:174; Norway: Norsk Retstidende (Rt.) 1990 p. 257, Rt. 1990 p. 312, Rt. 1990 p. 319, Rt. 1990 p. 1221; Sweden: Supreme Court 1988:108, 1988: 28. Most of these cases are discussed in Scheinin (ed.) 1996.

domestic legal order. In Finland, the constitutional rights reform of 1995 included a similar provision (Section 16a, subsection 1), even if most human rights treaties *have been* incorporated through an Act of Parliament. Section 16a (Section 23 in the new Constitution of 1999) can be said to afford human rights treaties with a *quasi-constitutional* status. In 1995 a clause was inserted into the Swedish Constitution Act (Instrument of Government, IG) stating that the *legislature* must respect the ECHR (Chapter 2, Section 19). As a consequence of this provision, a law that is in conflict with the ECHR and hence has been enacted in contradiction with the mentioned provision is unconstitutional and can thus be set aside by a court; since 2011, this does not any longer require that the contradiction should be manifest (see Swedish Constitution Act, Chapter 11, Section 14, which was changed in 2011, thus making judicial review easier).

In 1995 both Iceland and Finland adopted a new constitutional catalogue of fundamental rights. The Finnish constitutional rights reform was of a higher level of ambition. One of the proclaimed aims of the reform in Finland was to strengthen the judicial application of constitutional rights provisions.[3] This aim was sought primarily through the doctrines of fundamental-rights-conform interpretation and direct applicability of fundamental rights (Scheinin 1991, 198–208), without touching the traditional doctrine that courts are prohibited from examining the constitutionality of laws adopted by Parliament. International human rights treaties served as a strong source of inspiration for the reform and for the formulation of individual provisions in the new catalogue of rights. In addition, there was a deliberate effort to afford *better protection* in areas where the international standards were seen not to be ambitious enough. At least some of the provisions on economic, social and cultural rights were given a more precise and concrete formulation compared to existing international human rights treaties.

There are thus good grounds to state that the 1990s meant a revolution or paradigm shift in Nordic legal thinking on rights, mainly because of the changes in the operation of courts in applying the ECHR and other human rights treaties. This is an important change compared to traditional Nordic legal thinking. It is now understood that courts have the competence and even the duty to apply a catalogue of fundamental rights, even of a "foreign" origin, as a normative basis for reviewing decisions or other measures taken in the application of domestic law. In some cases it is possible to state that courts have given *priority* to the ECHR, in relation to domestic laws (Supreme Court of Iceland 1992, 174; Supreme Court of Norway 1984, 1174; 1994, 610). In the other Nordic countries except Finland this change occurred *prior* to the formal incorporation of the ECHR which took place in 1992 in Denmark, in 1994 in Iceland, in 1995 in Sweden and in 1999 in Norway.

Although this change has primarily been related to the ECHR and hence to traditional civil liberties (civil and political rights), the courts in the Nordic countries have occasionally referred also to treaties on economic and social rights. In 1991 the Swedish Supreme Administrative Court (Regeringsrätten) cited the European

[3] See the mandate of the Commission established to draft a new fundamental rights catalogue, letter by the Ministry of Justice 21 September 1989 No. 3077/061/89 OM.

Social Charter in its reasoning on why asylum seekers from Russia could not be denied certain social assistance benefits (Supreme Administrative Court 1991, case No. 4642–1989). It is to be noted that the convention in question has *not* been incorporated into Swedish law and hence does not form a part of the formally constituted Swedish legal order.

Denmark

The beginning of a somewhat bolder attitude from the Supreme Court in issues related to judicial review may be traced back to 1996, when the President of the Court Judge Niels Pontoppidan declared in a newspaper interview (in the weekly journal *Weekend-Avisen*) that the Supreme Court was henceforth going to make a more thorough review of the constitutionality of Danish laws, in line with the general international development towards a stronger position of the courts in the modern society. Only about a month later, the Supreme Court then declared – in a decision after an appeal there had been made – that the Court of Appeal in Copenhagen (*Östre Landsret*) should review the constitutionality of the Danish law on accession to the Maastricht Treaty, in particular in relation to the above-mentioned art. 20 on transfer of competencies to international organisations.

After the Court of Appeal did not find that law unconstitutional, the issue was finally dealt with by the Supreme Court in a landmark judgment from April 1998, which resembles the German Maastricht judgment from 1993 (BVerfGE 1993, 155;UfR 1999, 800 H) very much. The treaty and thus the Danish law on accession was found to be compatible with the Constitution, but only after a very restricted interpretation of it had been made, in which the superiority of the Danish Constitution in relation to EU law, in case of conflict between the two, was strongly stressed.

Even more spectacular, and contrary to the ancient, cautious attitude from the courts, was a judgment from the Supreme Court a year later, in February 1999, in which a law was actually set aside (UfR 1999, 841 H). The case concerned a certain school (*Tvind*), which is considered as radically left-wing leaning and has for a long time been controversial. According to a new law, the Parliament could decide which schools outside the regular, public education system that should be granted money from public funds or not, a right it used to cut down all subsidies to the Tvind schools operating in Denmark and third-world countries. The Supreme Court found in an interesting judgment that this was not something that should be decided by the Parliament, since that would disturb the principle of separation of powers established in art. 3 (but never before applied by a Danish court)! According to the court, the Parliament could only enact laws, while decisions on support to various schools or other bodies should be made by the Government, in this case by the Ministry of Education. The judgment was met with huge surprise, but also interest. It is also a clear sign that stronger judicial review for the courts is not a factor that will always benefit rich and strong actors in the society, which is sometimes claimed by left-wing opponents to judicial review and separation of powers (at least in the Nordic countries).

In this respect, also the fact that the European Convention on Human Rights was incorporated into national, domestic Danish law in 1992 is of course of a certain importance. This also contributed to a somewhat bolder and more open attitude from Danish courts in relation to judicial review, although no really interesting or important cases have occurred during after 1999.

One example of this was a case from 1994 (UfR 1994, 536), where a person had been sentenced for a gambling offence by the local court in Frederiksberg, Copenhagen. He argued before the Court of Appeal (once again Östre Landsret) and the Supreme Court that the fact that the judge who had sentenced him was not a regular judge, but a person who had his regular post at the Ministry of Justice. Both courts, however, found that this practice was not contrary to art. 3 or art. 64, which regulates the legal position of judges. The Supreme Court here interpreted those articles very restrictively, but as far as the relation between the Danish system and the European Convention was concerned, the court was more generous. Here, it reached the conclusion that it was in fact not certain or clear, given the jurisprudence of the Strasbourg court, that the Danish system was contrary to art. 6 of the ECHR, but since it could be argued with some force that so was the case, it must be held that the applicant had not been given a fair trial in consideration of the requirements of the European Convention. The judgment was thus repealed and the case was sent back to the local court.

Otherwise, international law has never been considered as being part of the national legal system. Denmark is thus, as the other Nordic countries, traditionally dualistic. The assumption has always been, instead, that Danish laws should be interpreted as being compatible with the requirements of international law.

Finland

The ECHR was incorporated into Finnish law in 1990. Paradoxically, one can in Finland identify certain elements of genuine rights thinking according to which individual rights serve as limits to the operation of the democratic process of majority decision-making. Within Finnish legal theory Scandinavian realism never had as strong a position as in Scandinavia. Finnish legal scholars have sought inspiration from Germany and, after World War II, even France. It is a part of the paradox that it was the exclusion of judicial review over the constitutionality of legislation that in Finland led to the development of an institutionalised system of *preview* over the constitutionality of laws under consideration. This preview is in the hands of the Constitutional Law Committee of Parliament (Jyränki 1989). As a part of the preview process the Committee regularly hears legal experts which has led to a situation where Professors of Constitutional Law, together with the M.P.:s sitting on the Committee, many of whom are lawyers, compose a de facto *Conseil Constitutionnel* (Riepula 1973; Länsineva 1991). Through the operation of the Committee many of the provisions of the 1919 Constitution Act gradually gained, since the latter part of the 1940s, legal albeit not judicial application and significance. Due to shifts in political constellations the institution was first developed in the post-war years to protect property rights (Kastari 1948, 191–223) but later on giving recognition to civil rights and liberties in the 1970s[4] and the right to work in the 1980s.[5] This development shows that even if the idea of constitutional rights as a limitation to the legislator's' competence was first used to protect a specific category of political aspirations, the legal institution, once created, has been available also for the promoters of quite different political aims.

We may look at the various basic rights in the Constitution Act of 2000 a little bit more in detail. Chapter 2 of the constitution, articles 6–23, does now contain a fairly modern catalogue or bill of rights, which starts by declaring that everyone is equal before the law and that any discrimination based on e.g. gender, age, origin, language, religion, conviction or health is prohibited.[6] Also the equality between men and women is mentioned here, like the rights of children and their legal position.

According to art. 7, everyone has the right to personal freedom and integrity. Death penalty and torture or other kind of inhuman behaviour is strictly prohibited. No one may be deprived of his liberty without a due process of law and penalties including prison may only be given by a court. It is of course also important to respect the principle of legality, which is protected in art. 8, according to which no one may be convicted for an action that was not seen as a crime when the deed was committed, or given a harder or more severe penalty than the law prescribed at that time.

According to art. 9, Finnish citizens as well as foreigners who lawfully stay in the country have the right to move freely within the country as well as to leave the country, though that right may be limited through law. While Finnish citizens may never be expelled or prevented from travelling into Finland, similar rights for foreigners are regulated by law, though it may be noted that foreigners may never be expelled or sent back to a country, if that would mean that they run the risk of being sentenced to death, tortured or treated inhumanly. Also the more general right to privacy is protected through art. 10, which does however permit certain intrusions into persons homes in order to combat crime, given that those intrusions are provided by law.

The freedom(s) of religion and conscience, speech and information (which also includes transparency and access to documents, in the same way as in Sweden), meeting and assembly as well as the right to form and join associations are covered in art. 11–13., while art. 14 protects the right to vote in general elections for citizens

---

[4] In Opinion No. 2 of 1971, related to security checks at airports, the constitutional clauses on the liberty and integrity of the person were, for the first time, taken seriously in examining the constitutionality of a Government Bill.

[5] In 1972, the Finnish Constitution Act was amended by inserting a new clause on the right to work. From 1980 onwards, the Constitutional Law Committee of Parliament insisted, in a row of Reports or Opinions, that the old Employment Act was not in harmony with the Constitution and should be replaced with a law that would guarantee an individual right to a job, at least for persons belonging to certain groups and for a certain time. Finally, the reform was implemented through the adoption of a new Employment Act (No. 275 of 1987).

[6] As opposed to Sweden, this enumeration of prohibited forms of discrimination in art. 6 does not explicitly mention sexual orientation, though it is likely that it will be effective also in such cases.

who are at least 18 years old. Like in Sweden, foreigners older than 18 years and permanently residing in Finland have the right to vote in municipal elections (as well as in elections to the European Parliament, though that is not mentioned in the Constitution).

The right to property is mentioned in art. 15, which is however quite short and does not really show or indicate the extent to which this right has traditionally been strong in Finland. On the other hand, the right to exercise a trade or profession freely is well covered in art. 18, that also mentions the right not to be fired without lawful reasons, though that right is probably weaker and in any case more rarely invoked.

Some other rights, like the right to education and culture in art. 16 and the obligation of the public bodies to promote employment in art. 18, are social or economic and more general to their nature. The same is true concerning the protection of the environment, art. 20. It would probably be difficult to base any legal claim before a court on any of those rights, while the right for everyone to face courts and other public bodies in either Finnish or Swedish, in art 17, on the other hand imposes a clear legal obligation on those bodies.

From that particular point of view, i.e. the so-called *enforceability* of a certain right, the right to social protection and security in art. 19 is probably the most difficult to grasp, like in many other countries. It looks very likely that claims based on this article are often made before Finnish courts, but its real legal status is unclear and the likeliness for success in those cases thus difficult to ascertain. Still, there may of course be room for a certain legal development in this area.

An article that is definitely both important and enforceable, on the other hand, is the right to a fair and public trial and the general right to a review by a court concerning any kind of civil rights and obligations, art. 21. This rule is very similar to art. 6 in the European Convention of Human Rights, a fact that will most likely guarantee its impact not least in the area of administrative law.

It should be noted that anyone whose basic rights have been violated is entitled to financial compensation from the state, according to art. 118. This rule is very modern and reflects a current European tendency towards increased protection of the individuals, in a "post-Francovich" European legal setting (Cfr C-6/90; Cfr C-9/90; ECR 1991, 5357). The provision is similar, for instance, to rules in the British Human Rights Act from 2000.

Sweden

A few words could also be said concerning the background of the incorporation of the European Convention of Human Rights into Swedish law. As mentioned *above*, Sweden is a typical example of what is normally called a *dualist* state in terms of its relations with international law, i.e. a state where international law, whether in the terms of international customary law or of international conventions which Sweden has ratified, does not take effect within the national legal system without a special act of transformation that turns them into domestic law (NJA 1973, 423; RÅ 1974,

121). During the 1980s, however, the two highest Swedish courts gradually came to consider the ECHR as an important source of interpretation and inspiration (Cameron 2006, 153). Swedish laws were thus interpreted in the light of the convention and the case law from the Strasbourg court (NJA 1988, 572; 1989, 131; 1990, 636; 1991, 188, 512; RÅ 1990, ref. 75, note 492).

However, the incorporation nevertheless took place in a problematic way, in particular from a legal point of view. Due to a political compromise, the ECHR, despite being referred to in former IG Chapter 2, Article 23 (now Chapter 2, Article 19) was not given constitutional status, but is as such incorporated through an ordinary law.[7] IG 2:19 simply states that 'No act of law or other provision may be adopted' which contravenes Sweden's undertakings under the ECHR. Thus, this may be seen as a rule directed to the legislator rather than the courts (Cameron 2006, 155; Bernitz 2002, 81), an impression that is strengthened by the fact that since ECHR is incorporated as an ordinary law, the restrictions and limitations on judicial review imposed by IG 11:14 apply with even greater force in relation to ECHR than in relation to the national constitution(s) (Bohlin and Warnling-Nerep 2004, 334). The situation, should a law passed either before or after 1 January 1995 be in conflict with the ECHR, was in the *travaux préparatoires* handed to the courts to deal with by the use of ordinary means of interpretation (e.g. rules on *lex posterior* and *lex specialis*).

What does this mean in practice, then? It could of course be seen to indicate that when a conflict, which is not manifest, will arise between the ECHR and a Swedish law or ordinance, the law or ordinance shall be applied.[8] But on the other hand, it must be noted that in the travaux préparatoires, both from the government and the Constitutional Committee of the Parliament, mentioning is made of the 'special character' and status of ECHR, which ought to give it a certain weight of its own in future conflicts with domestic laws (or ordinances).[9] On the basis of those remarks, Swedish courts ought to be able to find at least some room for *manoeuvering* if they want to secure the respect (if not supremacy) of ECHR.

Still, which is perhaps not entirely surprising against this background, the Swedish courts were for a long time reluctant to use the ECHR, at least when this would mean setting aside a national law. In one case from 1998 (NJA 1998, 817), the Supreme Court even refused to uphold the Convention (as well as the FSA) against a demand from Swedish and Norwegian authorities to execute a penal judgment from a Norwegian court (which was all the more embarrassing since Norway was 6 months later condemned by ECtHR for violating the ECHR concerning that same issue) (Bladet Tromsö and Stensaas v. Norway 1999, case 21980/93). At the same time, both the highest courts have been very clear in terms of acknowledging e.g. the impact of the principle of proportionality, flowing from ECHR (NJA 2001, 409).

---

[7] The number of which is 1994:1500.

[8] Of course, it shall also be noted that the similarities between ECHR and Chapter 2 IG, which contains a rights catalogue, are striking. The main difference is that the protection of personal integrity and family life (Article 8 ECHR) is definitely weaker in the Swedish constitution(s), given not least the wide right to access to documents in Sweden.

[9] Prop 1993/94:117, p. 37 s as well as KU 1993/94:24, p. 19 s.

In the last few years, questions related to administrative tax sanctions (or penalties) and the possibility for Swedish courts to impose damages when the Convention has been violated have been in the focus of the discussion (Södergren 2002, 659–682). In both areas, it seems clear that while EctHR has found that certain violations of ECHR had taken place in Sweden, Swedish courts have been slow or even reluctant to take the full consequences of those judgments and come to the same conclusions as the ECtHR did in almost identical cases (*Janosevic and Västberga Taxi/Vulic* v. *Sweden* 2002, 34619 and 36985/97). As far as economic compensation for violations of the convention is concerned, Swedish courts have tended, until 2005, when a new important case was decided (NJA 2005, 462), to view this as an exclusive competence of the EctHR, though this is in fact not quite in line with the case-law of that court, nor with the ECHR itself.

At the same time, however, ECHR is regularly being invoked and applied in a number of criminal law cases, not least in relation to the procedures applied. Thus, the picture is mixed and it seems too early to make a full evaluation of how ECHR is being dealt with by Swedish courts. While waiting for that, it may be noted that a number of new monographic studies on the topic reveal a considerable interest in it from law scholars.[10] And the tendency is definitely clear, that the courts are becoming ever more interested in giving ECHR priority before regular national laws.

Sweden is a typical example of what is normally called a *dualist* state in terms of its relations with international law, i.e. a state where international law, whether in the terms of international customary law or international conventions which Sweden has ratified, does not take effect within the national legal system without a special act of transformation that turns them into domestic law (NJA 1973, 423; RÅ 1974, 121). During the 1980s, however, the two highest Swedish courts gradually came to consider the ECHR as an important source of interpretation and inspiration, as mentioned above (Cameron 2002, 153). Swedish laws were interpreted in the light of the convention and the case law from the ECtHR in Strasbourg, which means that a move towards always giving ECHR priority before national laws would probably not be too difficult (NJA 1988, 572; 1989, 131; 1990, 636; 1991, 188, 512; RÅ 1990, ref. 75 and note 492).

Such a development has also been given new impetus by the events surrounding the well-known *Åkerberg Fransson* case (Supreme Court 2013, C-617/10). A few words may now be said about the background of this case – that never went to the Supreme Court – and its repercussions in Swedish law.

Mr Åkerberg Fransson was a self-employed fisherman with only one fishing boat. He ran his financial activities as a sole trader and was therefore personally

---

[10] *See* apart from the highly respected standard comment by Hans Danelius, Mänskliga rättigheter i europeisk praxis: en kommentar till Europakonventionen om de mänskliga rättigheterna, Stockholm 2002 also two dissertations on the right to property from recent years; Karin Åhman, Egendomsskyddet – Äganderätten enligt artikel 1 första tilläggsprotokollet till den Europeiska konventionen om de mänskliga fri-och rättigheterna, Uppsala 2000 and Gudrun Gauksdottir, The Right to Property and the European Convention on Human Rights – A Nordic Approach, Lund 2004. Judge Danelius also contributes regular comments on the case-law of EctHR to the periodical Svensk Juristtidning.

responsible for paying income tax and VAT. He fished vendace in the north of Sweden, at the mouth of the Kalix River. Vendace is full of valuable roe, *Kalix löjrom*, which is an expensive and delicious speciality that enjoys a protected designation of origin in the EU. Mr. Åkerberg Fransson sold *Kalix löjrom* to buyers in Sweden, primarily first class restaurants, but he had also sold a smaller amount of eviscerated vendace as mink food in Finland.

The Swedish Tax Agency scrutinised the tax returns and the book-keeping of Mr. Åkerberg Fransson, assessing that there were errors in the book-keeping for the sale of roe and deciding to increase Mr. Åkerberg Fransson's declared income and declared VAT for 2004 and 2005 with approximately SEK 500,000 and the VAT with approximately SEK 150,000 (ca € 16,000). The Tax Agency also decided to charge a tax surcharge as the tax returns were found unsatisfactory. For the income part the surcharge was 40 % and for the VAT part 15 %. Mr. Åkerberg Fransson did not appeal the Tax Agency's decision.

Despite the fact that Mr. Åkerberg Fransson had been ordered to pay a tax surcharge, he was summoned to appear before Haparanda District Court in 2009 on charges of serious tax offences. Given the circumstances, he risked a prison sentence of some 6–8 months. His defence counsel pleaded that the case should be rejected, invoking the *ne bis in idem* principle. In December 2010, the District Court decided to request a preliminary ruling from ECJ, asking whether the Swedish policy of double procedures and sanctions could be regarded as being compatible with the prohibition against *ne bis in idem* in Article 50 of the Charter. In its request to the ECJ, the District Court stressed that the tax surcharge partly concerned VAT (NJA 2011, 444).

The issue whether it was legally possible under ECHR to apply separate legal proceedings for tax surcharge and tax offences based on the same information in a tax return had been debated in Sweden for a long time. In 2002, the ECtHR had concluded in two cases that the Swedish system with tax surcharges was of a criminal kind.[11] However, the decisions by the ECtHR did not change the Swedish legislation. Neither did the courts change their practice. However, the sharpened definition of what constitutes *ne bis in idem* in the Zolotukhin judgment in 2009 made the problem urgent. The Supreme Court ruled on the matter in two new decisions in 2010 resp. 2011. In the 2010 decision, which focused on ECHR, the majority of the justices took the view that the Zolotukhin judgment did not give "clear support" to the need to change Swedish practice (NJA 2010, 168).

In the 2011 case (NJA 2011, 444), the defendant in particular invoked the ne bis in idem principle in Article 50 of the Charter. The case dealt partly with tax surcharges for undeclared VAT. A Supreme Court majority of three justices concluded that the Swedish legal provisions on tax offences and tax surcharges lay outside the scope of the Charter, and that, thus, a preliminary ruling was not required. Two dissenting justices took a different view and concluded that the legal position was not clear as regards the possible applicability of the Charter and that a preliminary ruling should thus be requested. In reality, the Supreme Court voted on whether a preliminary ruling

[11] Janosevic v. Sweden, App. No. 34619/97 and Västberga Taxi and Vulk v. Sweden, App. No, 36985/97.

should be requested by the ECJ or not. As is well-known, according to Article 267 sect. 3 TFEU, the highest instance is obliged to request a preliminary ruling if a case pertains to EU law, unless the legal position is clear (*acte clair*, as follows from the well-known CILFIT case). Obviously, the Supreme Court did not observe that obligation, which was even sharper as the ECJ at that time had not clarified its position on the scope of the Charter. In its *Åkerberg Fransson* judgment the ECJ found it necessary to include a reminder – obviously addressed to the Supreme Court – about the duty to observe Article 267 TFEU as interpreted in the CILFIT case.[12]

In Sweden, decisions from the Supreme Court are not formally binding on judges in lower courts, but nevertheless hitherto always observed and followed. However, in this case, some judges in lower courts found the position of the Supreme Court clearly wrong and refused to follow it. This much observed "revolt" among Swedish judges is an important part of the background to the *Åkerberg Fransson* case, in which a district court judge in a small town thus decided to call in question the established Swedish system by asking the ECJ for a preliminary ruling.

In the Åkerberg Fransson judgment, then, ECJ as we know emphasised the importance of CfR and underlined the need for national courts to apply it whenever possible, i.e. when the case is within the scope of EU law. After the Åkerberg Fransson judgment, the Swedish Supreme Court in two other rulings in June and July 2013 based on the *ne bis in idem* principle totally reversed the practice to impose a tax surcharge on a person and then also prosecuting the same person for a tax offence in different legal proceedings.[13] In the first ruling, a unanimous plenary ruling in June 2013 (NJA 2013, 502), the Supreme Court found that the established Swedish double sanction system (tax surcharge and criminal sentence), applying two different legal procedures for providing false information in a tax return, was not compatible with the *ne bis in idem* principle. It is obvious that this important change in the Swedish legal position was brought about by the decision of the Court of Justice in the *Åkerberg Fransson* case.

Later, in July 2013 (NJA 2013, 746), the Supreme Court established that a result of this change in the law is that everyone has the right to a new trial if he or she has paid a tax surcharge and in addition been sentenced in a criminal procedure for tax offence. The Supreme Court set the "birth" for the use of this extraordinary legal remedy to the 10th February 2009, the date of the ECtHR judgment in the *Zolotukhin* case (NJA 2013, 502). In the following months, a substantial number of persons serving sentences for tax offences were thus released from prison and many ongoing tax offence prosecutions were terminated in cases where the accused persons had had to pay a tax surcharge.

Thus, it is clear that the Åkerberg Fransson judgment had very important repercussions in Swedish constitutional law, strengthening both human rights and judicial

[12] Case 283/81, Cilfit and Others [1982] ECR 3415, para 47 in the Åkerberg Fransson judgement.

[13] The literature on this subject is now large. See in English D. Sarmiento, Who's afraid of the Charter?, CMLRev 2013, p. 1267 ff., I Kargopoulos, Ne bis in idem in Criminal Proceedings, Swedish Studies in European Law, Vol. 5, Oxford 2014, p. 85 ff, Ola Zetterquist, *Ne Bis in Idem* and the European Legal Tsunami of 2013: A Vision from the Bench and Magnus Gulliksson, Effective Sanctions as the One-dimensional Limit to the *Ne Bis in Idem* Principle in EU Law and, both in (J. Nergelius/E. Kristoffersson (eds.), Human Rights in Contemporary European Law – Swedish Studies in European Law, vol. 6, Oxford 2014, pp. 131–40 and 141–89, respectively.

review. The Supreme Court has, also in other cases, been eager to stress the increased importance of ECHR and the fact that Swedish laws will normally not be upheld should they violate or be in conflict with the Convention (NJA 2013, 746).

Bibliography

Books

Åhman, Karin. 2002. *Egendomsskyddet – Äganderätten enligt artikel 1 första tilläggsprotokollet till den Europeiska konventionen om de mänskliga fri-och rättigheterna*. Uppsala: Iustus.

Bernitz, Ulf. 2002. *European law in Sweden: Its implementation and role in market and consumer law*. Stockholm: Juridiska fakulteten vid Stockholms universitet.

Bohlin, A., and W. Warnling-Nerep. 2004. *Förvaltningsrättens grunder*. Stockholm: Norstedts Juridik.

Cameron, Iain. 2002. *An introduction to the European convention on human rights*, 4th ed. Uppsala: Iustus Förlag.

Cameron, Iain. 2006. *An introduction to the European convention on human rights*, 5th ed. Uppsala: Iustus Förlag.

Danelius, Hans. 2002. *Mänskliga rättigheter i europeisk praxis: en kommentar till Europakonventionen om de mänskliga rättigheterna*. Stockholm: Norstedts Juridik.

Eckhoff, Thorstein. 1976. Höyesterett som grunnlovens vokter, in Jussens Venner, pp 1–34.

Gyllenswärd, Jan. 1975/76. *Nytt juridiskt arkiv*. Register 1964–1973 jämte Högsta domstolens minnesbok för samma tid. Stockholm: Norstedt.

Gauksdottir, Gudrun. 2004. *The right to property and the European convention on human rights – A Nordic approach*. Lund: Lund University.

Jyränki, Antero. 1989. *Lakien laki*. Helsinki: Lakimiesliiton kustannus.

Kastari, Paavo, 1948. Socialiseringssträvandena och egendomens grundlagsskydd i de europeiska länderna, Tidskrift for Rettsvitenskab, pp 191–223.

Länsineva, Pekka. 1991. The Constitutional Committee of Parliament: The Finnish model of norm control. In *The Finnish constitution in transition*, ed. M. Sakslin, 68–80. Helsinki: Hermes-Myynti Oy.

Nergelius, Joakim. 1996. *Konstitutionellt rättighetsskydd: Svensk rätt i ett komparativt perspektiv*. Stockholm: Norstedts Juridik.

Riepula, E. 1973. Eduskunnan perustuslakivaliokunta perustuslakien tulkitsijana, Vammala.

Smith, Eivind. 1990. Domstolskontroll med lovgivning i Norge etter ca. 1970, Tidskrift for Rettsvitenskab, pp 88–120.

Södergren, Jan. 2002. Axplock II – ur svensk konventionstillämpning, Europarättslig tidskrift, p 664 et seq.

Scheinin, Martin. 1991. *Ihmisoikeudet Suomen oikeudessa*. Jyväskylä: Akateeminen kirjakauppa.

Scheinin, Martin. 1996. General Introduction. In *International human rights norms in the Nordic and Baltic countries*, ed. Martin Scheinin. Boston: The Haguen.

Decisions

ECtHR. 27 October 1986. Boden and Pudas. Series A, 125-A, 125-B.

ECtHR. 19 November 1991. Joint cases, Andrea Francovich and Danila Bonifaci and others v Italian Republic. C-6/90 and 9/90, ECR I-05357.

ECtHR. 23 September 1982. Bosphorus Hava Yolları Turizm ve Ticaret Anonim Şirketi v. Ireland Series A 52.

ECtHR. 24 May 1989. Hauschildt v. Denmark. Series A 154, case 10486/83.

ECtHR. 7 July 1989. Tre Traktörer Aktiebloag v. Sweden, case 10873/84.
ECtHR. 20 May 1999. Bladet Tromsö and Stensaas v. Norway, case 21980/93.
ECtHR. 23 July 2002. Janosevic and Västberga Taxi/Vulic v. Sweden, case 36985/97.
Entscheidungen des Bundesverfassungsgerichts (BVerfGE). 1993. vol. 89, 155.
Human Rights Committee. 2 April 1990. Torres v. Finland, Communication No. 291/1988, UN Doc. CCPR/C/38/D/291/1988.
Human Rights Committee. 7 April 1989. Antti Vuolanne v. Finland, Communication No. 265/1987, UN GAOR.
NJA 1984: 170.
NJA 1973: 423.
NJA 1988: 28.
NJA 1988: 108.
NJA 1988: 572.
NJA 1989: 131.
NJA 1990: 636.
NJA 1991: 181.
NJA 1998: 817.
NJA 2001: 409.
NJA 2005: 462.
NJA 2010: 168.
NJA 2011: 444.
NJA 2013: 502.
NJA 2013: 746.
Supreme Administrative Court of Finland. 1993. A 26–29.
Supreme Administrative Court. 12 June 1991, case No. 4642–1989.
Supreme Court of Finland. 1992: 73.
Supreme Court of Finland. 1993: 19.
Supreme Court of Finland. 1993: 58.
Supreme Court of Iceland. 1990: 2.
Supreme Court of Iceland. 1990: 92.
Supreme Court of Iceland. 1990: 93.
Supreme Court of Iceland. 1992: 174.
Ugeskrift for Retsvaesen. 1990.12 HK.
Ugeskrift for Retsvaesen. 1990.181 H.
Ugeskrift for Retsvaesen. 1994.536 H.
Ugeskrift for Retsvaesen 1994.988 H.
Ugeskrift for Retsvaesen. 1999.800 H.
Ugeskrift for Retsvaesen. 1999.841 H.
Supreme Court of Norway Rt. 1984. 1174.
Supreme Court of Norway Rt. 1994. 610.
Norsk Retstidende. 1990. pp. 257, 312, 319 and 1221.
Arbetsdomstolens domar 1972. Ref. 75.
Regeringsrättens årsbok. 1974. Ref. 121.
Regeringsrättens årsbok. 1990. Ref. 75.

Legislation

Constitution of Finland, Section 106 (Act No. 731 of 1999).
Finnish Constitution Act of 1919. Section 92.2.
Ministry of Justice. 21 September 1989. No. 3077/061/89 OM.

Fundamental Freedoms and Rights in Contemporary Europe

Bogusław Banaszak

Abstract Regulation of individual freedoms and rights in constitutions and treaties take into account, both in the catalogue of such rights and freedoms and specific provisions concerning them, norms of international law and customs binding on European countries, as well as constitutional standards existing in democratic states and Member-states of EU. As there is a multitude of concepts of human rights and liberties, it is reasonable in this article to restrict the discussion only to these which in the past substantially influenced or are currently influencing normative regulations concerning individual rights, focusing solely on their most fundamental assumptions. The discussed concepts were: legal-natural, liberal, concepts typical of the so-called social state ruled by law. The common values and the EU law implementing them stimulate the identification of citizens of EU member states with the Union as a whole. This serves the purpose of increasing their interest in public life. For the purpose of implementing this task it is important that European integration is in its form and content an expression of a broad social consensus, a result of compromise between various social groups and political powers. From this perspective it may be observed that the Union strives to implement these objectives and that the proposals of differentiating the rate of integration within two-speed Europe or unjustified criticism of new EU members wishing to voice their views have become the thing of the past.

Introduction

Constitutional regulation of rights, freedoms and duties of an individual in every country does not form an accidental set of norms, but is rather determined by a particular concept of the status of the individual in the state. This does not necessarily mean that it must reflect such a concept and that constitutions based on the same concept should be exactly alike. In fact, we must be mindful of the fact that any basic law does not come into existence in a vacuum and often applies to institutions or

B. Banaszak (✉)
University of Zielona Góra, Zielona Góra, Licealna 9, Poland
e-mail: bbanaszak@o2.pl

R. Arnold (ed.), *The Convergence of the Fundamental Rights Protection in Europe*, Ius Gentium: Comparative Perspectives on Law and Justice 52,
DOI 10.1007/978-94-017-7465-9_6

solutions existing in a given country. On the other hand, despite widespread acceptance of one concept by the authors of an organic law, they may find it necessary to admit some elements typical of another (e.g. Declaration of Rights of Man and Citizen of 1789 connected liberal ideas with elements of the natural-law concept). Moreover, concepts of the status of an individual themselves are not monolithic. They maintain only certain fundamental assumptions, but are subject to modification in respect of other questions and apply different approaches in resolving detailed issues. The result is that some – and sometimes far-reaching – differences can exist between individual countries, even those whose constitutional norms concerning rights, freedoms and duties of an individual have been based on the same concept.

Generally speaking, regulation of individual freedoms and rights in constitutions and treaties take into account, both in the catalogue of such rights and freedoms and specific provisions concerning them, norms of international law and customs binding on European countries, as well as constitutional standards existing in democratic states and Member-states of EU.

Concepts of Human Rights and Liberties Influencing International, Supranational and Internal Normative Regulations

As there is a multitude of concepts of human rights and liberties, it is reasonable to restrict the discussion only to these which in the past substantially influenced or are currently influencing normative regulations concerning individual rights, focusing solely on their most fundamental assumptions and ignoring detailed analyses, presentations of their different versions, etc. After all, every concept may to a greater or lesser degree be modified and adapted to the current social, economic and political premises. This is an issue constituting a separate subject of research, which can not be elaborated here.

Legal-Natural Concepts

Legal-natural concepts constitute an internally diversified group, which results from the possibility of adopting various assumptions for their existence – philosophical, religious, historical or biological. Leaving aside a detailed discussion, a general thesis may be formulated, proposing that all the natural concepts are characterised by the recognition that people are equal and free by nature and that they are entitled to certain inherent rights. Positive law only declares natural law, which already exists, and so does not enact them. Its primary task is to restrict rights in the interest of individuals co-existing in an organised society. It thus acquires a negative character identified with interference in the sphere of natural rights with an aim of restricting them in exceptional cases. In this view law is secondary in character, while natural rights are primary. This view, focusing on an individual, does not take into consideration the fact that the law and the state are indispensable for the development of an individual and implementation of his or her natural rights. Therefore, some proponents of legal-natural concepts maintain that these do not deny the need to protect inherent rights of an individual by positive law, as exemplified by the following view of H. Waśkiewicz: "positive law plays the same role for natural rights as executory provisions do for a statute".

Legal-natural concepts frequently influence the interpretation of the significance of individual rights in international and national scales, which does not necessarily have to result in legal nihilism and negation of the letter of positive law, although undoubtedly one of the functions of natural law – especially from the point of view of American natural law jurisprudence – is countering legal positivism.

It is interesting that after considerable restriction of the role of legal-natural concepts in the nineteenth century, they enjoyed a considerable revival after World War II.

Liberal Concept

Nineteenth century constitutional regulations of individual rights emerged under an overwhelming influence of liberalism (e.g. the constitution of Belgium from 1831). They no longer emphasised a legal-natural character of individual rights but interpreted them "as an expression of the will of the state, which is totally independent in their establishment". The state was to be a mere instrument providing social order and internal security, concurrently protecting society and creating conditions for its development as well as the development of the individuals constituting it. The status of an individual in a state, and the scope of his or her rights, depends on the positive law existing in a given state or the common law which the state accepted. A rule was adopted that individual rights are guaranteed solely for the citizens of a given state and only in exceptional circumstances for non-citizens. Constitutional provisions provided grounds for normative regulation of civic rights but, due to their general character, had to be elaborated and specified in statutes, owing to which they could be adapted to the changing social reality as the process of resolving statutes or their amendment is easier than amending the constitution.

The grounds for the liberal catalogue of individual rights were constituted by the notions of personal freedom and freedom of business, protection of property and ownership, religious tolerance and restriction of the Church's influence, freedom of assembly and freedom of speech. These freedoms were to protect an individual against interference from the state, while at the same time liberalism perceived the state as a guarantor and protector against anti-liberal tendencies and threats.

The liberal concept perceives an individual as an isolated entity. The concept's basic premise was the idea of a self-regulating, free society, which was more or less directly expressed in the works of G. Hegel, J. Bentham, A. Smith. It assumes that a society consists of equal, free individuals who encounter resistance from other individuals when attempting to implement their needs and interests. Various individual interests work in different directions and therefore it is eventually possible to establish a solution benefiting the whole society. Individuals tend to compromise and are by themselves able to evaluate legal, political and economic problems rationally. Common interests are stronger than what divides people.

The liberal concept perceived individual rights as an expression of division of competences between an individual (a society) and a state, which resulted in juxtaposing a state and a society, and a state and an individual.

Concepts Typical of the So-called Social State Ruled by Law

The purpose of such a state, in contrast to the liberal state, is to direct the processes of social development and to ensure impartial distribution of its fruits. In order to achieve its goals, it may apply not only the traditional means (i.e. commands and prohibitions) but also a wide spectrum of other measures designed to direct one's personal conduct (e.g. through taxation or subsidies). The state and society are not treated as mutually opposing forces, although they are not identical to each other. The social state ruled by law is separated from society, which guarantees freedom of the individual, but is also closely connected with it, thereby guaranteeing progress and social justice. This corresponds with the departure from regarding an individual as an isolated subject whose links with society are recognized. On the one hand, this makes it possible to emphasize individual responsibility for deciding the fate of the community and leads to re-evaluation of duties consigned to him/her, which, having received a wider social context, become instruments for implementing new tasks of the state. On the other hand, the state has been obliged to care for the subsistence of an individual and ensure the provision of opportunities for an individual development as guaranteed in the constitution. This leads to a change in the character of individual rights that begin to function as an aim of the state's activities. Formal guarantees do not suffice, and the state is compelled to undertake political, environmental, social and other activities in order to carry out the programme formulated in provisions of the constitution relating to them. Rights and freedoms do not protect only the individual sphere of liberty of the person, but also play some social functions and, therefore, an enjoyment thereof should be socially oriented, i.e. when protecting interests of an individual they should also serve the common good.

The concept of human rights and liberties typical of the so-called social state ruled by law underlines political rights of citizens. They play an important role in the functioning of the democratic state. They not only stimulate democratic modifications of political institutions, but allow the growth of sense of law in society as well. They influence a wider range of realization of other rights and freedoms.

Confirming the significance of social rights, the social state ruled by law treats them in a different way from political or personal rights (Banaszak 2012, 17–20). They do not found any claims by an individual for a particular behaviour on the part of the state or any concrete performance, but are rather an imposition on the state of an obligation to undertake activity for their accomplishment. The social state ruled by law, as compared to the liberal state, reverses the principles concerning the substantial scope of rights, freedoms and duties contained in the constitution. While under the liberal conception they relate, above all, to citizens, and only in exceptional situations – to non-citizens, under the concept of the social state ruled by law, it is assumed that provisions of the constitution specifying the status of an individual are addressed to all persons staying in the territory of a given state, except for the rights, freedoms and duties explicitly reserved for citizens.

Lack of Common Concept of Human Rights in the Initial Period of Forming the EEC and EU

The attitude to human rights in the EEC, and subsequently in the EU, underwent an interesting evolution. Their regulation was deliberately omitted in the treaties constituting the European Communities as the issue was on the one hand regulated by member states' internal laws (mainly the constitutions) and on the other – by both universal and regional public international law. The creators of European integration did not want to duplicate both the standards of protection and the catalogues of human rights.

Initially the European Tribunal of Justice restrictively interpreted the treaty provisions and rejected the concept of the existence of fundamental rights of an individual in the community law. It changed its position in the mid-1970s acknowledging that these rights are part of unwritten community law. The Tribunal began drawing its own catalogue of fundamental rights, closely linked with four freedoms rooted in the treaties, and vital for uniform European market. The rights that were protected were solely within the scope essential for the functioning of the community law.

In this situation, when the system of fundamental rights was based on the principles proposed by the Tribunal, the EU lacked legal acts concerned with fundamental rights, which legally bind EU bodies and member states as well as coherent procedures serving the purpose of their protection. The problem could be resolved in two ways – either by implementing a new treaty which would offer complex regulation of fundamental rights within the EU law or by the EU joining the Convention on the Protection of Human Rights and Liberties. Over 50 years of experience in the implementation of the Convention would enable to avoid numerous inconveniences resulting from introducing new legislation.

Charter of Fundamental Rights

Initially, a third way was adopted. The Charter of Fundamental Rights (CFR) adopted by the European Parliament, Council and Commission at the summit in Nice on 7 December 2000 was an agreement between institutions and was by no means a legally binding act. The situation changed after ratification of the Treaty of Lisbon.

Thanks to the Charter, the EU, for the first time, has adopted a complex attitude to the issue of the protection of the rights of an individual. The protection comprises all the categories of rights – apart from personal and political – including those widely understood as social, cultural and economic rights. In view of para. 5 of the Charter's preamble, the catalogue of protected rights comprises "the rights resulting especially from constitutional traditions and international agreements adopted by all the member states [...] as well as the judicature of the Tribunal of Justice of European Communities and the European Tribunal of Human Rights". A new attitude towards all rights – including the traditional ones, universally included in the catalogue of protected rights – may be observed, aiming at regulating possibly all contemporary issues resulting from their implementation. This attitude enables not only to account for the threats resulting from the development of civilisation but also to reformulate some of the rights. Thus the Charter comprises new potential in the application of the rights and includes the regulation stimulating changes in their understanding and protection.

Within its subjective scope the Charter aims at protecting not only EU citizens, but also everyone staying in the EU territory, which conforms with the tendency in the EU legislation, which determines that by definition the EEC and the EU legal acts concerned with rights of an individual extend their subjective scope onto everyone present in the area where the EU law is in effect.

Even though the Charter does not recognize *expressis verbis* the implementation of its provisions in the case of legal persons, this "does not denote that in singular cases legal persons could not cite the Charter's provisions if it they are applicable in their situation".[1]

The complex character of the Charter is favored by the manner of regulation of particular rights. "While some rights and liberties are formulated in such a way that they may be directly implemented, there are numerous ones which offer guidelines as to the policy of community bodies [...]. This method [...], avoiding difficulties resulting from finding a formula enabling implementation of the rights by courts, confirms that all the rights and liberties are binding. This denotes that everyone may demand their implementation, even though not in each case their implementation can be vindicated in legal proceedings".[2]

Multiplicity of sources concerned with the rights of an individual implies existence of diversified terminology, which, in turn, due to interpretation of concrete notions, is of practical significance for implementation of particular rights on the basis of a normative act applied in a given situation. In the case of international and supranational law, all this is affected by problems resulting from translating legal notions into national languages of the countries where they are implemented.

Realizing this, the creators of the Charter did not want it to be yet another element in the kaleidoscope of acts concerned with the rights of an individual. In its very title

[1] Stanowisko Rady Doradczej do spraw Praw Człowieka przy Ministrze Spraw Zagranicznych, [w:] Karta Praw Podstawowych Unii Europejskiej, Ministerstwo Spraw Zagranicznych, Warszawa 2001, p. 62.

[2] Ibidem, p. 57.

they aimed at referring to the notion of fundamental rights developed in the judicature of the European Tribunal of Justice from the late 1960s. Simultaneously, striving to ensure the Charter's compatibility with the European Convention on Human Rights, they formulated the principle in art. 53, para. 3 of the Charter stating that "Within the scope in which this Charter includes the rights corresponding to the rights guaranteed by the Convention on the Protection of Human Rights and Liberties, their interpretation and scope are congruent with the those conferred by the Convention".

In the legal sciences for some authors the relation between the Charter and European Convention of Human Rights is not clear. The good example is the opinion of Polish scholar A. Bisztyga: "European Convention for the Protection of Human Rights and Fundamental Freedoms enjoys good opinion of the constitutional act orders European legal space of human rights. The pearl in the Convention crown is the European Court of Human Rights, whose case-law creates European standards of human rights in a contemporary way. Being obligatory, the Lisbon Treaty and Charter of Fundamental Rights of European Union change the previous situation. The instrumentation of the human rights protection in Europe has been enriched. However a number of questions about the relation between Convention and Charter arise and the relation between European Court of Human Rights and Court of Justice of European Union as well as the case-law of both European courts. Are the relations going to be complementary or use confrontation?" (Bisztyga 2009, 188).[3]

It should be underlined that the notions used by the Charter also refer to the terms employed by the constitutions of most EU member states, which legal sciences are well acquainted with even in the countries which do not employ appropriate terms in their legislation (e.g. human dignity).

All these measures enable states to create not only a complex catalogue of fundamental rights, but also to interpret them in a largely uniform way both in widely understood European law (EU and Council of Europe) and in the EU member states' internal law. According to the Charter, the European Tribunal of Justice has a significant role to play in the process of interpretation of the Charter's provisions. In this context it is interesting to quote the following stance of the Polish Constitutional Tribunal: "Interpretation of the EU law by the European Tribunal of Justice should fall within the scope of functions and competences delegated to the Communities by the member states. It should also correlate with the principle of subsidiarity determining the activity of the Community and EU institutions. The interpretation should be also based on the assumption of mutual loyalty between the Community and EU institutions and member states. This assumption obliges the European Tribunal of Justice to support local legal systems, while the member states are obliged to apply the highest standards of respecting community norms [...]. Member states retain the right to evaluate whether EU legislative bodies acted within the delegated competences and whether they exercised their authority in congruence with the principle of subsidiarity while issuing a legal act (legal provision). The principle of priority of the community law is not applicable in the case of the acts (provisions) issued in excess of the above restrictions" (OTK ZU 2005).

[3] Cf. also Lenaerts (2000).

The Charter does not refer to the category of the rights of an individual already present in international law and internal law of many countries, i.e. their division into rights and liberties and further division into two groups: personal and political as well as economic, social and cultural. This typology frequently caused controversy in the legal doctrine, but it has been universally accepted, which is substantiated by two UNO Human Rights Pacts constituting the basis for the system of protection of human rights adopted by the UN and the presence of European Social Charter together with the European Convention on Human Rights in the regional European system of their protection.

Instead of adopting the already existing typology, the Charter creates six categories corresponding to its first six chapters, which is intended by the Convent elaborating the Charter to provide it with its complex character and enable to extend the protection over new areas exceeding the traditional scope of regulation, universally adopted in international and internal law. The headings of the chapters – groups of rights – are linked with value–ideas (Chrostowski 2001, 304) especially important for the EU. In this way "the Charter seems to break with historically formed division and by rejecting the hierarchy of fundamental rights, based on the division mentioned above, [the Charter – B. B.] creates a new concept of fundamental rights" (Capitant 2006, 13–14). The concept is not rooted in the traditional science of law. It is not yet fully mature, while the accompanying axiology has not been universally adopted. It emerged under the strong, predominating influence of social democratic thought[4] and only in a very limited degree does it take into consideration other philosophical trends. Despite that, it lacks coherence, which is substantiated by the need to prepare explanations to the Charter's provisions after it was adopted. On the initiative of the Great Britain the Presidium of the Convent elaborated explanations, which by virtue of para. 7 art. 52 of the Charter serve the purpose of its interpretation and should be taken into consideration by the courts of the EU and member states.

As a result it would be difficult to assume that the Charter creates new standards and one concept of human rights or provides a more or less uniform interpretation of individual rights both within the scope of widely understood European law (EU and Council of Europe) and internal law of EU member states.

The proponents of the Charter, supporting such a wide catalogue of rights guaranteed by it, perceive it as a virtue and a testimony of a complex character of its regulations. However, they admit that "the Charter's wide catalogue has been designed for future, extended EU competences".[5] They indicate possible restriction in the scope of rights regulated in the internal law of the member states, which is exemplified by possible opposition of the Union to the introduction of death penalty in the countries tightly co-operating with the USA in combating terrorism.[6]

The EU seems to lack acceptance of one, universally adopted concept of human rights, which substantially hinders further integration and protection of human

---

[4] This is the opinion of other scientists analysing the text of the Charter of Fundamental rights – cf. Hogan (2006, 65).

[5] E.g. C. Castello and V. Browne – cf. ibidem, p. 68.

[6] E.g. C. Castello and V. Browne – cf. ibidem, p. 68.

rights. As an example I may quote the contentious issue of including the regulation concerning social rights in the Charter of Fundamental Rights. The comparison of the catalogue of constitutional human rights common to all the EU member states shows that its core is formed by traditional (classic) personal liberties and political rights. Social, cultural and economic rights (with the exception of property rights) are to a varying degree present in individual constitutions and in their case no elements common for them all can be determined. This is caused by the controversy in the science of law and among various political movements concerning the need of and extent of constitutional regulation of social rights and the whole social sphere.

Opponents of subjecting social rights to constitutional regulation maintain that since the degree of their implementation always depends on current and constantly changing economic situation, the matter should thus be subject to statutory legislation. In their view the regulation's place in the legal hierarchy should not determine the extent of social effects of state's effort. They also emphasize that social rights have a postulatory character. In their case a state must first elaborate and then implement complete social programs (cf. Müller 1981, 41–44, 203). If, apart form the norms of postulatory character, the constitution included social rights enabling an individual to claim benefits from the state, to meet these it might have to take over the control of economy, which would contradict the provisions of property rights and economic freedom (cf. Horner 1974, 225). In this context it is the essence of the constitution that is important, the role it is to play in the state. This is referred to by W. Martens, who writes: "Where [...] the guarantee of freedom is interpreted as the guarantee of existence, a constitution devoted to the principle of liberty contradicts itself" (Martens und Häberle 1972, 33). From this perspective, including social rights in the constitution is prevented by fear of undermining the effectiveness of political rights and civil liberties in a situation where the same catalogue would protect an individual against the state and would simultaneously authorize him or her to demand benefits from it. Because of this "the constitution [...] is transformed from the act which determines the limits of authority into the act which determines the sphere of the authority's obligations. Consequently, this transforms the constitution into a peculiar charter of social life" (Ciemniewski 1995, 68–69). Additionally, the state is not obliged to guarantee social rights and to provide actual conditions enabling individuals and social groups to benefit from their constitutionally guaranteed rights. This aims at preventing the use of other rights included in the constitution to satisfy social claims.

The viewpoint that social rights should not be included in a constitution has many proponents in the doctrine of constitutional and European law in several developed democracies. It is held that such rights have a programmatic nature and that in this respect the state must implement whole social programs. Personal and political rights and freedoms require that the state and EU create adequate institutional guarantees or only refrains from interfering with the legally protected autonomy of the individual. They may be accomplished more easily and quickly, and EU or state activity is in this respect determined to a smaller degree by economic factors.

At this point, it might be said that "even in most advanced democratic systems of government, there have been observed permanent or occasional departures from the proclaimed principles. This mostly relates to social and cultural rights whose extent, and, particularly, level of realization is very often determined by the stage of the business cycle, depending on place and time. Any instances of international or domestic recession result in trends towards the reduction of social benefits" (Zwierzchowski 1992, 22).

Proponents of regulation of social rights in EU law advocate the need of departing from the treatment of fundamental rights and liberties as the means of merely protecting individuals against the interference on the part of the state. The guarantee of civil liberties and political rights thus requires taking into account economic, social and cultural conditions, i.e. introducing social rights into the constitution. According to P. Häberle, in the contemporary state "a complex tool develops, which includes the following elements: guarantee of fundamental rights as widely-understood social rights, as the aim of the constitution, as the subjective entitlement to benefits and as the interpretation guidelines for the judiciary" (Martens and Häberle 1972, 73). He also notes that "absence of or modest presentation of social matter in the constitution does not prevent the state from the possibility of conducting broad social policy transforming it into a welfare state. Presence of precise and elaborate social matter in the constitution determines this direction. Therefore, from the point of view of the majority of citizens who will benefit from social rights [...] it is desirable that [...] the constitution includes elaborate and precise regulations of the social matter" (Zawadzka 1996, 94).

For the proponents of social rights in the states lacking constitutional regulation of the matter or where this regulation is limited, the Charter of Fundamental Rights has a great significance for two reasons. Firstly, the Charter includes the statements distinctly indicating the existence of social rights, thanks to which they, interpreted as fundamental, would be indirectly introduced into the legal systems of these states. Secondly, the charter enables to grant a social function to the rights already included in the constitution which are not treated as social. Then "classic fundamental civic rights are mixed with fundamental social rights which may be appealed from as being directly applicable and as subjective constitutional law" (Müller 2001, p. 78). Pursuant to these citizens could demand the state to provide certain benefits, both of material character and as means enabling them to take advantage of the regulations created by the state aiming at providing social conditions for their implementation.

Another example is provided by the Charter's regulations concerned with marriage and family. Art 51, para. 2, of the Charter seems to state in a way excluding any doubts that "the Charter does not extend the scope of implementation of the EU law beyond the Union's competences, it does not introduce new competences or tasks for the EU". On the other hand certain formulations of the Chart's provisions may indicate a different tendency or are devoid of legal significance. An Irish scientist G. Hogan, who analyzed them, states: "elementary rights, which the Charter will protect, are *de facto* not designed to be applied by the Union of precisely restricted competences but by a federal state or even a centralized or Unitarian state. For example, art. 9 of the Charter states that 'the right to marry and establish a family are guaranteed in accordance with member state statutes regulating the implementation of these rights'. Yet, what is missing – at least now – is any EU competence concerning the right to marry. Therefore a question arises why the right is to be protected at the level of the new European constitution. [...] In other words, in what circumstances could a member state statute concerned with the right to marry contravene art. 9 of the Charter of Fundamental rights? If the answer is that it is impossible, as the right to marry is regulated solely by the member state law, then we return to the basic question, why an attempt has been made to include [in the Charter] the right to marry and establish a family as well as its protection if it is protected at the state level by the constitutions and by art. 12 of the European Convention on Human Rights? The same concerns the majority of rights included in the Charter, such as the provisions concerned with the rights of children, the right for just legal proceedings or the right for the health protection" (Hogan 2006, 67–68).

It should be underlined that the EU includes countries with restrictive regulation concerning divorce (Malta) and the countries which accept homosexual marriage (e.g. Spain, France). At the forum of EU institutions and in many individual member states this dispute about the role of family and marriage has become a dispute about the role of freedom of speech and religion.

People inspired by Christianity or Islam find it difficult to accept a departure from a traditional notion of a family. Therefore, those who view this notion differently frequently attack mainstream Churches and religions in Europe and treat them as hypocrites, which the Catholic Church brings to attention. In his document *The Family and Human Procreation* published in 2011 cardinal A. Lopez Trujillo, the head of the Pontifical Council for the Family, points out at the tendency to "overshadow God" in contemporary culture.

This act of dissociating from the values shaping European culture for two millennia, which is best exemplified by absence of reference to God in the proposed EU constitution, distorts the past. As M. Pera wrote in his book *Deprived of Roots* "People (and nations) who forget about their roots are neither free nor serious".

Criticism of views negating non-traditional values is sometimes treated as reprehensible and punishable hatred. This obviously affects the notion of freedom of speech and forces public authority to undertake inquisitional activity – as in the case of the reverend Ake Green. Equaling a critical view, proposing different values, attack results in suspension of freedom of speech and delegating to the state the power of decision as to what is permitted. R. Descartes said that he may disagree with someone's views but he is ready to sacrifice his life so that the view may be propagated. A. de Tocqueville warned that it is the whole of the citizens of a democratic country and not public authority who have the power of deciding whether someone's views are right or wrong. Once an attempt to restrict this power is made, there will be no end to further restrictions.

It should be remembered in this context that when a new Polish constitution was resolved in 1997, the text of its preamble caused a heated political and ideological dispute. Eventually a compromise formula was adopted referring to the ten centuries of the history of the state and the nation and indicating a significant role of Christian heritage. It was also emphasized that opening to Europe and the world does not contradict the sense of national identity and attachment to cultural roots.

In this context the following view of the Polish Constitutional Tribunal is worth quoting: "The interpretation of EU law by the European Court of Justice should not exceed the functions and competences delegated by member states to EU. It should also correlate with the principle of subsidiarity determining the activity of the community-EU institutions. The interpretation should also be based on the assumption of mutual loyalty between the community-EU institutions and the member states. The assumption generates – on the Court's part – the obligation to favor national legal systems, while on the part of member states – the obligation to observe community norms to the highest achievable standards [...] Member states reserve the right to evaluate whether the community (EU) legislative bodies resolving a given act (of law) observed delegated competences and whether they exercised their powers in accordance with the principles of subsidiarity and proportionality. Exceeding this framework results in the fact that the principle of the priority of the community law does not apply to the acts (provisions) resolved in excess of these limitations" (OTK ZU 2005).

The Polish Constitutional Tribunal emphasized that "relative autonomy of legal systems, based on their own internal hierarchical principles, is not tantamount to absence of mutual influence. It also does not eliminate the possibility of collision between the regulations of the community law and the provisions of the Constitution. The latter would take place when there was irrevocable contradiction between a constitutional norm and the norm of the community law, a contradiction which could not be eliminated with the use of interpretation respecting relative autonomy of the European law and the national law. Such a situation can not be ruled out but it may – due to [...] common character of assumptions and values – appear only exceptionally" (OTK ZU 2005).

For the so-called new member states of EU, which include Poland, it is especially important that the disputes concerning values discussed above were, as emphasized by Ioan Ganfalean, resolved respecting the principles of "solidarity, consensus and in the spirit of compromise" (Ganfalean 2008, 123). The values on which the whole EU legal system is based cannot be imposed on any country by another country, neither can they be imposed on a minority by a majority currently in power within individual states.

It must be remembered that common values and the EU law implementing them stimulate the identification of citizens of EU member states with the Union as a whole. This serves the purpose of increasing their interest in public life and their contribution to influencing the will of their own countries and the Union – e.g. by participating in the elections to the European Parliament. For the purpose of implementing this task it is important that European integration is in its form and content an expression of a broad social consensus, a result of compromise between various social groups and political powers. This multiplicity must form an integrated whole, which in its turn affects its ability to perform economic and political functions of a new entity. The EU law may constitute the basis of the social development of united Europe only when it is accepted by the citizens, when it protects their interests, ensures freedom and the possibility of the development of an individual, guarantees internal peace by creating mechanisms of solving social conflict, provides the citizens with the possibility of exercising authority not only in their own country but also in EU and supervising not only the national but also European institutions. From this perspective it may be observed that the Union strives to implement these objectives and that the proposals of differentiating the rate of integration within two-speed Europe or unjustified criticism of new EU members wishing to voice their views have become the thing of the past.

The Treaty of Lisbon enables us to hope that new decision-making mechanisms will enable us to reach a compromise in determining new values influencing the quality and form of integration.

Bibliography

Banaszak, B. 2012. Constitutionalisation of social human rights – necessity or luxury? *Persona y Derecho* 1–2(2012): 17–20.

Bisztyga, A. 2009. Europejska Konwencja Praw Człowieka a Karta Praw Podstawowych Unii Europejskiej - stan kompatybilności czy konkurencyjności?. *Przegląd Prawa Konstytucyjnego*: 7/2009.

Capitant, D. 2006. Die Charta der Grundrechte der Europäischen Union in der französischen Rechtsordnung. In *Kölner Gemeinschaftskommentar zur Europäischen Grundrechte-Charta*, ed. P.J. Tettinger and K. Stern, 9–18. München: C.H. Beck.

Chrostowski, W. 2001. *Czynić sprawiedliwość w miłości*. Warszawa: Wydawnictwo Uniwersytetu Kardynała Stefana Wyszyńskiego.

Ciemniewski, J. 1995. Konstytucja państwa socjalnego czy konstytucja państwa liberalnego?. *Prawo w okresie przemian ustrojowych w Polsce*: 68–69.

Ganfalean, I. 2008. The Implementation of European Law in Romania. *Annales Universitatis Apulensis, Series Jurisprudentia*: 11/2008.

Hogan, G. 2006. Der Einfluss der Europäischen Grundrechte–Charta auf die irische Verfassung. In *Kölner Gemeinschaftskommentar zur Europäischen Grundrechte-Charta*, ed. P.J. Tettinger and K. Stern. München: Verlag C. H. Beck.

Horner, F. 1974. *Die sozialen Grundrechte*. Salzburg und München: Pustet.

Karta Praw Podstawowych Unii Europejskiej. 2001. Warszawa: Ministerstwo Spraw Zagranicznych.

Lenaerts, K. 2000. Fundamental rights in the European Union. *European Law Review* 25: 575–600.

Martens, W., and P. Häberle. 1972. Grundrechte im Leistungsstaat. *Veröffentlichungen der Vereinigung der Deutschen Staatsrechtslehrer*. Vol. 30. Berlin/New York: Walter de Gruyter.

Müller, J.P. 1981. *Soziale Grundrechte in der Verfassung?* Basel, Frankfurt am Main: Nomos.

Müller, J.P. 2001. Katalog i zakres obowiązywania praw podstawowych. In *Konstytucja Federalna Szwajcarskiej Konfederacji z 1999 r. i Konstytucja Rzeczypospolitej Polskiej z 1997 r*, ed. Z. Czeszejko-Sochacki. Białystok: Temida.

OTK ZU Nr 5/A/2005.

Stanowisko Rady Doradczej do spraw Praw Człowieka przy Ministrze Spraw Zagranicznych. 2001.

Zawadzka, B. 1996. *Prawa ekonomiczne, socjalne i kulturalne*. Warszawa: Elipsa.

Zwierzchowski, E. 1992. *Wprowadzenie do nauki prawa kanstytucyjnego państw demokratycznych [An introduction to the teaching of constitutional law of democratic states]*. Katowice: PWN.

Human Rights in Romanian Courts: A European Perspective?

Bianca Selejan-Guţan

Abstract The perception and application of the European Convention on Human Rights by various national jurisdictions depends fundamentally on the way in which the Convention has been introduced into national law, as well as, in some countries, by how constitutional jurisdictions shaped this relationship. The article examines the reception of the Convention by a few European states, with a special regard on the case of Romania. Romanian courts, including the Constitutional Court and the supreme court, had a hesitant approach of the principle established by 1991 Constitution of the priority of international law of human rights over domestic law. In the context of the diversity of sources of the European law of human rights, there is an active effort at the European level to create a more coherent order amongst this plurality of human rights protection instruments, in the context of the imminent adhesion of the European Union to the European Convention and of the high number of states-parties to the Convention. The most recent example is the adoption of Protocol no. 16 to the Convention, on 17 July 2013, which will help domestic jurisdictions in their efforts to incorporate the Convention's standards into the internal law of the states-parties. With the analysis of all these aspects, the paper is aiming to contribute to the topical debate on the convergence of fundamental rights in Europe.

List of Abbreviations

ECHR	European Convention on Human Rights
ECtHR	European Court of Human Rights
HCCJ	[Romanian] High Court of Cassation and Justice
RCC	Romanian Constitutional Court
SCJ	[Romanian] Supreme Court of Justice
SCM	[Romanian] Superior Council of Magistracy

B. Selejan-Guţan (✉)
Lucian Blaga University of Sibiu, Sibiu, Romania
e-mail: bianca.gutan@ulbsibiu.ro

R. Arnold (ed.), *The Convergence of the Fundamental Rights Protection in Europe*, Ius Gentium: Comparative Perspectives on Law and Justice 52,
DOI 10.1007/978-94-017-7465-9_7

Brief Remarks on the Reception of the European Convention on Human Rights in the Domestic Law of the State Parties

Human rights have become a constant topic of political and legal discourse in Europe, especially after the fall of the Iron Curtain and the European integration of most post-communist countries. Not only have states configured and reconfigured their legislative, constitutional and institutional constructions around this common denominator, but the supranational European organization, presently called the European Union, has also done likewise. These states have all assumed, to differing degrees and in different successive steps, the development of a specific system of human rights protection, at the same time integrating into the most powerful existing regional human rights system, namely that of the Council of Europe.

Evidently, the perception and application of the European Convention on Human Rights by various national jurisdictions depends fundamentally on the way in which the Convention has been introduced into national law, as well as, in some countries, by how constitutional jurisdictions shaped this relationship.

Only by 2003 had the Convention been incorporated, in one way or another, into the domestic law of *all* states parties. In any case, the normative incorporation of the Convention has been a variable geometry construction from the beginning, and not all state parties adopted the same techniques consecrated by international law, as the Convention's text does not impose a direct applicability in states' domestic law. As a result, the two preferred methods of incorporation exemplify both the monist and dualist visions on the relationship between national and international law of the respective countries: integration by transposition (dualist states: United Kingdom, Ireland, Norway, Denmark, Germany etc.) and integration by direct incorporation by effect of constitutional dispositions (mostly monist states: France, Spain, Italy, Bulgaria, Romania etc.).

Beyond the classical distinction between monism-dualism, the reception of the ECHR also presents other peculiarities. As a general rule, in "monist" states, the Convention has become a part of domestic law as an effect of ratification, whereas in "dualist" states, special laws of transformation or transposition were necessary. Moreover, some monist states confer a privileged status in domestic law to all international treaties and others only to human rights international treaties.

France, for instance, created a privileged regime for all international treaties. Article 55 of the Constitution says "the treaties or agreements ratified or approved according to the law have, from the moment of publication, an authority superior to the laws, under the reservation, for any treaty or agreement, of its application by the other Party". Therefore, in French law, the European Convention on Human Rights has an equal position with the other international treaties ratified or approved, having a supra-legislative and infra-constitutional value (Hourquebie 2012, 149).

In Germany, Article 59 paragraph 2 of the Fundamental Law reflects a dualist view. Thus, for an international law to become a part of domestic law, besides ratification, it must be "transposed." In German law, treaties thus introduced have a supra-legislative position, but one evidently inferior to the constitution (Arnold 2005, 805). The main difference from the French system, as was noted in German doctrine, is that the French judge directly applies the treaty which became part of the national law as a result of ratification, while the German judge applies the law of approval, by virtue of which the treaty entered the domestic legal order.

The United Kingdom was among the last state parties to introduce the Convention in their domestic legal order. Dualist *par excellence*, the British legal system was very reluctant to accept the incorporation of human rights international rules. Incorporation finally happened in 1998, when the famous *Human Rights Act* came into force. As a consequence, Convention rights became a part of the British legal system. However, the actual incorporation was and still is a long-term process and it depends to a large degree on the attitude of the British courts.

Post-communist Romania partially followed the French model, reflecting its monist orientation, but several sources suggest that inspiration came from the Constitution of Spain. Article 11 paragraph 2 of the 1991 Constitution says that international treaties, ratified by the parliament, are a part of domestic law. The Constitution thus confers a direct applicability to international treaties, on the basis of the law ratifying the treaty (Popescu 2012, 117–122). A special position is given to the human rights treaties. By virtue of the Law on Treaties (590/2003), human rights treaties must be ratified by law, thus being automatically included in the category covered by Article 11 of the Constitution. Secondly, human rights treaties have a privileged constitutional status, given by Article 20, which subordinates the interpretation and application of the Constitution and of all the other internal laws to the ratified human rights treaties, subject to the principle of subsidiarity (i.e. with the exception of dispositions of international law which would be less favourable than domestic law). Similarly in the Czech Republic, which is closer to the French model, Article 10 of the Constitution, introduced in 2001 as part of the "Euro-amendments" of the fundamental law, says that "promulgated treaties, to the ratification of which Parliament has given its consent and by which the Czech Republic is bound, form a part of the legal order; if a treaty provides something else than the statute, the international treaty shall apply" (Kokes 2011, 182).

The problem of reception of the ECHR reveals its true complexity when it comes to the practical application of norms, especially by national courts. That is why a brief comparative overview is useful in assessing the true impact of the Convention upon national law and for the detection of a so-called European judicial culture of human rights. This overview should prove much more useful than a mere, dry analysis of the normative reception.

The European Court of Human Rights' Jurisprudence and European National Courts

It is almost commonplace to say that a legal text means nothing in the absence of adequate interpretation and application. Between the well-known "extremes" of the legal and constitutional world (total creativity *versus* total submission to the "letter of the law"), the former of which exemplified by the US Supreme Court, the reception of international law and especially of the international law of human rights may present surprising peculiarities. A Constitution, regardless of whether it may be the result of a legal transplant, becomes an asset of a certain legal system, and the courts – ordinary and/or constitutional – are sometimes free to interpret and even to recreate it partially. Conversely, an international treaty will always be "foreign law", even in a monist state, because it only fictionally, *par ricochet*, represents the "expression of the general will".

The ratification of a treaty is frequently made for political reasons, in order to adhere to certain organisations and not always through consultation, by referendum, with the sovereign. Even in this context, human rights treaties are a special case, because they are ratified for the benefit of the individual and his rights and do not create obligations based on reciprocity. However, the national courts, even in the case of such treaties, may feel that their full freedom of appreciation on individual rights is undermined. In other words, a human rights treaty, introduced in the domestic legal order with or without precedence over domestic law, may become an irritant for domestic courts, which may manifest a certain resistance to such "imperialism".

In Germany, the best known decision of the Federal Constitutional Tribunal regarding the application of the European Convention by national courts is the one given in *Görgülü case*, in 2004 (BVerfG 2004). Here, the Court said that, firstly, in Germany, the Convention has the legal value of a federal statute. Secondly, in case of a conflict, except when the domestic law gives more extensive rights, German courts have an obligation to interpret the domestic law, including constitutional law, in conformity with the Convention "as read by the ECtHR" (Lübbe-Wolff 2006, 141; Arnold 2005, 811–812; Papier 2006, 1). According to the Constitutional Court, it is the duty of national courts "to integrate a judgment of the ECtHR in the relevant sector of the domestic legal order" (the so-called method of the "evaluative consideration" – *wertende Berücksichtigung*) (Arnold 2005, 813). However, differing positions of national courts are still possible, as long as they find themselves within the margin of appreciation allowed by the Strasbourg jurisprudence. Thus, the Constitutional Court uses the wording "must take into account" when referring to the national courts' obligation towards Strasbourg case law.

In France, the distinction between the conventionality review and the constitutionality review (*contrôle de conventionnalité/contrôle de constitutionnalité*) is well known. The former is done by ordinary courts, whereas the latter is within the competence of the Conseil Constitutionnel which, in its famous 1975 *Décision sur la loi concernant l'interruption volontaire de grossesse*, declined its competence to declare a law incompatible with an international treaty. Therefore, this task would belong to ordinary judges. The Constitution could not be used as a norm of reference in this control, therefore, due to the absence of individual access to constitutional review until 2008–2009, most applicants preferred to appeal to ordinary courts against laws contrary to fundamental rights and use the method of *contrôle de conventionnalité*. The introduction into the French Constitution of the *question prioritaire de constitutionnalité* (QPC) was meant to put an end to this inconsistency (Gaïa 2013, 230; Dutheillet de Lamothe 2008, 293). Like in other countries (Burgorgue-Larsen 2008, 265), the QPC became a complementary means of action against laws contrary to fundamental rights, with priority vis-à-vis the conventionality control. Although Article 61–1 of the Constitution does not expressly provide, the organic law says that "when the court is consulted with issues contesting the conformity of a legal provision of the Constitution *and* with international engagements of France, the court must rule firstly on the issue of constitutionality."

In practice, before as well as after the 2009 reforms, French judges have used the European Convention to correct national law, to complete it, in addition to enriching its contents, by taking into account the Strasbourg standards (de Gouttes 1999, 9; Lamanda 2008, 325), in fields such as: the right to an independent and impartial tribunal, the right to a defence (ECtHR 1993a, b), the right to liberty and security (pre-trial detention), right to privacy [the telephone tapping cases (ECtHR 1990a, b), the transsexual rights cases (ECtHR 1992)], and the right to access to remedies in appeal (the *Cour de Cassation* declared incompatible with Article 6 of the Convention a disposition similar to the one on the annulment appeal from Romanian law.)

A more particular situation is that of the United Kingdom. British courts are in principle bound by the provisions of Section 2(1) of the Human Rights Act 1998, which states that: "A court or tribunal determining a question which has arisen in connection with a Convention right must take into account any judgment, decision, declaration or advisory opinion of the ECtHR (…)". The key expression here is "must take into account" which may cause ambiguity in interpretation. As already noticed in the doctrine, "the juxtaposition of the obligatory [*must*] and the permissible [*take into account*] is unusual and a little ambiguous. While it is clear that courts are obliged to take into account the Strasbourg jurisprudence, it is not clear to what extent this process will entail giving effect to, or following, the Strasbourg case-law" (Wicks 2005, 406). Thus, a set of questions had been raised by the British doctrine, among which: is it sufficient for a court to cite the relevant case law? Should the judgments be analysed? Do convincing reasons need to be given for a departure from established Strasbourg jurisprudence? etc. As a consequence of this ambiguity, British courts have taken different paths in their approach to applying the Convention, according to Section 2(1) HRA. In some instances the judge would be "blindly following" the European Court's case-law and would not depart from it without very good reason. Other judges would disregard or "pay insufficient regard" [in a very British "translation" (Wicks 2005, 415)] to ECtHR judgments. Not surprisingly, there are also judges in British courts who would assess the relevance of the Strasbourg jurisprudence by reference to their own opinion on the merits, that is, a moderate approach between the two aforementioned extremes. And, finally, as a most controversial subtype of the latter, there are judges who would consciously depart from the European Court's views (Wicks 2005, 410–423).

Romanian Courts and the European Perspective

Although the Constitution had created the possibility of introducing the international human rights catalogues into domestic law ever since 1991, and despite the fact that Romania had become a party to the European Convention on Human

Rights relatively early, in 1994, these international instruments and especially the ECHR had rarely been mentioned by judges in the first decade of the transition period. Even the constitutional texts on fundamental rights were applied with reluctance by national authorities and judges.

One of the main general criticisms of the Romanian judicial system during the transitional period has been the absence of a jurisprudential coherence and a lack of understanding of its role as a guarantee of fundamental rights: "Misused or misunderstood, functional independence of judges combined with a more and more complex legal system, brought diversity and uneven case law, which was found to be counterproductive and against the very principles of a state governed by the rule of law" (Tănăsescu and Deaconu 2013, 326; Selejan-Gutan 2010, 289–292). These unfortunate features applied even more evidently in the field of fundamental rights protection and especially in the acknowledgement, by ordinary judges, of the existence and application of fundamental rights catalogues with superior legal value, including the Constitution and the international law.

In cases related to the right to liberty and security (especially the conditions of pre-trial detention) one could find, in the 1990s, arguments like "judges are only subjected to apply the law and not the Constitution". In a famous 1999 decision, the Supreme Court of Justice expressed a common attitude among judges of that time: "the provisions of the Constitution are not addressed directly to the ordinary courts, which apply the ordinary law, but only to the legislator, who must comply with the Constitution and bring changes to the ordinary laws. The Constitutional Court decisions have the same status (…). The courts are bound to apply the present ordinary law and not directly the Constitution; only the legislator is bound to comply with the constitutional provisions and principles, bringing changes to the legislation in this respect" (SCJ 1999). This "national legal nonsense" (Popescu 2006, 197) was a dominant mentality amongst judges towards constitutional principles, and the relationship of national law with international human rights law.

The Constitutional Court started to invoke international human rights instruments more frequently from 2000, in a period of more active case law on fundamental rights protection. The Supreme Court of the land (presently called the High Court of Cassation and Justice – HCCJ) followed in its steps rather shyly at first, but its position strengthened in time and was followed by lower courts (appellate courts, tribunals, first instance courts). However, the approach of European rules and case law was mostly a "parallel" one, without a true integration of principles and without exercising a true "conventionality control".

Despite the recent interest of the national courts to know and apply the "Strasbourg law", one can still detect certain confusion in their approach to the different catalogues of rights. In 2011–2012, there were many Romanian judges who did not make the distinction between the EU law, the community law and the Council of Europe's law. They addressed the European Court of Justice with numerous preliminary ruling requests in which they asked for the interpretation of the European Convention on Human Rights (Şandru et al. 2013, 127–155). There were also courts which, understanding the differences between the catalogues, rejected applications for such preliminary rulings for lack of relevance. Even the

Constitutional Court had its part in this chain of confusion, but this does not demean its role as the guardian of fundamental rights (Popescu 2007, 1–3).

On the other hand, neither the Constitutional Court nor the High Court of Cassation developed a strong jurisprudence similar to the *Görgülü* decision of the German Federal Constitutional Tribunal. In fact, such jurisprudence would theoretically hardly be necessary, as Article 20 of the Constitution is clear enough; although, it might lead to a more constant reference to international catalogues of human rights, as well as avoid positions like the one expressed by the Supreme Court of Justice in 1999. However, the highest jurisdictions did give two decisions of principle in which they affirmed the priority of the Strasbourg jurisprudence. In 1994, the Constitutional Court stated that interpretation of the European Court ['s judgments] is compulsory for national jurisdictions, by virtue of the subsidiarity principle (RCC 81/1994; Popescu 2012, 138), and in 2003, the Supreme Court stated that the judgments of the Strasbourg Court represent "interpretation precedents" (RCC 102/2003). As a result, it has been stated that "although both constitutional and ordinary judges have occasionally wrongly interpreted and applied the Strasbourg case-law the very text of the Convention, they never dared to reverse a judgment of principle and put themselves in open rebellion against the European judge" (Popescu 2012, 139).

It is also worth mentioning that Romanian judges do not achieve what in French law is called a *contrôle de conventionnalité*. Very frequently, they only acknowledge ECtHR case-law arguments to underpin their decisions, although Article 20 of the Constitution would allow them to directly examine the conformity of national laws with the European Convention. Few judges exercise this power which would associate them with conventionality control and which is, simultaneously, an expression of the subsidiarity principle.

In a recent survey among Romanian judges, of all levels, regarding the relationship of Romanian law with European law (Gutan 2014, 239–242) including Strasbourg law, a very interesting result came in response to the question: "How do you explain why Romania was repeatedly found in violation of Article 6 of the Convention and of Article 1 Protocol 1?" 93.07 % of the judges who answered the poll said that it was because of bad legislation. Therefore, they were not even conscious of the power, given to them by Article 20 of the Constitution, to review legislation contrary to HR treaties. To the same question, 17 % of the judges answered that it may be explained by the fact that "the Roman-Germanic legal family does not allow precedent as source of law", whereas 13.85 % said that Romanian judges are responsible for ignoring the European Court's case law. At the same time, surprisingly, 84.84 % of these same judges consider the European Court's Jurisprudence to have the legal value of precedent for Romanian courts!

The Constitutional Court does not exercise a conventionality control: it has stated, as early as 2001, that it is the guardian of the Constitution and not of the conventionality of the Constitution or laws, and therefore it cannot invalidate a constitutional disposition as being allegedly unconventional, as this would amount to a constitutional amendment and a transgression of its own jurisdiction. As a result, the Court mostly refers to the ECtHR case-law in support of its own arguments, but sometimes, as has happened in the case of social rights, the Court's interpretation, although formally based on some European judgments, departed substantially from the one consecrated *par ricochet* by the Strasbourg Court. In other cases, the Constitutional Court refers to the Strasbourg Court's judgments but its arguments are totally different. Finally, there are cases where the Constitutional Court's decision is in total disagreement with the established case law of the European Court.

The most famous and recent example of a case contradicting the Strasbourg views is the one of *Decision no. 206 of 2013* where, by exceeding its substantial competence (as regards the object of the control) as well as its formal competence (as a negative legislator), the Constitutional Court also ignored the meaning of the constant jurisprudence of the ECtHR regarding freedom of expression and the repeated encouragements of the European Court to remove the criminal sanctions for insult and libel from legislation (ECtHR 2013).

Instead, the Constitutional Court preferred to declare a decision of the HCCJ as unconstitutional, a decision of jurisprudential unification. The history of this unconstitutionality decision began in 2006, when the Parliament decided to decriminalize the offences of insult and libel, by changing the Criminal Code. In 2007, the Court adopted a decision in which it declared the unconstitutionality of the new law and of the decriminalisation of the old, saying that the civil law remedies were not sufficient to protect human dignity in cases of breach by insult or libel. Beyond the arguments on merits, the most important technical problem arising from this decision was the effect upon the criminal norm. The Romanian doctrine is unanimous that a Constitutional Court decision, as "negative legislator", may not have the effect of replacing an abrogated legal decision back into force. The Constitution, on the other hand, says that legal dispositions declared unconstitutional by the Constitutional Court cease to apply 45 days after the decision's publication (having been suspended during those 45 days). What should a judge do in such a case? Confronted with a divergent jurisprudence from various courts, the HCCJ tried to put some order into the chaos created by the legislator's lack of intervention following the Court's decision (the legislator apparently wanted to maintain its decriminalisation policy) and, in October 2010, adopted a decision of jurisprudential unification (in an "appeal on points of law"), in which it stated that the norms incriminating insult and libel were not in force. In subsequent decisions, in 2011, the HCCJ reversed its decision and declared that ordinary judges should take the Constitutional Court's decision of 2007 into account. In 2013, by the abovementioned Decision no. 206, the Court declared that "the solution given by the HCCJ to the legal problem" [i.e. the 2010 decision] was unconstitutional.

It is important to emphasize here that the Constitution does not give the Constitutional Court the power to review judicial decisions. At any rate, the *dictum* of the Decision 206/2013 is peculiar, as the Court "*admitted* " the exception of unconstitutionality of the article of the Code of Criminal Procedure [which establishes the competence of the HCCJ to adopt compulsory decisions], but "*declared unconstitutional* " the "solution given to the legal problem" by the high court. Thus, the Constitutional Court does not state anything on the object of the exception – the abovementioned article from the Code of Criminal Procedure – not even as an interpretative decision ("constitutional *insofar as*"). Instead, it declared the unconstitutionality of a judicial decision exceeding its limited powers given by the Constitution.

As a conclusion on this point, I would say that this legislative and jurisprudential pandemonium on the standards of freedom of expression comes from the fact that the Constitutional Court should not have decided on a matter which pertains to the exclusive competence of the legislator: decriminalizing an offence such as insult or libel is a matter of legislative policy and should not become the object of a constitutional review except for an extremely serious case of discrimination or violation of other fundamental constitutional principles. This was obviously not the case.

This type of uncertain situation regarding national law may create a difficult task for an ordinary judge, who may find himself in the presence of a "conflict of fundamental rights catalogues". The Constitution protects the freedom of expression, but the interpretation of the Constitution by the Constitutional Court is at odds with the European Court of Human Rights case law. On the other hand, the same Constitution gives priority to the European law of human rights and implicitly to the case law of the ECtHR, which is already commonly accepted as part of the European law of human rights. Therefore, the constitutional provisions according to Article 20 §1, should be interpreted and applied in accordance with the conventional dispositions. It is a difficult dilemma, and one that is not foreign to other constitutional and legal systems.

In this case, the legislator, following the "indirect" pressures of European judgments, especially those against Romania in the context of the freedom of the press (*Cumpana and Mazare, Stangu and Scutelnicu* etc.), decriminalized insult and libel. The Constitutional Court, setting aside the law, raised "human dignity" as a constitutional value. The High Court of Cassation and Justice tried to solve an incoherent jurisprudence based on this legal uncertainty, but has itself had an inconsistent position (at first upholding the law, but then later changing its mind, saying that the courts must obey the Constitutional Court – even if its decision exceeded its competence and may not replace into force an abrogated norm). The legislator, in all this time, didn't take any action. Then the Constitutional Court came back with an even more imperative decision, but one with the same technical faults as the others. What should the ordinary judge, confronted with a complaint for insult or libel, do? To which of these norms and decisions should he or she give priority? The Constitution? The European Convention on Human Rights and the case law of the Strasbourg Court? The Constitutional Court? The HCCJ? Who will be responsible for potential further Strasbourg convictions?

This is a good example, albeit an extreme one, of the relationship between national courts and international law and international jurisprudence.

Certainly, it is possible to find many examples of a more coherent relationship with the international law of human rights in the Romanian Constitutional Court's case law. The Court gave, in many cases, concrete effect, of a palliative and sometimes of a corrective nature, to the European Convention. Thus, the Court's role in the "constitutionalisation" of the legal system, by permeating it with European human rights standards, cannot be contested. One of the most famous examples is the one regarding an annulment application (*recurs in anulare*) and the Court's contribution, although belated, to the elimination of this procedure from the Romanian legal system, as it was contrary to the legal certainty principle and the right to a fair trial (RCC 73/1996; 110/1997).

In 2008, however, the Superior Council of Magistracy (the Romanian Judicial Council) gave a striking decision in which the Council described the relationship to be developed by national judges with the European Court of Human Rights jurisprudence: "as regards the alignment of the supreme court to the solution given by the European Court in the case *Beian v. Romania* (2008), in which Romania was found to be in violation of the Convention for a divergent practice at the level of the supreme court, one must take into account the dispositions of Article 124 §3 of the Constitution, according to which judges are independent and submitted only to the law and not to judicial precedent: therefore, to claim that the judge would be "bound" by past decisions is *illegal and foreign to the spirit of the Romanian legal system*. The State must find the most adequate instruments to avoid a divergent practice, as a judgment of the European Court does not represent, as such a basis for a [national] solution formulated in the abovementioned terms".

Therefore, a relative resistance to European standards, as expressed by the Strasbourg court, existed in the 1990s and even, with this SCM decision, in the first decade of the years 2000. This resistance is rooted in a mentality inherited from the totalitarian regime, according to which there may be no superior authority above judges and is manifest also as regards the Constitutional Court and its jurisprudence. Nevertheless, this resistance did not become a general phenomenon and when it existed, it was determined more by inertia and ignorance than by a general and conscious act from the part of national judges (Selejan-Gutan 2008, 108–111).

Conclusions

Despite all the jurisprudential incoherence discussed above, there are no true normative conflicts between the international law of human rights and national law in Romania. Certainly, the supranational human rights judges, in their important and difficult task of finding a common denominator to establish the standards of protection, turn more and more to national jurisprudence and especially to that of the constitutional courts. In any case, National judges have already been considered as better placed than international judges to establish the exact contents of human rights, due to their "direct and constant contacts with the living forces of their countries (ECtHR 1976)." This was the start of the margin of appreciation doctrine in the Strasbourg case law. Although it was formulated over 35 years ago, the argument is still valid. What's new is the greater need for judicial dialogue at all levels: "l'action conjuguée des jurisprudences pour une lecture "constructive" de la norme européenne passe par le dialogue"/ *the combined action of jurisprudences for a "constructive" reading of the European norm passes through dialogue* (Potvin-Solis et al. 2004, 25). The Strasbourg Court makes more and more reference to national law and uses comparative law for interpretive purposes and for defining autonomous concepts. The evolutive interpretation of the Convention – a *living instrument* – would not even be possible without considering the latest developments of national legal systems, especially in controversial fields like assisted human reproduction, euthanasia, the freedom of expression *versus* private life etc. Legal comparison gained "an invisible role in the interpretive process of the ECtHR" (Mahoney 2004, 149), in a coherent manner – as Paul Mahoney put it – which is natural if one thinks that the Convention system is built on the common democratic values of the states parties.

Nevertheless, one must emphasise the great difference between the position of the national jurisdictions in Western countries and in post-communist countries, towards the supranational jurisdictions and the international law of human rights. If the former have had periods of resistance or conflict, it was because, as President Jean-Paul Costa said, referring to the French case, "Il y a parfois aussi une irritation parce que ces hautes juridictions considèrent, à juste titre d'ailleurs, que depuis de décennies elles défendent les libertés publiques et les droits de l'homme et que la Cour de Strasbourg vient parfois leur donner des leçons de procédure interne, ce qui les agace" (Potvin-Solis et al. 2004, 50)/*There is sometimes also an irritation because these high courts think, with good reason, that they have, for decades, defended public liberties and human rights and that the Strasbourg Court comes to teach them lessons of domestic procedure, which annoys them.* However, the dialogue and cooperation found their place in this relationship, especially with respect to the Luxembourg Court, by means of the preliminary rulings procedure, but also with the Strasbourg Court: "en ce sens, les juridictions nationales (...) considèrent de plus en plus qu'elles doivent tenir compte, non seulement de la Convention, mais de la jurisprudence de notre Cour, et en tenir compte même pour modifier leur propre jurisprudence" (Costa 2002, 3148; Potvin-Solis et al. 2004, 30)/*in this respect, national jurisdictions consider more and more that they must take account not only of the Convention, but also the case-law of our Court, even in order to change their own case-law.*

In contrast, constitutional courts and supreme courts of post-communist countries were not "born" continuing a tradition of European judicial culture, containing human rights as a salient element. They were entrusted with the task to build, immediately, by themselves, an already Europeanised judicial culture. This is an extremely difficult task, especially if we take into account the inheritance of a totalitarian past. These courts have mostly been created by new constitutions, based on new principles inspired by post-war Western law. Nevertheless, they were born in post-communist transitional regimes, in extremely difficult economic and political circumstances. They have given their early decisions under extraordinary external pressure and most of the time they have not risen to the task. However, there was little space left for conflict, given the political will of these countries to become part of the European Union. That is why the two situations are not yet comparable. What the Western jurisdictions achieved in over 50 years, the post-communist ones were required to do in less than 20. The most difficult task in this context is, thus, not changing norms, but mentalities. And, although great improvements have been made, this is still a work in progress for the Romanian judiciary. Recent CVM reports on Romania (July 2012 and January 2013) seem to note better progress in achieving the established benchmarks, but also highlighted points which are still pending: the actual entry into force of the new adopted codes, jurisprudential unification, an update of the jurisprudential database, and, not least, a "significant progress in the handling of high level corruption cases".

However, the Commission was very critical towards the process of jurisprudential unification and pointed out the existence of a mentality issue: "The High Court of Cassation and Justice has the primary responsibility for the unification of jurisprudence. A number of important steps have been taken since 2007. The Small Reform Law amended the appeal in the interest of the law procedure, with a view to strengthening its efficiency. The new procedure codes introduce a preliminary ruling mechanism as a new instrument for legal unification, as well as reforming jurisdictional arrangements to help unification (…). Failure to respect the High Court's rulings in appeals on points of law, as well as decisions of the Constitutional Court, has now become a potential ground for disciplinary measures. However, these mechanisms have not yet been able to overcome inconsistency, which is a major frailty of the Romanian judicial system. Part of the problem seems to lie in the insufficient awareness of the importance of legal unification among the magistracy, perhaps linked to an extreme interpretation of independence" (European Commission 2012).

There is an active effort at the European level to create a more coherent order amongst this plurality of human rights protection instruments, in the context of the delayed but still foreseen adhesion of the European Union to the European Convention and of the high number of states-parties to the Convention. The most recent development in this respect is the adoption of Protocol no. 16 to the Convention, on 17 July 2013, which provides the possibility for the highest jurisdictions of the states parties to obtain, from the European Court of Human Rights (in Grand Chamber composition), advisory opinions on questions regarding the interpretation or application of rights and freedoms defined by the Convention and its protocols. Romania has signed the Protocol on 14 October 2014 and declared the domestic Courts that will have jurisdiction to request advisory opinions from the European Court, within the meaning of the Protocol, are the High Court of Cassation and Justice, the Constitutional Court and the Courts of Appeal.

The main purpose of this new instrument is the enhancement of the dialogue between national and international judges, with a view to clarifying the Convention dispositions and the impact of the Court's case law. This new competence of the Court had been envisaged since 2005 and it will certainly enrich the European *acquis* in the field of human rights and will contribute to a better understanding of European human rights standards by national judges.

Bibliography

Arnold, Rainer. 2005. La Cour constitutionnelle fédérale allemande et la Cour européenne des droits de l'homme. *Revue Internationale de Droit Comparé* 57(3): 805–818.

Burgorgue-Larsen, Laurence. 2008. L'influence de la Convention Européenne sur le fonctionnement des Cours constitutionnelles. *Revue Internationale de Droit Comparé* 60(2): 265–282.

BverfG. 14.10.2004. 2 BvR 1481/04, Absatz-Nr. (1–73). http://www.bverfg.de/entscheidungen/rs20041014_2bvr148104en.html

Conseil Constitutionnel. 2009. Decision no. 2009–595 of 3 December. In *Les Grandes Décisions du Conseil Constitutionnel*, no. 41.

Constitution of France. 1958.

Constitution of Spain. 1978.

Costa, Jean-Paul. 2002. La Cour européenne des droits de l'Homme: interview de Jean-Paul Costa. *Recueil le Dalloz* 42: 3148–3150.

de Gouttes, Régis. 1999. La Convention Européenne des Droits de l'Homme et le juge en France et au Pays-Bas. *Revue Internationale de Droit Comparé* 57(1): 7–20.

Deaconu, Stefan. 2013. Analogical reasoning as a dialectical instrument. In *The use of foreign precedents by constitutional judges*, ed. Groppi Tania and Marie-Claire Ponthoreau. Oxford: Hart Publishing.

Dutheillet de Lamothe, Olivier. 2008. La Convention Européenne et le Conseil Constitutionnel. *Revue Internationale de Droit Comparé* 60(2): 293–308.

European Commission. 2012. Report on Romania, COM(2012) 410 final.

European Court of Human Rights. 1976. Application no. 5493/72, *Handyside v. United Kingdom*, 07.12.1976.

European Court of Human Rights. 1990a. Applicaton no. 11105/84, *Huvig v. France*, 24.04.1990.

European Court of Human Rights. 1990b. Application no. 11801/85, *Kruslin v. France*, 24.04.1990.

European Court of Human Rights. 1992. Application no. 13343/87, *B. v. France*, 25.03.1992.

European Court of Human Rights. 1993a. Application no. 14647/89, *Saidi v. France*, 20.09.1993.

European Court of Human Rights. 1993b. Application no. 11444/85, *Delta v. France*, 19.12.1990.

European Court of Human Rights. 2013. Application no. 26118/10, *Eon v. France*, 14.03.2013.

Gaïa, Patrick. 2013. Chestiunea prioritara de constitutionalitate si controlul de conventionalitate. In *Excepţia de neconstituţionalitate in Romania si Franta*, ed. Simina Elena Tanasescu, 229–241. Bucuresti: Universul juridic.

Gutan, Manuel. 2014. The Romanian judicial culture and the application of the European court of human rights' case-law. An empirical research. In *Europeanization and judicial culture in contemporary democracies*, ed. Manuel Gutan and Bianca Selejan-Gutan, 220–246. Bucharest: Hamangiu.

Hourquebie, Fabrice. 2012. La réception des règles européennes de protection des droits de l'homme dans l'ordre juridique national français. In *Approches franco-roumaines face au défi européen*, ed. Tănăsescu Elena Simina, 145–154. Iaşi: Institutul European.

Kokes, Marian. 2011. The application of the law of the human rights treaties in the Czech Republic. *The Vienna Journal on International Constitutional Law* 5(2): 175–187.

Lamanda, Vincent. 2008. La Convention Européenne et la Cour de Cassation. *Revue Internationale de Droit Comparé* 60(2): 325–335.

Lübbe-Wolff, Gertrude. 2006. ECtHR and national jurisdiction – the Görgülü case. *Humboldt Forum Recht* 12–2006: 138–147.

Mahoney, Paul. 2004. The comparative method in judgments of the European court of human rights: Reference back to national law. In *Comparative law before the courts*, ed. Guy Canivet, Mads Andenas, and Duncan Fairgrieve, 135–152. London: British Institute of International and Comparative Law.

Papier, Hans-Jürgen. 2006. Execution and effects of the judgments of the European court of human rights from the perspective of German national courts. *Human Rights Law Journal* 27(1): 1–4.

Popescu, Corneliu-Liviu. 2006. L'exception d'inconstitutionnalité en tant que recours interne avant une requête individuelle devant la Cour européenne des droits de l'homme. In *Liber Amicorum Ioan Muraru, Despre constituţie şi constituţionalism*, ed. Simina Tănăsescu and Ştefan Deaconu, 184–198. Bucureşti: Hamangiu.

Popescu, Corneliu-Liviu. 2007. Comentariu la Decizia Curţii Constituţionale nr. 588/2007. *Curierul Judiciar* 9: 1–4.

Popescu, Corneliu-Liviu. 2012. L'intégration des règles internationales en matière des droits de l'homme dans l'ordre juridique roumain. In *Approches franco-roumaines face au défi européen*, ed. Elena Simina Tănăsescu, 115–144. Iaşi: Institutul European.
Potvin-Solis, Laurence, et al. 2004. Le concept de dialogue entre les juges en Europe. In *Le dialogue entre les juges européens et nationaux: incantation ou réalité?* ed. François Lichère et al., 19–58. Bruxelles: Bruylant.
Romanian Constitutional Court. 04.06.1996. Decision 73/1996. *Monitorul Oficial al României*, 1996, 255.
Romanian Constitutional Court. 15.07.1994. Decision 81/1994. *Monitorul Oficial al României* 14/25.01.1995, 250.
Romanian Constitutional Court. Decision 102/2003. *Monitorul Oficial al României* 27.03.2003, 201.
Romanian Constitutional Court. Decision n°110/1997. *Monitorul Oficial al României* 22.12.1997, 370.
Romanian Constitutional Court. Decision n°145/2000. *Monitorul Oficial al României* 16.12.2000, 665.
Selejan-Gutan, Bianca. 2008. *Spatiul european al drepturilor omului*. Bucuresti: C.H.Beck.
Selejan-Gutan, Bianca. 2010. Transitional constitutionalism and transitional justice in post-communist states – the Romanian case. *Romanian Journal of Comparative Law* 2: 9–36.
Superior Council of Magistracy. 2008. Resolution no. 981 of 2 October. http://www.csm1909.ro/csm/linkuri/05_11_2008__18491_ro.pdf. Consulted on 5 July 2013.
Supreme Court of Justice. 1999. Decision no. 1813 of 17 June.
Şandru, Daniel Mihail et al. 2013. Interpretarea şi aplicarea dreptului UE şi a Convenţiei pentru apărarea drepturilor omului şi a libertăţilor fundamentale în cererile privind trimiterile preliminare în faţa instanţelor din România. In *Mai este Curtea Europeană a Drepturilor Omului un mecanism judiciar eficient?*, ed. Raluca Bercea, 127–155. Bucureşti: Universul Juridic.
Wicks, Elizabeth. 2005. Taking account of Strasbourg? The British judiciary's approach to interpreting convention rights. *European Public Law* 11(3): 405–428.

Fundamental Rights and Freedoms in Turkey and the Turkish Constitutional Court

Merih Öden and Selin Esen

Abstract The article titled "Fundamental Rights and Freedoms in Turkey and the Turkish Constitutional Court" illustrates the influence of the European human rights standards in Turkey. First, the article examines the key features of the fundamental rights and freedoms regime under the 1982 Constitution. Second, it discusses the Turkish Constitutional Court's approach on fundamental rights and freedoms within the framework of the decisions on some of the specific issues that have proven controversial in Turkey, i.e. "gender equality", "freedoms of political parties", "social rights" and "emergency-law decrees". This article reveals that the European human rights documents and the rulings of the European Court of Human Rights are indispensable elements for Turkish legislation and the Constitutional Court, even though it seems that sometimes they do not fully embrace the principles. Accordingly, the Turkish case suggests the "Convergence of Fundamental Rights in Europe".

Introduction

The 1961 Constitution of Turkey gave Rights and Freedoms a special and privileged place. Indeed, the Constitution recognized them in a more comprehensive way than the previous constitutions of the country. In Article 2, it identified the Turkish state as a Republic 'based on human rights'. The 1982 Constitution maintained this approach, however it also gave priority to the authority of the state if the concepts of freedom and authority were ever in conflict. Accordingly, the 1982 Constitution placed more emphasis on the limits of freedom rather than the exercise of rights and freedoms. The 1982 Constitution identified the state as a Republic "respecting human rights" in Article 2, showing a weaker emphasis on human rights than the 1961 Constitution's Formula.[1] Unlike the 1961 Constitution, according to the 1982

[1] However, we note that, as we will discuss the new version of Article 14 that prohibits abuse of fundamental rights and freedoms adopted in 2001 diminished this difference between two constitutions.

M. Öden (✉) • S. Esen
Law Faculty, Ankara University, Ankara, Turkey
e-mail: merihoden@gmail.com; oden@law.ankara.edu.tr; selin.esen71@gmail.com

R. Arnold (ed.), *The Convergence of the Fundamental Rights Protection in Europe*, Ius Gentium: Comparative Perspectives on Law and Justice 52,
DOI 10.1007/978-94-017-7465-9_8

Constitution, fundamental rights and freedoms are also comprised of the duties and responsibilities of the individual. Furthermore, while the 1982 Constitution's approach in the original text on fundamental rights and freedoms was based on their restriction, the 1961 Constitution provided a broad space to enjoy rights and freedoms. These differences between the two constitutions stem from different understandings of democracy, the rule of law, and constitutionalism. Even though both of the constitutions were written after military coups, they had different points of view on limitations of power and the strength of the state's authority. Thus, while the 1961 Constitution gave special importance to the freedoms and limited the government by various means, the 1982 Constitution's aim was to strengthen the state's authority by empowering the executive branch and restricting freedoms.

In this paper, first we will examine how the 1982 Constitution drew up the fundamental rights and freedoms and explore the key features of the fundamental rights and freedoms regime within the framework of relevant the Turkish Constitutional Court (TCC) decisions. Secondly, we will discuss the TCC's approach on some of the specific issues. In order not to miss the historical perspective, we will make note of the 1961 Constitutional provisions and some of the rulings of the Court ruled in this period, where relevant.

An Overview of Fundamental Rights and Freedoms in the 1982 Constitution

Constitutional Guarantees on Fundamental Rights and Freedoms

The 1982 Constitution provides a long list of rights and freedoms that are included in most of the liberal democratic constitutions. The Constitution draws up rights and freedoms under three chapters, namely: "individual rights and duties", "social and economic rights and duties" and "political rights and duties", in accordance with the classical classification based on negative, active and positive rights. However, the rights of each category are not always true to the spirit of this tripartite classification. To give an example, the freedom to work and conclude contracts, the right to organize trade unions, and the right to collective bargaining and strike actions are deemed negative rights, but the Constitution places them in the chapter of "social and economic rights and duties".

According to the Constitution, rights and freedoms may be restricted either directly by the Constitution or by law in accordance with the principles written in the Constitution. The Constitution directly stipulates some comprehensive restrictions in relevant provisions. Some of these limitations can be applied directly in nature. To give an example, consider Article 42, which guarantees the right to education, but prohibits teaching in any language other than Turkish as a mother tongue to Turkish citizens, at any institutions of training or education. Article 68 explicitly prohibits affiliation with a political party for judges and prosecutors, members of higher judicial organs, civil servants, members of the armed forces and students who are not yet in higher education institutions. However, some of the constitutional restrictions are ambiguous, such as disallowing individuals "*to exploit or abuse religion or religious feelings, or things held sacred by religion, in any manner whatsoever, for the purpose of personal or political influence, or for even partially basing the fundamental, social, economic, political, and legal order of the state on religious tenets*" (Art 24). Article 27 outlaws the exercise of the right to disseminate for the purpose of changing the provisions of Articles 1, 2 and 3 of this Constitution.[2] Article 54 provides that the right to strike and lock-out shall not be exercised in a manner contrary to the principle of goodwill to the detriment of society. Such abstract and undefinable restrictions require clarification by the law and courts in order to put them into practice. Hence, such limitations in the Constitution give law-makers large discretion to restrict rights and freedoms.

The Constitution also limits fundamental rights and freedoms in other ways, namely excluding acts of the President of the Republic on matters of his or her own competence, some decisions of the Supreme Military Council, and those of the Supreme Council of Judges and Public Prosecutors from the scope of judicial review (Art 125 and 148). In addition, emergency decrees, which possess the force of law (decree-laws), issued by the executive authority during a state of emergency and martial law fall outside the judicial review (Art 91).

Article 13 of the Constitution provides principles for the limitation of fundamental rights and freedoms.[3] Accordingly, they may be only limited by law, so long as their essence is not infringed upon. Thereby, decree-laws, by-laws or any other administrative regulations may not impose limitations on rights and freedoms. However, one should distinguish social and economic rights from others. According to Article 91, "*Individual rights and duties included in the First and Second Chapter of the Second Part of the Constitution and the political rights and duties listed in the Fourth Chapter, cannot be regulated by decree-laws*".

The limitations of the law should be in conformity with the letter and spirit of the Constitution. Namely, limitations should be compliant with the constitutional guar-

---

[2] **Article 1**. The Turkish State is a Republic.

Article 2. The Republic of Turkey is a democratic, secular and social state governed by the rule of law; bearing in mind the concepts of public peace, national solidarity and justice; respecting human rights; loyal to the nationalism of Atatürk, and based on the fundamental tenets set forth in the Preamble.

Article 3. The Turkish state, with its territory and nation, is an indivisible entity. Its language is Turkish.

Its flag, the form of which is prescribed by the relevant law, is composed of a white crescent and star on a red background.

Its national anthem is the "Independence March".

Its capital is Ankara.

[3] Article 13 as amended in 2001, "Fundamental rights and freedoms may be restricted only by law and in conformity with the reasons mentioned in the relevant articles of the Constitution without infringing upon their essence. These restrictions shall not be in conflict with the letter and spirit of the Constitution and the requirements of the democratic order of the society and the secular Republic and the principle of proportionality."

anties and prohibitions. In addition, Parliament should take the whole of the Constitution into consideration when restricting rights and freedoms. To give an example, the Preamble of the Constitution depicts the political regime as a "liberal democracy". Accordingly, the parliament should proceed under the principle that "freedom is the rule, restriction is the exception". This is the principle upon which democratic regimes are based (Sabuncu 2006, 63).

The original text of Article 13 envisaged a cumulative restriction system for fundamental rights and freedoms. Accordingly, Article 13 cited general reasons for restrictions; namely, the aim of safeguarding; the indivisible integrity of the state with its territory and nation, national sovereignty, the Republic, national security, public order, general peace, the public interest, public morals and, public health. Furthermore, the Constitution stipulated specific reasons for the limitation of every fundamental right and freedom in its relevant article. Consequently, the Turkish Grand National Assembly (TGNA) could restrict them in accordance with the general reasons in Article 13 and/or specific reasons mentioned in the relevant articles. The 2001 constitutional amendments rewrote Article 13, repealing general grounds in accordance with the European Convention of Human Rights (ECHR). However the specific reasons in the related articles remained. Nevertheless, the amended restrictive regime certainly provides more liberal sphere for constitutional rights and freedoms.

What is the limit upon these limitations of fundamental rights and freedoms? The 1961 Constitution had envisaged a guarantee of the "essence" of fundamental rights and freedoms inspired by the 1949 Constitution of Germany. We may describe the "essence" of a fundamental right or freedom as its indispensable element and essential core. Yet it is not possible to make a general definition of the "essence". The concept should be identified separately for each right and freedom in accordance with its specific nature. The original version of the 1982 Constitution lifted the principle of the essence and introduced the criterion of the "requirements of the democratic social order" imported from the ECHR. In the beginning, this principle raised doubts as to whether it guarantees universal standards of democracy, because the Preamble of the Constitution refers to liberal democracy as the one set forth in said Constitution. In the beginning, the TCC interpreted the "democratic social order" as "democratic order adopted by the 1982 Constitution" (TCC E. 1985/21, K. 1986/23). However, the Court changed its opinion shortly thereafter and interpreted the expression of "democratic order adopted by the 1982 Constitution" as "contemporary liberal democratic order" (TCC E. 1985/8, K. 1986/27), interpreting this principle in the context of universal standards (TCC E. 1985/8, K.1986/27; E. 1988/2, K. 1988/1). The Court used the principle of the "requirements of the democratic social order" alongside the principle of the essence. The 2001 constitutional amendment, adding the principle of essence to Article 13, provided an additional guarantee for the protection of fundamental rights and freedoms. Together with such improvements, the guarantee that restrictions should not be in conflict with the requirements of the democratic social order was also maintained (Özbudun 2007, 181).

According to Article 13, proportionality is another principle that must be considered while limiting fundamental rights and freedoms. This principle is derived from the jurisprudence of the German Constitutional Court and the European Court of

Human Rights (ECtHR) (Case of Soering v. United Kingdom1989). Even though the Constitution did not explicitly place importance on the proportionality principle, the formula of '... *grounds for restrictions of fundamental rights and freedoms ... shall not be imposed for any purpose other than those for which they are prescribed'* in the original version of Article 13 embraced the core of the principle of proportionality. This principle was explicitly inserted into the Constitution in 2001. However, we should note that the TCC used this principle in its decisions before 2001, associating it with the principle of fulfilling the requirements of the democratic social order. According to the Court, freedoms can only be limited exceptionally and to the extent required by the continuity of democratic social order (TCC E. 1985/8, K.1986/27).

Finally, "secular Republic" is another criterion for the restriction of fundamental rights and freedoms. Accordingly, the limitations of the rights and freedoms should be in conformity with the requirements of the secular Republic. The inclusion of this criterion in to Article 13 in 2001, in fact, signifies the importance of this issue in Turkish society and the commitment of the elite to republican secular principles This amendment can be seen as the expression of this broad-based sensitivity (Gönenç 2004, 100).

Derogation of the Exercise of Fundamental Rights and Freedoms

According to the Constitution, in times of war, mobilization, martial law, or state of emergency, the exercise of fundamental rights and freedoms can be partially or entirely suspended, and even measures which derogate the guarantees stipulated in the Constitution (Art 15) can be taken. "Suspension" or "derogation", refers to a much wider range of intervention in freedoms than "limitation". Namely, in "extraordinary regimes" such as times of war, mobilization, martial law or a state of emergency [fundamental rights and freedoms may be restricted in broader terms than usual, and their exercise may be partially or entirely suspended (Sağlam 1982, 180–181). The TCC describes suspension of the fundamental rights and freedoms as postponement of their exercise for a certain period of time (TCC E. 1992/36, K. 1993/4).

On the other hand, Article 15 stipulates three principles to protect the fundamental rights and freedoms under extraordinary regimes. Firstly, measures taken under states of exception will not violate Turkey's obligations under international law. This principle refers to international treaties and agreements duly put into effect in the area of fundamental rights and freedoms and general principles of international law. Secondly, measures must be taken to the extent required by the exigencies of the situation, i.e. conform with the principle of proportionality. Thirdly, rights and freedoms named in the second paragraph may not be violated even under states of exception. Accordingly, a right to life, and the integrity of his or her material and spiritual entity shall be inviolable, except where death occurs through a lawful act of warfare; no one may be compelled to reveal his or her religion, conscience, thought or opinion, nor be accused on account of them; offences and penalties may not be made retroactive, nor may anyone be held guilty until so proven by a court judgment. Hence, the Constitution draws up an untouchable core area composed of a few rights and freedoms. However, this core area serves no useful purpose because the Constitution disallows judicial review of decree-laws issued during states of exception.

Prohibition to Abuse Fundamental Rights and Freedoms

The Constitution prohibits the abuse of fundamental rights and freedoms to endanger the state. According to Article 14, revised in 2001, no one may use constitutional rights and freedoms in order to violate the indivisible integrity of the state's territory and nation, and endanger the existence of the democratic and secular order of the Turkish Republic based upon human rights.

The second paragraph of Article 14 stipulates that any of the provisions of this Constitution shall not be interpreted in a manner that enables the state or individuals to destroy the fundamental rights and freedoms embodied in the Constitution or to stage an activity with the aim of restricting them more extensively than stated in the Constitution.

The second paragraph repeats, almost verbatim, Article 17 of the ECHR. While Article 17 of the ECHR basically safeguards the fundamental rights and freedoms in the Convention against their destruction or limitation to a greater extent than is provided for in the Convention, the first paragraph of Article 14 of the Turkish Constitution aims first and foremost at preventing the destruction of the state, as well as the democratic and secular republic, through the exercise of rights and freedoms in the Constitution (Gönenç 2004, 102).

Protection of Fundamental Rights and Freedoms

The fundamental rights and freedoms may be protected by extra judicial and judicial mechanisms.

The Petition Committee, The Human Rights Inquiry Committee, and The Committee on Equal Opportunity Between Man and Woman in the TGNA, the Human Rights Institution of Turkey and the Ombudsperson may be considered extra judicial mechanisms in Turkey. The Petition Committee receives all kinds of complaints against administrative acts. The Human Rights Inquiry Committee, founded in 1990, scrutinizes allegations regarding human rights violations and prepares annual reports. The Committee on Equal Opportunity Between Woman and Man, formed in 2009, investigates claims concerning violations of gender equality and discrimination. We should note that the committees do not have significant influence on protecting human rights for two reasons. Firstly, they are composed of political party groups in Parliament that are represented in proportion to their number of members. Thus, the political party which forms the government holds a majority in these committees. Secondly, the decisions of the committees are not binding.

The Human Rights Institution of Turkey was founded in 2012 to work on matters relating to the protection and promotion of human rights. However, this institution is designed as a state organization, i.e. it is affiliated with the office of the Prime Minister. Members are appointed at the discretion of the government. The impartiality and independence of the institute is not guaranteed.

The institution of the Ombudsperson or Ombudsman, charged with acting as a mediator between state and citizens, and with assessing complaints about the functioning of the administration, was founded in Turkey in 2012 in conformity with the constitutional amendment of 2010. The institution of the ombudsperson is established under the TGNA Presidency. The Constitution does not provide strong autonomy for this institution. The Chief Ombudsperson shall be elected by the TGNA for 4 years by a "simple majority" (receiving the greatest number of votes). The law provides for five ombudsmen to work under the chief ombudsperson, a secretary, and other personnel. Appointments have already been criticized, calling into question the effectiveness of the new institution. One instance has been the election of a judge, with a history of failing to respect standards of human rights, being elected Chief Ombudsman, while other ombudsmen have ties with the ruling party.

As a matter of fact, a thumping majority of human rights violations stem from state actions. This is why, national human rights bodies must be absolutely independent from state institutions and political power, because a potential violator cannot play a protective role at the same time. The Paris Principles establish the same criteria for national human rights institutions (Human Rights Watch 2012). Accordingly, we argue that the newly established human rights institutions contradict the spirit and essence of the Paris Principles and therefore will most probably be ineffective in protecting rights.

Another instrument for protecting human rights in Turkey is ordinary judiciary procedure. Turkey is part of the international human rights systems. Turkey signed the ECHR in 1954, recognized the right of an individual to have a recourse to the European Commission of Human Rights in 1987, and accepted the jurisdiction of the ECtHR in 1989. Additionally, Turkey ratified the Convention on the Elimination of the All Forms of Discrimination against Women in 1985, the European Convention for the Prevention of Torture and Inhuman or Degrading Treatment or Punishment in 1988, the United Nations Convention against Torture and Other Cruel, Inhuman or Degrading Treatment or Punishment in 1988, and the European Social Charter in 1989. More recently, Turkey has become party to the International Covenant on Civil and Political Rights; the International Covenant on Economic, Social and Cultural Rights, the Convention on the Elimination of All Forms of Racial Discrimination, the Convention on the Rights of the Child; and the Protocol Six of the European Convention on Human Rights concerning the death penalty. Turkey also ratified 35 ILO Treaties.

Turkey's integration into international human rights systems, e.g. the ECHR system, instigated the adoption of some constitutional and statutory rules in the country. For this purpose, in 2004, Parliament re-established the position of international treaties concerning human rights within domestic law. According to the original version of Article 90.5 of the Constitution, "*International agreements duly put into effect bear the force of law. No appeal to the Constitutional Court shall be made regard to these agreements, on the grounds that they are unconstitutional*". However, the formulation of this provision has raised some problematic issues since the era of the 1961 Constitution. The confusion derived from the prohibition to appeal to the Constitutional Court against an international agreement. Some authors have interpreted this provision as: 'international agreements had the same value and force with laws' (Özbudun and Yazıcı 2004, 32). Another group of authors have argued that the prohibition to appeal to the Constitutional Court for the international agreements put them in a different position in the legal system. Because it was not possible to annul international agreements with a *lex posterior* or *lex specialis* domestic law, they became embodied of a common will of states or common cultural heritage (Batum 1990, 261). Besides an intention to eliminate this hot argument in the constitutional legal literature, the necessity of adaptation of the EU regulations into the domestic law as a candidate country led the TGNA to make an addition to Article 90.5 in 2004. According to the new provision, "*In case of contradiction between international agreements regarding basic rights and freedoms approved through proper procedure and domestic laws, due to different provisions on the same issue, the provision of international agreements shall be considered*". Hence, the amendment made it clear that international human rights agreements have priority over domestic laws (Gönenç and Esen 2006, 490–497). However, if an international treaty conflicts with the Constitution, the latter will still be binding.

Additionally, the TGNA changed some of the statutes in order to protect fundamental rights and freedoms in domestic law in accordance with the decisions of the ECtHR. Hence, in 2002 the Code of Civil Procedure and the Code of Penal Procedure, in addition to the Code of Administrative Procedure in 2003, were amended to allow for retrial in light of the decisions of the ECtHR for civil, criminal and administrative law cases. In 2011, a new Law on the Establishment and Rules of Procedure of Constitutional Court also introduced the possibility of retrials for the Constitutional Court's decisions on dissolutions of political parties and trials of statesmen, in a process known as the "Grand Tribunal". This is an important step to render the jurisprudence of the ECtHR directly applicable to the legal system.

We should also add that, the institution of "constitutional complaint", the so called "individual application" in the Constitution, was introduced to the Turkish legal system with the 2010 constitutional amendments. This enables individuals to access to the Constitutional Court directly on the grounds that one of their fundamental rights and freedoms, guaranteed by the Constitution together with the ECHR, is being violated by public authorities. The Court began to accept complaints under this provision in September 2012.

The Turkish Constitutional Court's Approach on Fundamental Rights and Freedoms

In this part, we will discuss the TCC's approach on some specific issues. A very wide range of the Court decisions are related to the fundamental rights and freedoms and exhaustive discussion of all case law would clearly exceed the limits of this paper. Therefore, we have chosen four specific issues that have proven controversial in Turkey. That is to say, we will argue the TCC's approach on fundamental rights and freedoms within the framework of the decisions on "gender equality", "freedoms of political parties", "social rights" and "emergency-law decrees". In this way, we will argue for freedoms of political parties which are part of the freedom of association, in addition to union rights and freedoms under "social rights" which acquire special importance in a democratic regime.

Gender Equality

Both the 1961 and 1982 Constitutions describe the principle of equality as "equality before law". According to Article 10.1 of the 1982 Constitution "*All individuals are equal without any discrimination before the law, irrespective of language, race, colour, sex, political opinion, philosophical belief, religion and sect, or any such considerations.*" Hence, the Constitution places importance on the "prohibition of gender discrimination" combined with the principle of "general equality" (Öden 2003b, 126–133). This particular prohibition clearly outlaws discrimination against women. Sensitivity on discrimination against women has been increasingly growing in Turkey, as we observe, in many other countries. As a result of this sensibility, a new paragraph was added in the form of "*Women and men have equal rights. The state shall have the obligation to ensure that this equality exists in practice*" to Article 10 of the Constitution in 2004, and the sentence, "*Measures taken for this purpose shall not be interpreted as contrary to the principle of equality.*" was inserted in 2010. Moreover, within the 2010 amendments, a sentence that specifies that "*the family is based on the equality between the spouses*" was added to Article 41 of the Constitution regarding "protection of family." We should also note that Turkey is a party of some of the international human rights treaties concerning women, such as CEDAW *(Convention on the Elimination of all Forms of Discrimination Against woman)*. Hereinafter, we will discuss the TCC's jurisprudence concerning equality between men and women, and how the Court has responded to the increasing attention of society on this matter.

First of all, we should remark that decisions of the TCC regarding discrimination between men and women generally rest on the principle of "general equality". The TCC reads the equality clause in the Constitution as follows: "*the principle of equality in Art 10 provides equal treatment between people who are legally in equal status and allows to be treated differently of those who are in different status*". This does not mean that every person will be treated equally if they have a different status. On the contrary, the Court construes that, "equals should be treated equally and nonequals should be treated according to their differences" (Öden 2003b, 323–334).

In some cases, the TCC declared unconstitutional, statutory provisions that deprived women from some of their rights. In 1990, the Court annulled the provision of the Civil Code of 1926, which grants a husband the right to exercise control over his wife's professional or artistic activities, based on the principle of equality in Article 10 and right to work in Article 49 of the Constitution (TCC E. 1990/30, K. 1990/31). The Court ruled in this case that equality between men and women should be construed as to make women equal with men when they are in a "similar" situation. If women are deprived from some of the rights which are afforded to men in similar situations, it will be contrary to the principle of equality. However, different legal regulations result from dissimilarities between the two genders, such as allowing women maternity leave, shall not infringe the principle of equality (TCC E. 1990/30, K. 1990/31). Additionally, we should note that in this case, the Court explicitly paid attention to provisions of the Universal UN Declaration of Human Rights, the ECHR and its Protocol 7 and the CEDAW in interpretation of the principle of equality according to the Constitution.

The TCC decreed unconstitutional in 1996 the provision of Penal Code of 1926, which discriminated between men and women in the definition of adultery as a criminal offence in favor of men on the ground that such differences infringed the principle of equality. Indeed, Article 440 and Article 441 of the Penal Code provided that, while one sexual act with a man other than her husband was sufficient for a conviction of adultery for a married woman, a married man could not be convicted of adultery unless it was proven that he was living with another woman other than his wife. According to the Court, this statutory difference concedes a legal advantage to husband against his wife. There is no justifiable cause to concede such an advantage to a husband in conjugal community, because there is no difference between husband and wife in terms of mutual fidelity obligation. Legislators cannot use their discretionary power to discriminate between husband and wife, since they are in the same position as parties of conjugal community (TCC E. 1996/15, K.1996/34). In this case, the TCC interpreted the principle of constitutional equality taking into consideration provisions of the Universal UN Declaration of Human Rights, the ECHR, and the CEDAW. Further, the Court stated expressly that there is no fundamental difference between constitutional and international standards regarding the principle of equality and sexual discrimination.

Two years later, the TCC also decreed the unconstitutionality of Article 441 of the Penal Code. The Court stated that a wife should have in the same legal status as a husband in the conjugal community. Despite the fact that adultery is not an offence anymore for a husband, it is still a crime for wife in the Penal Code. This is incongruous with the principle of equality provided in Article 10 of the Constitution (TCC E. 1998/3, K. 1998/28). In this case, the Court reads the principle of equality between man and woman in accordance with its previous decision referring international human rights standards.

In another case in 2007, the TCC declared unconstitutional the statutory provision that stipulates that women working in agriculture, in the position of householder, are to benefit from compulsory social security. According to the Court, this provision violates Articles 10.2 and 60 of the Constitution, which guarantees the principles of equality and right to social security (TCC E. 2003/81, K. 2007/50).

In 2011, the TCC declared unconstitutional a provision of the Act of Family Name of 1934, stipulating that a child will take his father's family name, even in cases of annulment of marriage, or divorce, even if child was placed under his mother's custody. The Court came to the conclusion that spouses have the same legal rights and responsibilities during marriage and divorce. The provision granting only the father the right to choose his children's last name as part of custodial rights prompts discrimination between men and women based on sex, as well as between wife and husband (TCC E. 2010/119, K. 2011/165). The Court also based its legal ground on the CEDAW, International Covenant on Civil and Political Rights, ECHR and ECtHR decisions, together with the Constitution (TCC E. 2010/119, K. 2011/165).

Nevertheless, the Court often tends to interpret the principle of equality, regarding women, to limit their rights rather than validate them. The TCC acts as protectively as possible of women, if the issue fits within the traditional understanding of patriarchal Turkish Society. Yet, it acts as conservatively as possible if the identity of woman threatens family values. The Court bases its decisions on "public interest" and "public safety" concepts. On the other hand, in some of its decisions we observe an egalitarian approach, however this has not been consistent.

The Court's conservative approach may be noted clearly in cases concerning a woman's right to use her maiden name during marriage. Under Article 153 of the old Turkish Civil Code of 1926, which is no longer in force, a married woman had to bear her husband's name throughout her married life. The provision was altered in 1997, enabling married women to keep their maiden names in front of their husband's surname. The Civil Code of 2002 repeats this provision verbatim in Article 187. The unconstitutionality of both provisions were reviewed by the TCC in 1998 and 2011, respectively.

Meanwhile, the original provision of Article 153 of the Civil Code of 1926, stating "*Married women shall bear their husband's name…*" was brought in front of the European Commission of Human Rights by Ayşe Ünal Tekeli in 1995. The ECtHR reached a verdict in 2004 by taking into account final version of the relevant article (Ünal Tekeli v. Turkey 2004; Leventoğlu Abdülkadiroğlu v. Turkey 2013; *Tuncer Güneş v. Turkey 2013*; *Tanbay Tüten* v. *Turkey* 2013).

In its first verdict, the TCC stated that, "*The rule according to which married woman bears her husband's name derives from certain social realities and is the result of the codification of certain customs that have formed over centuries in Turkish society. According to the family law doctrine, the purpose of the rule is to protect women, who are "created differently" from men, strengthen family bonds, nurture the prosperity of the marriage, and to prevent bicephalous authority within the family. For the sake of protecting family union the legislature has recognised the priority of the husband's family name over the wife's. Considerations of public interest and policy have been decisive. Moreover, under the new provision women are now allowed to keep their maiden name in front of their surname.*

Furthermore, the principle of equality within the meaning of Article 10 of the Constitution does not mean that everyone is subject to the same rules of law. The special characteristics of each person or each group of persons may reasonably justify the application of different rules of law…" (TCC E. 1997/61, K. 1998/59).

The grounds on which the Court based its decision seem legally weak. The Court failed to explain how the values of family union can be reflected by choosing the husband's surname as the family name, but not just as well by choosing the wife's surname or a joint name chosen by the couple. As the ECtHR states in its Tekeli case (2004), the objective of reflecting family union through a joint family name cannot provide a justification for the gender-based difference in treatment (Ünal Tekeli v. Turkey 2004).

A case concerning the same issue was brought one more time before the TCC in 2009. The Court concluded the case in October 2011. According to the Court, this rule was legislated for the sake of public interest and public order, such as the protection of the family union and the strengthening of family bonds, keeping population records, and designating parentage. According to the Court, the disputed provision achieves continuity of the union and integrity of the family, which is the essence of Turkish society. The legislator has discretionary power to provide public order and public interest, thus the provision does not infringe the principle of the rule of law. Nevertheless, the TCC reiterates its description of the principle of equality and concludes that the provision does not violate Article 10 of the Constitution. The Court indirectly accepts that a last name is an inherent fundamental right however the legislator can limit this right for the reasons of public order and public interest (TCC E. 2009/85, K. 2011/49). Even though the TCC rests its arguments on considerations of public order and public interest, it does not go any further to interpret these concepts. So, all argumentation based on public interest and order falls short and vague. The Court also concludes that the provision does not conflict with Article 13 of the Constitution, which provides criteria to restrict fundamental rights and freedoms.

Finally, in this case the TCC deliberately ignores Article 90 of the Constitution. As we have mentioned above, according to Article 90, in case of a conflict between international agreements in the area of fundamental rights and freedoms duly put into effect, and domestic laws, due to differences in provisions on the same matter, the provisions of international agreements shall prevail. Since Turkey is part of the CEDAW and the ECHR systems, these conventions and the ECtHR rulings are binding in domestic law. This is why, the TCC should interpret the Constitution in conformity with the Conventions and the decisions of the European Court. Unfortunately, in this case the Court disregarded the European Court's precedent on this issue, i.e. Ünal Tekeli case (Öden and Esen 2013, 817–836). In this respect, we may observe a remarkable difference in approach between this case and other three decisions of the Court we have indicated above.

We should note that the same issue regarding the constitutionality of Article 187 of the Civil Code was brought before the TCC through individual application in 2013. This time the First Section of the Court decided that the application of the statutory provision, which the Court declared constitutional in 2011, violates Article 17 of the Constitution that guarantees the right to protect and develop material and spiritual entity of the individual (TCC 2013, 2013/2187; TCC 2014, 2013/4439). According to the Court, the Constitution requires that fundamental rights and freedoms should only be restricted by law (Art 13) in order to admit interference within Article 17 of the Constitution that meets the requirement of legality, it should be bounded by law. The First Section states that according to the ECtHR disallowing married women to keep their maiden names is incongruous with the ECHR. Additionally the TCC notes that the International Covenant on Civil and Political Rights (Art 23.4) and the CEDAW (Art 16.1-g) proscribe to provide equality between man and woman and prevent discriminations against women. Hence, the Court states that the aforementioned provision conflicts with the ECHR, International Covenant on Civil and Political Rights and the CEDAW.

The TCC interprets Article 90.5 of the Constitution that refers international agreements regarding human rights. According to the Court, Article 90.5 of the Constitution implicitly eliminates enforceability of a law (implied abrogation) that is in conflict with international agreements concerning fundamental rights. The Court states that, "*...In accordance with the fifth paragraph of Article 90 of the Constitution, agreements are part of our legal system and they can be applied as laws. According to the same paragraph, should a conflict between a statutory provision and an international agreement provision regarding fundamental human rights exist in practice, it must be prevailed agreement provision. This is an implied abrogation rule that eliminates the application capability of a statutory provision which is inconformity with an international agreement provision regarding fundamental rights and freedoms*" (TCC 2013, 2013/2187; TCC 2014, 2013/4439). Thus, in the present case, domestic courts should adjudicate the dispute regarding married woman's maiden name according to the provisions of international agreements instead of Article 187 of the Law No. 4271. The judgements of the courts which are not predicated on the ECHR and the ECtHR case-law are interference without any legal basis with the right to use a name which is guaranteed within the spiritual existence of the applicant. The Court concludes that there is a violation of Article 17 of the Constitution that guarantees the right to protect and improve her spiritual existence.

Clearly, the Court's verdict is a positive development towards protection and implementation of women's rights. Also this decision yields up the importance of the international human rights agreements, particularly the ECtHR precedents regarding protection of women's right. It is also noteworthy that the Court reads Article 90.5 of the Constitution as a conflict-norm, that is to say, domestic law which is in conflict with an international agreement regarding human rights or an international court's precedents must be eliminated.

However we may not draw a conclusion that this decision illustrates a radical change of the TCC's approach on equality between man and woman and women's rights. The Court did not discuss constitutionality of the provision regarding married woman's last name. The verdict is based on the application of Article 187 of the Civil Code instead of ECHR and the ECtHR precedents. The First Section of the Court disregards its previous decision (TCC E. 2009/85, K. 2011/49) taken by the General Assembly. Accordingly, we may not claim that the First Section deems that Art 187 of the Civil Code infringes the Constitution (Art 10, 11 and 17). Yet, it is not clear that the decision taken by the First Section will be followed by the General Assembly of the Court. To put another way, the decision of the First Section does not suggest a change of the TCC's conservative approach on gender equality and women's rights matters.

In fact, some other decisions of the TCC illustrate the Court's conservative approach has gained continuity as a general trend. To give an example, the TCC also ruled constitutional the provision of the Civil Code of 1926 that requires a judge's permission for a married woman take on debt for the benefit of her husband. According to the Court, the intent of the law was to protect the wife and the family union by preventing the wife from falling into debt without being aware of its extent and the consequences thereof. Accordingly, this provision aims at assuring family union by inhibiting the deterioration of the wife's economic power under the influence of her husband. The provision intends to ensure public interest through protecting the family union and by conforming with the requirements of the democratic social order.[4] Hence, the Court adopted once more a traditional view towards woman.

In another case the TCC deemed the provision of Law No.1593 dated 4 July 2012 that bans C-section surgery upon mothered the provision of Law No.1593 to perform C-section surgery without a medical necessity unless a vaginal delivery would put baby's or mother's life or health at risk does not violate the Constitution (TCC E. 1997/27, K. 1998/43; E. 1999/47, K. 1999/46). This provision prevents a mother to choose a delivery method. According to the Court, the law aims at providing a healthy way of living by restricting practices which is deemed unhealthy. This aim is a result of the positive duty of the state which is obliged by the Constitution (Art 5, 17 and 56). The state has a positive obligation to protect everybody's right to life from public authorities, other persons, and person's own actions. An individual may have a limited disposing power on his/her own body. Disposing of a third person's actions towards an individual is barred even when the individual concerned permits this action. For instance in the field of health a patient cannot force the physician to perform a treatment or an operation that the physician does not approve. This is why determination of treatment method is mainly physician's duty and right as well. Physician who will determine a treatment method cannot be forced by the patient to a diagnosis and/or treatment that conflicts with the physician's scientific opinion.

Accordingly, the Court views the C-section delivery in conformity with the law as a "disposing power" that can be applied only in case of a "medical necessity", but not a method that may be performed according to the joint preference of the patient and the physician. The TCC entirely disregards the patient's choice and restricts the physician's preference. It does not strike a balance between the patient's right to choose the treatment and the state's obligation to protect the right to live of the patient and the physician's right not to perform a method that he/she will not approve. We should note that the Court does not refer in the decision constitutional provisions and international human rights documents concerning women's rights. In sum the TCC disregards domestic and international standards.

[4] Decisions of the TCC: E.1997/27, K.1998/43, 30 June 1998, Official Gazette 15 January 2000-23934; E.1999/47, K.1999/46, 28 December 1999, Official Gazette 10 March 2000-23989.

Conversely, the TCC upholds some statutes which recognize certain social rights applicable only to women, for the purpose of the "protection of woman and family union" (TCC E. 2006/166, K. 2009/113). The Court has decreed "special treatment" for protected categories in several decisions relating to woman's status in the family. However, even these decisions reflect the traditional and conservative view of the Court. In a case in 2006, the Court reviewed the constitutionality of a provision of the Labor Code, which allows a woman to demand severance pay from her employer if she terminates her contract within a year of the date she got married. However the law does not grant the same right to a man in the same situation. The TCC concluded that the provision is not unconstitutional, because it aims at protecting women and the family union. According to the Court, social realities, such as the responsibilities and duties that women assume in society and the family, may demand the legislation of different rules and implementations to the advantage of woman employees. These kinds of regulations shall not infringe the principle of equality (TCC E. 2006/156, K. 2008/125). The Court also grounded its decision in the CEDAW, the European Social Charter and other international treaties and recommendation resolutions concerning social matters together with the Constitutional provisions, intended to protect woman and family, i.e. Articles 10, 41 and 50. However, in this case the Court misses the point. The provision aims at protecting social rights of the female employees who have to abandon work life after the marriage, not safeguarding family. In other words, the purpose of the legislature is not to protect family, but to remedy de facto inequality in work life against female employees.

The TCC's decision regarding the legal protection provided to female children in the Retirement Fund Law may be given as another example. As stipulated in the law, female children are eligible unless they are married, but male children must be disabled or under the age of 21 in order to qualify as the principle beneficiary. According to the Court, the Constitution and its laws embrace equality between men and women as a fundamental principle. Nonetheless, this principle cannot be implemented in Turkish society due to historical, economical, and social reasons. Because of the economic disempowerment, lack of education and traditional values, it is necessary to support women's status in society through affirmative jurisprudence and legislation. So, the Court concluded that such protective measures cannot be considered discrimination (TCC E. 1996/10, K. 1996/40).

Consequently, the Court's approach on woman is problematic, because it validates special protective treatments for women only in their role as a wife, a mother, or a daughter but not as an individual. The TCC uses the principle of affirmative action, aimed at protecting women in a traditional family structure, in order to provide them minimum economic independency. Here we should note that, the TCC considers that women require special protection because of the requirements of the traditional family, but not due to their unequal position throughout history.

Freedom of Political Parties

The 1961 Constitution recognized political rights and freedoms and for the first time, political parties. The Constitution also imposed ideological bans on political party activities, inspired by an understanding of militant democracy found in the German Constitution. The Constitution stipulated that the Constitutional Court had the power to dissolve political parties which engaged in activities contrary to the constitutional prohibitions (Art 57(1)). The 1982 Constitution embraced the same approach. However, this Constitution extended bans on political parties excessively (Article 68–69). Moreover, the 1983 Law on Political Parties (LPP) no. 2820 broadened constitutional bans.[5] Provisions concerning political parties in the 1982 Constitution underwent significant changes in 1995 and 2001. Namely, these alterations narrowed bans and made the dissolution of political parties more difficult (Öden 2003(a), 54–102). Article 68.4 of the 1982 Constitution stipulates that, "*The statutes and programs, as well as the activities of political parties shall not be in conflict with the independence of the state, its indivisible integrity or with its territory, nation, human rights, the principles of equality and the rule of law, sovereignty of the nation, the principles of the democratic and secular republic; they shall not aim to protect or establish class or group dictatorship or dictatorship of any kind, nor shall they incite citizens to crime.*"

According to Article 69 of the Constitution a political party may be banned in three circumstances: Firstly, if the status and program of a party are in conflict with the principles set forth in Article 68.4. Secondly, if the activities of a political party violate the principles of the Constitution in Article 68.4 and have become a center for the execution of such activities. Thirdly, if a political party accepts financial aid from foreign states, international institutions, persons, and/or corporate bodies. Under the first two circumstances the TCC may impose a lesser penalty instead of dissolving the party altogether. The concerned party may be deprived of state aid wholly or in part, depending on intensity of its actions (Article 69.7. The TCC may sentence a political party to closure by two thirds majority (Article 149.3).

To date, the TCC has dissolved 14 political parties since the 1982 Constitution came into force. Only five of them were prohibited in the 1961 Constitution era. The vast majority of its decisions were based on grounds of violation of the principles of integrity of the state with its territory and nation and/or secular state. So we will discuss the Court's approach to political parties, limiting the discussion to cases involving the violation of the principle of indivisible integrity of the state with its territory and nation.

The 1982 Constitution refers to the principle of 'indivisible integrity of state with its territory and nation' not only in Article 68.4 as one of the elements that political

[5] The Provisional Article 15 of the Constitution exempted laws adopted between 12 September 1980 and the date of the formation of the Bureau of the Turkish Grand National Assembly which was to convene following the first general elections from the constitutional review. Accordingly, Law on Political Parties was the scope of this prohibition. The constitutional provision was finally lifted in 2010.

parties must obey, but also in the preamble and several provisions. To give an example, the Preamble denotes "*the eternal existence of the Turkish nation and motherland and the indivisible unity of the Turkish state*" in the first paragraph and "*the recognition that no protection shall be accorded to an activity contrary to Turkish national interests and, the principle of the indivisibility of the existence of Turkey with its state and territory*" in the fifth paragraph. Also Article 3.1 stipulates that the Turkish state, with its territory and nation, is an indivisible entity and prohibits any alteration of this provision. Furthermore, the Constitution in Article 14.1 considers the exercise of the rights and freedoms recognised in the Constitution in the form of activities aiming to violate this principle as abuse of fundamental rights and freedoms.[6] Furthermore, the Constitution in Article 14.1 considers whether the rights and freedoms recognised in the Constitution could be exercised to denounce this principle as an abuse of fundamental rights. The LPP of 1983 also specifies the principle of indivisible integrity of the state in an even more restrictive way. For example, political parties are banned from aiming and acting to change the principle of the unitary state (Article 80). This prohibits claiming the existence of national, religious, cultural, racial and linguistic minorities in the country, aiming and acting to destroy national unity through creating minorities by means of protecting, developing and disseminating other languages and cultures aside from that of the Turkish language and culture, using other languages than Turkish (Article 81), and aiming to and acting for regionalism or racism (Article 82).

The TCC interpreted the principle of 'indivisible integrity of the state with its territory and nation' in the matter of the dissolution of political parties narrowly, in accordance with the Constitution and the PPA, giving priority to the protection of ideology over rights and freedoms (Aslan 2002, 11).

The Court construed the principle of "indivisible integrity of the state with its territory" in a manner consistent with the unitary state. According to the Court, the unitary state is the basis of the existence of the Turkish nation and this basic principle cannot be compromised or refuted (TCC E. 1991/2, K. 1992/1; E. 1992/1, K.1993/1). According to the reading of the Court, the principle excludes the creation of ethnic or religious minorities and, the advocating of regionalism, and racism. However, one may argue that the principle of indivisible territorial integrity of the state in fact refers to nation-state. In a nation-state, this principle not only is one of the central elements of the unitary state but also federalism and regionalism. Since the Constitution does not explicitly prohibit some of these nation-state formations, the constitutionality of the TCC's interpretation, based on Article 80 of the PPA, is controversial (Özbudun 2010, 128).

The TCC also applied this restrictive interpretation of the principle of indivisible integrity of the state with its nation. The Court asserted that to allocate certain territory to a race group and to give special rights to an ethnic group would mean dividing up national unity. In the case of the United Communist Party of Turkey in 1991,

---

[6] The Constitution also refers to this principle in Article 28.4 (freedom of press), Article 58 (protection of the youth), Article 81 and 103 (oath text that deputies and the president of the republic must take to assume office) and Article 130.4 (institutions of higher education).

the Court ruled that some statements in the statute and program of the political party referencing the 'Kurdish question' encouraged separatism and the division of the Turkish nation. The Court deemed that this was in violation of the principle of the indivisible integrity of the state, and closed the party permanently shortly after it was founded (TCC E.1990/1, K.1991/1). The TCC used similar legal grounds, i.e. the undermining of the territorial integrity and the unity of the nation, to ban political parties in later decisions, on the grounds that said parties had intended : "*to encourage separatism, to create minorities within the country while stating the existence of the 'Kurdish nation' as separate from the 'Turkish nation', to advocate the establishment of a Kurdish-Turkish federation, to defend self-determination for the so-called 'Kurdish people' and religious minorities, to conduct judicial and educational services in Kurdish language*" (TCC E.1992/1, K.1992/1; E.1993/1, K.1993/2; E. 1993/3, K.1994/2) through statements in their statutes and programs (TCC E.1990/1, K.1991/1; E.1993/1, K.1993/2) and/or their activities (TCC E.1992/1, K.1992/1; E. 1992/1, K.1993/1). In this context, the Court differentiates between culture and politics. According to the Court, there are different cultural groups that freely follow their own traditions. To follow a tradition is permissible, however to make political claims is illegitimate as it gives rise to separatism (Kogacioğlu 2003, 265). According to the Court, the definition of 'minorities' in Turkey is restricted to non-Muslim communities, e.g. Armenians, Orthodox Greeks, and Jews, as these are the only groups mentioned by the Lausanne Treaty, which recognized the foundation of the Turkish state with its current borders. Therefore other ethnic groups, such as Kurds, which are not recognized in the treaty, could not be considered as minorities. The TCC also established the existence of a close relationship between democracy, the existence of the state, and established ideology. According to the Court, political activities that aim to demolish the state should not be considered as an exercise of rights and freedoms (TCC E. 1993/3 K.1994/2; E.1995/1, K.1996/1; E. 1999/1, K.2003/1).

The Court makes good use of the Convention, sometimes emptying its content, only to justify its own, conflicting, ideology-based rationale. For instance in some cases the Court made a controversial interpretation stating that to argue for a national and unitary state based on ethnic differences is forbidden by international human rights documents, such as Articles 11 and 17 of the ECHR. The Court, however, did not propose a persuasive explanation (TCC E. 1993/1, K. 1993/2; E. 1993/3, K. 1994/2; E. 1996/1, K. 1997/1). In the Socialist Party case (TCC E. 1991/2, K. 1992/1), without discussing differences or common points of the Convention and the Constitution, it held that 'there is no doubt that the activities of the Socialist Party were found to be in breach of the Constitution, and will thus also be in violation with the provisions of this Convention'.

To sum up, according to the TCC the principle of the indivisible integrity of the state with its territory and nation is comprised of 'independence and unitary of the state, territorial integrity, equality among citizens, prevention to create minorities, prohibition of regionalism and racism. The Court reads this principle in accordance with the restrictive provisions of the PPA (Kaboğlu 2002, 434–435, 359–360; Öden

2003a, 120). However, The ECtHR does not construe the Convention articles concerning freedom of political parties as the TCC does. The rulings of the Strasbourg Court in cases originating from Turkey concerning the prohibition of political parties prove this argument. Indeed, the ECtHR found a violation of the Convention in all Turkish cases, except for the Welfare Party case. It is obvious that the original text of the 1982 Constitution brought heavy restrictions on political parties. The PPA was even more restrictive, imposing additional legal grounds for prohibition. However, Article 90.5 of the Constitution could raise the possibility of enabling the Constitutional Court to interpret the restrictive domestic law under a right-based approach, giving the ECHR and the ECtHR decisions priority. But the Court has not used this opportunity. It decided that the ECHR may not be directly applied and that the PPA may not be omitted for two reasons. First, the latter is *lex specialis*, and second, the Convention does not contain specific provisions to be applied on the matter of dissolution of political parties (TCC E.1996/3, K.1997/3).

The TCC's approach to the illegalization of political parties has been undergoing change in recent times. The Court has started to use the ECtHR substantially in some of recent cases, though the perception of the Court's view still continues to be controversial in some ways. We will analyze the Court's approach based on two recent dissolution cases: The Rights and Freedoms Party (Hak-Par) and Democratic Society Party (DTP). Even though the case's legal ground concerned the violation of the principle of secularism, we will also consider the Justice and Development Party (AKP) closure case, since the Court sets forth some criteria for the dissolution of a political party within.

In the case of Hak-Par, the Court used a "clear and present danger" test, and noted that statements about "the Kurdish question" in the party's statute and program should be deemed to be within the scope of freedom of expression, unless these statements pose a clear and present danger for the democratic regime. In short, political parties should not be banned in democratic countries unless they create a serious threat for the regime. Furthermore, the 1982 Constitution is predicated upon attaining the standards of contemporary civilization. This is why one may not construe that Article 68.4 of the Constitution allows the government to ban a political party because of its statute and program. Secondly, the Court did not find any evidence that Hak-Par would intend to use unlawful methods to implement its goals. The suit against the Hak-Par was brought before the Constitutional Court shortly after the party was founded. According to the TCC, any sanction based on statements in the statute and the program without testing the constitutionality of the party's activities would be a grave intervention to the freedoms of association and expression, and is not a necessary measure in a democratic society (TCC E.2002/1, K. 2008/1). Consequently, the Court dismissed the case.[7] As we see, this time the TCC followed the principles of the ECtHR and, departing from its previous

[7] However, we should note that the Constitution required three fifth majority of the TCC judges for dissolution until 2010. The decision was not made by the majority. Accordingly, it is not clear that the Court has changed its precedent in this case.

decisions, made a narrow interpretation of Article 68.4, instead reading the provision based on freedom.[8]

The TCC continues the same approach in the AKP case (TCC E. 2008/1, K. 2008/2), in which the ruling party was faced with the dissolution sanction on the grounds that the party had become a center for the execution of activities, which violated the principle of secularism. In that case, the Court clearly noted that Article 90.5 of the Constitution aims at providing parallelism between the legal order of the country, and the principles and practices of contemporary democracies. Thus, one should take international standards into consideration, in favor of freedoms. Constitutional norms, ruling cases of the ECtHR, and criteria set out by the Venice Commission regarding political parties, not only guarantee political freedoms, but also justify dissolution of political parties as a last resort to protect and strengthen the democratic order. Accordingly, the Court takes into consideration other provisions of the Constitution which emphasize the special importance of political parties. The Court, therefore, has three criteria for the dissolution of political parties. Firstly, a political party's statute, program or activities must contradict with the principles in Article 68.4 to a substantial degree. So, not just any single contradiction will be enough to dissolve a political party. Secondly, the statute, program or activities must 'aim at eliminating' the principles defined in Article 68.4. Thirdly, the statute, program or activities must present a "clear and present danger" to democracy. Evidently, the TCC goes a step further in this case than in its previous judgement and introduces, explicitly, the fundamental requirements for the banning of a political party in conformance with international law, i.e. ECtHR.[9]

The latest case, in which the TCC used the thinking of the ECtHR when deciding whether to dissolve a political party, is the DTP case. The Court unanimously dissolved DTP based on evidence that it had become a center for the execution of activities which violated the state's indivisible integrity with its territory and nation. The Court also found that the party had provided assistance and support to the Kurdistan Workers' Party (PKK), a terrorist organization (TCC E.2007/1, K.2009/4).

The TCC repeated the formulation first set out in the AKP case regarding the place of Article 90.5 of the Constitution. According to the Court, the Constitutional provisions should be interpreted in conformity with the ECHR, the ECtHR decisions,

[8] A good example concerning the TCC's ongoing hesitation about observing European standards on political parties is its recent ruling about the retrial of party dissolution cases. The Criminal Procedure Act of 2004 (Art 311) provides a right to retrial for criminal cases which are later found to be in violation of the Convention by the ECtHR. Nevertheless, the TCC, disregarded to apply this provision for dissolved parties and refused the application of the United Communist Party of Turkey for retrial in 2008 due to the lacking of a new material fact (E.2003/6, K.2008/4, 8 January 2008 (Official Gazette, 22 March 2008-26824). We should note that the TCC concluded both the case of HAKPAR and the application of the TBKP for retrial within the same month. This indicates that the Court has not fully adhered to the European standards. The TGNA was prodded to enact a provision parallel to the Criminal Procedure Act in Law of the Organisation and Trial Procedures of the Constitutional Court of 2011 to eliminate the restrictive ruling of the Court.

[9] However, the Court's ruling is controversial in AKP case but we will not discuss it since the case is based on the violation of principle of secularism.

and the principles of the Venice Commission. Besides conformity with the ECtHR rulings, the TCC indicated that the existence of multiple political parties and a diversity of political programs among said parties are necessary to provide democratic legitimacy. The TCC intensively uses some principles set forth by international institutions, such as the principle that the sanction of dissolving a political party should be used only in an exceptional situation. It referred to some of the international documents on freedom of association and terrorism such as the ECHR, the Charter of Paris, the UN Security Council resolution 1624, as well as quoting from various cases of the ECtHR, such as Karatepe, Zana, TBKP and Batasuna. The TCC stated that the international documents do not justify terrorism by any means in a democratic society and denoted the PKK as a terrorist organization, referring to the Turkish Court of Cassation's decision and the EU's list of terrorist organizations. After stating expressly that the PKK was a terrorist organization, the TCC – departing from its previous rulings – based its judgement on the DTP's support of terrorism and on its organic relationship with the PKK. The Court came to the conclusion that there was a substantial connection between the terrorist group and the political party.

The latter was using terror as an instrument to destroy the indivisible integrity of the State. This ruling was based on evidence such as: the fact that the party leaders did not condemn the PKK's terrorist activities, in fact tolerating them; the political party's views that the PKK's terrorist activities constituted a "war", "proud fight", and "rightful resistance"; the provision by some party members of weapons, supplies and information to the terrorist organization; and documents depicting the PKK's propaganda and photographs of the members of the terrorist organization, which were found in the political party's offices. At this point, the Court took lessons from the ECtHR rulings, especially the Batasuna case.

However, the TCC's second legal ground for the dissolution of the party is the violation of the principle of "indivisible integrity of the state with its territory and nation" (TCC E.2007/1, K.2009/4). Even though the Court provides a strongly worded description of this principle in its previous cases, it continues to interpret the integrity of territory and nation as a historically indispensable and fundamental element. According to the Court, repeating its previous rulings, this principle prohibits endeavouring to create minorities within the country, by region and race. Thus, the TCC notes that political parties should avoid any kind of action that might spoil this integrity. On the contrary, they should work to strengthen it. Political parties cannot act to spoil the state's indivisible integrity with its territory and nation whilst enjoying democratic rights and freedoms. Subsequently, the Court stresses that political parties which support or receive support from terrorism cannot survive as legal entities. Apart from violence or terrorism, to endeavour to create minorities within the country, through regionalism and racism, is still considered to be unconstitutional by the TCC (TCC E. 2007/1, K. 2009/4).

In this case, the Court considered both real links with terrorism as well as some of the conduct and statements of party members which were not necessarily related to terrorism, but infringed upon the principle of indivisibility nevertheless. Hence, the TCC continued to read this principle in a broad sense, citing some actions and statements of party members, which did not contain violence or even support violence.

The ECtHR adjudicates one more time in the recent HADEP case that even if a political party advocated the right to self-determination of the Kurds, this would not in itself be contrary to democratic principles and could not be equated to supporting acts of terrorism. Taking such a stance would imperil the possibility of dealing with related issues in the context of a democratic debate (Hadep and Demir 2010, para. 79). Furthermore, referring the case of Herri Batasuna and Batasuna v. Spain, the ECtHR notes that to dissolve a political party because of links between a political party and a terrorist organisation should objectively be considered as a threat to democracy.[10] The TCC refers to additional international human rights documents and uses the principles of the ECHR and the ECtHR, especially in the field of freedom of association, i.e. political parties, in its recent cases.

Even though there has been improvement, the TCC does not seem to entirely embrace the essence of the principles of the ECtHR on the matter of political parties. It seems that the TCC has recently been caught in-between the European standards and its own established more conservative approach. As I have argued regarding the DTP case, the TCC cannot make a clear distinction between actions aiming to infringe the state's integrity and actions supporting terrorist organization. A political party can aim to infringe the integrity of the state by advocating a radical change in the constitutional framework, respecting fundamental democratic principles and values. On the other hand, a political party may support violence without aiming to alter the constitutional order. However, we still may predict that the importance of the European standards on human rights to the constitutional judiciary will continue to rise.

Social Rights

The 1982 Constitution provides for the principle of the social state in Article 2. Under Article 5, the Constitution states that, "*The fundamental aims and duties of the state are; to safeguard the independence and integrity of the Turkish Nation, the indivisibility of the country, the Republic and democracy; to ensure the welfare, peace, and happiness of the individual and society; to strive for the removal of political, social and economic obstacles which restrict the fundamental rights and freedoms of the individual in a manner incompatible with the principles of justice, and of the social state governed by the rule of law, and to provide the conditions required for the development of the individual's material and spiritual entity.*"

[10] Decision of the ECtHR: Case of HADEP and Demir, Date of Judgement 14 December 2010 (Application no. 28003/03), at para 80. For a brief comparison between the DTP case of the TCC and the Batasuna case of the Spanish Supreme Court *see* Selin Esen, "How Influential Are the Standards of the European Court of Human Rights on the Turkish Constitutional System in Banning Political Parties?", *Ankara Law Review*, v.9 n.2, 2012, pp.151–152.

The Constitution thus draws up the requirements of the social state, and establishes various social rights.[11]

The TCC describes the social state as, "a state which is obliged to provide true equality, namely social justice and social balance by protecting the weak against the strong" (TCC E. 1988/19 K. 1988/33; E. 1972/2, K. 1972/28; E. 1972/16, K. 1972/49; E. 1973/38, K. 1975/23; E. 1990/27, K. 1991/2; E. 1996/17, K. 1996/38). In this context, the Court noted that this understanding of the social state requires social rights to be effectively provided (TCC E. 1976/36, K. 1977/2). In its recent decisions, the Court establishes a relationship between the principle of the social state, human dignity and social justice. According to the Court the social state aims at protecting "human dignity" and in order to achieve this goal it endeavours to establish social justice. This principle provides for an individual to maintain a dignified life which is a birthright to enjoy his/her right and power to develop his/her material and spiritual entity to this effect (TCC E. 2005/139, K. 2007/33). The social state is a state that provides at least a minimum living standard for the citizens and strikes a balance between individual and public interest. It promotes social solidarity towards the highest level, achieves social justice by protecting people who are socially and economically in a disadvantaged position (TCC E. 2011/136, K. 2012/72; E. 2011/132, K.2012/82; E. 2012/87, K.2014/41). According to the Constitutional Court, social security and social justice are the conditions for the protection of individual rights and the foundation of a state governed by the "real rule of law" (TCC E. 1972/16, K.1972/49; E. 1973/38, K. 1975/23; E. 1990/27, K. 1991/2).

As we have stated above, Article 2 of the 1982 Constitution characterizes the Republic as a social state governed by the rule of law. Hence the Court reads both principles together taking into consideration Article 5 of the Constitution. "Social state governed by the rule of law" provides a cohesion between the principles of "rule of law" and the "social state" by harmonizing individual freedom, social justice and social security with each other (TCC E. 2005/139, K. 2007/33). Article 5 of the Constitution specifies that endeavouring to provide the conditions required for the development of the individual's material and spiritual entity is among the fundamental aims and duties of the state. The aims and duties of the state include goals such as to make people happy, to ease their struggle for life, to provide them life that they will live proudly beseeming dignity (TCC E. 2006/111, K. 2006/112).

"Social state governed by the rule of law" respects human rights and freedoms, guarantees individuals to live in peace, welfare and contentment, strikes a balance between individual and society, protects workers and proved them to live humanely

[11] Under Article 2, the 1961 Constitution characterized the State as "social state" for the first time in Turkey. The Constitution included a broad list of social rights and drew up the requirements of the social state. According to the Article 10.2 of this Constitution, "The state shall remove all political, economic and social obstacles that restrict the fundamental rights and freedoms of the individual in such a way as to be irreconcilable with the principles embodied with the rule of law, individual well-being and social justice. The state prepares the conditions required for the development of the individual's material and spiritual entity". We should note that, the 1961 Constitution has a stronger emphasis on the duties of the State than Article 5 of the 1982 Constitution.

by taking social, economic and financial measures in order to ensure improvement of working life in stability, prevents unemployment, takes necessary measures in order to distribute national income equitable, protects the weak against the strong (TCC E.1999/50, K.2001/67; E.2005/56, K.2009/94; E.2008/56, K.2011/58).

We should note that some of the social rights guaranteed in the Constitution are considered negative rights, while others have a positive right character. Positive rights, such as the right to work, to earn a fair wage, social security and health may be exercised only if state takes proactive actions. These rights, recognized by the Constitution, shall not grant individuals subjective public rights that they can directly exercise per se. To put it another way, using such rights is conditional upon legal regulations in related fields legislated by the TGNA. According to Article 65 of the Constitution, "*the state shall fulfil its duties as laid down in the Constitution, in the social and economic fields, within the capacity of its financial resources, taking into consideration the priorities appropriate to the aims of these duties.*"

According to the TCC the legislature has a large discretion in the implementation of such social rights that permit or require state action. As a result the Court concluded that Parliament has a broad discretionary power in the field of social security to provide some positive rights (TCC E. 1963/138, K. 1964/71; E. 1986/16, K. 1986/25). Therefore the TCC does not consider the state's failure to promote positive social rights as unconstitutional. However, the Court does state that once the legislature provides a specific social right within the limits of "financial resources", it must include everyone involved in the law (TCC E. 1963/138, K. 1964/71).

The Court annulled statutory provisions which set a time limit to the health care provided by social security institutions. The Court underlined that there is a strong link between the rights to health and social security (Cons. Art 56 and 60), and the rights to "life" and to "protect and improve his/her material and spiritual entity" (Art 17). In other words, the right to life can be protected by establishing a right to health and social security. Thus, the TCC ruled that the state may not legislate restrictions that prevent the enjoyment of rights or make their utilisation difficult when it fulfills its duties regarding rights to health and social security (TCC E. 1990/27, K. 1991/2; E. 1996/17, K. 1996/38). Recently, the Court has gone to a step further characterizing the right to health as a "natural right". The Court states that the right to health is one of the inherent rights which is inalienable. Repeating its previous precedents, the Court establishes a relationship between the right to health and Article 17 of the Constitution, indicating that the right to "life" and the right to "protect and improve his/her material and spiritual entity" are inalienable and have strong ties with each other (TCC E. 2012/103, K.2013/105). We should acknowledge that this precedent has made a substantial contribution to the implementation of social rights.

By way of contrast, the 1961 Constitution prioritized union rights. Some of the decisions of the TCC on union rights gave rise to the general impression that the Court adopted a liberal approach in accordance with the Constitution. The TCC stated in one of its decisions that the Constitution provides two things in order for workers and individuals who are economically weak to live humanely and to improve their working life decisively. The Constitution obliges the state to protect employees, to promote labor to take measures to prevent unemployment and the exploitation of labor force. Furthermore, it recognizes certain rights for employees, including the right to establish trade unions in order to regulate and improve their living and working conditions. According to the Court, constitutional provisions concerning freedom to join a trade union ought to be understood and interpreted the way they are understood in western democracies (TCC E. 1963/336, K. 1967/29). Accordingly, the Court annulled the provisions that made union membership difficult (TCC E. 1970/48, K.1972/3), and dismissed the applications claiming unconstitutionality against the provisions which strengthen trade unions (TCC E. 1963/337, K. 1967/31).

Nevertheless, the TCC took a different approach to political and ideological prohibitions concerning trade union activities, when ruling them constitutional (TCC E. 1963/336, K. 1967/29). The Court described trade unions as "organizations which participate in the state's life in solving social and economic problems and assist the state in fulfilling its duties" (TCC E. 1963/336, K. 1967/29). Accordingly, some scholars suggest that the Court consider union rights as "functions that ought to be used depending on purpose" rather than as "freedoms" (Tanör 1978, 355).

We should also touch on the TCC's approach on the right to strike. The Court described striking as a "way of social war, according to circumstances, that has very destructive effects" and deemed law that recognized striking under some conditions, such as holding collective bargaining meetings, to be constitutional. According to the Court, to acquire a right through "social war" such as "striking" rather than "social peace" such as "collective bargaining" can never be justified and deemed appropriate for the public interest (TCC E.1963/337, K.1967/31). We should note that, even though the 1961 Constitution gave importance to union rights, the TCC did not adopt a right-based approach on the right to strike. Far from approving a right to strike, the Court found the right of a firm to lock-out to be constitutional. According to the Court, the Constitution obliged the state to strike an economic and social balance between employers and employees to take measures to prevent exploiting capital versus labor force and labor force versus capital. The goal of the democratic social state ruled by law is not to allow one class to oppress another one at the cost of development and thus create an imbalance between the classes. The state should not weaken the capitalist whilst attempting to prevent unemployment. As a requirement of fair legal order, laborers' and employers' interests should be accommodated (TCC E. 1963/336, K. 1967/29).

The original text of the 1982 Constitution, in contrast to the 1961 Constitution, substantially narrowed union rights and drew limits by imposing various political and ideological prohibitions (m. 51–54).[12]

---

[12] *See* Article 46 (the 1961 Constitution): Employees and employers are entitled to establish trade unions and federations of trade unions without having to obtain prior permission, to enroll in them as members, and to resign from such membership freely.

For those engaged in public services other than physical labor similar rights shall be regulate by law.

The by-laws, the management, and the operation of trade unions and federations thereof shall not conflict with democratic principles.

Some of the decisions of the TCC during this period that protect freedom of trade union within the limits of the Constitution merit attention. To give an example, the original text of the Constitution (Art 51) guaranteed the right to establish trade union only to labourers. The Court took this constitutional restriction into account

---

Article 51 (the original text of the 1982 Constitution): Workers and employers have the right to form labour unions and employers' associations and higher organisations, without prior permission, in order to safeguard and develop their economic and social right and the interests of their members in their labour relations. In order to form unions and their higher bodies, it shall suffice to submit the information and documents prescribed by law to the competent authority designated by law. If this information and documentation is not in conformity with law, the competent authority shall apply to the appropriate court for the suspension of activities or the dissolution of the union or the higher body.

Everyone shall be free to become a member of or withdraw from membership in a union.

No one shall be compelled to become a member, remain a member, or withdraw from membership of a union.

Workers and employers cannot hold concurrent membership in more than one labour union or employers' association.

Employment in a given workplace shall not be made conditional on being, or not being, a member of a labour union.

To become an executive in a labour union or in higher organisations of them it is a prerequisite condition that the workers should have held the status of a labourer for at least ten years.

The status, the administration, and the functioning of the labour unions and their higher bodies should not be inconsistent with the characteristics of the Republic as defined in the Constitution, or with democratic principles.

Article 51 (as amended in 2010): Employees and employers have the right to form labour unions, employers' associations and higher organizations, without obtaining permission, and they also possess the right to become a member of a union and to freely withdraw from membership, in order to safeguard and develop their economic and social rights and the interests of their members in their labour relations. No one shall be forced to become a member of a union or to withdraw from membership.

The right to form a union shall be solely restricted by law for purposes of safeguarding national security and public order and preventing crime and protecting public health and public morals and the rights and freedoms of others.

The formalities, conditions and procedures to be applied in exercising the right to form union shall be prescribed by law.

The scope, exceptions and limits of the rights of civil servants who do not have a worker status are prescribed by law in line with the characteristics of their job.

The regulations, administration and functioning of labour unions and their higher bodies should not be inconsistent with the fundamental characteristics of the Republic and principles of democracy.

Article 52 (original text of the 1982 Constitution): Labour unions, in addition to being under the general restrictions set forth in Article 13, also shall not pursue a political cause, engage in political activity, receive support from political parties or give support to them, and shall not act jointly for these purposes with associations, public Professional organisations, and foundations. The fact of engaging in labour union activities in a workplace shall not justify failure to perform one's work.

The administrative and financial supervision of labour unions by the State, and their revenues and expenditures, and the method of payment of membership dues to the labour union, shall be regulated by law.

Labour unions shall not use their revenues beyond the scope of their professional aims, and shall keep all their funds in State banks. Artical 52 was repealed in 1995.

and found the provision that fails to recognize the rights to collective bargaining and to establish union for contract personnel in the state-owned enterprises to be unconstitutional (TCC E. 1988/5, K. 1988/55; E. 1990/12, K. 1991/7). According to the TCC, legislation has a wide margin of appreciation to guarantee the right to trade unions for workers other than labourers. However, the Court found the provision that deprives labourers from trade union rights by changing their status to contract personnel unconstitutional (TCC E. 1988/5, K. 1988/55; E. 1990/12, K. 1991/7).

The constitutional amendments of 1995 and 2001 repealed some of the limitations on trade union rights. These changes also influenced the TCC's approach on this matter. For example, the Court, in a recent decision, annulled the provisions of the law that authorized the government to carry out a wide range of administrative and financial supervision on trade union activities, on the grounds that the concerned constitutional provision was revoked in 1995 (TCC E. 2009/50, K. 2011/89). The Court concluded that, maintaining trade unions and their ability to function freely in line with their objectives is an "integral part of the freedom of union".

In another case, the TCC defined unions as an "indispensable element of the democratic social state ruled by law" and stressed that the unions must be independent in order to fulfil their functions. It is noteworthy that the Court used relevant international treaties, i.e. ILO Conventions no. 98 and 151 when interpreting the Constitutional provisions concerning union rights and freedoms (TCC E. 2006/94, K. 2009/92).

Additionally, in one of its recent decisions the Court establishes a relation between the right to form a trade union and the principle of social justice. According to the TCC, workers are individually in a weak position against employer. They increase their bargaining power against entrepreneur by organizing and unionizing. They are in an active position to protect their rights and interests and solve their problems. In this regard, unionizing is an important democratic tool that serves to establish social justice (TCC E. 2013/130, K. 2014/18).

The Court reviewed the constitutionality of the statutory prohibitions regarding the right to form and join a union of some public servants. In a case, the law bans the right to form and join trade unions of civilian public servants and government officials who work in the Turkish Armed Forces. The Court stated that considering the importance of the Armed Forces in homeland defence, the Parliament has a discretionary power to prescribe peculiar regulations within the constitutional limitations in order to provide necessary strict discipline for uniformed military personnel who actively carry out homeland defence that requires using weapons. In fact, according to the Court the ILO Convention No. 87 concerning freedom of association and collective bargaining vests a discretionary power to the states, stating that "The extent to which the guarantees provided for in this Convention shall apply to the armed forces and the police shall be determined by national laws or regulations".

However, the right to form a union of civilian personnel will not infringe the military discipline. Trade unions of the civilian personnel will not affect negatively the hierarchical structure in the military institutions, since the members of these trade unions will be only civilians. Accordingly, depriving civil personnel from the right to form and join trade unions by the reason of discipline is neither a necessity, nor is conformity with the nature of the service. In fact, there is no absolute prohibition for civil servants on the right to organize unions in other democratic countries. While annulling the provision the TCC also referred Article 11 of the ECHR and Case of Demir and Baykara v. Turkey of the ECtHR stating that the right to form a union of civil servants may be subject to lawful restrictions if there are convincing and compelling reasons (TCC E. 2013/21, K. 2013/57).

The TCC reviewed the constitutionality of another similar statutory provision that prohibits all police to form and join trade unions. In this case the Court declares unconstitutional the provision for civilian personnel who work at the police department. According to the TCC civilian personnel is not principal element of the domestic security service. They only carry out tecnical and logistics services. Since these services do not require strict discipline, it is not necessary to deprive civilian personnel from the right to form a union. Disruption of these services caused by less strict discipline will not result in damages which are difficult or impossible to compensate. This is why the prohibition is not conformity with the requirements of the democratic social order.

On the other hand, the Court found the provision constitutional for the police. According to the Court, some professions including policing require strict discipline and hierarchical order. Trade unions have a potential to effect strict discipline negatively. Superior public interest to maintain the democratic social order cannot disregard potential negative effects of trade unionism on discipline for professions based on discipline and this can be a justifiable cause to ban trade unionism for these professions. The Court refers one more time the ILO Convention No. 87 and comes to the conclusion that it is not unconstitutional that legislation exercises its discretionary power to ban the right to form and join trade unions for police personnel (TCC E. 2013/130, K. 2014/18).

Constitutional amendments not only influenced the decisions of the TCC on the right to establish trade unions, but also on the right to strike. We have observed above that the TCC interpreted the "democratic social order" as "democratic order adopted by the 1982 Constitution" (TCC E. 1985/21, K. 1986/23). In the same judgement, the Court took into consideration economic interests resulting from the establishment of free trade zones together with "public interest" and, deemed constitutional the provision that prohibits employees in free trade zones to exercise the right to collective bargaining and to strike for a period of 10 years (TCC E. 1985/21, K. 1986/23). Thus the TCC interpreted the constitutional provisions prohibiting and postponing strike actions in a way that left legislation a wide margin of appreciation. We may consider that, this decision indicates the Court's extremely timid attitude regarding the right to strike.

As we have mentioned above, the TCC changed its opinion about "democratic order" and reinterpreted "democratic order adopted by the 1982 Constitution" to mean "contemporary liberal democratic order" (TCC E. 1985/8, K. 1986/27). The Court has expanded this approach and interpreted constitutional prohibitions concerning the right to strike more narrowly. Accordingly, the Court annulled a legal provision that deemed any action of workers, other than collective bargaining, to be an illegal strike warranting criminal sanctions (TCC E. 2002/71, K. 2008/44). According to the Court, the right to strike recognized by Article 54 of the Constitution is also acknowledged as the most effective fighting tool of workers in international treaties. The Constitution recognizes the right to strike for workers if a dispute arises during the collective bargaining process and prohibits some actions enumerating numerous clauses in Article 54 (2 and 7). Besides, workers can act collectively if the action is a work struggle or a form of expression. Such actions lie outside the sphere of both collective bargaining and the prohibitions against striking. Therefore, these prohibitions ought to be interpreted narrowly and the actions of workers intended to protect and improve their economic and social rights and interests in labor relations should be considered within the scope of freedoms (TCC E. 2002/71, K. 2008/44). We may remark that this case indicates the Court's changing understanding on the right to strike and that the TCC has made a significant jurisprudential contribution regarding the protection of union rights. We should also note that prohibitions on the right to strike in the Constitution (Art 54(7)) were lifted in 2010.

However, it seems that the Court has not thoroughly abandoned its restrictive approach on union rights. Indeed, the TCC ruled constitutional a legal provision that prohibits going on strike and lock-out in places of work relating domestic capital markets including the stock exchanges (TCC E. 2013/24, K. 2013/133). According to the Court, in a democratic country to recognize the right to strike and the right to lock-out when a disagreement arises between two parties is a requirement of the regime. However, there is no doubt that these fighting instruments may be subject to some limitations and restrictions when it is taken into consideration their negative impacts on national economy and public order, influence of strike to the rights of third persons who bear no relation. Strike is a very effective tool for workers to seek their rights. According to the TCC, because of the "*society's right to maintain economic welfare*" and negative impacts of the strikes on the national economy, firms, banks and citizens, banning to strike in the financial markets will not infringe the public interest. Therefore, the Court considers that financial markets are strategically important. Prohibition to strike for implementing the public interest falls within the scope of duty of the state provided in Article 49 of the Constitution[13] when it is considered economic impacts of the strike that may occur because of delays of works in the institutions.

The reasoning of the Court seems problematic. Firstly, the TCC places financial markets a "strategic importance". According to the Freedom of Association Committee of the ILO, the right to strike may be restricted or prohibited either in the public service only for public servants exercising authority in the name of the state or in essential services in the strict sense of the term, that is, services the interruption of which would endanger the life, personal safety or health of the whole or part of

[13] Article 49- Everyone has the right and duty to work.

The State shall take the necessary measures to raise the standard of living of workers, and to protect workers and the unemployed in order to improve the general conditions of labour, to promote labour, to create suitable economic conditions for prevention of unemployment and to secure labour peace.

the population (ILO 2006, para. 576). Clearly, financial sector does not fall within this definition.

Secondly, the Court creates a new right, so called the "society's right to maintain economic welfare" in order to uphold the prohibition of the right to strike. We may note that this ambiguous expression is open to dispute. In addition, the TCC remarkably excuses the prohibition the possible negative effects of the strikes to the national economy. Clearly, strikes inherently may cause undesirable and uncomfortable conditions for employers and in some cases for society as well. Right to strike will be meaningless and ineffective if it does not cause any negative consequences. As the Freedom of Association Committee has noted, "by linking restrictions on strike action to interference with trade and commerce, a broad range of legitimate strike action could be impeded. While the economic impact of industrial action and its effect on trade and commerce may be regrettable, such consequences in and of themselves do not render a service "essential", and thus the right to strike should be maintained" (ILO 2006, para. 592).

Thirdly, Article 49 of the Constitution does not provide any constitutional basis for the prohibition. On the contrary the state should provide necessary conditions for workers in order to enjoy their constitutional rights. Obviously, labor rights are very important tools in order to "raise the standard of living of workers" and "secure labour peace". We may conclude that the TCC still does not fully embrace right-based approach and international human rights standards on labor rights.

Emergency Decree-Laws

The 1982 Constitution provides for two separate types of decree-laws, namely ordinary decree-laws and emergency decree-laws. In Articles 91, 121 and 122 the Constitution establishes significant differences between the two kinds of decree-laws. While only the Council of Ministers headed by the President of the Republic may issue emergency decree-laws, the Council may pass ordinary decree-laws without the presence of the President. In other words, ordinary decree-laws may be passed with counter-signature. Unlike ordinary decree-laws, emergency decree-laws do not require a prior enabling act of the TGNA. Also they can regulate areas of civil and political rights that cannot be regulated by ordinary decree-laws. Under Article 148 of the Constitution, the constitutionality of emergency decree-laws cannot be reviewed by the Constitutional Court, while there is no such restriction for ordinary decree-laws. Once they are ratified by the Assembly however, emergency decree-laws become ordinary laws and then may be subject to judicial review. This restriction on the competence of the Constitutional Court has been criticized since some of the worst violations of human rights take place during the periods of states of emergency or martial law.[14] Also, as we have mentioned before, the restriction

[14] The 1982 Constitution stipulates two types of state of exception, i.e. state of emergency and martial law. According to the Constitution, states of exception are declared by the Council of

counteracts the untouchable core area composed of a few rights and freedoms in Article 15 of the Constitution. Given the fact that some 41 years of its 90 years Turkey has been under an extraordinary regime, such limitation on judicial review gains even greater significance.

The TCC partly eliminated adverse consequences of this restriction with two decisions in 1991 (TCC E. 1990/25, K.1991/1; E.1991/6, K.1991/20; Esen 2008, pp. 278–286; Öden 2009, 659–691). The Constitutional Court pointed out that emergency rules are limited "legal regimes" deriving from the Constitution. Accordingly, state of emergency and martial law are legal regimes within the understanding of "democratic state governed by the rule of law".[15] The Court ruled that while the Constitution recognizes the power of the government to issue decree-laws in state of emergency and martial law (Art 121 and 122), it also limits this power in various ways. That is to say, emergency decree-laws can be issued only during the time of emergency and on matters necessitated by emergency situations. If the state of emergency is declared for one part of the territory instead of throughout the country, the power to issue emergency decree-laws also is limited geographically to the regions for which the state of emergency is declared. Furthermore, the Constitution stipulated that some matters concerning emergency regime would be regulated by law.[16] In that case, such decree-laws cannot alter or repeal the law. Thereby, the TCC concluded that Article 148 of the Constitution only excludes judicial review of decree-laws issued within the foregoing limits. To put it another way, the Court accepted that it could review the constitutionality of emergency decree-laws and judge whether they exceed the limits provided in Articles 121 and 122 of the Constitution (TCC E. 1990/25, K.1991/1; E.1991/6, K.1991/20). In these cases, the Court declared unconstitutional some of the emergency decree-laws, which exceeded the limits. Notwithstanding, the TCC employs a broad interpretation of the discretionary power of the executive authority when assessing whether a decree-law provision is a "necessary measure" for the state of emergency (TCC E. 1990/25,

---

Ministers, presided over by the President of the Republic, and are immediately submitted to Parliament for approval.

[15] According to Article 2 of the Constitution "The Republic of Turkey is a democratic, secular and social state governed by the rule of law; bearing in mind the concepts of public peace, national solidarity and justice; respecting human rights; loyal to the nationalism of Atatürk, and based on the fundamental tenets set forth in the Preamble."

[16] Article 121.2 "The financial, material and labour obligations which are to be imposed on citizens in the event of the declaration of state of emergency under Article 119 and, applicable according to the nature of each kind of state of emergency, the procedure as to how fundamental rights and freedoms shall be restricted or suspended in line with the principles of Article 15, how and by what means the measures necessitated by the situation shall be taken, what sort of powers shall be conferred on public servants, what kind of changes shall be made in the status of officials, and the procedure governing emergency rule, shall be regulated by the Law on State of Emergency."

Article 122.5 "In the event of martial law, mobilization and state of war, the provisions to be applied and conduct of affairs, relations with the administration, the manner in which freedoms are to be restricted or suspended and the obligations to be imposed on citizens in a state of war or in the event of emergence of a situation necessitating war, shall be regulated by law."

K.1991/1; E.1991/6, K.1991/20). We may conclude that, the Court approaches this issue cautiously.

In 2003 the TCC enlarged the scope of its precedent. The Court ruled that the power of the government to issue emergency decree-laws was not only limited by Articles 121 and 122, but also by other relevant provisions of the Constitution (TCC E. 2003/28, K.2003/42).[17] The Court interpreted the phrase "matters necessitated by the state of emergency" in Article 121 in a broad perspective, taking all rules of the Constitution concerning emergency rule into consideration. Consequently, the Constitutional Court took into consideration Article 125.6 of the Constitution[18] and annulled the emergency decree-law, which excluded administrative acts of the governor in the state of emergency region from the scope of judicial review (TCC E. 2003/28, K.2003/42).

We should note that, this precedent of the Court made a significant contribution to protect fundamental rights and freedoms in states of emergency and martial law. Thereby, the TCC did not allow emergency regime to become either an "extra-legal regime", or to change its extraordinary character turning it into an "ordinary regime".

However, it is not clear whether the Court will review the constitutionality of emergency decree-laws with respect to the conformity of the guarantees under Article 15.2. One may suggest that if the Court enlarges the scope of the constitutional review on emergency decree-laws, then Article 148.1 of the Constitution, which exempts emergency decree-laws from judicial review, will become ineffective. This is why we believe that the best solution would be to repeal this prohibition from the Constitution.

Conclusion

The original text of the 1982 Constitution restricted the field of fundamental rights and freedoms significantly more than the 1961 Constitution. Nevertheless, many constitutional amendments, especially those made in 1995, 2001 and 2004, enlarged and strengthened the scope of fundamental rights and freedoms. Also some of the constitutional changes made in 2006 and 2010 were in favor of the rights and freedoms. One of the most important legal guarantees of the fundamental rights and freedoms in Turkey is the Constitutional Court. The institution of the "constitutional complaint", the so called the "individual application" adopted in 2010 also gives the Court much more important role in protecting fundamental rights and freedoms in the Turkish legal system. Even though the institution is newly

---

[17] Decision of the TCC: E. 2003/28, K.2003/42, 22 May 2003 (Official Gazette, 16 March 2004–25404).

[18] Article 125.6 "The law may restrict the issuing of an order on suspension of execution of an administrative act in cases of state of emergency, martial law, mobilization and state of war, or on grounds of national security, public order and public health.

established, the TCC receives many applications. However it is still premature to predict if it will be an effective judicial remedy to protect human rights since the Court continues to set case-law.

The Court generally reads constitutional provisions regarding the general regime of fundamental rights and freedoms, so as to strengthen said freedoms. The precedent of the TCC, developed for emergency regimes and emergency decree-laws, illustrates this understanding.

However, we do not always observe the same approach in other matters. For instance, the Court interprets the discretion of the legislature providing equality between men and women, and social rights broadly. Yet, the decisions of the TCC regarding gender equality generally establish a conservative approach based on traditional values that give priority to the principle of the "family and family union". According to the Court's general view, women should be protected as a "member of a family", a "mother" and a "wife", but not as an "individual".

We may also observe that the Court develops a special sensitivity concerning the political and ideological limits of the fundamental rights and freedoms, especially in the field of freedom of association. Actually, the TCC places a special emphasis on constitutional limitations concerning union rights and prohibitions on political parties. To give an example, the Court significantly curtails the legitimate field of politics concerning the "unitary state" as an integral part of the principle of 'indivisible integrity of the state with its territory and nation'. We may note that the Court's approach on equality between men and women, political party freedoms, and union rights fall far behind international standards.

Finally, the Court increasingly places weight on international documents on human rights when making its decisions. The TCC applies international norms and case-law to support its interpretation on constitutional provisions. Yet, it acts selectively when referring to international human rights treaties and the ECtHR case-law. The Court uses them only to support its decisions. We may observe this attitude especially when reviewing cases concerning gender equality and prohibitions on political parties. We may also note that sometimes the TCC misses the essence of the ECtHR rulings, as it did in the DTP case.

Bibliography

Aslan, Zühtü. 2002. Conflicting paradigms: Political rights in the Turkish constitutional court. *Critical Middle Eastern Studies* 11: 9–25.

Batum, Süheyl. 1990. *Avrupa İnsan Hakları Sözleşmesi ve İnsan Haklarına Etkileri*, PhD. Thesis, Istanbul.

Decision of the ECtHR: Case of Soering v. United Kingdom, Date of Judgement 7 July 1989. Application no. 14038/88.

Decision of the ECtHR: Case of HADEP and Demir, Date of Judgement 14 Dec 2010. Application no. 28003/03.

Decision of the ECtHR: Case of Ünal Tekeli v. Turkey, Date of Judgement 16 Nov 2004. Application no. 29865/96.

Decision of the ECtHR: Case of Leventoğlu Abdülkadiroğlu v. Turkey, Date of Judgement 28 May 2013. Application no. 7971/07.
Decision of the ECtHR: Case of Tuncer Güneş v. Turkey, Date of Judgement 3 September 2013. Application no. 26268/08.
Decision of the ECtHR: Case of Tanbay Tüten v. Turkey, Date of Judgement 10 December 2013. Application no. 38249/09.
Decision of the TCC: E. 1963/138, K. 1964/71, 11 December 1964. *Official Gazette*, 2 Apr 1965: 11969.
Decision of the TCC: E. 1963/336, K. 1967/29, 26–27 September 1967. *Official Gazette*, 19 Oct 1968: 13031.
Decision of the TCC: E. 1963/337, K. 1967/31, 19 and 20 October 1967. *Official Gazette*, 2 May 1969: 13188.
Decision of the TCC: E. 1970/46, K. 1971/24, 2 March 1971. *Official Gazette*, 4 Aug 1971: 13916.
Decision of the TCC: E. 1970/48, K.1972/3, 8 and 9 February 1972. *Official Gazette*, 19 Oct 1972: 14341.
Decision of the TCC: E. 1972/2, K. 1972/28, 23 May 1972. *Official Gazette*, 21 Nov 1972: 14368.
Decision of the TCC: E. 1972/16, K.1972/49, 17 October 1972. *Official Gazette*, 1 Mar 1973: 14463.
Decision of the TCC: E. 1973/38, K. 1975/23, 11–14 and 25 February 1975. *Official Gazette*, 3 Dec 1975: 15431.
Decision of the TCC: E. 1976/36, K. 1977/2, 25 January 1977. *Official Gazette*, 9 May 1977: 15932.
Decision of the TCC: E. 1985/8, K.1986/27, 26 November 1986. *Official Gazette*, 14 Aug 1987: 19544.
Decision of the TCC: E. 1985/21, K. 1986/23, 6 October 1986. *Official Gazette*, 14 Mar 1987: 19400.
Decision of the TCC: E. 1986/16, K. 1986/25, 21 October 1986. *Official Gazette*, 31 Jan 1987: 19358.
Decision of the TCC: E. 1988/2, K. 1988/1, 8 February1988. *Official Gazette*, 16 May 1989: 20167.
Decision of the TCC: E. 1988/19, K. 1988/33, 26 October1988. *Official Gazette*, 11 Dec 1988: 20016.
Decision of the TCC: E. 1988/5, K. 1988/55, 22 December 1988. *Official Gazette*, 25 July 1989: 20232.
Decision of the TCC: E. 1990/30, K.1990/31, 29 November 1990. *Official Gazette*, 2 July 1992: 21272.
Decision of the TCC: E. 1990/25, K.1991/1, 10 January 1991. *Official Gazette*, 5 Mar 1992: 21162.
Decision of the TCC: E. 1990/27, K. 1991/2, 17 January 1991. *Official Gazette*, 19 Aug 1991: 20965.
Decision of the TCC: E.1991/6, K.1991/20, 3 July 1991. *Official Gazette*, 8 Mar 1992: 21165.
Decision of the TCC: E. 1990/1, K.1991/1, 16 July 1991. *Official Gazette*, 28 Jan 1992: 21125.
Decision of the TCC: E. 1991/2, K. 1992/1, 10 July 1992. *Official Gazette*, 25 Oct 1992: 21386.
Decision of the TCC: E. 1990/12, K. 1991/7, 4 April 1991. *Official Gazette*, 13 Aug 1991: 20959.
Decision of the TCC: E. 1992/36, K. 1993/4, 20 January 1993. *Official Gazette*, 19 Mar 1993: 21529.
Decision of the TCC: E. 1992/1, K. 1993/1, 14 July 1993. *Official Gazette*, 18 Aug 1993: 21672.
Decision of the TCC: E. 1993/1, K. 1993/2, 23 November 1993. *Official Gazette*, 14 Feb 1994: 21849.
Decision of the TCC: E. 1993/3, K.1994/2, 16 June 1994. *Official Gazette*, 30 June 1994: 21976.
Decision of the TCC: E. 1995/1, K. 1996/1, 19 March 1996. *Official Gazette*, 23 Oct 1997: 23149.
Decision of the TCC: E. 1996/15, K.1996/34, 23 September 1996. *Official Gazette*, 27 Dec 1996: 22860.
Decision of the TCC: E. 1996/17, K. 1996/38, 16 October 1996. *Official Gazette*, 9 Aug 1997: 23075.

Decision of the TCC: E. 1996/10, K. 1996/40, 22 October 1996. *Official Gazette*, 21 Oct 1997: 23147.
Decision of the TCC: E. 1996/1, K. 1997/1, 14 February 1997. *Official Gazette*, 26 June 1998: 23384.
Decision of the TCC: E. 1996/3, K. 1997/3, 22 May 1997. *Official Gazette*, 2 June 2000: 24067.
Decision of the TCC: E. 1997/61, K. 1998/59, 29 September 1998. *Official Gazette*, 15 Nov 2002: 24937.
Decision of the TCC: E. 1997/27, K. 1998/43, 30 June 1998. *Official Gazette*, 15 Jan 2000: 23934.
Decision of the TCC: E. 1998/3, K.1998/28, 23 June 1998. Official Gazette, 13 March 1999: 23638.
Decision of the TCC: E. 1999/47, K. 1999/46, 28 December 1999. *Official Gazette*, 10 Mar 2000: 23989.
Decision of the TCC: E. 1999/1, K. 2003/1, 13 March 2003. *Official Gazette*, 19 July 2003: 25173.
Decision of the TCC: E. 2003/28, K. 2003/42, 22 May 2003. *Official Gazette*, 16 Mar 2004: 25404.
Decision of the TCC: E. 2003/81, K. 2007/50, 17 April 2007. *Official Gazette*, 9 Nov 2007: 26695.
Decision of the TCC: E. 2003/6, K. 2008/4, 8 January 2008. *Official Gazette*, 22 Mar 2008: 26824.
Decision of the TCC: E. 2002/71, K. 2008/44, 17 January 2008. *Official Gazette*, 03 Apr 2009: 27189.
Decision of the TCC: E.2002/1, K. 2008/1, 29 January 2008. *Official Gazette*, 1 July 2008: 26923.
Decision of the TCC: E. 2005/139, K.2007/33, 22 March 2007. Official Gazette, 15 December 2007: 26731.
Decision of the TCC: E. 2005/56, K.2009/94, 25 June 2009. Official Gazette, 26 November 2009: 27418 bis.
Decision of the TCC: E. 2006/111, K.2006/112, 15 December 2006. Official Gazette, 30 December 2006: 26392 bis.
Decision of the TCC: E. 2006/156, K. 2008/125, 19 June 2008. *Official Gazette*, 26 Nov 2008: 27066.
Decision of the TCC: E. 2008/1, K. 2008/2, 30 July 2008. *Official Gazette*, 24 Oct 2008: 27034.
Decision of the TCC: E. 2006/166, K. 2009/113, 23 July 2009. *Official Gazette*, 19 Mar 2010: 27526.
Decision of the TCC: E. 2007/1, K. 2009/4, 11 December 2009. *Official Gazette*, 14 Dec 2009: 27432.
Decision of the TCC: E. 2009/85, K. 2011/49, 10 March 2011. *Official Gazette*, 21 Oct 2011: 28091.
Decision of the TCC: E. 2009/50, K. 2011/89, 2 June 2011. *Official Gazette*, 15 Oct 2011: 28085.
Decision of the TCC: E. 2006/94, K. 2009/92, 25 June 2009. *Official Gazette*, 10 Nov 2009: 27402.
Decision of the TCC: E.2010/119, K.2011/165, 8 December 2011. *Official Gazette*, 14 Feb 2012: 28204.
Decision of the TCC: E. 2012/87, K.2014/41, 27 February 2014. Official Gazette, 26 July 2014: 29072.
Decision of the TCC: E. 2012/103, K.2013/105, 3 October 2013. Official Gazette, 17 December 2014: 29208.
Decision of the TCC: E. 2013/21, K.2013/57, 10 April 2013. Official Gazette, 12 July 2013: 28705.
Decision of the TCC: E. 2013/24, K. 2013/133, 14 November 2013. *Official Gazette*, 22 July 2014: 29068.
Decision of the TCC: E. 2013/130, K. 2014/18, 29 January 2014. *Official Gazette*, 13 May 2014: 28999.
Decision of the TCC: Case of Sevim Akat Ekşi, Date of Judgement 19 December 2013. Application no. 2013/2187.
Esen, Selin. 2008. *Karşılaştırmalı Hukukta ve Türkiye'de Olağanüstü Hal Rejimi*. Ankara: Adalet Yayınevi.
Gönenç, Levent. 2004. The 2001 amendments to the 1982 constitution of Turkey. *Ankara Law Review* 1(1): 89–109.

Gönenç, Levent, and Selin Esen. 2006. The problem of less protective international agreements in domestic legal aystems: Article 90 of the Turkish constitution. *European Journal of Law Reform* 8(4): 490–497.

Human Rights Watch. 2012. http://www.hrw.org/news/2012/12/09/turkey-reconsider-appointment-key-rights-body. Accessed 10 Dec 2012.

ILO. 2006. *Freedom of Association: Digest of decisions and principles of the Freedom of Association Committee of the Governing Body of the ILO*, Fifth (revised) edition, Geneva: International Labour Office.

Kaboğlu, İbrahim Ö. 2002. *Özgürlükler Hukuku*. Ankara: İmge Kitabevi.

Kogacioğlu, Dicle. 2003. Dissolution of Political Parties by the Constitutional Court in Turkey. Judicial Delimitation of Political Domain. *International Sociology* 18: 258–276.

Öden, Merih. 2003a. *Anayasa Hukukunda Siyasi Partilerin Anayasaya Aykırı Eylemleri Nedeniyle Kapatılmaları*. Ankara: Yetkin Yayınları.

Öden, Merih. 2003b. *Türk Anayasa Hukukunda Eşitlik İlkesi*. Ankara: Yetkin Yayınları.

Öden, Merih. 2009. Anayasa Mahkemesi ve Olağanüstü Hal ve Sıkıyönetim Kanun Hükmünde Kararnamelerinin Yargısal Denetimi. *AÜHF Dergisi* 58(3): 659–691.

Öden, Merih, and Selin Esen. 2013. Anayasa Mahkemesi ve Evli Kadının Soyadı. In *Prof. Dr. Erdal Onar'a Armağan*, 817–836. Ankara: Ankara Üniversitesi Basımevi.

Özbudun, Ergun. 2007. Democratization Reforms in Turkey, 1993–2004. *Turkish Studies* 8(2): 179–196.

Özbudun, Ergun, and Serap Yazıcı. 2004. *Democratization Reforms in Turkey*. Istanbul: TESEV.

Özbudun, Ergun. 2010. Party Prohibition Cases: Different Approaches by the Turkish Constitutional Court and the European Court of Human Rights. *Democratization* 17: 125–142.

Sağlam, Fazıl. 1982. *Temel Hakların Sınırlanması ve Özü*. Ankara: AÜSBF Yayını.

Sabuncu, Yavuz. 2006. *Anayasaya Giriş, Baskı 7*. Ankara: İmaj Yayınları.

Tanör, Bülent. 1978. *Anayasa Hukukunda Sosyal Haklar*. İstanbul: May Yayınları.

United Nations Human Rights Commission by Resolution 1992/54 of 1992, and by the UN General Assembly in its Resolution 48/134 of 1993. http://www2.ohchr.org/english/law/paris-principles.htm

Fundamental Rights Protection in a New Constitution: The Example of Kosovo

Arbëresha Raça Shala

Abstract The role of the individual in the society is undeniable and his fundamental rights that are protected by normative acts do not remain only at the level of national protection but they go further in the international legal protection. In fact, Kosovo's constitutional provisions expressly highlight and define as a value the respecting of the fundamental rights and freedoms. The individual is guaranteed judicial protection of his/her rights but he/she is at the same time empowered to refer violations by public authorities of the fundamental rights and freedoms in the jurisdiction of the Constitutional Court. In the constitutional review where the individual was an authorized party before the constitutional jurisdiction, the convergence of fundamental rights adjudicated and the violation of the fundamental rights and freedoms has been decided upon.

Basic Rights and Freedoms in the Constitution of Kosovo

The Constitution of Kosovo, of 15 June 2008, in a similarity with other democratic constitutions, represents the highest and the most sublime act of a state. This Constitution is grounded upon the highest standards of modern and democratic standards of human rights and freedoms. The Constitution of Kosovo stipulates on human rights overview in Chapter II, specifically articles 21 up to 56.

Article 21, of the Constitution of Kosovo in a rather clear articulation on General Principles, defines the human rights and freedoms as being, "*indivisible, inalienable and inviolable and are the basis of the legal order of the Republic of Kosovo*". Whereas Article 22 specifies on international treaties and instruments, guaranteeing their direct application in Kosovo, with a priority of application in case of conflict with domestic laws and other acts embrace the following:

1. Universal Declaration of Human Rights.
2. European Convention for the Protection of Human Rights and Fundamental Freedoms and its Protocols.

A.R. Shala (✉)
Basic Prosecutor Office, Palace of Justice, Hajvali, Building C, Prishtine, Kosovo
e-mail: arberesha.shala@gmail.com

R. Arnold (ed.), *The Convergence of the Fundamental Rights Protection in Europe*, Ius Gentium: Comparative Perspectives on Law and Justice 52,
DOI 10.1007/978-94-017-7465-9_9

3. International Covenant on Civil and Political Rights and its Protocols.
4. Council of Europe Framework Convention for the Protection of National Minorities.
5. Convention on the Elimination of All Forms of Racial Discrimination.
6. Convention on the Elimination of All Forms of Discrimination Against Women.
7. Convention on the Rights of the Child.
8. Convention against Torture and Other Cruel, Inhumane or Degrading Treatment or Punishment.

In scrutinizing the purposes of the Constitution of Kosovo and its set-up, these constitutional-normative inclusion of international instruments, make clear the legitimacy of constitutional observation, promoted and protected by each public authority exercising powers in Kosovo, their protection by the judicial system, and also by the Constitutional Court.

The Constitution of the Republic of Kosovo, in its Article 23 avers *Human Dignity* as inviolable, and the basis of all human rights and fundamental freedoms.

Independently of the various situations, violation of these rights and fundamental freedoms is excluded in all circumstances, which may include:

- *Equality before Law*, Article 24, because all are equal before the law, and all enjoy the right to equal legal protection without discrimination.
- *Right to Life*, Article 25, which asserts on prohibition of (capital) death penalty.
- *Prohibition of Torture, Cruel, Inhuman or Degrading Treatment*, Article 27.
- *Prohibition of Slavery and Forced Labor*, Article 28; (*Labor or services provided by law by persons convicted by a final court decision while serving their sentence or during a State of Emergency declared in compliance with the rules set forth in this Constitution shall not be considered as forced labor*) including prohibition of trafficking of human beings.
- *Right to Liberty and Security*, Article 29; (*No one shall be deprived of liberty except in the cases foreseen by law and after a decision of a competent court, in cases provided expressly and by procedure designated by constitutional and legal provisions*).
- *Right to Fair and Impartial Trial*, Article 31; (guaranteed equal protection of rights in the proceedings before courts, other state authorities and holders of public powers).
- *The Principle of Legality and Proportionality in Criminal Cases*, Article 33; (observation of the principle *"nullum crimen, nulla poena sine lege"*, excluding offences which at the time of commission, as provided by international law, consisted of genocide, war crimes or crimes against humanity).
- *Right not to be Tried Twice for the Same Criminal Act*, Article 34.
- *Right to Marriage and Family*, Article 37.
- *Freedom of Belief, Conscience and Religion*, Article 38.

Nevertheless, on the same human rights and fundamental freedoms the Constitution of Kosovo provides a way out for their renunciation during a state of emergency, though through a ridged interpretation when necessity of circumstances demands so with regard to:

- *Right to Legal Remedies*, Article 32.
- *Right to Personal Integrity*, Article 26; (right to body control, right not to undergo medical treatment against his/her will, the right not to participate in medical or scientific experiments without her/his prior consent).
- *Rights of the Accused*, Article 30.
- *Freedom of Movement*, Article 35.
- *Right to Privacy*, Article 36.
- *Religious Communities*, Article 39; (establish religious schools and charity institutions).
- *Freedom of Expression*, Article 40; (right to express, disseminate and receive information, opinions and other messages).
- *Right of Access to Public Documents*, Article 41.
- *Freedom of Media*, Article 42.
- *Freedom of Gathering*, Article 43, right to organize gatherings, protests and demonstrations and the right to participate in them.
- *Freedom of Association*, Article 44, (right of everyone to establish an organization without obtaining any permission, to be or not to be a member of any organization and to participate in the activities of an organization. Freedom to establish trade unions and to organize).
- *Freedom of Election and Participation*, Article 45, vote is personal, equal, free and secret.
- *Protection of Property*, Article 46.
- *Right to Education*, Article 47.
- *Freedom of Art and Science*, Article 48.
- *Right to Work and Exercise Profession*, Article 49.
- *Rights of Children*, Article 50.
- *Health and Social Protection*, Article 51. (Basic social insurance related to unemployment, disease, disability and old age shall be regulated by law).
- *Responsibility for the Environment*, Article 52; and
- *Judicial Protection of Rights*, Article 54.

In summary, one may say that with all the assurances offered by the Constitution, only law, to a necessary extent, may limit human rights. The constraint of rights and freedoms guaranteed by this Constitution, in no way can be argued to infringe the essence of those guaranteed rights. As a result, one might argue that none of public institutions may behave in a way of abusing the essential fundamentals of human rights standards sustaining in Chapter II of the Constitution of Kosovo. This line of argumentation fits with the findings of International Court of Justice (ICJ) with regard to states obligation in terms of adhering to fundamental principles, specifically, ICJ's assertion reads that, "where a State or an international organization has created the legitimate expectation that it would act in a certain manner, it is under a legal obligation to fulfill that expectation" (Istrefi 2012, 81–93). Indeed, since Kosovo is aspiring to be part of international community order, there is no justification why Kosovo's constitutional order won't be fully flagged member respecting fundamental rights.

In fact, the manner of application of human rights norms in Kosovo as explained is found in Article 22 ad also Article 53 as it will be explained later throughout this discussion. Since, Article 22 provides direct application of various international documents including ECHR human rights standards, the Constitution of Kosovo widely provides to the progression of convergence of Fundamental Rights in Europe through its Constitutional Court of Kosovo.

One must also emphasize the fact that the limitation of rights by domestic acts cannot exceed the restrictions provided by the Universal Declaration of Human Rights and ECHR and in event of the limitation; the rights must be proportional to the cause or the condition, which brought such limitation. Always, the essence – the core of guaranteed rights must be preserved, and may never and in any circumstance be denied. Similarly, the rights of marginalized communities and their members, as distinctive rights, may be limited to a certain extent, in compliance with the law, and by not violating the rights of other persons.

The Constitution of the Republic of Kosovo contains 33 Articles providing on human rights and fundamental freedoms, including the special category of the rights of communities and their members.[1] In fact, the human rights provisions of Kosovo's constitution contain a merged contemporary core rights due to the fact that a mixed commission of international and national members has drafted it.

Worth highlighting that the constitutional provisions are grouped into two categories: provisions that may not be waived, in any circumstance, and provisions, which may be provisionally waived, under certain circumstances, until these circumstances prevail.

In comparison with Constitution of the Republic of Kosovo, the Constitution of the Republic of Albania (Albanian Constitution, Art. 15–58) groups human rights and fundamental freedoms into three categories:

(I) *Individual rights and freedoms*, provided by Articles 15–44: the right to life, freedom of expression, freedom of media, right to information, freedom of conscience and religion, prohibition of torture, cruel, inhuman or humiliating punishment or treatment, prohibition of forced labor, right to private property.
(II) *Political freedoms and rights*, provided by Articles 45–48*; right to elect and be elected, right to collective organization, freedom of peaceful and unarmed assembly.*
(III) *Economic, social, and cultural freedoms and rights*, provided by Articles 49–58: right to earn means of livelihood by lawful work, employees' rights to strike, right to social insurance of old age, right to marriage and family, right

[1] Constitution of the Republic of Kosovo, 2008, quoted: Rights of Communities and their Members, Articles 57–62. The Constitution of Kosovo – the state recognizes these persons' special rights, along with the rights and freedoms enjoyed by the majority of the population. The State is obliged to provide the members of non-majority communities with adequate conditions for enjoying special rights as guaranteed by the Constitution. For more, see quoted case law of the Constitutional Court of Kosovo, elaborated in this work.

to medical care by the state, right to obtain information on environment and its protection, right to education, and freedom of artistic creation and scientific research.

The state is bound to observe and protect human rights, because they are the values of the constitutional order in the Republic of Kosovo. Moreover, constitutional order of Kosovo is well advanced with other trends of other constitutional orders in Europe like the Constitution of Albania. There are other constitutional provisions, apart from the Chapter II, stipulating on duties of the public authorities *"with full respect for internationally recognized fundamental human rights and freedoms, as well as protection of the rights of and participation by all Communities and their members"* (Kosovar Constitution, Art. 3), duties for legislative, executive and judicial authorities.

Furthermore, the following constitutional provisions underline the following issues related to human rights:

- Article 17, providing that the Republic of Kosovo participates in international cooperation for promotion and protection of peace, security and human rights.
- Article 18, providing on the duty of the Assembly of Kosovo to ratify by two thirds (2/3) vote of all deputies of the Assembly international agreements relating to the fundamental rights and freedoms.
- Article 62, providing on Representation in the Institutions of Local Government, and stipulating that the Deputy Mayor shall also be responsible for reviewing claims by Communities or their members that the acts or decisions of the Municipal Assembly violate their constitutionally guaranteed rights. In the event the Municipal Assembly chooses not to reconsider its act or decision, or the Vice President deems the result, upon reconsideration, to still present a violation of a constitutionally guaranteed right, the Vice President may submit the matter directly to the Constitutional Court, which may decide whether or not to accept the matter for review.

The Protection of the Fundamental Rights by the Constitutional Court

The Constitution of Kosovo lays foundations of Constitutional Court of Kosovo. The combination of theoretical and practical part avers role model where universal human rights are integrated domestically. Human rights and fundamental freedoms, as the basic principles and standards of international treaties and highest legal acts of a state, in democratic countries, although widely proclaimed, are not observed and implemented comprehensively. Despite the constitutional guarantees, even judicial authorities in adjudicating matters or disputes may cause violations or infringements of such rights. It never suffices only to provide and guarantee with the highest legal acts of a state, and therefore mechanisms ordering and binding respect and observation of such rights are necessary. Thus, even though rights and freedom are protected at every instance of trial, they may be violated/infringed as well, thus, here it comes in the significance of Constitutional Court as a forum of convenience for individuals in order to address their complains.

Among the basic principle of this constitutionalism is the statement of rights and a fundamental freedom that in case of Kosovo is enshrined in Chapter II of the Constitution. This Chapter is a pillar that supports and legitimizes any exercise of constituent power, now and into the future (Hasani 2013, 139). This means that Chapter II of the Constitution of Kosovo is the essence or hart of the Constitution of the Republic of Kosovo. Priority is set on implementation of international agreements and instruments in case of conflicts with other legal acts and norms.

From constitutional viewpoint, out of all eight documents mentioned in Article 22, ECHR is the most applicable one in the Republic of Kosovo. At the same time it is the most visible aspect of Constitutions impact to the practice of convergence of Fundamental Rights in Europe. Beyond that, in terms of reference Constitutional Court to the Strasbourg Court case law, Article 53 of the Constitution expressly specifies, *"that human rights and fundamental freedoms guaranteed by this Constitution shall be interpreted consistent with court decisions of the European Court of Human Rights"*. It has binding obligations for the Constitutional Court to interpret the human rights provisions, as guaranteed with the Constitution of Kosovo, in compliance with decisions of the European Court for Human Rights. Therefore, the Constitutional Court of Kosovo consolidates its own case law referring to the case law of the Strasbourg Court, not only in terms of substantial rights, but also in procedural matters (Botusharova 2012, 82).

Article 53 of the Constitution spells out binning obligation upon Constitutional Court of Kosovo when asserting pith and substance of each particular case occurred in front of this court. The same article makes its clear that Constitutional Court interpretation must be read in compliance with long established jurisprudence of the Strasbourg Court. In addition, reading in conjunction Articles 22 and 53 of the Constitution of Kosovo with the practices of European Court of Human Rights shows the coherence of Constitutional Court leave no room for other interpretation, other than adhering to the practices ECtHR. In short, Kosovo's constitutional court is well advanced with best practices European Court of Human Rights.

Consequently this study asserts the Constitutional Court of Kosovo (CCK) makes regular reference to the ECtHR decided cases. Enormous decided by Constitutional Court of Kosovo shows the consistency of making reference to ECtHR. Otherwise stated, CCK complies entirely with jurisprudence of ECtHR and cannot avoid doing so due to its constitutional legitimacy.

Important examples of such transnational principles are: the anthropocentric approach of constitutional law – the paramount position of the individual in comparison with state interests, culminating in the recognition of dignity as a supreme value; the efficiency of fundamental rights based on this value, and the limitation of public power, including that of the legislator, to restrict the guarantee of these rights (Arnold 2007, 5). The complaint of an affected individual whose constitutional rights is claimed to have been violated is generally the basis for appropriate proceedings of protection in which the protection of rights by the Constitutional Court is only one out of a number of other legal remedies for protection (Mavčič 2011, 4).

In reality the Constitutional Court of Kosovo is not a court of fact, whereby it will ascertain the factual condition of a certain matter. Rather, its primary function is to find out whether or not violations of human rights and freedoms has taken place, and all respective authorities are bound to comply with the decision rendered by the Court. In turn, as it will be discussed shortly in most of the decides cases decided by CCK makes reference to the long practice jurisprudence of the Strasbourg Court.

The convergence process of the CCK with ECtHR is also noted in procedural aspects. Procedures in individual claims are also in compliance with ECtHR procedural rules in many terms. They are specific in the sense of elaborating the claims as required by legal provisions, in terms of timelines, since the referral must be filed within 4 months from the receipt by the party of the court ruling, and in the sense of procedural costs, since the individual is not charged with court fees, when his/her referrals are grounded and admitted.[2] To put it differently, when we talk about admissibility criteria, it is worth pointing out that Constitutional Court of Kosovo applies to great extend the practice of ECtHR.

In consideration of the above, one may say that the Constitutional Court is not a "fourth instance" court, because it enjoys no competency in ascertaining the factual condition. This Court may decide on matters referred by the individuals *if decisions by public authorities violate human rights guaranteed by the Constitution.* It is visibly clear that the Constitutional Court has no jurisdiction of reviewing appeals as a higher instance, but it only has jurisdiction to protect human rights and freedoms, upon finding a violation, infringement or denial of such rights in rulings of state authorities. Apart from this, it has been found and the concluded that the "constitutional court, because of its jurisdiction over concrete review referrals and individual complaints, comes to behave as a kind of supreme or appeal court for the judiciary, involving itself in the latter's tasks of fact-finding and rule application; and the techniques of constitutional decision making become an important mode of argumentation and decision making in the ordinary courts" (Sweet 2007, 90).

While the Constitution provides upon and guarantees a series of rights, it also reflects the role of the Constitutional Court in relation to regular courts in terms of violations of rights and freedoms. Its special role, *sui generis*, is contained in its other jurisdiction, which is protection of rights and freedoms in any case in which they are infringed by actions of public authorities, including the violations of public authorities administering justice, such as courts.

The role of the Constitutional Court as the main guarantee for human rights and fundamental freedoms is specifically emphasized in cases when such protection is requested. In the dimension of experience of constitutional adjudication, Kosovo might have the shortest experience in constitutional reviews, and might be the youngest in Balkan and Europe in protecting rights and freedoms, nevertheless, it

[2] For more, see Articles 28, 46–50 of the Law on the Constitutional Court of the Republic of Kosovo, Law No. 03/L-121, December, 2008.

has established the foundations of constitutional justice, since the addressing and review of cases for rights and freedoms has its specific meaning and importance.

The Constitution has clearly and precisely provided on the cases in which an individual may put the Constitutional Court in motion. Article 113.7 provides that "Individuals are authorized to refer violations by public authorities of their individual rights and freedoms guaranteed by the Constitution, but only after exhaustion of all legal remedies provided by law". The submission of individual referrals does not only include the natural persons, but also legal persons, for as much provisions of Chapter II of the Constitution apply. Individual referrals filed with the Constitutional Court have different names in constitutional law, such as "constitutional complaints", "constitutional claims", and "individual complaints". Independently of the denomination, they contain a single aim – the possibility of an individual to subject to review the alleged violations by public authorities, thereby giving real and overarching sense to the democratic spirit of the state.

Consequently, the protection of individual rights is not less important than the normative control in practice. Developed countries with a high level of democracy put *priority over priority* on the protection of human rights, along other priorities. In procedures of reviewing merits of individual constitutional referrals/complaints, the Court has also a direct role in developing and promoting rights and freedoms guaranteed by the Constitution. One cannot rule out the stance that in normative control procedures, the Constitutional Court protects human rights guaranteed by the Constitution, in an *"in abstracto" manner*. Talking in this context, the Constitutional Court of Albania has interpreted widely and creatively on the Constitution in protecting individual rights. "Its decisions have not only elaborated on the guarantees provided by the Constitution, but have also affirmed new elements of guaranteeing such rights" (Methasani-Cani 2008, 22).

Like in the Albanian constitutional jurisprudence, we can draw similarities also in Kosovo's constitutional justice. Thus, on issues of protection of human rights aroused upon individual's as well as other parties request in one hand, and the demand to address those alleged violation of rights in compliance with the constitution, laws, decrees, or municipal statuses on the other hand, demand proper institution to be in place. In this aspect of addressing referrals filed either by an individual or by an authorized institution, the constitutional justice in Kosovo showed to able to deal those matters and provided prompt answers – decisions.

Additionally, in scrutinizing the decision-making process based on statistical data provided from the Bulletin of Case Law (Bulletin of Case Law 2009–2011, 2012/I, 2012/II), Table 1, shows the type of the decision issued by constitutional court.

Based on above, constitutional justice rendered a total of 294 decisions between 2009 and 2012, on which 38 or 13 % were judgments and 256 or 87 % were decisions on inadmissibility.

The total numbers of 38 judgments, out of them 26 judgments were on individual referrals, and 12 referrals were from other authorized parties. It must be emphasized that the practice of the Constitutional Court of Kosovo is that they render a single

Table 1 Type of the decision issued by the constitution court of Kosovo 2009–2012

2009–2010		2011		2012		2009–2012	
Judgment (J)	Resolution on inadmissibility (R)	Judgment (J)	Resolution on inadmissibility (R)	Judgment (J)	Resolution on inadmissibility (R)	(J)	(R)
9	48	12	117	17	91	38	256
16 %	84 %	9 %	91 %	16 %	84 %	13 %	87 %

judgment for more than one referral. Otherwise stated, on a number of joint referrals[3] the Constitutional Court treats all together at once. Consequently, the court renders a single judgment for multiple referrals.

For instance a typical case of this nature is the case no. KI 40/09, whereby the Court concluded by a single judgment[4] with regard to a joined of 49 individual referrals from former employees of the Kosovo Energy Corporation (KEK). They demanded constitutional review of individual judgments rendered by the Supreme Court on compensation of their salaries. In reviewing each referral, the Constitutional Court made several references upon decided cases by ECtHR (Kopecký v. Slovakia 2004; Prince Hans-Adam II of Liechtenstein v. Germany 2001, para 82–83; Gratzinger and Gratzingerova v. the Czech Republic 2002, para 69) while assessed and weighed the referrals in three dimensions:

- Twelve (12) referrals were found inadmissible, since their demands were premature, and the cases were under ongoing proceeding with regular courts.
- Five (5) referrals were found partially admissible, due to the fact that five of the applicants had the age of 65, and had at least 15 years of working experience. In fact, they had reached the retirement age, and had acquired the right to pension, with an amount guaranteed by law.

---

[3] Regarding the joined of referrals, Rules of Procedure of the Constitutional Court of the Republic of Kosovo, on Rule 37, provides: (1) The Secretariat shall provide notice to the President and the Judge Rapporteur that the referral may be related in subject matter to another referral before the Court and directed against the same act of a public authority. The President, upon the recommendation of the Judge Rapporteur may order the joinder of those separate referrals. (2) If a referral addresses two or more laws or other acts of public authority, the Judge Rapporteur shall notify the Secretariat and the President. Upon the recommendation of the Judge Rapporteur, the President may order a separate consideration of the respective elements of the referral if joint consideration does not favor a fair and expeditious determination of the issues. (3) If a party disagrees with the Court's decision to join or sever referrals, it shall request reconsideration of the decision, together with any factual or legal arguments, within fifteen (15) days of the date of the President's Order to join or sever referrals.

[4] Judgment in the case no. KI 40/09, Applicant Imer Ibrahimi and 48 former employees of the Kosovo Energy Corporation, Constitutional Review of 49 individual judgments of the Supreme Court of the Republic of Kosovo, Ref. no. AGJ 30/10, of 23 June 2010, the Constitutional Court of the Republic of Kosovo (cases were joined because the Court found that they had an identical subject matter, deriving from the same essential problem, and therefore, in compliance with procedural rules, the individual referrals were joined, and were decided by a single judgment upon review).

- Thirty-two (32) referrals were admissible, and were found to have contained violations of property rights and the right to fair and impartial trial (including violations found in the five partially admissible referrals), as guaranteed by Articles 46 and 31 of the Constitution. Articles are also related to the Article 1, Protocol 1, and Article 6 of the European Convention on Human Rights (Article 1, Protocol 1, provides that "*every natural or legal person is entitled to the peaceful enjoyment of his possessions. No one shall be deprived of his possessions except in the public interest and subject to the conditions provided for by law and by the general principles of international law*").

At the same issue, there were four other judgments rendered in reviewing referrals of other former KEK employees, with the same subject matter as the judgment mentioned above, namely constitutional review of individual judgments of the Supreme Court of the Republic of Kosovo. These four judgments were similar in their reasoning. From the judgments rendered in 2010, one should mention two (2) cases:

- Case KI 58/09 and 15 other cases joined,[5] the judgment related to demands of 16 former KEK employees, where violations of property rights and rights to fair and impartial trial were found. Only one referral was found partially admissible, and all judgments of the Supreme Court on individual cases were invalidated; and
- Case no. KI 08/10, and 24 other cases,[6] the judgment was related to 25 referrals, where 5 were found partially admissible, and also, all judgments of the Supreme Court on individual cases were invalidated.

One judgment was rendered in 2011, related to case no. KI 76/10, and 20 other cases,[7] and only 6 referrals were found partially admissible out of 21 referrals filed, and all judgments of the Supreme Court were invalidated; and a judgment rendered

[5] Cases no. "(KI 58/09, KI 59/09, KI 60/09, KI 64/09, KI 66/09, KI 69/09, KI 70/09, KI 72/09, KI 75/09, KI 76/09, KI 77/09, KI 78/09, KI 79/09, KI 03/10, KI 05/10, KI 13/10, case of Gani Prokshi and 15 other former employees of the Kosovo Energy Corporation, against individual judgments of the Supreme Court of the Republic of Kosovo, Ref. no. AGJ 62/10, of 15 October 2010.)" In the decision making process the Constitutional Court references upon decided cases by ECtHR as are mentioned the cases *"Prince Hans-Adam II of Liechtenstein v. Germany, no. 42527/98*, paras 82–83, ECHR 2001-VIII" and *"Gratzinger and Gratzingerova v. the Czech Republic* (dec.) [GC], no. 39794/98, para. 69, ECHR 2002-VII).; Case García Ruiz v. Spain [GC], no. 30544/96, paragraph 28, European Court on Human Rights [ECHR] 1999-I); Case Edwards v. United Kingdom, App. No 13071/87 adopted on 10 July 1991); Case Ruiz Torija v. Spain, judgment of 9 December 1994, Series A no. 303-A, § 29).

[6] Judgment in the cases no. KI 08/10, KI 16/10, KI 22/10, KI 24/10, KI 27/10, KI 36/10, KI 41/10, KI 42/10, KI 45/10, KI 53/10, KI 54/10, KI 56/10, KI 57/10, KI 58/10, KI 59/10, KI 60/10, KI 61/10, KI 63/10, KI 64/10, KI 65/10, KI 66/10, KI 67/10, KI 68/10 KI 71/10, KI 74/10, KI 76/10; Applicant Isuf Mërlaku and 25 other former employees of the Kosovo Energy Corporation, against individual judgments of the Supreme Court of the Republic of Kosovo, Ref. no. AGJ 90/11, 10 March 2011.

[7] Judgment in the cases no. KI 76/10, KI 82/10, KI 83/10, KI 102/10, KI 111/10, KI 122/10, KI 127/10, KI 11/11, KI 15/11, KI 18/11, KI 45/11, KI 47/11, KI 48/11, KI 50/11, KI 57/11, KI 60/11, KI 69/11, KI 71/11, KI 73/11, KI 75/11, KI 79/11, Applicant Ilaz Halili and 20 other former

in 2012 was related to the case no KI 132/10 and 16 other cases[8] where the same violations were found again. Eight referrals were found partially admissible, while all judgments of the Supreme Court on individual cases were invalidated.

The decisions of the Constitutional Court on the referrals filed by the former KEK employees stated, in their enacting clause, that judgments of the Supreme Court were returned for reconsideration. From this enacting clause, the Constitutional Court further underlined that its role is not to ascertain the factual situation, and that it is not a court of fact, and it only reviews and finds violations of human rights and freedoms as guaranteed by the Constitution and international treaties. Specifically, the Constitutional Court stated, *"it remains seriously seized of the matter of the case, and expecting the enforcement of its judgment"*.

Additionally, the analysis of the case law of the Constitutional Court appears to be that the decided judgments upon individual referrals, the court found the following violations of human rights and freedoms, as guaranteed by Chapter II of the Constitution of Kosovo:

- In five individual cases: KI 25/10, KI 108/10, KI 103/10, KI 06/12,[9] and KI 51/11, the right to fair and impartial trial was violated, Article 31.
- In two individual cases: KI 50/11 and KI 08/09, the right to fair and impartial trial and protection of property, were violated, Articles 31 and 46.
- In the case KI 129/11, the right to fair and impartial trial and judicial protection of rights, were violated, Articles 31 and 54.
- In the case KI 72/12 the right to fair and impartial trial, the right to legal remedies, and legal protection of rights, were violated, Articles 31, 32, and 54.
- In the case KI 04/12, equality before law, the right to fair and impartial trial, the right to legal remedies, and judicial protection of rights, were violated, Articles 24, 31, 32 and 54.
- In the case KI 32/10, violations of right to vote and participate in voting, and judicial protection of rights were found, Articles 45 and 54.
- In the case KI 06/10, violations of freedom of movement and judicial protection of rights were found, Articles 35 and 54.
- In the case KI 47/12, violations of right to legal remedies and judicial protection of rights were found, Articles 32 and 54.

---

employees of the Kosovo Energy Corporation, against individual judgments of the Supreme Court of the Republic of Kosovo, Ref. no. AGJ 181, dated 27 December 2011.

[8] Judgment in the cases no. KI 132/10, KI 28/11, KI 82/11, KI 85/11, KI 89/11, KI 100/11, KI 104/11, KI 109/11, KI 118/11, KI 123/11, KI 142/11, KI 143/11, KI 144/11, KI 154/11, KI 01/12, KI 02/12, KI 14/12, Applicants Istref Halili and 16 other former employees of the Kosovo Energy Corporation, against individual judgments of the Supreme Court of the Republic of Kosovo, Ref. no. AGJ 309/12, of 01 October 2012.

[9] The Constitutional Court references upon decided cases by ECtHR: *Judgment in the case Akdivar v. Turkey judgment of 16 September 1996; judgment in the case of Pressos Compania Naviera S.A. v. Belgium of 20 November 1995, para. 27; Radio France c. France, no. 53984/00, decision of 23 September 2003, para. 33 and* see, *mutatis mutandis*, Hornsby v. Greece, judgment of 19 March 1997, *Reports* 1997-II, p.511, para. 41.

Table 2 183 reviewed individual cases – 2009–2012

Rendered by decision-resolution on inadmissibility Constitutional court of Kosovo			
Inadmissibility criteria	Constitution of Kosovo Law on C. court rules of procedure	Number of cases	%
Referral filed after legal deadline	Rule 36.1b	43	24
Manifestly ill-founded	Rule 36.2	37	20
Legal remedies not exhausted	Rule 36.1a	36	19
No evidence "*prima facie*"	Rule 36.2a	26	14
No reasoning of allegation on violation	Rule 36.2b	20	11
Incompatible "*Ratione temporis" with* Constitution	Rule 36.3 h	13	7
Referral filed by an unauthorized party	Rule 36.3c	3	1.50
Referral not allowed	Article 46, Law on CCK	2	1.30
Referral withdrawn by the party	Rule 32	1	0.80
Insufficient legal grounds	Rule 36.3e	1	0.80
Referral doesn't meet submission criteria	Article 22, Law on CCK	1	0.80
Inadmissibility criteria on the decision issued by the Constitution Court of Kosovo		**183**	**100**

- In the case KI 55/11, violations of judicial protection of rights were found, Article 54.
- In the case KI 104/10, violation of property rights was found, Article 46.

Furthermore, the assessment stresses the fact that the violation of human rights and freedoms is committed by the "bodies administering justice" themselves, i.e., the regular courts. Almost in all decided cases, except in two cases,[10] human rights and freedoms were violated by other public authorities. For instance, in one case, the Municipal Assembly in Peja committed the violation, while in the other the Ministry of Internal Affairs and the Municipal Court/Kosovo Judicial Council.

Having into consideration and based on statistical findings (see Table 2), 256 cases were concluded by decision-resolution on inadmissibility. Out of 256, this paper has reviewed 183 cases and all were dismissed as inadmissible, thus in compliance with the Constitution of Kosovo, Law on the Constitutional Court of Kosovo (Law on C. Court), and Rules of Procedure of the Constitutional Court of Kosovo

[10] Judgment Case no. KI 06/10, Applicant Valon Bislimi vs. Ministry of Internal Affairs, Kosovo Judicial Council and Ministry of Justice, (the case was referred *upon decided cases by ECtHR, as it mentioned: "see, mutatis mutandis, Hornsby v. Greece, judgment of 19 March 1997, Reports 1997-II, p. 511, para. 41);* Judgment in the case KI 32/10, Applicant Fahrudin Megjedoviq, Deputy Chairperson for Communities of the Municipal Assembly of Peja, Constitutional review of the Decision of the Municipal Assembly of Peja appointing the Deputy Mayor of Municipality for Communities, dated 15 February 2010. Apart from this, there were three judgments of the Constitutional Court of the Republic of Kosovo where no violations of human rights and freedoms were found in these individual cases KI 39/9, KI 55/09 and KI 09/10. For more, see Bulletin of Cases of the Constitutional Court for year 2009–2010 and Bulletin of Cases of the Constitutional Court 2011.

(Rule of CCK), since the referrals filed did not meet the requirements of admissibility during the reviewed procedure. The following table indicates clearly the cases treated by Constitutional Court of Kosovo of this nature.

Based on such data, it may clearly be seen that in 43 cases, authorized parties have not had the necessary knowledge on the timelines of submitting referrals to the Court, while in 36 cases they have not exhausted their legal remedies, which is the first and the key requirement for the individuals to defend their rights and freedoms against violations by public authorities. In our opinion, the cases that have been found by the Court to be admissible, and the large number of individual referrals, demonstrates that the organization of consultative meetings on constitutional procedures is necessary, not only with Municipal Assembly members, but also members of other institutions, and the legal community/lawyers and citizens.[11] This would be a necessary measure, for the constitutional referrals to be submitted with proper justifications. This process would also reduce the decisions found inadmissible, due to non-exhaustion of legal remedies, and due to the fact that the parties had filed their referrals after the legal deadline.

Ultimately as a comparison example we have brought three individual decisions of the Albanian Constitutional Court, related to individual referrals. One was related to annulling court decisions; the second on the violation of the right to a due process and third was related to failure to execute the ECtHR decision.

Decision no. 4, of 10.02.2012, (V-4/12), where an individual applicant, through his representative, had requested the annulment as incompatible with the Constitution of the Republic of Albania of the decisions of the First Instance Court for Serious Crimes, the Court of Appeal for Serious Crimes, and the Criminal Panel of the Supreme Court – Advisory Chamber. According to his claims, the courts had violated his rights to a fair trial, due to the *infringement of the right to defense and the right to be immediately and specifically informed on the charges brought. The Court* had decided to admit the referral, and had annulled as incompatible with the Constitution of the Republic of Albania the decisions mentioned above, ordering the reopening of the case at the First Instance Court for Serious Crimes.

Another case of the Constitutional Court of the Republic of Albania, Decision no. 12, dated 05.03.2012, (V–12/12), where the individual applicant claimed an infringement of the constitutional right to a fair trial, due to the failure to hold trial within reasonable time. The applicant had filed the case to the Court in December 2006, but until May 2011, when the Constitutional Court had already begun review, there was no decision on the allegations of the applicant. Therefore, the Applicant had not exhausted the legal remedies, since she did not have a final court decision. In this case, the Court decided to accept the referral, and found the violation of the constitutional right to a fair trial, as a result of not holding trial within a reasonable time, and violation of Article 6 of the ECHR.

[11] In relation to this "education", the Constitutional Court has organized consultative meetings on constitutional procedures with Municipal Assembly members in several municipalities. For more, see Annual Report 2010, 2011, Constitutional Court of the Republic of Kosovo.

A specific case was the decision of the Constitutional Court of the Republic of Albania, no. 20/11 (Constitutional Court of Albania, 01.06.2011), where the individual applicant had requested:

- Annulment as unconstitutional of the decision of the Criminal Panel of the High Court.
- Suspension of the relevant decision of the Criminal Panel of the High Court, and order the state institution to enforce the decision of the European Court of Human Rights.
- Suspension of the decision of the Criminal Panel of the High Court until entry into force of the final decision of the Constitutional Court.

An interesting fact was that the individual had addressed the European Court for Human Rights, which had found, amongst other, that the risk of an error from proceeding authorities or a court must be taken by the state, and errors cannot be compensated to the detriment of the individual. As a conclusion, this court had decided to accept the application of the Applicant, and according to the Court, the proper manner for restoring the violated right would be the reconfirmation by relevant authorities of the respective decision, by which the admission of the application and suspension of the case was decided, since he had not committed the criminal offence charged upon him. Since the decision of the ECtHR was not recognized by Albanian state authorities, the applicant had addressed the Constitutional Court to acknowledge his innocence in the criminal offence of murder, and enforcement of the decision of the European Court, while the Constitutional Court had decided to turn down the application, designating the High Court to be the competent authority for fulfilling requirements of the ECtHR decision.

The Criminal Panel of the High Court had decided to turn down the revision request, since it had found that while the ECtHR had decided that there was a violation of the right to fair trial of the citizen mentioned, this is an indication for initiating a constitutional review, and not a revision procedure.

Finding that the interpretation made by the Criminal Panel of the High Court is erroneous, and in contradiction with constitutional provisions of Article 46 of the ECHR, the Constitutional Court had ultimately decided on:

- Unanimous annulment of the decision by the Criminal Panel of the High Court – Advisory Chamber, and had sent the case for revision at the High Court, and
- Rejection, by a majority vote, of the request for suspending the decision of the Criminal Panel of the High Court, due to the lack of jurisdiction.

Constitutional Review of Decisions of Regular Courts

It is already clear that all rights and freedoms are constitutional items, and enjoy judicial protection, since in any case of infringement they may be defended before regular courts. Article 54 of the Constitution of Kosovo provides that: *"Everyone enjoys the right of judicial protection if any right guaranteed by this Constitution or by law has been violated or denied and has the right to an effective legal remedy if found that such right has been violated"*. Based upon the conviction that human rights have an important place in the development of a country, they should be the essence and the most difficult item of all matters (Donnelly 2006, 64). They are a difficulty in terms of effective implementation and protection thereof by the Courts. The Constitutional provisions of Kosovo have stipulated that the powers of regular courts and specialized courts are unique and independent, and within this power, the Supreme Court is the highest authority in administering justice.

Article 32 of the Constitution of the Republic of Kosovo guarantees the right to remedies, specifically providing that "*Every person has the right to pursue legal remedies against judicial and administrative decisions which infringe on his/her rights or interests, in the manner provided by law*". These guarantees are there for the protection of natural and legal persons, because it enables them, in cases of infringement of rights, freedoms and interests, to request from a competent public administration authority the revocation, abolishment or modification of an administrative act, suspension of application of an administrative act, so as to defend their rights and interests.[12] In any administrative and judicial proceeding, discontented or interested parties may address at higher instance, always after having exhausted all other possibilities or legal remedies. Therefore, the complaint (appeal) is an institutional manner of protecting human rights and freedoms, also enshrined in the Constitution and laws, and not only in judicial proceedings, but also in administrative procedure.

The right of appeal is recognized also for the civil servants, in internal procedures of recruitment, against administrative decisions issued by employing authorities. This right is provided upon by the Article 12 of the Law on "the Independent Oversight Board", which explicitly provides that "A civil servant who is unsatisfied by a decision of an employing authority in alleged breach of the rules and principles set out in Law on Civil Service in the Republic of Kosovo, shall have the right to appeal to the Board". A decision by this Board is considered to be "a final administrative decision and shall be executed by the senior managing officer or the person responsible at the institution issuing the original decision against the party". Execution shall be effected within fifteen (15) days from the day of receipt of the decision.[13] In addressing the enjoyment of the right of appeal against administrative decisions at first instance, the author has used the cases referred to the Constitutional Court of the Republic of Kosovo during the period 2009–2012, cases contesting

[12] Law no. 2/L-28, on Administrative Procedure, Official Gazette of the Provisional Institutions of Self-Government in Kosovo, dated 1 January 2007. For more, see Articles 126, 127. Article 126 provides: "Natural and legal persons are entitled to request revocation, abolishment or modification of administrative act in compliance with the rules for administrative appeal set out under this Law. The entitlement referred may be exercised through a request for redress or review submitted to the person responsible for the act, or through appeal sent to higher bodies.

[13] Law on Independent Oversight Board of the Civil Service of Kosovo, no. 03/L-192, 16 August 2010. For more, see Articles 12, 13 and 14.

decisions of regular courts. In eight cases, from a total of 514 cases[14] registered, the individuals had filed complaints with the Independent Oversight Board against administrative decisions at first instance. This Board had rendered a decision, but against the decisions, discontented parties had used their legal remedies before the Court, or had requested from the Court to allow execution of a final administrative decision.

Countries with administrative courts existing and operating have an advantage in resolving administrative issues, in order for the citizens to effectively enjoy their rights.

Our rationale and preference for administrative courts are grounded on the fact that an international view, since the latter half of the nineteenth century, administrative courts have existing to review administrative cases; such is the case of the Administrative Tribunal of the International Labour Organization (ATILO). An illustrative case can be taken from a decision from the ATILO, on the claims of UNESCO employees, which was further reviewed by the International Court of Justice, which had given its consultative opinion on the nature of adjudication of the ATILO, and had emphasized the binding nature of its advisory opinion on the case (Zaganjori 2010, 139–142). We consider that along other changes, the establishment of administrative courts within the country would be much necessary, because only in this manner the judicial system is specialized, while the regular courts would be relieved of the administrative cases.

Until the end of 2012, while the Law on Regular Courts was in application, there was a special panel within the Supreme Court of Kosovo, adjudicating administrative matters, but in many monitoring reports issued by the OSCE, a delay in resolving cases had been found, along with many other problems, notably the overwhelming numbers of such cases.[15] Nevertheless, the Law now applicable since 1 January 2013, has provided that the adjudication of administrative cases related to final decisions, should be left to the competency of regular courts,[16] while the future should show the working results in proceeding and resolving administrative issues reflecting such changes.

---

[14] On the use of right of appeal against an administrative decision at first instance, see cases referred to the Constitutional Court of the Republic of Kosovo, namely: paragraph 16, case 55/11; paragraph 11, case KI 81/10; paragraphs 9–11 of case 120/11; paragraphs 12, 14, 15, 16, case 129/11; paragraph 9 case KI 04/12. The case challenging a final administrative decision, see case 120/11, paragraphs 12 and 21.

[15] Report on the Administrative Justice System in Kosovo, April 2007 – Organization for Security and Co-operation in Europe Mission in Kosovo.

[16] Law on Courts, no. 03/L-199, 22 July 2010, superseding the Law on Regular Courts of the SAPK, UNMIK Regulations and Law on Minor Offences; Upon the entry into force of this Law any reference in any Law, regulation, directive, rule or other act vesting first instance jurisdiction in the Minor Offenses Court, Municipal Court, District Court, Commercial Court, or Supreme Court shall be construed to mean the Basic Court. Any reference in any Law, regulation, directive or rule vesting second instance jurisdiction in the High Minor Offenses Court, District Court, or Supreme Court shall be construed to mean the Court of Appeals; the Law entered into force on January 1, 2011 for Articles 29, 35, 36 38 and 40, while for other Articles it shall begin to be implemented from January 1, 2013

According to our research, final decisions of the Independent Oversight Body for civil servant in Kosovo (IOBCSK) were appealed before regular courts,[17] while decisions of the Constitutional Court[18] had found violations of human rights by the courts that had reviewed the IOBCSK decisions before. This proves the fact that decisions of regular courts have not a unified system of case law in material competency, namely in labor relations.[19] In seven cases, the claims of authorized parties – individuals were about application or execution of such court decisions, while one was a request to annul a Judgment of the Supreme Court, because the case, according to the Applicant, had been decided on the basis of legal provisions which would be subject to constitutional review by the Court, and in this case, the court would have suspended the proceeding until a verdict is rendered by the Constitutional Court. The reasons referred to by the Constitutional Court in reviewing and annulling decisions of the Supreme Court are mainly the failure of the Supreme Court to preserve reliability and integrity of the proceeding, thereby causing violation of constitutional rights to a fair and impartial trial, as provided by Article 31 of the Constitution, and the Article 6 of the ECHR (Hasani et al. 2012, 68).

Referring back to the aspects we addressed above, it is worth mentioning that a considerable number of regular court decisions have been contested before the Constitutional Court of Kosovo. Specifically, out of total number – 514 cases submitted by authorized parties to the Constitutional Court from its establishment until 2012, 381 cases were disputes of decisions rendered by regular courts. The Table 3, reflects the number of cases referred to the Court and the subject matter thereof. In this statistical analysis, one may see that in the majority of referrals/cases, or 74 %, authorized parties have requested constitutional review of regular court decisions, while only in 133 referrals/cases or in 26 %, they have had another issue to be review by constitutional justice.

---

[17] Decisions of the Supreme Court of Kosovo: Decisions: A.no. 678/2010, 23.02.2011; A. no. 1029/2009, 27.05.2012; A.no. 2898/2010, 23.02.2011; A.no. 11/2010, of 23.02.2012 and Judgments: A. no. 2504/2007. 27.02.2009; A.no. 2376/2007, dated 26.08.2009 and A.no. 551/2011. For more, see Report on the Administrative Justice System in Kosovo, April 2007, Legal System Monitoring Section, Department of Human Rights, Decentralization and Communities, Organization for Security and Co-operation in Europe Mission in Kosovo, for remarks and criticism in the operations – namely decisions of the Supreme Court related to labour disputes involving civil servants. It also states that there are contradictory judgments, and failure to observe the principle of resolution of cases in a reasonable timeline, pp. 19–20.

[18] See unenforced decisions of the IOBCSK, related to disputing of court decisions, in cases KI 81/10, KI 55/11, KI 120/11, KI 129/11, KI 140/11, all cases decided by the Constitutional Court by the end of December 2012, while KI 80/12 and KI 112/12, left to be reviewed in 2013. One of the cases demanding review of Judgment of the Supreme Court A.no. 551/11, of 20 June 2011, by referral filed by the Ministry of Health, in the case 120/11, it was proposed also that the Constitutional Court of the Republic of Kosovo review the constitutionality of the Law on the Independent Oversight Board of Kosovo, no. 03/L-192, concretely Articles 13 and 14.

[19] See Decisions of the Supreme Court quoted. Decisions when the Supreme Court of Kosovo declares incompetent to decide on the claim of claimant against the decision of the Independent Oversight Board of Kosovo, thereby transferring the case to the Municipal Court, and judgments in which this court approves the claims, thereby annulling decisions of the Independent Oversight Board of Kosovo, and reviews and adjudicates these cases as a competent court.

Table 3 Subject matter of the cases/referrals submitted from the parties to the Constitutional court 2009–2012

2009		2010		2011		2012		2009–2012	
79 cases submitted		132 cases submitted		164 cases submitted		139 cases submitted		514 cases submitted	
Review of the regular court decisions	Other	Review of the regular court decisions	Other	Review of the regular court decisions	Other	Review of the regular court decisions	Other	Review of the regular court decisions	Other
48	31	93	39	139	25	101	38	**381**	**133**
Cases	Cases	Cases	Cases	Cases	Cases	Cases	Cases	Cases	Cases
60.7 %	**39.3 %**	**70.5 %**	**29.5 %**	**84.7 %**	**15.3 %**	**72.7 %**	**27.3 %**	**74 %**	**26 %**

Furthermore, the Constitutional Court of Kosovo, since its first decision, has throughout this time referred to the ECHR decisions, thereby transmitting and enforcing directly the effect of ECtHR decisions in its case law, but also further into the legal system of Kosovo. Moreover, its role as a Constitution defender and guarantor amount to a "linking bridge" between the Constitutions of the Republic of Kosovo and the European Convention on Human Rights.

The observation of provisions of the ECHR and protocols to it, and enshrinement of constitutional mechanisms in Kosovo for the protection of fundamental human rights and freedoms, derive from the Article 22 of the Constitution of Kosovo, directly affecting implementation and imposing superiority on the constitutional system. The paper highlights the challenges and achievements of Kosovo's constitutional jurisprudence in defending fundamental human rights and freedoms.

All this brings to a clear conclusion that the Constitutional Court of Kosovo's practice is in line with the best European practices, not only by simply incorporating international norms in the its constitution but also from view point of consistent interpretation with practices of the ECtHR. Undoubtedly, the trend of development of the constitutional jurisprudence of Kosovo is a reality of closely following ECtHR practices.

Conclusion

In addressing matters related to such rights and freedoms, one must point out the role of the Constitutional Court as the high guarantee for human rights and freedoms. It has been found and emphasized that the constitutional review of the individual cases referred to the constitutional justice of Kosovo has decided that there were violations of individual rights and freedoms. In judgments related to individual complaints, it was found that the violation of human rights, namely: the right to fair and impartial trial, right to legal remedies, judicial protection of human rights, equality before law, electoral rights and participation, freedom of movement, and property rights. These cases speak of violation of human rights and freedoms by the "justice administration bodies", precisely by regular courts, almost in all decided cases, excluding two judgments, fundamental rights and freedoms were violated by other public authorities.

On the other hand, according to the decisions of the Constitutional Court in the years 2009–2012, there have been a considerable number of individual cases in which the Court has rejected the referrals of the parties, and decided on them by resolutions on inadmissibility. As it was delineated throughout this paper the jurisprudence of Constitutional Court of Kosovo heavily draws from the long practice jurisprudence of European Court of Human Rights.

The consolidation of constitutional justice in Kosovo dealing with cases regarding the protection human rights were challenging for the newly established Constitutional Court of Kosovo. Consequently, they are a special success story of the Kosovo society, related to the rule of constitutional legal order, the rule of law, and protection of human rights in a young state.

All in all, Articles 22 and 53 of the Constitution of Kosovo are key integrated elements of ECHR and jurisprudence of ECtHR into jurisprudence of Constitutional Court of Kosovo. Moreover, Therefore, it could be rightly argues that fundamental rights jurisprudence of the Kosovo Constitutional Court follows fully the European Convention of Human Rights and the Strasbourg jurisprudence, and that therefore the Kosovo Court contributes to the process of convergence of Fundamental Rights in Europe.

Bibliography

Books & Articles

Arnold, Rainer. 2005. The European Constitution and the Transformation of National Constitutional Law. Accessed on 14 Feb 2014. www.ecln.net/elements/conferences/book_prag/ArnoldFinal.pdf

Arnold, Rainer. 2007. The emergence of a European Constitutional Law. *Electronic Journal of Comparative Law* 11: 3. Accessed on 14 Feb 2014. http://www.ejcl.org/113/article113-26.pdf

Constitutional Court of Kosovo. 2009–2010. Bulletin of case law. http://www.confeuconstco.org/en/congress/congress-XVI/Bulletin_of_Case_Law_-_E.pdf

Constitutional Court of Kosovo. 2011. Bulletin of case law. http://www.gjk-ks.org/repository/docs/BULETINI%202011%20ANG.pdf

Constitutional Court of Kosovo. 2012. Bulletin of case law I. http://www.gjk-ks.org/repository/docs/buletini_ang_vol_1.pdf

Constitutional Court of Kosovo. 2012. Bulletin of case law II. http://www.gjk-ks.org/repository/docs/buletini_ang_vol_2.pdf

Hasani, Enver. 2013. Constitutional protection of the head of state: The case of Kosovo. *Vienna Journal International Constitutional Law, ILC* 7: 2.

Hasani, Enver, Paczolay, Petar, and Riegner, Michael (eds). 2012. Constitutional justice in Southeast Europe, Constitutional Courts in Kosovo, Serbia, Albania, and Hungary between Ordinary Judiciaries and the European Court of Human Rights, Baden.

BoIstrefi, Kushtrim. 2012. The application of Article 103 of the United Nations Charter in the European Courts: The quest for regime compatibility on fundamental rights. *European Journal of Legal Studies* 5(2): 81–93.

Botusharova, Snezhana, (eds). 2012. *The Constitutional Court of Kosovo and the European Court of Human Rights*. In: Constitutional Justice in Southeast Europe, Constitutional Courts in Kosovo, Serbia, Albania, and Hungary between Ordinary Judiciaries and the European Court of Human Rights, Baden

Donnelly, Jack. 2006. *International human rights*, 3rd ed. Boulder: Westview Press.

Mavčič, Prof. Dr. Arne Marjan. 2011. Individual complaint as a domestic remedy to be exhausted or effective within the meaning of the ECHR – comparative and Slovenian aspects. Accessed on 14 Feb 2014 at: https://www.google.com/#q=The+Effects+of+the+Judgments+of+the+European+Court+of+Human+Rights+According+to+the+German+Constitutional+Court

Methasani-Cani, Eralda. 2008. Garancitë e të drejtave dhe lirive themelore të njeriut, Jus & Justica, nr.2/2008, Universiteti Evropian i Tiranës, Tiranë, (Scientific Journal of the Law Faculty, European University of Tirana).

Sweet, Alec Stone. 2007. The politics of constitutional review in France and Europe. *I•CON* 5(1). Accessed on 14 Feb 2014 at: http://islandia.law.yale.edu/alecstonesweet/PDFs/politics%20con%20review%20france%20europe.pdf

Zaganjori, Xhezair. 2010. The constitutional court as a guarantor of the fundamental human rights and freedoms. Accessed on 14 Feb 2014 at: http://www.umk.ro/images/documente/publicatii/Buletin19/2_the_constit.pdf

Normative Acts/Reports

Annual Report. 2010. Constitutional Court of the Republic of Kosovo.
Annual Report. 2011. Constitutional Court of the Republic of Kosovo.
Constitution of the Republic of Albania. Mar 2009.
Constitution of the Republic of Kosovo. June 2008.
Constitutional Court of the Republic of Albania. 01.06.2011. Decision no. 20.
Constitutional Court of the Republic of Albania. 05.03.2012. Decision no. 12.
Constitutional Court of the Republic of Albania. 10.02.2012. Decision no. 4.
European Convention for the Protection of Human Rights and Fundamental Freedoms. 1950.
Law on Administrative Procedure. 1 January 2007. Official Gazette of the Provisional Institutions of Self-Government in Kosovo, no. 2/L-28.
Law on Independent Oversight Board of the Civil Service of Kosovo. 16 August 2010. no. 03/L-192.
Law on the Constitutional Court of the Republic of Kosovo. December 2008. Law No. 03/L-121.
Report on the Administrative Justice System in Kosovo. April 2007 – Organization for Security and Co-operation in Europe Mission in Kosovo.
Rule of Procedure of the Constitutional Court of the Republic of Kosovo. November 2010. No.185/1/2010.
Supreme Court of the Republic of Kosovo. 01 October 2012. Istref Halili and 16 other former employees of the Kosovo Energy Corporation, against individual judgments of the Supreme Court of the Republic of Kosovo, no. KI 132/10, KI 28/11, KI 82/11, KI 85/11, KI 89/11, KI 100/11, KI 104/11, KI 109/11, KI 118/11, KI 123/11, KI 142/11, KI 143/11, KI 144/11, KI 154/11, KI 01/12, KI 02/12, KI 14/12, ref.no. AGJ 309/12.
Supreme Court of the Republic of Kosovo. 10 March 2011. Isuf Mërlaku and 25 other former employees of Kosovo Energy Corporation, Constitutional Review of 26 Individual Judgments of the Supreme Court of the Republic of Kosovo, KI 08/10, KI 16/10, KI 22/10, KI 24/10, KI 27/10, KI 36/10, KI 41/10, KI 42/10, KI 45/10, KI 53/10, KI 54/10, KI 56/10, KI 57/10, KI 58/10, KI 59/10, KI 60/10, KI 61/10, KI 63/10, KI 64/10, KI 65/10, KI 66/10, KI 67/10, KI 68/10 KI 71/10, KI 74/10, KI 76/10 Applicant, ref. no. AGJ 90/11.
Supreme Court of the Republic of Kosovo. 12 June 2012. Bajrush Gashi, case No 06/12, Pzd. no. 67/2011, ref. no. AGJ 262.
Supreme Court of the Republic of Kosovo. 14 December 2010. Kimete Bikliqi versus The Central Election Commission, no. KI 09/10, ref. no.: 67/10.
Supreme Court of the Republic of Kosovo. 15 October 2010. *Gani Prokshit* other former employees of Kosovo Energy Corporation, Constitutional Review of 21 Individual Judgments of the Supreme Court of the Republic of Kosovo, KI 58/09, KI 59/09, KI 60/09, KI 64/09, KI 66/09, KI 69/09, KI 70/09, KI 72/09, KI 75/09, KI 76/09, KI 77/09, KI 78/09, KI 79/09, KI 03/10, KI 05/10, KI 13/10, Applicant, ref. no. AGJ 62/10.
Supreme Court of the Republic of Kosovo. 16 July 2012. Islam Thaçi, rev. no. 188/2009, KI 47/12, ref. no.: AGJ/278/12.
Supreme Court of the Republic of Kosovo. 23 June 2010. Imer Ibrahimi and 48 other former employees of Kosovo Energy Corporation versus 49 individual judgments of the Supreme Court of the Republic of Kosovo, KI 40/09, ref. no. AGJ 30/10.
Supreme Court of the Republic of Kosovo. 27 December 2011. Ilaz Halili and 20 other former employees of the Kosovo Energy Corporation, against individual judgments of the Supreme

Court of the Republic of Kosovo no. KI 76/10, KI 82/10, KI 83/10, KI 102/10, KI 111/10, KI 122/10, KI 127/10, KI 11/11, KI 15/11, KI 18/11, KI 45/11, KI 47/11, KI 48/11, KI 50/11, KI 57/11, KI 60/11, KI 69/11, KI 71/11, KI 73/11, KI 75/11, KI 79/11, ref.no. AGJ 181.

Supreme Court of the Republic of Kosovo. 27 May 2009. *Avni Kumnova*, KI 39/09, no. 142/07, ref. no. AGJ 82/11 November 2011.

Supreme Court of the Republic of Kosovo. 3 March 2011. Fahrudin Megjedovic, Deputy Chairperson for Communities of the Municipal Assembly in Peja Constitutional review of the Decision of the Municipal Assembly of Peja on the appointment of the Deputy Mayor of Municipality for Communities, KI 32/10, ref. no. AGJ 85/11.

Supreme Court of the Republic of Kosovo. 30 October 2010. Valon Bislimi versus Ministry of Internal Affairs, KI 06/10, ref. no. AGJ 63/10.

Supreme Court of the Republic of Kosovo. 6 April 2011. NTSH Meteorit, no. KI 55/09, Decision No. 2407/2006.

Supreme Court of the Republic of Kosovo. 7 June 2010. Arsic Draza, no. K1 104/10, GZ no. 78/2010 of the District Court of Gjilan, ref. no.: AGJ221/12.

Protection of Human Rights in the European Union

Viktor Muraviov and Olena Sviatun

Abstract The article analyzes the system of human rights protection in the European Union and its relationship with the human rights protection of the Council of Europe. The special focus is made on the legal nature and framework of the EU Charter of Fundamental Rights and the progress of the European Union's accession to the European Convention on the Protection of Human Rights and Fundamental Freedoms.

Respect for and protection of human rights is one of the leading activities of the European Union in accordance with the aim and principles of the organization, enshrined in the founding treaties. Any European State that respects the values of freedom, democracy, respect for human rights and fundamental freedoms and the rule of law may apply to become a member of the EU, as provided by Articles 6 and 49 of the Treaty on the European Union (TEU) (Official Journal, 26 October 2012, C 326). The criteria to be met by the candidate countries for accession to the European Union (the Copenhagen criteria) were approved by the European Council in Copenhagen in June 1993. According to these criteria, membership in the EU, from the perspective of political standards, requires that the candidate country secures the stability of institutions, thus guaranteeing democracy, the rule of law, respect for human rights and protection for minorities.

Countries wishing to become members of the EU should not only consolidate democracy and the rule of law into their constitutions, but also implement those principles in everyday life. Their constitutions must guarantee democratic freedoms, including political pluralism, freedom of speech and freedom of conscience. They should establish democratic institutions and independent judiciary, bodies of constitutional jurisdiction. This will in turn create conditions for the normal functioning of state institutions, free and fair elections, the periodic change of the ruling parliamentary majority, as well as recognition of the important role of the opposition in political life.

V. Muraviov (✉) • O. Sviatun
Institute of International Relations, Taras Shevchenko National University of Kyiv,
36/1 Melnikova St, 308, 04119 Kyiv, Ukraine
e-mail: vmour@visti.com

R. Arnold (ed.), *The Convergence of the Fundamental Rights Protection in Europe*, Ius Gentium: Comparative Perspectives on Law and Justice 52,
DOI 10.1007/978-94-017-7465-9_10

In the European Union, there is no integrated mechanism to protect human rights. National human rights protection systems that operate in every EU Member State complement the human rights protection system of the Union. Additionally, the protection of human rights is an integral part of the activities of the Council of Europe. All 28 EU Member States are members of the Council of Europe. Evolvement of the legal framework at the EU level to ensure the protection of rights and freedoms was previously gradual, but the system has great potential for development.

In the early stages of its evolution the EU did not pay much attention to human rights. It was believed that such issues were outside the goals of economic integration and that the list of human rights should thus not be included in the founding treaties of the European Community. Furthermore, in the decisions of the Court of Justice (Stork 1959, Geitling 1960), the provisions of the EU law were interpreted as having primacy over the provisions of national constitutions of the Member States regarding human rights and freedoms. This caused fear on the part of EU institutions that Member States might be required to bring the provisions of EU law in accordance with their domestic law for the protection of human rights.

On the other hand, the competence of institutions of the European Community in the field of human rights was limited. The European Court of Justice (ECJ) did not have criminal jurisdiction, narrowing its ability to engage in the protection of human rights and freedoms. While hearing cases, the ECJ had to deal with political and social rights only occasionally. Therefore, the ECJ did not consider the issue of human rights systematically. However, it was for the Court of Justice to begin to confer the Community competence in the sphere of human rights. National Courts placed pressure on the ECJ, refusing to recognise the primacy of European Community Law if it failed to guarantee protection of human rights.

First principles of human rights law in the European Communities were recognized by the Court of Justice in the case 29/69 Stauder v City of Ulm [1970].[1] In this case, a German citizen protested that his fundamental right to human dignity, protected by Article 1 of the German Grundgesetz (the German Constitution) was being infringed by having his name on his coupon when claiming reduced-price butter by the Community. The Court of Justice held that the Commission's decision in 1969 that had given the Member States permission to establish preferential prices for certain categories of the population, did not contain anything that could violate the basic human rights protected by the Court of Justice and enshrined in the general principles of Community law. So there was no infringement of fundamental human rights by the EU institutions. The activities of the national authority to amend its legislation according to the provisions of the adequate Community law were the reasons for violation. The requirement to indicate personal data on the coupon, which violated human rights, was not necessary. Thus, the concept of basic human rights was in this instance recognized as a general principle of European Community law (Forster 2008, 82) for the first time.

[1] Judgment of the Court of 12 November 1969. – Erich Stauder v City of Ulm – Sozialamt. – Reference for a preliminary ruling: Verwaltungsgericht Stuttgart - Germany – Case 29–69.

In the case 11/70 Internationale Handelsgesellschaft [1972][2] which dealt with the introduction of licenses for the export of agricultural products within the common agricultural policy, the Court of Justice held that fundamental human rights are part of the constitutional principles common to the Member States of the European Community. The Court of Justice was therefore supposed to protect basic human rights by applying the relevant provisions of the constitution and international agreements on human rights to which both the Member States were party. In this case, the Court of Justice decided that it should protect fundamental rights, taking into account the basic principles of the Community. Protection of these rights, in accordance with the common constitutional traditions of the Member States, should be provided within the structure and goals of the European Communities. The Court of Justice further stated that the source of the validity of the concept of human rights was the legal framework of the European Communities. In such instances, the Court of Justice should apply national constitutions and international treaties of the Member States relating to the protection of human rights, not as the source of European Community law, but as the source of cognition of law to educe the fundamental rights taking into account interests of Communities.

In the case 136/79 National Panasonic [1980], the European Court of Justice held that although the European Convention for the Protection of Human Rights and Fundamental Freedoms of 1950 was not the part of the EU legal order, its provisions should nevertheless be implemented. Therefore any measures adopted within the EU would not be valid if they were contrary to the provisions of the Convention (National Panasonic (UK) Limited v Commission of the European Communities 1980). So by virtue of the practice of the Court of Justice human rights were attributed to the general principles of European Community law.

Gradually in Europe, two independent systems of human rights protection began to evolve – within the Council of Europe and the European Communities. However, the human rights protection system created by the Community was fragmented. In the early stages of its existence, it mostly comprised of economic rights as the ideology of "market human being" was prevailing at the time.

The further development of European integration, its extension in the political sphere and in the sphere of justice and home affairs was accompanied by the adoption of further rulings in the Member States. According to those rulings, Member States refused to acknowledge the primacy of Community law over internal constitutional law concerning human rights and freedoms. This prompted the Member States and Community institutions to pay more attention to the protection of human rights. At this time, a number of documents were adopted which attempted to determine the fundamental rights and freedoms of human beings within the European Community. These include the European Social Charter (1961), the Declaration of Fundamental Rights and Freedoms (1989), the Charter of Fundamental Social Rights of Workers (1989), amongst others.

---

[2] Judgment of the Court of 17 December 1970. – Internationale Handelsgesellschaft mbH v Einfuhr- und Vorratsstelle für Getreide und Futtermittel. – Reference for a preliminary ruling: erwaltungsgericht Frankfurt am Main – Germany – Case 11–70.

Of fundamental importance for the recognition of human rights as a component of EC law, was the adoption of the Single European Act in 1986. Its preamble referenced the European Convention on Human Rights and Fundamental Freedoms 1950 (ECHR) as the grounds for supporting democracy.

After the European Union was founded in 1993 the efforts to create a catalogue of fundamental rights were intensified. This catalogue was to take into account the provisions of the European Convention as of 1950, and to contain the fundamental rights attributed to the Union's citizens. The Article F was included into the Treaty on European Union. This Treaty also contained the provision that the EU respects the fundamental rights guaranteed by the European Convention of 1950, as well as the general principles of Community law commonly provided by all Member States' constitutional traditions. This provision was transposed as Article 6 into the Treaty of Amsterdam on the European Union in 1997. However, the EU refused to sign the Convention itself, leaving this issue for the Member States to decide.

The main organization in charge of the protection of human rights and freedoms has traditionally been the Council of Europe, established in 1949. According to the Statute of the Council of Europe, the Organization is to promote the spiritual and moral values, which are the common heritage of their peoples and the true source of individual freedom, political liberty and the rule of law. In short, principles which form the basis of all genuine democracies.[3]

Since its inception, the European Community has maintained a close relationship with the Council of Europe. The Treaty establishing the European Community contained a separate Article 303 (Official Journal, 24. December 2002, C 325, 33–184) (now Article – 220 of the Treaty on the Functioning of the EU), which reinforced the need to establish appropriate forms of cooperation with the Council of Europe. In practice, a European country cannot join the EU if it is not a member of the Council of Europe. Within the Council of Europe, an effective system of human rights protection was established. The main documents on which it is based are the European Convention (1950), the European Social Charter (1961), the European Convention against Torture and Inhuman or Degrading Treatment or Punishment (1983), and the Framework Convention for the Protection of National Minorities (1995). The implementation of these documents by the member States of the Council of Europe is monitored by a system of control authorities, which all have the appropriate competencies.

The European Convention for the Protection of Human Rights and Fundamental Freedoms of 1950[4] is the most important of the documents adopted by the Council of Europe. It sets the standards of conduct for States Parties in the sphere of the protection of human rights and fundamental freedoms. The Convention not only contains the catalogue of rights enshrined in the Universal Declaration of Human

[3] Statute of the Council of Europe, 1949: http://conventions.coe.int/Treaty/en/Treaties/Html/001.htm.

[4] Конвенція про захист прав людини і основоположних свобод з поправками, внесеними Протоколами №№ 11 та 14. [Електронний ресурс]. – Режим доступу до докум.: http://www.echr.coe.int/NR/rdonlyres/888FC791-E2C0-4096-AF5E-D843F09C0E24/0/UKR_CONV.pdf.

Rights (1948), but also charges the European Court of Human Right with monitoring the activities of Member States to promote those rights. The decisions of the European Court of Human Rights are binding for the High Contracting Parties of the European Convention.

The EU recognizes the European Convention of 1950 but is not currently party to it because the Convention does not form part of EU law. Although the Union does not claim a leading role in protecting human rights in Europe, there is competition between the Council of Europe and the European Union. The European Court of Justice decided against accession to the European Convention without amending the founding documents of the European Union. One important reason for this decision was that such accession would imply borrowing rules of law without taking into account the specific nature of the EU and its legal order. Another reason was the absence, in the European Convention (1950), of the expanded catalogue of social, economic and cultural rights contained in another Council of Europe legal source: the European Social Charter (1961), revised in 1996. On the other hand, the Court was unwilling to subordinate its jurisdiction to the European Court of Human Rights. As EU citizens, in order to protect their rights, can apply to the judicial authorities of the EU and of the European Convention of 1950, a problem arises as to whose judgment would have priority in a case of collision. A partial solution to these issues was found within the Lisbon Treaty and the EU Charter of fundamental rights as revised in 2007.

Even before the signing of the Treaty of Lisbon, first steps for the separation of powers of the European Court of Human Rights and the Court of Justice were being made. The European Court of Human Rights, in a number of its judgments, applied the doctrine of limited interference with the jurisdiction of the EU if the EU legal order provides equivalent protection of human rights within the Union. The doctrine's essence lies in the recognition, by the European Court of Human Rights, of equivalent protection if the person on the territory of the Union has the opportunity to appeal against acts of the EU institutions that violate the human rights guaranteed by the European Convention of 1950.

The system of norms and mechanisms to protect human rights and freedoms in the EU includes various documents that have both mandatory and declarative power. The Treaty on European Union (TEU) contains several provisions relating to human rights. Article 2 states that the Union is founded on the values of respect for human dignity, freedom, democracy, equality, the rule of law and respect for human rights, including the rights of persons belonging to minorities. These values are common to all Member States in a society in which pluralism, non-discrimination, tolerance, justice, solidarity and equality between women and men prevail. Article 6 TEU establishes the principle of respect for fundamental rights and freedoms. It emphasizes that the fundamental rights guaranteed by the European Convention for the Protection of Human Rights and Fundamental Freedoms are common to the constitutional traditions of all Member States, which in turn constitute the general principles of Union law.

Part two of the Treaty on the Functioning of the European Union (TFEU) is entitled "Non-Discrimination and Citizenship of the Union". In addition to establishing EU citizenship, this Part of the Treaty provides for such rights and freedoms of EU citizens, such as the right to free movement and residence in the territory of the Member States, the right to vote and stand as a candidate at municipal elections in the Member States and European Parliament elections, the right to diplomatic and consular protection and the right to address claims to the institutions or bodies of the European Union.

Part Three of the TFEU establishes freedom of movement for workers, freedom of establishment and the principle of equal salaries for men and women.

The TFEU also sets out safeguards to protect the rights and freedoms: compensating damages caused by the activities of the EU institutions and or by its servants (Article 340).

Judgments of the Court of Justice define the basic principles of human rights and freedoms in the EU.

Among the documents that are declarative in nature, one should mention the Declaration of Fundamental Rights and Freedoms and the Community Charter of the Fundamental Social Rights for Workers.

The Charter of Fundamental Rights of the European Union, adopted in 2007 (Official Journal, 26 October 2012, C 326, 394–407), holds a special status in EU law. The Charter includes a detailed catalogue of fundamental rights and the freedoms attached to those rights that are attributed to every human being within the territory of the European Union, covering civil, political, economic, social and cultural rights. By virtue of the Charter's provisions, all these rights have the same legal regime, thus marking the final departure from the concept of "market human being".

The Charter has the same legal value as the Treaties, although it is not a part of them.

A new ideological approach regarding the human being and his/her place in the world was accepted as the basis for the Charter. The Preamble of the Charter proclaims that an individual and his/her interests are central to the Union. Unlike the vast majority of international legal instruments that classify fundamental rights according to the subject matter of the right protected, the classification of rights and freedoms in the Charter is made on the basis of the values they protect. These values are human dignity, individual freedom, equality and solidarity. The rights and freedoms to be protected by these values are enshrined in titles under their respective names (Titles I–IV). Separate titles are devoted to citizenship and justice (Titles V and VI).

The catalogue of fundamental rights and freedoms is divided into several categories. This includes personal rights and freedoms, political rights and freedoms, economic, social and cultural rights, and the main responsibilities of Member States. These rights are complemented by the guarantees of rights and freedoms of the individual.

The principle of equality ensures equal conditions for the implementation of all rights and freedoms, thus preventing discrimination. Its main elements are the legal, social and political equality. Articles 20, 21, 23 implement formal equal opportunities for individuals. The idea of positive discrimination is also taken into account and compensation is provided for individuals who, for objective reasons relating to their condition in society, need special treatment in the form of special conditions and provisions with additional legal options. This applies to children's rights (Article 24), the rights of the elderly (Article 25) and persons with physical and mental disabilities (Article 26).

Article 22 of the Charter is intended to guarantee cultural, religious and linguistic diversity. Equality in this area is aimed at creating a pan-European human rights culture for further integration in the EU, based on the recognition of human values.

Legal equality implies equality of all individuals before the law. Social equality means equality regardless attribution to any particular social group (gender, race, religion, age, sexual orientation etc.). Political equality means equality regardless person's nationality.

Individual rights and freedoms (Titles I and II) belong to the natural and inherent rights of every person from birth. These include the right to human dignity, right to life, the right to integrity of the person, the right to liberty and security of person, the right to respect for private and family life, the right to protection of personal data, the right to marry and to found a family, freedom of thought and religion, freedom of expression and freedom of information, freedom of movement and choice of residence, and the right to asylum.

Title II "Freedoms" contains not only traditional (negative) rights such as the right to freedom of expression, freedom of religion, freedom of assembly etc. but also rights of the second generation (positive), including the right to choose an occupation and engage in work, the right to housing and so on. Implementation of the latest requires assistance from state and society.

Political rights and freedoms are closely related to the functioning of the state and the European Union. At the EU level they are clearly connected to European citizenship. These include voting rights, freedom of assembly and association, the right to good governance, the right of access to official documents, and the right to petition.

Economic, social and cultural rights are based on the principle of the welfare state. They are enshrined in Title II, "Freedom", Title III "Equality" and Title IV "Solidarity". These rights include the right to property, freedom of economic activity, employment and related rights of employees, social and economic rights of people in need of increased social security, the right to protection of family, mother and child, the right to social security and social assistance, the right to healthcare, the right of access to services of general importance, freedom of the arts and sciences, the right to education, and the guarantee of a high level of protection for environmental law and consumer rights.

The main responsibilities of the Charter refer to the duty to respect and protect human dignity, to adequately consider the interests of children, to provide free compulsory education, and to promote and enhance environmental protection.

The Charter also includes provisions on the abuse of rights (Article 54). These provisions prevent the authorities or private individuals from elimination or excessive restrictions on the rights and freedoms of others.

Safeguards for rights and freedoms in the European Union are covered by institutional, procedural and substantive measures.

Institutional safeguards include non-judicial and judicial protection in the form of the Ombudsman of the European Union, the Commission, and the European Data Protection Supervisor and the diplomatic and consular missions of the Member States in the third countries.

Procedural safeguards include the right to a fair and public trial within a reasonable time by an independent and impartial tribunal (Article 47.2), the right to legal aid (Article 47.2), the presumption of innocence (Article 48.1), the principle of legality and proportionality of criminal offences and penalties (Article 49), the principle of inadmissibility of criminal prosecution for an offense for which the person was already tried or punished in the Member States (Article 50), prohibition of imprisonment for debt, and the right of appeal in relation to criminal cases.

Material safeguards compensate for damage caused to individuals by others, as physical and legal entities, such as the EU and Member States may be subject to financial responsibility.

Financial responsibility of individuals and entities is regulated primarily by the domestic law of Member States.

Financial responsibility of Member States for violation of subjective rights is established by the provisions of the European Union law and EU case-law (case Francovich).

Financial responsibility of the EU may result from the activity or inactivity of Union institutions or bodies, as provided for in Article 340 TFEU.

Title VII "General Provisions Governing the Interpretation and Application of the Charter" (Articles 50–54) is the final section. Its purpose is to define the conditions and procedures for application of the Charter by the EU and Member States, as well as to resolve the difficult issue regarding co-relation of its provisions with other sources of fundamental rights adopted at the universal, European and domestic levels.

First, one should note the limited scope of the Charter (Article 51.1). Despite the fact that the Charter enshrines the fundamental rights and principles of the legal status of people and citizens in all areas, only EU institutions, bodies, offices and agencies, on the one hand, and the Member States on the other, are recognized formally as "addressees".

However, EU member states are the " addressees" of the Charter provisions only when they are "implementing the EU Law", in other words, when acting in the exercise of its founding treaties, international agreements, regulations and the European Court of Justice case-law.

In areas that are not regulated by EU law (e.g. election of national parliaments, religion, marriage and family relations), the Charter provisions have no power over Member States. If these areas affect the fundamental rights and freedoms of the individuals or citizens (e.g. freedom of conscience and religion), the individual concerned must seek protection under the provisions of other legal documents, e.g. national constitutions and/or the European Convention on Human Rights.

Article 53 of the Charter guarantees the inviolability of other sources of fundamental rights and freedoms of individuals and citizens. It refers to international legal acts at both the universal and regional level (United Nations International Covenants on Civil and Political Rights and Economic, Social and Cultural rights (1966), the European Convention of Human Rights (1950), the European Social Charter and other human rights conventions of the Council of Europe, etc.), national constitutional law (fundamental rights incorporated in the constitutions of the Member States, including the constitution of the federation, for example, in Germany), and finally to other sources of European Union law that provide basic human and civil rights.

Separately, the Charter installs an instrument for application and interpretation particularly for the provisions borrowed from other fundamental rights sources. If any right is recognized in the text of the Charter and in EU founding treaties, it should be exercised under conditions and within the limits of the Treaties (Article 52.2). This applies to all fundamental rights of the Union's citizens that, as was mentioned above, are enshrined in the Part Two of the Treaty on Functioning of the European Union. The same applies, for example, to the right of citizens of the Union to engage in work in any Member State (Article 15.2 of the Charter), which is the key element of the freedom of movement for workers within the EU internal market.

If the rights enshrined in the Charter, "correspond" to the rights enshrined in the European Convention of Human Rights and Protocols hereto, their meaning and scope are recognized as being the same as those laid down in the Convention (Article 52.3). This mainly includes personal and political rights (right to life, the right to security of person, freedom of assembly, etc.). Most of the rights in the text of the Charter have been transposed directly from the European Convention on Human Rights, and are thus identically worded. At the same time, this provision does not prevent the EU from expanding the contents of the corresponding rights and guarantees beyond those provided for in the Convention (Article 52.3). The European Convention on Human Rights, interpreted by the European Court of Human Rights, retains the role of setting the minimum standard of fundamental rights to which the Union should accede as a High Contracting Party. Accordingly, in matters of interpretation and application of human rights there is a clear trend of Union law keeping with the standards of the Council of Europe.

Finally, for those provisions of the Charter that result from the common constitutional traditions of the Member States (for instance, Article 20 "The principle of equality before the law"), it is provided that their interpretation should be in harmony with these traditions.

In addition to the above mentioned principles, Title VII of the Charter of Fundamental Rights enshrines other "general provisions". These provisions indicate that the Charter is not intended to expand the competence or the scope of EU law beyond the powers of the Union (Article 51.1), rather it provides for the grounds and limits of permissible restrictions on rights and freedoms enshrined in the Charter (Article 52.1). The Charter is required to take full account of laws and enforcement practices of Member States in cases where the Charter refers directly to the relevant legislation and/or practice – for example, in when implementing the right to marry and found a family, the freedom of thought, conscience and religion, and the many other social rights (Article 52.6).

Special rules are provided for those articles of the Charter which do not enshrine individual rights as such, but rather more abstract principles, such as: the principle of recognition and respect for the rights of elderly to a decent life (Article 25), to ensure a high level of consumer protection (Article 38) and others. These provisions do not have direct effect, but they are effective through legal measures that the Union and the Member States adopt to implement them. Natural and legal persons may invoke such provisions of the Charter in the courts, but only in order to interpret and/ or to control the legality of the acts of the relevant public authorities (Article 52.5).

Special conditions concerning the application of the Charter of Fundamental Rights of the European Union have also been established for Poland and the United Kingdom, which achieved some exceptions for themselves while drafting the Lisbon Treaty. These issues are enshrined in Protocol (No 30) "Protocol on the Application of the Charter of Fundamental Rights of the European Union to Poland and the United Kingdom." In Poland and the UK, the Charter does not extend the ability of the Court of Justice of the European Union, or any court or tribunal of Poland or of the UK, to find that the laws, regulations or administrative provisions, practices or actions of Poland or of the UK are inconsistent with the fundamental rights, freedoms and principles that it reaffirms. This prohibition does not apply to other sources of European Union law, even if they fix the provisions similar to those contained in the articles of the Charter. These sources (founding Treaties, regulations, directives and other EU legal acts, international treaties of the Union, etc) are fully covered by the action of the rule of law in all Member States, including Poland and the UK.

Social rights arising from Title IV "Solidarity" generate subjective rights which are subject to legal protection in Poland and the UK, only when similar rights are provided for in the national legislation of these countries. Such approach is set for all the provisions of the Charter which refer to national legislation and national practices (e.g., the right to marry and found a family – Article. 9). These provisions apply to Poland and the UK only to the extent that they are recognized in the law or practices of either country.

Protocol No 8 of TFEU provides that the agreement on accession of the Union to the European Convention on Human Rights (ECHR) (Official Journal, 26 October 2012, C 326, 273) should include the provisions aimed at preserving the specific nature of the EU and its legal system. In particular, it concerns specific arrangements for the Union's possible participation in the control bodies of the ECHR, as well the mechanisms necessary to ensure that proceedings by non-Member States and individual applications are correctly addressed to Member States and/or the Union as appropriate.

Such agreement shall ensure that accession of the Union to the ECHR does not adversely affect the competence of the Union and the powers of its institutions.

It will also ensure that it does not change the status of Member States in relation to the ECHR, especially with regard to the Protocols thereto, measures taken as a derogation from the obligations under the Convention during emergencies in accordance with Article 15 ECHR and reservations made by Member States in accordance with Article 57 ECHR.

After the Union accession to the ECHR, citizens and other subjects of fundamental rights guaranteed by the Convention will be able to apply to the European Court of Human Rights against the actions or failure to act of not only the national government (of the States Parties to the ECHR), but also of supranational authorities (EU institutions, bodies and agencies). Thus in both cases, current operating conditions will be kept concerning the exhaustion of domestic remedies (in the case of the EU – claims to the Court of Justice).

Actual activities on preparing the accession of the EU to the European Convention on Human Rights were launched earlier. In March 2001 the Committee of Ministers of the Council of Europe authorized the Steering Committee for Human Rights to study the legal and technical aspects for the Council of Europe to face, in case of eventual EU accession to the ECHR. In June 2002, the Steering Committee prepared a report [5]on the results of the above issues.

The report of the Steering Committee noted that the European Union will be able to accede to the ECHR, in contrast to countries that sign and ratify the Convention. Article 17 of the Protocol No 14 to the ECHR, signed in 2004, provides for amending Article 59 ECHR with new paragraph 2 to read as follows: "2. The European Union may accede to this Convention". It should be noted that the text of the Convention would need to undergo additional amendments to ensure a connection from a legal and technical point of view. The Steering Committee supported the position that such changes may be made either by the adoption of an additional protocol to the Convention, or by an agreement between the European Union on the one hand, and the Member States of the Convention on the other. Although the Steering Committee stressed the desirability of the latter option, it was determined not to include into Protocol No 14, provisions regarding an accession agreement, in order to leave the future open for all options. In January 2010, the last of the 47 Member States of the Council of Europe, the Russian Federation, ratified the Protocol No 14, which in turn became effective June 1, 2010. So, all obstacles to EU accession to the Convention on Human Rights of the Council of Europe were removed.

For this purpose, on 4 June 2010, the EU Ministers of Justice gave the European Commission the mandate to conduct negotiations on their behalf. On 26 May 2010, the Committee of Ministers of the Council of Europe gave an ad-hoc mandate to its Steering Committee for Human Rights (CDDH) to elaborate, in co-operation with the European Commission, the necessary legal instrument for the accession.

---

[5] Study of technical and legal issues of a possible EC/EU accession to the European Convention on Human Rights. Report adopted by the Steering Committee for Human Rights (CDDH) at its 53rd meeting (25–28 June 2002). – DG-II(2002)006, [CDDH(2002)010 Addendum 2]. – 37.

The CDDH entrusted the informal working group (CDDH-UE) with this task. It was composed of 14 experts from the Council of Europe member states (7 from EU member states and 7 from non-EU member states). The group held 8 meetings between July 2010 and June 2011.[6]

Apart from the issues discussed in connection with the accession to the ECHR (including problems concerning accession to different protocols, the possibility of making reservations etc.), the EU authorities in the Council of Europe raised the question of the necessity of making technical amendments to the text of the Convention to ensure the effectiveness of the protection of human rights provisions introduced by the ECHR (including the financial side of the EU participation in this system), and the ability to make these amendments to the ECHR system, taking into account the specific nature of the legal system of the EU.

On 14 October 2011, the Steering Committee for Human Rights of the Council of Europe transmitted a report to the Committee of Ministers on the work done, and the draft legal instrument in appendix. Given the political implications and some issues that were raised, on 13 June 2012, the Committee of Ministers instructed the CDDH to pursue negotiations with the EU within the ad hoc group "47 + 1" and to finalise the legal instrument dealing with the accession modalities. The ad hoc group held 5 meetings in Strasbourg. The last meeting was held on 2–5 April 2013 when the negotiators finalised the draft accession agreement of the European Union to the European Convention on Human Rights. It consists of a package of texts, equally necessary for the accession of the EU to the ECHR: a draft agreement on the accession of the EU to the ECHR and a draft explanatory report, a draft declaration by the EU, a draft rule to be added to the Rules of the Committee of Ministers for the supervision of the execution of judgments and of the terms of friendly settlements in cases to which the EU would be a party, a draft model of a memorandum of understanding. Unfortunately, December 18, 2014 the European Court of Justice delivered its binding Opinion 2/13 declaring that the agreement envisaged was not compatible with the provisions of founding Treaties of the EU.

Thus, over the past 60 years the European Union has come a long way to establish its own human rights protection system: from full deflection of the idea that human rights can take advantage of to the provisions of EU law, to developing its own catalogue of human rights – the Charter of Fundamental Rights. In addition, the entry into force of the Lisbon Treaty introduced a legal basis for the EU's accession to the European Convention on Human Rights. This poses the question of whether Ukraine needs to improve its own human rights system, as according to the criteria of EU accession only a State with the appropriate level of respect for human rights and fundamental freedoms can become a full member of the European Union.

[6] Accession of the European Union to the European Convention of Human Rights: http://www.coe.int/t/dghl/standardsetting/hrpolicy/Accession/default_en.asp.

Bibliography

Accession of the European Union to the European Convention of Human Rights. 2002. http://www.coe.int/t/dghl/standardsetting/hrpolicy/Accession/default_en.asp. CDDH, 25–28 June 2002.

Forster, Nigel. 2008. *European law, directions*, 2nd ed. New York: Oxford University Press.

Judgment of the Court of 4 February 1959. Friedrich Stork & Cie v High Authority of the European Coal and Steel Community. Case 1/58.

Judgment of the Court of 15 July 1960. Präsident Ruhrkolen-Verkaufsgesellschaft mbH, Geitling Ruhrkohlen-Verkaufsgesellschaft mbH, Mausegatt Ruhrkohlen-Verkaufsgesellschaft mbH and I. Nold KG v High Authority of the European Coal and Steel Community. Joined cases 36, 37, 38–59 and 40–59.

Judgment of the Court of 12 November 1969. Erich Stauder v City of Ulm – Sozialamt. Reference for a preliminary ruling: Verwaltungsgericht Stuttgart – Germany. Case 29–69.

Judgment of the Court of 17 December 1970. Internationale Handelsgesellschaft mbH v Einfuhr- und Vorratsstelle für Getreide und Futtermittel. Reference for a preliminary ruling: Verwaltungsgericht Frankfurt am Main – Germany. Case 11–70.

Judgment of the Court of 26 June 1980. National Panasonic (UK) Limited v commission of the European communities. Competition: Investigations by the commission. Case 136/79.

Official Journal, 24 December 2002, C 325.

Official Journal, 26 October 2012, C 326.

Конвенція про захист прав людини і основоположних свобод з поправками, внесеними Протоколами №№ 11 та 14. [Electronic resource]. Mode of access to the document. http://www.echr.coe.int/NR/rdonlyres/888FC791-E2C0-4096-AF5E-D843F09C0E24/0/UKR_CONV.pdf.

Access to Services of General Economic Interest Under Article 36 of the Charter of Fundamental Rights EU and the National Law

Jiří Zemánek

Jean Monnet Professor of European Law at the Charles University in Prague; Justice of the Constitutional Court of the Czech Republic.

Abstract European Community law has reflected since the very beginning (TEEC Article 90, section 2) a need to allow preferential treatment of undertakings which, under conditions accessible to everyone, provide services in particular economic sectors or in territorially disadvantaged (remote) areas, i.e. those running at a loss. It allowed for a deviation at the required level from its market rules, e.g. balancing losses from public budgets. These services of general economic interest (SGEI) impact on fundamental freedoms of the internal market, however, the provision thereof is regulated by national laws or by decisions of public authority at a national level. Differences between national laws were so significant and politically sensitive that they have been moderated through the harmonisation at the EU level only in high-profile cross-border relations, e.g. in the area of electronic communication.

Questions of the Lisbon Treaty

European Community law has reflected since the very beginning (TEEC Article 90, section 2) a need to allow preferential treatment[1] of undertakings which, under conditions accessible to everyone, provide services in particular economic sectors or in territorially disadvantaged (remote) areas, i.e. those running at a loss. It allowed for a deviation at the required level from its market rules, e.g. balancing losses from

[1] We can speak about a failure of incentive function of the market which is set to a standard relationship between an offer and demand, about reasons of strategic nature, etc.

J. Zemánek (✉)
Faculty of Law, Charles University, nam. Curievych 7, 11640 Praha 1, Czech Republic
e-mail: zemanek@prf.cuni.cz

R. Arnold (ed.), *The Convergence of the Fundamental Rights Protection in Europe*, Ius Gentium: Comparative Perspectives on Law and Justice 52,
DOI 10.1007/978-94-017-7465-9_11

public budgets. These services of general economic interest (SGEI) impact on fundamental freedoms of the internal market, however, the provision thereof is regulated by national laws or by decisions of public authority at a national level. Differences between national laws were so significant and politically sensitive that they have been moderated through the harmonisation at the EU level only in high-profile cross-border relations, e.g. in the area of electronic communication.

There was no legislative definition of SGEI in European law.[2] These services are considered in the practice of EU bodies to be "market activities carried out in the interest of everyone and connected thereby with special obligations of member states for the benefit of the common good" (Commission Communication 1996, C 281/3; 2001, C 17/4). The term 'service' is interpreted broadly, including the supply of commodities, e.g. gas (Meyer 2011, Art. 36 para. 11). 'Generality' of the interest in the provision of the service flows from the fact that it can be guaranteed only by a state, or by a state-authorised undertaking. The (non-)profit orientation of the provider is irrelevant. Therefore, member states have considerable discretion in deciding which goods will fall into the category of SGEI. It may, on the other hand, make the authorised undertakings feel insecure regarding whether or not the exemption from Union rules they rely on is in reality incompatible with the Treaty.

The Lisbon Treaty reinforced the responsibility of the Union for setting rules and conditions for the provision of SGEI by member states on the one hand, and made access to these services – in the form of the Charter of Fundamental Rights EU (the Charter) – a part of the binding primary law. This leads to the question of whether or not some space for a new conception of SGEI in European law has been created. Does it only go beyond the framework of mere exemption of SGEI from the Union rules, namely rules of economic competition, if necessary, in well-grounded cases, for the preservation of their function in society (TFEU Article 10, section 2)? Or does it also grant individuals an enforceable claim to these services? Or does it oblige member states to ensure the provision of SGEI in the given extent and under the given conditions?

It is a case of Article 14 TFEU, which newly authorises the European Parliament and the Council of the EU, while maintaining the powers of member states to provide, contract for or finance these services as a part of 'Union values', to set the 'rules and conditions' of the administration of this national authority. Furthermore, it is a case of the Protocol (no.26), newly attached to the Treaties as their integral part, which considers the essentials of SGEI. In addition, there was a shift in setting the objectives of the Union: the former principle of "open market economy with free competition" (TFEU Article 4, section 1) was replaced and amended by clauses on "highly competitive social market economy, aiming at full employment and social progress", by clauses on the support of "social equity and protection" and "economic, social and territorial cohesion and solidarity among member states"

[2] In French: *services d'intéret économique général*, in German: *Dienstleistungen vom allgemeinen wirtschaftlichen Interesse*.

(TEU Article 3, section 3). Article 36 of "the Charter" (European Convention 2007, C 303/02) sets forth that:

> The Union recognises and respects access to services of general economic interest as provided for in national laws and practices, in accordance with the Treaties, in order to promote the social and territorial cohesion of the Union.

While the first two amendments have been analysed elsewhere (Zemánek 2011, 84–106), an emphasis herein will be put on the human rights aspects of SGEI. The impulse for this paper is the compromise wording and terminology in the said article of the Charter, which leaves a road space for interpretation. The proper sense of said provision will emerge with its practical application and it may seem almost imperceptible at the beginning, but it will be determining in long-term prospects.

Development of the Position of SGEI in Europe

The basis for the analysis is the ascertainment of whether national regulations of SGEI correspond with criteria used by the Court of Justice EU (ECJ) when developing Union law, which also became a benchmark for the human rights Convention (2000) at its unparalleled codification work.

ECJ's sources of knowledge of fundamental rights as general principles of Union law are mainly constitutional traditions common to all member states (Internationale Handelsgesellschaft mbH v Einfuhr- und Vorratsstelle für Getreide und Futtermittel, 1970; Hauer v Land Rheinland Pfalz, 1979; Eugen Schmidberger, Internationale Transporte und Planzüge 2003), as well as international conventions on the protection of human rights entered into, or adhered to, by all member states, in particular the European Convention on the Protection of Human Rights (ECHR) (Nold, Kohlen- und Baustoffgroßhandlung Case 4/73; Friedrich KremzowCase 299/95; Accession of the EU 2/94), social charters adopted by the Union, the Council of Europe and the United Nations, as well as the relevant case law of international judiciaries (Charter of Fundamentals Rights, Preamble). The method used by the ECJ is comparative (Hoechst AG Joined Cases 46/87 and 227/88), which however does not necessarily lead to the assumption of values incorporated spontaneously by the majority of national legal orders. A common solution becomes the one which, upon critical analysis, proves to be the best one regarding the level of protection granted to an individual (Oppermann 2005, Art. 6, para. 21).

The interference of a democratic state in the sphere of public goods and social equity in Western Europe in the post-war period led to the development of the state's new – social – function. However, it happened with a very different scope of authority and intensity in individual states, ranging from a limited domestic product redistribution to far-reaching state intervention measures to balance disharmonies between freedom and equity.[3] SGEI are not expressed in the form of a justiciable individual basic right. In the contemporary environment affected by world-scale economic and financial turbulences, a certain restraint position to the provision of SGEI is requested by budgetary pressures, which forces the states to reconsider their former approaches. The states are circumspect in undertaking international obligations which would result in lasting mandatory spending. To illustrate this, the German Federal Constitutional Court relies on the economic and political neutrality of the Basic Law, which "insulates" it against crucial budgetary impacts of changes in the EU Treaties (Jungbluth 2010, 472).

The situation is still more upset in the member states from Central and Eastern Europe, given the memento of their pre-accession experience. The explicit stipulation of public goods and social equity is missing among the values of the Czech Constitution and the access to SGEI is absent in the Czech Charter of Fundamental Rights and Basic Freedoms. The reminder of the former paternalistic state is still noticeable there. There are also principled objections which play a role: the burden on liberal democracy following from the express acknowledgement of the social function of state is said to impact the democratic principle of majority rule, if the extent of redistribution was directly predetermined by the constitution or by the constitutional court's case law, leaving no sufficient space for the assertion of the current parliamentary democratic majority. A feasible degree of solidarity, required by the provision of SGEI, shall be primarily set forth by the respective lawmaker, not prescribed "forever" by a constituent power. Social rights and public goods, including SGEI, may be sought solely within the statutes which can guarantee the financial and material background of their provision (Wintr 2013, 166).

This conception corresponds with the 'political question' doctrine[4] embodied in certain legal orders, e.g. of the U.S.A., which formally excludes legislative acts in certain fields from the review jurisdiction of (constitutional) courts. On the other hand, there is a conception adhered to, for example, in Germany, under which judicial review of legislative acts is not excluded but is only limited to review within the confines of the Constitution, which cannot be surpassed or overstepped by the legislator. Such confines are in particular the preservation of the nature and spirit of human freedom and dignity, which, being basic values, shall not be abandoned under the influence of technological and social changes by a decision of the current political majority. Thus, this conception avoids conceptually-positivist debates on the defining of *domaine reservé* for political decisions, and, unlike the doctrine of 'political question', it regards the constitutional protection of human rights in the field of public goods with favour (Papier 2009).

The right to the provision of SGEI is expressly guaranteed neither by ECHR nor by other regional or international treaties (Heselhaus et al. 2006, Art. 34, para. 2). Providing there is no substantive-law basis, i.e. regulation in at least a few member states, as a common denominator of their constitutional traditions, and the use of the

[3] For example Article 20, section 1 of the Basic Law of Germany (1949); Article 1 of the French Constitution (1958) or Article 1, section 1 of the Spanish Constitution (1978).

[4] Known as "acte de gouvernement" in French law.

benchmarking method of ECJ is ungrounded, the access to SGEI stipulated in Article 36 Charter cannot be deemed as a fundamental right – a part of the general principles of EU law. What is it then? Is it a principle to be relied on before a court solely for purposes of interpretation and review of legislative and executive acts of the Union and the member states, as stipulated in Article 52 Charter?

SGEI in EU Law

Whereas the mandate for the work of the human rights Convention of the EU (Conclusion No. 45 of the European Council 1999, Annex IV) approached its task as a codified consolidation of the existing case law of ECJ, not as a new law-making endeavour, the Convention went somewhat beyond the scope of its authorisation by adopting Article 36 of the Charter, since it has been pointed out above, SGEI do not form the general principles of EU law. A dispute between supporters of the codification of the right to SGEI led by France, who emphasised the social aspect of the equal access to SGEI, and their opponents headed by Great Britain, who warned of unpredictable domestic budgetary impacts of the grant of such a Community right, reflected different approaches to SGEI on the domestic front. Tensions should have been decreased by the affirmation according to which the provision of the Charter on the mere 'right to access' is in full accord with Article 14 of the TFEU and 'does not grant any new right', but it only stipulates the principle under which the Union, when practising its policies, respects the access to SGEI in the extent stipulated by domestic legal regulations.[5] This principle may be only understood together with noting the position of SGEI and its development in primary legislation of the Union and its development.

Article 106, section 2 TFEU contains the above mentioned compromise solution of the relationship between the principle, according to which undertakings authorised to provide SGEI in a member state are subject to Union rules of the internal market just like other undertakings, and an exception "in so far as the application of such rules does not obstruct the performance, in law or in fact, of the particular tasks assigned to them". The grant of an exception requires, like at other places in Union law, that the public undertaking or state bear the burden of proof regarding the justification thereof. They shall prove that the full application of Union rules in a given situation impedes 'legally or de facto' the providing of SGEI. The acceptance of such justifying reasons shall lead to the exempting of the undertaking providing SGEI from bans and restrictions of Union law, e.g. a ban on public subsidies, whose application would make impossible or frustrate, namely due to irreparable losses in profitability, the provision of said services. These least dubitable reasons are exemp-

[5] Cf.: Explanations originally executed under the Board of the Human Rights Convention and amended under the Board of European Convention (2007/C 303/02), which shall be, in compliance with Article 6 of the TEU, taken into consideration as a valuable interpretation instrument to clarify provisions of the Charter.

tions recognised by the Treaty itself, such as ensuring public order, security and health (TFEU Articles 36, 52), or by case law of ECJ reflecting the protection of other values of particular importance (*rule of reason*), such as so-called mandatory requirements (Rewe-Zentral AG C-120/78).[6] Other reasons connected for example with the ensuring of a certain standard of living and social welfare for nationals may or may not, depending on circumstances, be recognised as incompatible.

Upon the expiration of the transition period to build up foundations of the common market, i.e. since the end of the 1960s, Community liberalisation arrangements have started to spread to fields like postal services, telecommunications, media, transport infrastructure, waste disposal and energy supply, which used to fall into SGEI provided directly by the state or under its control. The state thereby got into an ambivalent position. It had to ensure full operation of common market rules on the one hand, while on the other it was supposed to protect national public interests – attending to the needs of nationals and ensuring the availability thereof, interfering where market mechanisms were insufficient, and substituting the profit-stimulating function of SGEI providers by remedying losses from public budgets.

First, it was the Commission that strived for the sustainability of both in that unstable situation; it came with a proposal to include the support of SGEI in Community objectives, and after appeal for a higher certainty of law when applying the rules of the single market, namely competition regulations, it focused on the economic viability of undertakings providing SGEI, as well as on the liability of the states, with regard to their constitutional functions, for arranging for those services (Commission Communication 1996 C 281/3; 2001 C 17/4; European Council COM 2001, 598). Eventually, it also analysed the possibilities and limits of potential Community regulation of SGEI, with scant outcomes, however (Green Paper 2003; White Paper 2004).

Faithful to its consistent approach, ECJ initially construed circumstances justifying an exception restrictively, in accordance with Article 106, section 2 TFEU. It insisted that an obstacle provably incompatible with the Treaty is solely the one which frustrates the provision of SGEI, and that its mere hampering is an insufficient reason for an exception (ECR 1985. 41/83; ECR 1991. C-179/90). It later modified its own stance by adjudicating that the term 'frustrating' shall also mean a mere 'hampering' of tasks in the field of SGEI assigned to an undertaking (Commission v. Netherlands 1997). That was the reason why ECJ rejected reasons raised as justifiable in favour of the full effect of rules of competition and free movement (Campus Oil Limited and others v Minister for Industry and Energy and others 1984). It then turned its attention to obstacles of fact, pointing out the economic unsustainability of the activity of undertakings in the field of unprofitable SGEI. In order to be able to provide such services in accordance with their authorisation on a long-term basis, the undertakings shall have the possibility of redistrib-

[6] ECJ considers those to be for example the environment, extending one's knowledge of the artistic and cultural heritage of the country, pluralistic non-commercial broadcasting, road safety, quality of craft industry, support of the national language, orderly course of a sport match, etc. – see the case law based on the judgment in *Cassis de Dijon*.

uting their revenues flowing from other fields of business activity. However, it may disadvantage them in competition with other organisations in the same fields; therefore, it is necessary to refuse the principle of equal treatment of the two groups when applying competition rules.[7] Case law of ECJ undoubtedly influenced the promotion of SGEI to 'common values of the Union' in the Amsterdam Treaty revision of Article 16 TEC, highlighting the importance of the care for economic and financial principles and conditions for their functioning by the Union and member states. Outputs arising from this development were assessed in different ways (Weis 2003, 186; Schwarze 2001, 13; Jungbluth 2010, Art. 16, par. 13, Art. 86, par. 49).

European Influence of French Concept of SGEI

The French theory of *service public*, which should have, being a counterweight to the theory of *puissance public* (public authority), as of the end of the nineteenth century manifested a transformation of the state previously defined against a citizen only in categories of superiority and inferiority into an institution which, based on the system of administrative law (statutes, administrative or judicial decisions), provides certain services to a citizen (Chapus 1968, 235). A later functional privatisation of some SGEI has led to a broadening of their definition: connection between a provider and a public corporation does not need to be solely direct (*établissement public*) but it can be indirect as well, for example through a concession granted to a subject of private law (*enterprise public*) (Chapus 1968, 432), in which the influence of the state is safeguarded by means of supervision or control.

Provision of SGEI on the basis of the discretion of the state or public authority (a self-governing territorial unit) shall meet the requirements of continuity (blanket and uninterrupted provision of SGEI), of adjustment (of the quality and quantity of provided SGEI to the requirements of user demand), and of equal access thereto under the same conditions for all users in the jurisdiction of the administrative body (which may also include, depending on circumstances, preferential treatment of socially disadvantaged or disqualified users). In order to enforce these principles, there is the possibility in French law of filing an individual administrative petition against the institution granting the concession (a state, self-governing territorial unit) which makes it possible to enforce the observance of these principles by a concession-holder. This concept was, on the part of France, an ideological support for the pressure on the integration of Article 36 into the Charter.[8] The principle of judicial enforceability of SGEI has not been met with support in countries outside the French legal culture, e.g. in Germany or in Scandinavia.

[7] Judgments in C-320/91 *Corbeau* (paras. 15 and foll..), C-393/92 *Almelo* (para. 49), C-159/94 *Commission v. France* (para. 96), C-280/00 *Altmark*.

[8] Even though there are not constitutional but only statutory bases.

Analysis of Article 36 Charter

European law does not define autonomously the main feature of SGEI, i.e. connection to the satisfying of needs of an economic nature as a subject of public interest, but it leaves the interpretation thereof upon the decision-making practice of Union bodies, upon national regulations, and upon national case law. The Treaty includes therein neither non-economic services,[9] e.g. educational, cultural, or social, nor services provided in order to satisfy purely particular, i.e. individual or group, needs without any link to public interest of the whole society.

The provision of Article 36 Charter opened to interpretation may, at first sight, allow for the construction in favour of deeper engagement of the state at securing public goods, including the potential Union obligation to provide SGEI to anyone residing within its jurisdiction.[10] The suggestion for integration of the access to SGEI into the rights of Union citizens was already discussed at an intergovernmental conference in Amsterdam (1997) (Prechal 2008, 69). Eventually, the efforts resulted in declaring SGEI a part of 'common values of the Union', which was intentionally phrased so that it allowed for encompassing various national concepts of these services (Nettesheim 2002, 40). Due to its generality, the provision of the Charter does not meet the requirements of direct effect (Tichý et al. 2014, 454) and does therefore create neither an enforceable individual right to the provision of SGEI, nor an opportunity for undertakings authorised to provide such services to oppose claims arising from such rights (Meyer 2011, Art. 16 Rn 2). Yet, incorporation of Article 36 into the Charter is perceived as the beginning of a gradual departure from a solely negative concept of SGEI in Article 106, section 2 TFEU as a reason for derogation exempting authorised public corporations from internal market rules to a positive concept leading towards a Community obligation of member states (Ross 2000, 23–24).

Nevertheless, careful reading of Article 36 Charter does not affirm the presumption of fundamental change in the concept of SGEI (their 'communitarisation'). The term 'right to access' does not mean that an objective right of each individual to a certain standard of these services with a corresponding general obligation of each member state to ensure provision thereof may be derived from it (Fiedziuk 2011, 236). Still, Article 36 has a certain 'added value'. It represents the recognition of a subjective right to SGEI in personal and material extent reinforced in a particular situation by laws and practices of a respective member state. Should these services be provided to all people on the basis of equal access (*principe d'égalité*, see above), like in France, an authorised undertaking shall not discriminate against users on the grounds of nationality.

---

[9] Protocol No. 26, Article 2.

[10] An inverse conclusion, i.e. that the provision of SGEI may be restricted by a member state to a certain group of users, may be arrived at through comparison with Article 35 Charter, which regulates the right of access to a special SGEI – healthcare in favour of anyone ("Everybody has the right…").

This interpretation is affirmed by the Explanations attached with the Charter, according to which this provision "does not confer any new rights".[11] Also, the position of Article 36 in the system of the Charter does not indicate another conclusion, as it is not incorporated in Chapter V – Civil Rights, but in Chapter IV – Solidarity, coming after the principles of Article 34 – Social Security and Social Assistance. Said Article, which contains similar wording ("The Union recognises and respects the entitlement to ...") and refers to national laws and practices, 'applies to cases where such services were introduced in order to provide certain benefits, but it does not mean that such services must be introduced if they do not exist'.[12] The condition of the accord of these regulations with the Treaty is replaced in Article 34 by a requirement 'in accordance with rules set forth by Union law', which are already in force in the field of social policy.

It means that no obligations flow from Union law for member states regarding SGEI provided by them. Such obligations are not based on primary legislation (Article 36 Charter, Article 14 TFEU) but on secondary legislation. Namely sector directives in the field of postal services,[13] telecommunications[14] and power engineering[15] (network services) impose an obligation of universal service which means "securing that certain services are available in the given quality to all consumers and users in the territory of the respective member state regardless of its geographical location and, taking particular national conditions into consideration, at a reasonable price (Green Paper 2003, sec. 50). Such supranational obligation is enforceable by means available under Union law. The fulfilment thereof is not subject to national (regional, local) control mechanisms which may have various weaknesses oftentimes caused by political pressures. Therefore, it is virtually more consumer or user friendly (Kahler and Lake 2009, 254). These directives require that national regulatory bodies, authorised to independently and transparently assign a universal service on competition-oriented non-discriminatory grounds and to oversee providers thereof taking the protection of consumer interests into account, exist.[16]

Suggestions *de lege ferenda*

As for sectors in which such institutional prerequisites of control on the basis of Union legislation do not exist, e.g. in the field of public radio and television broadcasting, the Commission has started to bond the granting of state subsidies under

[11] Explanation (note. 6) to Article 36 Charter.

[12] Explanation (note 6) to Article 34 Charter.

[13] Directive 97/67, on common rules for the development of internal market of postal services and on the improving of their duality.

[14] Directive 2002/22, on universal service and rights of users of electronic telecommunication networks and services.

[15] Directive 2003/54, on common rules for internal market with electric power.

[16] Footnote 14,15,16.

Article 107, section 3 TFEU with the formation thereof (Commission Communication 2009, sec. 53–54).[17] Spreading the legislation into other sectors may be expected in the future within a new competence, acquired by the Union by virtue of the Lisbon Treaty, which supplements Article 14 TFEU, under which the European Parliament and Council are authorised to set, in the form of a regulation arrived at through ordinary legislative procedure, principles and conditions of the functioning of SGEI, with a view to enabling the fulfilment of their tasks (Zemánek 2011, 100–101). After the Commission, which strived to adopt a framework horizontal directive on SGEI (Commission Communication 2005. C 297) but postponed it indefinitely (for the time being) upon the fall of the Constitutional Treaty, the role was assumed by the European Parliament, which, however, lacks the right of legislative initiative. Sector fragmented regulation and inconsistent case law[18] are good for the legal certainty of neither providers nor users of SGEI, regarding the financing thereof in particular: Aren't investments from public budgets contrary to Union rules for state subsidies, which impose an obligation upon a recipient to repay them together with interest thereon? Price impacts on consumers following therefrom have therefore been criticised by experts for a long period.

According to experts, a prospective consolidated or 'progressively developed' Union regulation should clarify especially competence issues regarding SGEI, the position of national regulators, rules for the selection of providers and financing, as well as the limits of applicability of internal market rules, in particular competition rules, to this special group of services (De and Sybe 2008; Krajewski 2008, 377). Although the final decision on the authorisation of undertakings to provide SGEI would henceforth remain in the hands of a member state, it should satisfy several conditions: The public service obligation shall be clearly defined; the scope of refunds to compensate losses arising therefrom shall be determined in a transparent way beforehand; these refunds from public budgets shall not exceed the necessary extent, i.e. they may truly cover only losses connected closely with SGEI and their amount shall either be minimised by a preceding competition of applicants for a public contract to provide SGEI or correspond to costs which would be incurred by a duly managed ordinary business undertaking in a similar situation (Altmark Trans GmbH and Regierungspräsidium Magdeburg 2003. para. 95).

Although a breakthrough in SGEI regulation from Union bodies themselves probably cannot be expected soon, as indicated above, the change might be brought about, in accordance with Article 11, section 4 TFEU, by a legislative initiative of at least 1mil Union citizens, to which the Commission would have to react. Even if consolidation of institutional and legal background for the provision of SGEI was achieved thereafter, major communitarization of the provision of SGEI leading towards the unification of their qualitative and quantitative standards across the Union would be impossible without further delegation of powers from member states to the Union. No sooner than with a new competence grounds would it be

---

[17] Commission Communication on the Use of Rules for State Support in Public Service of Radio and Television Broadcasting, Official Journal (2009) (2009) C 257/1, sec. 53–54.

[18] ECJ case law referred to SGEI indirectly, since the application of Article 106, sec. 2 of the Treaty on the Functioning of the EU itself has never been reviewed.

possible to look for a common denominator of a public interest, which is a defining feature of SGEI and differs in its nature from mere mechanical numbering of individual needs, satisfied through ordinary services provided on the basis of a standard market principle. Only then would it be possible to perceive the access to SGEI not merely as a programme principle but also as a truly enforceable right of an individual/Union citizen in accordance with the Charter.

Compatibility of National Regulation of SGEI with Union Law

Unions' 'recognition of and respect for' access to SGEI are expressed in passive acknowledgement of legal situations and practice connected with the provision thereof in member states, as well as active acceptance of the right to the access under respective national laws and practices, providing that such laws and practices are in accordance with Union law. Whereas there is no doubt about said condition in other language variants of Article 36 Charter, e.g. in English,[19] in French,[20] or in German,[21] the Czech wording relates the requirement of accord with Treaties to the Union obligation 'to recognise and respect' access to SGEI itself, not to national laws and practices.[22] It is an apparent mistake in the Czech wording. 'Compliance with Treaties' shall undoubtedly mean the ability of an undertaking authorised to provide SGEI with Article 106, section 2 TFEU, i.e. that its activity satisfies the condition for exemption from rules contained in the Treaties, the application of which would otherwise hamper or frustrate the fulfilment of special tasks assigned to such an undertaking by the state.

'Compliance with Treaties' shall also mean the observance of the prohibition of 'whatever discrimination' (direct or indirect) on the grounds of nationality under Article 18 TFEU incorporated in the national regulation of the access to SGEI. The ban only applies within the scope of the application of Treaties, unless a special provision sets forth otherwise. However, the operation of Treaties is interpreted widely by ECJ (Syllová et al. 2010, 246). The Court has ruled that prohibition of discrimination, being a general principle of Union law, applies not only to national legislation which immediately serves the implementation of legal rules of Union

[19] "The Union recognises and respects access to services of general economic interest as provided for in national laws and practices, in accordance with the Treaties, in order to promote the social and territorial cohesion of the Union".

[20] "L' Union reconnait et respects l'acces aux services d'interet économique général tel qu'il est prévu par les législations et pratiques nationales, conformément aux traités, afin de promouvoir la cohésion sociale et territoriale de l'Union".

[21] "Die Union anerkennt und achtet den Zugang zu Dienstleistungen von allgemeinem wirtschaftlichen Interesse, wie er durch die einzelstaatlichen Rechtsvorschriften und Gepflogenheiten im Einklang mit den Verträgen geregelt ist, um den sozialen und territorialen Zusammenhalt der Union zu fördern."

[22] "Unie v souladu se Smlouvami a s cílem podpořit sociální a územní soudržnosti ...".

law, but also to other legislation, be it in exclusive competence of a member state, which is, through its application effects, capable of influencing the status of Union citizens based on Union law. It regards mainly the status in the field of internal market under Part III, Chapter I TFEU (Ian William Cowan v Trésor public 1989; Data Delecta Aktiebolag and Ronny Forsberg v MSL Dynamics Ltd. 1996) and beyond, in the fields of all common policies of the Union, e.g. the right of free movement and stay of Union citizens under Article 20, section 2 TFEU. On the grounds of Article 18 TFEU, a member state shall accord to all Union citizens access to SGEI equal to that accorded to its own nationals.

Prohibition of discrimination on the grounds of nationality is also a manifestation of the principle of equality, which, being one of the values the Union is founded on Article 2 TFEU, binds member states,[23] regarding access to SGEI, in relation to all Union citizens. The equality of everyone before the law, an unwritten general legal principle of Union law,[24] has been codified as Article 20 Charter. It is binding in member states providing they apply Union law (Article 51, section 1 Charter), i.e. they either apply Union regulation directly or adopt implementing legislation to fulfil obligations following from the EU membership. As for SGEI, the Union obligations of member states do not include the ensuring of the provision of SGEI itself (from the point of view of kind or extent), but only the grant of the access thereto.

The aim of 'recognition and respect' under Article 36 Charter is to 'promote the social and territorial cohesion of the Union'. This provision, the same in terms of content as a similar provision in Article 14 TFEU, is mainly a programme postulate included among Union objectives in Article 3, section 3 TFEU, and it gives direction to the creation of Union policies. Their focus on, for example, deregulation of certain network sectors of the economy which leads to the entry of rival providers into the SGEI market should not fragment the contribution of these services to the building of a comparable (homogenous) economic and social environment in various locations of the Union territory. This provision also has a regulatory function as a referential standpoint for judicial review of the lawfulness of law-making and executive acts adopted by Union bodies within the scope of these policies, and for interpretation of these legal acts. It may be relied on solely for these purposes even before Union courts,[25] therefore, it is not possible to bring direct actions to compel bodies of the Union or of member states to act[26] to protect the rights of an individual in a given legal situation.

Another, no less important aim of the 'recognition of and respect for' access to SGEI under Article 36 Charter is the reinforcement of the fellow feeling of the citizens with the Union, which duly takes into consideration their status under national law in its policies (European Council COM 2000. 580).

---

[23] Cf.: reference to this article in the framework of conditions for the accession of new member states to the Union under Article 49 TFEU, and retributive mechanisms for the cases of material infringement of Union values by a member state under Article 1 TEU.

[24] E.g. ECJ, cases 283/83 *Racke*, 15/95 *EARL*, 292/97 *Karlsson*.

[25] Peculiarly in proceedings under Article 263 TFEU for annulment of a Union act, or in preliminary ruling proceedings under Article 267 TFEU regarding proper application of Union law at national courts.

[26] Article 52, sec. 5 Charter and Explanation thereto (note 6).

'Public interest' as a defining feature of SGEI reflects the indivisibility of the rights of a recipient of a particular service, whose status is determined by the dependence on the status of other recipients of the same service. It should not be confused with a particular interest as a mere nominal sum of individual (or group) consumer rights, which is the case of ordinary services provided on a purely commercial basis. A private entity authorised by a public authority to provide SGEI shall consistently distinguish this difference in its activity, even though the transition from one to the other may come about impliedly as a result of the change of condition on the Union internal market. Market-dictated conditions of economic management, previously influencing the profitability of a certain SGEI and thus the competitive ability of a provider thereof, may be changed for example as a result of global development, so an exemption from the application of the Union rules in the sense of Article 106, section 2 TFEU will lose grounds; or the other way around (Commission of the European Communities v Kingdom of Spain 2003). An obligation of a provider of SGEI that would also include a duty to contract is a restriction of freedom of contract, which would usually require legitimisation in national law (Heselhaus et al. 2006).

Conclusion

After the adoption of the Lisbon Treaty, Article 36 Charter does not form, beyond the scope of current Union competences, a classic basic right following the pattern of 'everybody has the right of access ...', neither does it extend rights following from the Union citizenship to a certain minimum standard of SGEI, inclusive of procedural instruments to be enforced by SGEI consumers against member states.[27] Nevertheless, with a growing migration of citizens between member states, there is a certain pressure on the spontaneous harmonisation of approaches (e.g. between French and German-Scandinavian tradition of SGEI). This is an important factual prerequisite for the possible embodying of a minimum standard of SGEI in selected economic sectors to serve as the frame of social and territorial cohesion in the future, and which would moderate imbalance, currently existing between member states, in the extent and quality of the provision of these services, including their budgetary impacts (Green Paper 2003, para. 63). Only on these bases would it be possible to embody the access to SGEI as another European constitutional right of Union citizens under Chapter V Charter.

The harmonisation of national legislation regarding SGEI in the spirit of the principle of equal treatment (in its full substantive-law sense) is impeded by a missing express Union authority[28] which cannot be assigned thereto as there is

[27] See the resumés of earlier debates on the topic of minimum standard generally binding in all member states in *Rodriguez, S.*, Les services publics et le Traité d'Amsterdam, 1998 Revue du Marché Commun, p. 4; or the opinion of the Economic and Social Committee of the EU, OJ 1999 C 368/51, para. 5.3.

[28] Therefore, the enhanced co-operation under Article 20 TEU, which requires the existence of joint (not sole) Union authority, cannot be relied on.

deficient political will of member states, anticipating the economic impacts of such a step, which are, for the time being, perceived as unsustainable in the long term. Redistribution of costs on the basis of solidarity would require would have to amount to a common European social fund, which seems to be rather unrealistic at present. The experience obtained from the recent financial crisis management shows, that references to the flexibility clause under Article 352 TFEU aiming at reinforcement of a policy area with substantial social impacts clashes with objection of the principle of subsidiarity. An extensive use of existing legislative powers granted to the Union under Article 14 sentence 2 TFEU for the installation of principles and conditions of the functioning of SGEI, as amended by the Lisbon Treaty, is more likely to be expected.

The SGEI have been perceived as an essential element of national social contract in some member states, as can be noticed from reactions of their population on austerity measures they are facing. Constraints against an excessive indebtedness of public budgets, cutting grants for SGEI, rather than stabilization of the level of their performance is taking place. For the same reason the SGEI are becoming commercialised at liberalised markets. The significance of the principles and conditions set by Union law will not be to protect SGEI against pressures by market competition, but to make their performance sustainable under the changed conditions.

Bibliography

Chapus, René. 1968. Le Service Public et la Puissance Public. *Revue du Droit Privé* 84: 235–282.

Charter of Fundamentals Rights.

Commission Communication. 1996. C 281/3. *Official Journal.*

Commission Communication. 2001. C 17/4. *Official Journal.*

Commission Communication. 2005. C 297. Community framework for a state subsidy in the form of compensation for public service. *Official Journal.*

Commission Communication. 2009. C 257/1. Communication from the Commission on the application of State aid rules to public service broadcasting. *Official Journal.*

Conclusion. 3–4 June 1999. No. 45, Annex IV. Cologne: *European Council.*

Directive 2002/22/EC of the European Parliament and of the Council of 7 March 2002 on universal service and users' rights relating to electronic communications networks and services (Universal Service Directive). *Official Journal*: L 108 of 24 April 2002.

Directive 2003/54/EC of the European Parliament and of the Council of 26 June 2003 concerning common rules for the internal market in electricity and repealing Directive 96/92/EC. *Official Journal:* L 176 of 15 July 2003.

Economic and Social Committee. 1999. C 368/51. *Official Journal.*

ECJ. Judgment of the Court. 17 December 1970, Internationale Handelsgesellschaft mbH v Einfuhr- und Vorratsstelle für Getreide und Futtermittel, Case 11/70. *European Court Reports*: 01125.

ECJ. Judgment of the Court of 14 May 1974. J. Nold, Kohlen- und Baustoffgroßhandlung v Commission of the European Communities. Case 4/73. *European Court Reports*: 00491.

ECJ. Judgment of the Court of 20 February 1979. Rewe-Zentral AG v Bundesmonopolverwaltung für Branntwein. Case 120/78. *European Court Reports*: 00649.

ECJ. Judgment of the Court of 13 December 1979. Hauer v Land Rheinland Pfalz, Case 44/79. *European Court Reports.*

ECJ. Judgment of the Court of 10 July 1984. Campus oil limited and others v Minister for industry and energy and others. Case 72/83. *European Court Reports*: 02727.

ECJ. Judgment of the Court (First Chamber) of 13 November 1984. Firma A. Racke v Hauptzollamt Mainz. Case 283/83. *European Court Reports*: 03791.

ECJ. Judgment of the Court of 20 March 1985. Italian Republic v Commission of the European Communities. Case 41/83. *European Court Reports*: 00873.

ECJ. Judgment of the Court of 2 February 1989. Ian William Cowan v Trésor public. Case 186/87. *European Court Reports*: 00011.

ECJ. Judgment of the Court 21 of September 1989. Hoechst AG v Commission of the European Communities, Joined cases 46/87 and 227/88. *European Court Reports*: 02859.

ECJ. Judgment of the Court of 10 December 1991. Merci convenzionali porto di Genova SpA v Siderurgica Gabrielli SpA. Case 179/90. *European Court Reports*: 05889.

ECJ. Judgment of the Court of 19 May 1993. Criminal proceedings against Paul Corbeau. Case 320/91. *European Court Reports*: 00223.

ECJ. Judgment of the Court of 27 April 1994. Municipality of Almelo and others v NV Energiebedrijf Ijsselmij. Case 393/92. *European Court Reports*: 01477.

ECJ. Judgment of the Court (Sixth Chamber) of 17 April 1997. EARL de Kerlast v Union régionale de coopératives agricoles (Unicopa) and Coopérative du Trieux. Case 15/95. *European Court Reports*: 01961.

ECJ. Judgment of the Court (Sixth Chamber) of 26 September 1996. Data Delecta Aktiebolag and Ronny Forsberg v MSL Dynamics Ltd. Case 43/95. *European Court Reports*: 04661.

ECJ. Judgment of the Court of 23 October 1997. Commission of the European Communities v French Republic. Case 159/94. *European Court Reports*: 05815.

ECJ. Judgment of the Court of 23 October 1997. Commission of the European Communities v Kingdom of the Netherlands. Case 157/94. *European Court Reports*: 05699.

ECJ. Judgment of the Court (Fifth Chamber) of 29 May 1997. Friedrich Kremzow v Republik Österreich. Case 299/95. *European Court Reports*: 02629.

ECJ. Judgment of the Court (Sixth Chamber) of 13 April 2000. Kjell Karlsson and Others. Case 292/97. *European Court Reports*: 02737.

ECJ. Judgment of the Court of 13 May 2003. Commission of the European Communities v Kingdom of Spain. Case 463/00. *European Court Reports:* 04581.

ECJ. Judgment of the Court of 12 June 2003. Eugen Schmidberger, Internationale Transporte und Planzüge v Republik Österreich. Case 112/00. *European Court Reports:* 05659.

ECJ. Judgment of the Court of 24 July 2003. Altmark Trans GmbH and Regierungspräsidium Magdeburg v Nahverkehrsgesellschaft Altmark GmbH, and Oberbundesanwalt beim Bundesverwaltungsgericht. Case 280/00. *European Court Reports*: 07747.

ECR. 1985. Italy v. Commission (British Telecommunication), 41/83, *CMLR*.

ECR. 1991. Merci convenzionali porto di Genova SpA v Siderurgica Gabrielli SpA. C-179/90, *European Court Reports*, I-05889.

European Commission. 2003. *Green paper on services of general interests*, COM (2003) 270 final (21 May 2003).

European Commission. 2004. *White paper on services of general interests*, COM (2004) 274 final (12 May 2004).

European Convention. 2007. C 303/02. *Official Journal.*

Fiedziuk, Natalia. 2011. Services of general economic interest and the Treaty of Lisbon: Opening doors to a whole new approach or maintaining the status quo. *European Law Review* 36: 226–242.

French Constitution. 1958.

Grundgesetz Deutschland. 1949.

Heselhaus, Sebastian and Nowak, Carsten. 2006. Handbuch der Europäischen Grundrechte, C.H.Beck/Linde/Stampfli & Cie.

Jung, Christian. 2011. In *EUV/EGV, das Verfassungsrecht der Europäischen Union mit Europäischer Grundrechtecharta, Kommentar*, ed. Callies, Christian and Ruffert, Matthias. München: C.H. Beck.

Jungbluth, David. 2010. Überformung der grundgesetzlichen Wirtschachaftsverfassung durch Europäisches Unionsrechts? *Europarecht* 4: 471–489.
Kahler, Miles, and David A. Lake. 2009. Economic integration and global governance: Why so little supranationalism? In *The politics of global regulation*, ed. W. Mattli and N. Woods, 242–276. Princeton: Princeton University Press.
Krajewski, Markus. 2008. Providing legal clarity and securing policy space for public services through a legal framework for services of general economic interest: squaring the circle? *European Public Law* 14(3): 377–398.
Meyer, Jürgen. 2011. *Charta der Grundrechte der Europäischen Union, 3. Aufl.* Baden-Baden: Nomos.
Nettesheim, Martin. 2002. Mitgliedstaatliche Daseinsvorsorge zwischen Wettbewerbskonformität und Gemeinwohlverantwortung. In *Europäische Union und mitgliedstaatliche Daseinsvorsorge*, ed. Rudolf Hrbek and Martin Nettesheim, 39–64. Baden-Baden: Nomos.
Opinion of the Court of 28 March 1996. Accession by the Community to the European convention for the protection of human rights and fundamental freedoms. Opinion 2/94. *European Court Reports*: 01759.
Opinion of the Economic and Social Committee on Services of general interest. 1999. Case 368/17, *Official Journal.*
Oppermann, Thomas. 2005. *Europarecht, ein Studienbuch*, 3rd ed. München: C.H. Beck.
Papier, Hans Jürgen. 23 November 2009. Verfassungsgerichtsbarkeit und Politik. Grusswort bei der internationalen Konferenz "Twenty Years of the Constitutional Court of Hungary" www.mkab.hu/index.php?id/conference.
Prechal, Sacha. 2008. Fundamental rights and the liberalization of service markets. In *The EU and WTO Law on Services: limits to the realisation of general interest policies within the services markets?* 55–74. Aalphen aan den Rijn: Kluwer Law International.
Report to the Laeken European Council. COM (2001) 598 final, 17 October 2001.
Rodriguez, Stéphane. 1998. Les Services publics et Traité d'Amsterdam: genèse et portée juridique du futur article 16 CE. *Revue du Marché commun et de l'Union européenne* 1: 37–46.
Ross, Malcom. 2000. Article 16 E.C. and services of general economic interest: from derogation to obligation? *European Law Review* 25(1): 22–38.
Schwarze, Jürgen. 2001. Einführung. In *Daseinsvorsorge im Lichte des Wettbewerbs*, ed. Jürgen Schwarze, 9–24. Baden-Baden: Nomos.
Spanish Constitution. 1978.
Syllová, Jindřiška, et al. 2010. *Lisabonská smlouva. Komentář*, 1st ed. Praha: C.H. Beck.
Tichý, Lubos, Rainer Arnold, Jiří Zemánek, Richard Král and Tomáš Dumbrovský. 2014. *Evropské právo. 5. vydání.* Praha: C. H. Beck.
Treaty on European Union. 1992. Maastricht.
Treaty establishing the European Economic Community. 1957. Rome.
Treaty on the Functioning of the European Union. 1958. Rome.
De Vries, Sybe A. 2008. Harmonization of services of general economic interest. In *The EU and WTO Law on Services: Limits to the realisation of general interest policies within the services markets?* 139–158. Aalphen aan den Rijn: Kluwer Law International.
Weis, Wolfgang. 2003. Öffentliche Unternehmen und EGV. *Europarecht* 38: 165–190.
Wintr, Jan. 2013. *Principy českého ústavního práva (s dodatkem principů práva evropského a mezinárodního).* Praha: Eurolex Bohemia.
Zemánek, Jiří. 2011. Hospodářsko-politické cíle EU po Lisabonské smlouvě a meze národní ústavní autonomie. In *XIX. Karlovarské právnické dny*, ed. V. Zoufalý, 84–106. Praha: Leges.

Human Dignity and European Constitutionalism: Flatus Vocis or Ratio Decidendi?

Antonio-Carlos Pereira-Menaut and María-Carolina Pereira-Sáez

Abstract After World War II human dignity successfully made its way into many constitutions and international treaties, as well as EU law. Yet, since it was not an entirely new concept, it should not be taken for granted that before 1945 it was quite irrelevant to Law. Its original roots can be found in the Judeo-Christian tradition, while its recent development comes mainly from the influential Kantian vision. Besides that, the latest philosophical and anthropological trends, the recent 'politicisation' of the human being, along with some developments in biotechnology, have brought dignity to the fore. However, we suggest that writing down dignity into legal texts, even in constitutional texts, does not fully settle the problem, as some relevant judicial decisions show.

1. The purpose of this paper is to reflect on the role of human dignity in the European Union constitutionalism. We assume that a European Union Constitution existed long ago even if without that name, and that, in a very unequal measure, it is formed by the Treaty on European Union (TEU), the Treaty on the Functioning of the European Union (TFEU), the European Charter of Fundamental Rights (the Charter), the European Convention on Human Rights (ECHR), some outstanding verdicts of the Court of Justice of the European Union in Luxembourg (ECJ), some verdicts of the Strasbourg Court and some principles. To this we must add – in a very unequal proportion, again – the constitutional traditions common to the

The original version of this chapter was included. The erratum to this chapter is available at: http://dx.doi.org/10.1007/978-94-017-7465-9_13

English translations, unless otherwise stated, are ours.

A.-C. Pereira-Menaut (✉)
School of Law, University of Santiago de Compostela, Galicia, Spain
e-mail: acp.menaut@usc.es; acp.menaut@gmail.com

M.-C. Pereira-Sáez
School of Law, University of Coruña, Galicia, Spain
e-mail: cpereiras@udc.es

R. Arnold (ed.), *The Convergence of the Fundamental Rights Protection in Europe*, Ius Gentium: Comparative Perspectives on Law and Justice 52,
DOI 10.1007/978-94-017-7465-9_12

member states[1] and their constitutional documents as well as the deposit made up of the main rulings of their constitutional jurisdictions. The sum of all this forms a constitutional magma lacking precise, definite borders but nevertheless real; a mixed, *composée* or compound Constitution, or, to put it another way, a constitutional block in which it is noticeable that the German constitutionalism holds a special place and all the more so when it comes to dignity.

We adopt the premise that dignity is more than rights: it is one of their foundations: were we not worthy, constitutional rights would not be 'absolute'. Like other such pre-legal basic notions – human person, personal consciences, life, tolerance, compassion, honour, and others – it shows considerable resistance to being captured *via* legal developments, provisions or articles, like water resists being caught in a basket. Human dignity is not like usufruct or a lease with option to buy a car, things that a good law can without much difficulty define appropriately. One way to recognise this is to say that it is a 'vague legal concept' *(un concepto jurídico indeterminado,* as Spanish legal conventional wisdom has it), but, after contenting us for a while, that phrase actually conceals the impotence of the law to give a full, satisfactory account of dignity. We do not consider that impotence to be bad news: not much would my dignity be if it could easily become a law article. We also think that the best thing for law to do with dignity is negative in character: not encourage it, even less create it, which is not in its hand, but protect it against possible attacks, repress whoever threatens it. Dignity will hardly generate a positive obligation on the legislator to follow a certain behaviour consisting of a *facere* (although it may also do this), while we can effortlessly see that it will generate a negative obligation to prohibit or reject behaviour that threaten it. This dimension of dignity – to feel more comfortable with 'negative' judgements, orders, rules or provisions than with 'positive' ones – suits well with the fact that law is rather 'negative' in nature: we feel more at home with *nemo iudex in causa* than with the constitutional mandate that "Spaniards shall be fair and beneficial" (Constitution of Spain 1812, Article 6).[2]

Not being a precise legal concept like 'lease' or 'nuncupative will', dignity does not go along smoothly with either law generally or Constitutional law. Anyone can see that in today's Spain, all social and opinion groups proclaim dignity, without this leading to much in practice: it is invoked by pro-abortion as well as pro-life sides, both by supporters of active euthanasia (who coined the term 'death with

---

[1] On constitutional traditions and principles, see the 1969 ruling of the then Court of Justice of the European Communities (ECJ) *Stauder v. City of Ulm* (case 29/69 ECR 419), originating from a European Commission decision that had been considered to be contrary to German fundamental rights. In the 1974 judgment *Nold, Kohlen-und Baustoffsgrosshandlung v. Commission* (case 4/73 ECR 491) the ECJ of the then Communities, to find a basis to protect fundamental rights, mostly unprotected by the Treaties at the time, was said to draw inspiration from the constitutional traditions common to Member States, that included fundamental rights (see paragraph 13).

[2] "Love of their fatherland is one of the main duties of Spaniards, as well as to be fair and beneficial" (the original reads: "*El amor de la Patria es una de las principales obligaciones de todos los españoles y, asimismo, el ser justos y benéficos*"). We do not mean all possible positive formulations are inconsistent with proper legal reasoning – just think of *pact sunt servanda* or *caveat emptor*.

dignity') and supporters of respecting human life from its natural beginning to its natural end. In the end, law does not get along well with anything that cannot be specified in a court ruling or principle (understood not as an organisational criteria but in the Romanist sense of 'principle' or *regula iuris*: not as 'principle of the rule of law' but as *prior tempore, potior iure*, for example).

Human Dignity and European Law

2. Human dignity is proclaimed by European constitutional law as one of its bases: article 2 of the TEU states that the Union is founded upon the value of respect for human dignity, among others. According to the Preamble and to article 1 of the Charter "human dignity is inviolable. It must be respected and protected", and the *Explanations Relating to the Charter* clarify that human dignity is not only a fundamental right in itself but constitutes the very foundation of fundamental rights – a correct view in that it does not conceive of dignity as just one among the rights but as a foundation of all rights. Article 10.1 of the Spanish Constitution also deals with dignity as the foundation of rights (and not only of rights), with an elegant wording that, in our view, could hardly be improved.[3] The *Explanations* refer then to the *Preamble of the Universal Declaration of Human Rights* of 1948, under which the recognition of the inherent dignity of all members of the human family is the foundation of freedom, justice and peace in the world. Later on, the Charter makes clear that none of the rights laid down therein may be used to harm the rights (including the dignity) of another person, and that dignity is part of the essence of the rights laid down in it, so that even when the exercise of a right has to be restricted, dignity must be respected (art. 52.1 plus art. 54).

Recognition of dignity in the TEU and later in the Charter was not a radical novelty. We could already find it in the constitutional tradition of some EU member states, particularly Germany and, some decades later, countries within its constitutional sphere of influence, such as Spain. Besides the German and Spanish

[3]The inclusion of dignity in the 1978 Spanish Constitution came to have further relevance since it influenced several Latin American constitutions that were amended or drafted *ex novo* after 1978. In a way we may say that the Spanish Constitution acted as a vehicle for expanding dignity in some Latin American contemporary constitutions. The wording of article 10.1 of the Spanish Constitution reads as follows: "The dignity of the person, the inviolable rights which are inherent, the free development of the personality, respect for the law and for the rights of others are the foundation of political order and social peace" (English official translation, webpage of the Spanish Parliament). It implies recognizing that human persons, their dignity and their rights come before the law, the Constitution, the political community and the very social contract that underlies it all. All those extremely important things are based on dignity, not vice versa. It may be noted that nothing in this wording suggests that dignity depends on the degree of self-awareness and autonomy, let alone on its appreciation by those around us (e.g., sterilisation of the mentally disabled, legalised in Spain since 1989); otherwise it would not be 'inherent'.

constitutions, those of Ireland (Constitution of Ireland 1999, preamble),[4] Italy (Constitution of Italy 1947, Articles 3.1 and 41),[5] Portugal (Constitution of Portugal 1976, Article 1),[6] Greece (Constitution of Greece 1975, Article 2.1),[7] Belgium (Constitution of Belgium 1994, Article 23),[8] Czech Republic (Constitution of the Czech Republic 1992, preamble),[9] Finland (Constitution of Finland 2000, ch. 1)[10] and Lithuania (Constitution of Lithuania 1992, Article 21)[11] now refer to dignity, yet with different intensities. Furthermore, at least in the *Netherlands v European Parliament and Council* case,[12] the European Court recognised its duty to protect human dignity in spite of not having, at the time, a literal basis in the Treaties (the Court had already done so with principles (Hartley 1998, 131–132)[13]). It is true that dignity was not present from the beginning in the bloodstream of European law, due in part to the mainly economic and commercial nature of European integration during its first decades. Since the inclusion of dignity in constitutions and bills of rights, as well as in case law, is relatively recent, today it is still uncommon to find many judgements in which dignity is the *ratio decidendi*[14] of the argumentation of judges, except in Germany (but since it has more faces than the merely chronological, we will come back again to this point later).

---

[4] "In the Name of the Most Holy Trinity, [...] We, the people of Éire [...] seeking to promote the common good, with due observance of Prudence, Justice and Charity, so that the dignity and freedom of the individual may be assured [...]".

[5] Article 31 ("All citizens have equal social dignity and are equal before the law, without distinction of sex, race, language, religion, political opinion, personal and social conditions") and 41 ("Private economic enterprise is free. It may not be carried out against the common good or in such a manner that could damage safety, liberty and human dignity" – it should be noted that dignity is now seen as a barrier or shield protecting persons against capitalist excesses).

[6] "Portugal is a sovereign Republic, based on the dignity of the human person and the will of the people".

[7] "Respect for and protection of human dignity constitute the primary obligation of the State".

[8] "Everyone has the right to lead a life in keeping with human dignity".

[9] "We, the citizens of the Czech Republic [...], Resolved to build, safeguard, and develop the Czech Republic in the spirit of the sanctity of human dignity and liberty [...]".

[10] "[...] The constitution shall guarantee the inviolability of human dignity and the freedom and rights of the individual and promote justice in society".

[11] "[...] The dignity of the human being shall be protected by law".

[12] ECJ, Judgment of 9 October 2001, (case C-377/98 ECR I-7079).

[13] According to Hartley, "the general principles are, therefore, an independent source of law and there can be little doubt that the Court would have applied them even if none of the Treaty provisions [...] have existed". See also Tridimas's opinion: "Among the sources of Community Law, [the general principles of law derived from the laws of Member States] occupy a different position. They are unwritten principles extrapolated by the Court from the laws of the Member States by a process similar to that of the development of the common law by the English courts" (Tridimas 2006, 7).

[14] This is Serna's view regarding Spanish constitutional case law, cf. Serna 1995, 287–306, 298–306.

Dignity and Law

3. The relationship between dignity and law (particularly rights) could be summarised as follows: dignity has always been a historical presupposition for rights; but during centuries it went on unmentioned.

There is little doubt that dignity, like freedom, equality, and the general belief in man, is one of the ethical and cultural assumptions of constitutionalism from its origins (Habermas 2010a, 464–480, 469)[15]: the novelty of constitutionalism – the recognition of inviolable, not granted, human rights which precede the Constitution – was made possible because of the spreading of certain characteristic notions of Western societies, especially the dignity of every human being *qua* human being and the essential, basic, equality of all men. In the seventeenth century we find widespread and, in several European countries specific, manifestations of the equal dignity of every human being, to which the first pronouncers of constitutionalism appealed (Habermas 2010b, 352–353).[16] In England, Rainborowe said to Cromwell in the discussions within the Parliamentary Army: "the poorest he that is en England hath a life to live as the greatest he."[17] The contemporary literature similarly reflects a clear perception of dignity by ordinary people: just see the works of Calderón de la Barca (1642)[18] or later on, in the nineteenth century, those of writers so diverse as Melville and Dostoievsky. The *starets* (monk) Zossima, a character in *The Brothers Karamazov*, wonders: "after all, what am I worth that another man, a fellow creature, made in the likeness and image of God, should serve me?" (Dostoievsky

[15] "[a]fter two hundred years of modern constitutional history, we have a better grasp of what distinguished this development from the beginning: human dignity forms the "portal" through which the egalitarian and universalistic substance of morality is imported into law".

[16] Habermas refers to Levellers.

[17] According to the *Oxford Dictionary of Quotations*, this phrase was uttered by Rainborowe in Putney in 1647. Other sources attribute it to other people. It could well have been said by more than one person, since in the Parliamentary Army, as well as among Levellers and Diggers, everything was discussed. Cromwell was not in favour of the greatest possible degree of democracy and constitutionalism, even by the standards at the time, a fact that would help explain reactions like these.

[18] (*El Alcalde de Zalamea*, written around 1642). Pedro Crespo, the mayor of the small, remote town of Zalamea de la Serena, faces Don Alvaro de Ataide, a nobleman and captain of the royal armies passing through this small town, who has kidnapped and raped his daughter. When another commander, Don Lope, says to Pedro that he is under the obligation to suffer these kinds of things because of his low social status, Pedro responds that he is obliged fully to the King "with my property, but not with my honour. My goods and chattels and my life are the King's; but my honour belongs to my soul, and that is but God's" (act. I, scene III; the original reads:"*Con mi hacienda, / pero con mi fama no. / Al rey la hacienda y la vida / se ha de dar, pero el honor / es patrimonio del alma, / y el alma sólo es de Dios*"). That perception of human dignity, undoubtedly clear and alive in popular culture, did not imply any significant constitutional development in Spain at that moment, nor later. The Spanish constitutional situation at that moment amounted, at most, to something similar to what Rawls calls a "decent hierarchical" regime (see Rawls 1999, 59 ff.). The fact that these Calderonian notions would smoothly pass censorship suggests their general acceptance (in Spain, as in other monarchies of that epoch, the responsibility for publishing books was the monarch's, so that all publications were subject to censorship).

1880)[19] The main idea of *Memories from the House of the Dead*, written out of his Siberian prison experience, is that human dignity survives even in the most depraved prisoners (Dostoievsky 1862).

In a dramatically different context we find the following phrases in the novel *Moby Dick*:

> Men may seem detestable as joint stock-companies and nations; knaves, fools, and murderers there may be; men may have mean and meagre faces; but man, in the ideal, is so noble and so sparkling, such a grand and glowing creature, that over any ignominious blemish in him all his fellows should run to throw their costliest robes. That immaculate manliness we feel within ourselves, so far within us, that it remains intact though all the outer character seem gone; bleeds with keenest anguish at the undraped spectacle of a valor-ruined man. Nor can piety itself, at such a shameful sight, completely stifle her upbraidings against the permitting stars. But this August dignity I treat of, is not the dignity of kings and robes, but that abounding dignity which has no robed investiture. Thou shalt see it shining in the arm that wields a pick or drives a spike; that democratic dignity which, on all hands, radiates without end from God; Himself! The great God absolute! The centre and circumference of all democracy! His omnipresence, our divine equality!
>
> If, then, to meanest mariners, and renegades and castaways, I shall hereafter ascribe high qualities, though dark; weave round them tragic graces; if even the most mournful, perchance the most abased, among them all, shall at times lift himself to the exalted mounts; if I shall touch that workman's arm with some ethereal light; if I shall spread a rainbow over his disastrous set of sun; then against all mortal critics bear me out in it, thou just Spirit of Equality, which hast spread one royal mantle of humanity over all my kind! Bear me out in it, thou great democratic God! Who didst not refuse to the swart convict, Bunyan, the pale, poetic pearl; Thou who didst clothe with doubly hammered leaves of finest gold, the stumped and paupered arm of old Cervantes; Thou who didst pick up Andrew Jackson from the pebbles; who didst hurl him upon a war-horse; who didst thunder him higher than a throne! Thou who, in all Thy mighty, earthly marchings, ever cullest Thy selectest champions from the kingly commons; bear me out in it, O God! (Melville 1851, ch. 26)[20]

4. In some sense the quotation of Melville could not be more opposed to that of Dostoievsky, and still more so their respective contexts, democratic North America on one side and Tsarist Russia on the other. They only agree regarding the equal dignity of all human beings and its foundation. Besides the Christian origin of American democracy and its belief in the common man, a human dignity that can never be lost appears in the quotation from *Moby Dick*: a dignity that radiates from

[19] Before becoming a *starets* (monk), Zossima had served as an officer in the Czar's army. His wonder came upon him precisely after brutally and unjustly beating his assistant, Afanasi. At the time of the action described in the novel, serfdom was legal in Russia, and army officers dealt with their assistants not much better than with beasts.

[20] Despite chronological and cultural differences, it is noteworthy that similar ideas can be found in another text fifteen centuries earlier: "What is it that is about to be created, that enjoys such honour? It is man that great and wonderful living creature, more precious in the eyes of God than all other creatures! For him the heavens and the earth, the sea and all the rest of creation exist. God attached so much importance to his salvation that he did not spare his own Son for the sake of man. Nor does he ever cease to work, trying every possible means, until he has raised man up to himself and made him sit at his right hand" (J. Chrysostom, *In Genesin Sermo*, 2.1; we borrow the modern English version from the *Catechism of the Catholic Church*, 358).

God, reaches the last man and cannot be lost even if everything else is lost, even moral character, and – what was then so important in whalers – courage.

As mentioned, human dignity has been a hidden or latent assumption of constitutionalism and human rights since its origins (and before its origins), but it was neither attributed any specific legal character nor did anyone attempt to make it into the articles of a legal text. Since it was a presupposition, and it was pre-legal in nature, it was taken for granted. Only after World War II, as stated, dignity began to be laid down in international legal instruments, bills of rights and constitutions, as a reaction against the crimes committed by totalitarian regimes and the other horrors of that war (Calo 2012, 473–499).[21] From that date it has kept on permeating through an increasing number of legal instruments, domestic as well as international, to the point that today it is rare to find a recent bill of rights or constitution that does not mention it – with different wordings and intensities, depending on the case. Outside the European Union the Constitutions of Chile (1980),[22] Brazil (1988),[23] Colombia (1991)[24] and Peru (1993),[25] among others, state, recognise or proclaim dignity.

On the other hand, the transformation of man and human life into a subject of public policies and legislation that has taken place in our days explains why dignity is being referred to in many important legal and ethical debates. However, it seems

[21] Speaks of an "explicit turn to dignity" after WWII that worked "as the linguistic and substantive basis for human rights norms [and] fulfilled dignity's democratic promise [, as well as bringing] human dignity into the main of legal and political discourse" (p. 474). Calo emphasises that although in 1948 there was general consensus about dignity, it has now become "deeply contested" (pp. 473 ff., 475). Interestingly, in September 2012 the Human Rights Council of the UN approved, at the request of Russia and sixty other states, a resolution stating that traditional values common to all mankind have a positive role in the promotion and protection of human rights: the HRC "[…] reaffirms that a better understanding and appreciation of traditional values shared by all humanity and embodied in universal human rights instruments contribute to promoting and protecting human rights and fundamental freedoms worldwide". The Resolution also "stresses that human rights derive from the dignity and worth inherent in the human person" (see HRC, Twenty-first Session, Resolution "Promoting human rights and fundamental freedoms through a better understanding of traditional values of humankind: best practices", A/HRC/RES/21/3, 9 October 2012). Unlike in 1948, the passing of this Resolution left behind victors and vanquished and was only approved after serious disagreements: not to mention the fact that in recent years quite a number of resolutions were passed of a different or opposite meaning.

[22] At the moment of the writing of this Constitution, in 1980, there were relatively few constitutions explicitly affirming human dignity. The drafters were familiar with German and Spanish constitutions, but they chose wording differing from most other constitutions and rather sober: "Men are born free and equal in dignity and rights" (art. 1, para. 1).

[23] Art 1.III: "The Federative Republic of Brazil, formed by the indissoluble union of the states and municipalities and of the Federal District, is a legal democratic state and is founded on: […] III – the dignity of the human person" (see http://www.v-brazil.com/government/laws/titleI.html).

[24] Art. 1: "Colombia is a legal social state organized in the form of a unitary republic, decentralized, with the autonomy of its territorial units, democratic, participatory and pluralistic, based on respect of human dignity, […]" (English version: webpage of confinder.richmond.edu).

[25] Art. 1: "The defense of the human person and respect for his dignity are the supreme purpose of society and the State" (English text issued by the Peruvian Congress of the Republic, August 2006).

that neither its meaning nor its effects are clear, since it is invoked to defend contrary claims, as in the above example of the debate on euthanasia. We may ask, then, if the inclusion therein of human dignity makes any serious difference to law. Do any specific legal requirements derive from it, so that, for example, dignity could be used to resolve cases? Can the law define it with a minimum degree of accuracy? Could the attempt to define it, even if motivated by the laudable intention of ensuring its respect, become in one way or another detrimental to dignity? After all, small matter would human dignity be if the legislator were to 'create' or define it, as he defines, say, 'usufruct'. Small would be its relevance to law if from being its foundation and presupposition, it became its object, thus to be configured, defined and shaped. Having dignity, then, would be to fit into a concept that others have decided to use as a recognition criteria, as Robert Spaemann explains referring to human rights.[26] In Victorian England, Bagehot famously said that "one cannot make men good by Act of Parliament"[27]; for the same reason, no legal text is going to dignify us if we are unworthy (although it may be able to punish other people's attacks against our dignity). When 'dignity talk', as has happened with 'rights talk', comes into vogue, does dignity *ipso facto* become something more to the law than a *flatus vocis*? We believe that, for the mere fact of being an assumption, dignity is already more than a *flatus vocis*, but its inclusion in an article of a constitution, treaty or other legal instrument does not change its nature, or turn it as if by magic into something so legally operating as, for example, the *accessorium sequitur principale* principle in a dispute over the allocation of interest on a debt. YeThere are yet nuances and differences according to countries and constitutional cultures: in Germany and Spain, their respective constitutional courts have not dealt with dignity in the same way: in the former, *Menschenwürde* has become a part of its 'constitutional identity' while in Spain things have not gone that way notwithstanding the role assigned to dignity by the wording of Constitution.

What Is Dignity?

5. In ordinary language dignity refers to deservingness: to be worthy of something means to deserve something, for example, to be treated with respect. Recognising human dignity would then imply recognising that every human being deserves always to be treated as such, with all the respect that our fellow men and women owe us simply because we are human beings – according to Stith, respect should be our basic response when we are before a human being.[28] However, what that appropriate, worthy treatment consists of, depends on the understanding of mankind that we are starting from: we will understand the conduct due to a man as we understand

[26] Cf Spaemann 1991, 66; apud Serna 1998, 23–79, 46.

[27] As quoted in the webpage of Hillwatch.com, *Quotations on Parliament, the House of Commons and Cabinet Government.*

[28] Cf Stith 2004, 165–84, *passim.*

him – and the perception of man and his nature have changed, and, additionally, has become a matter of government and legislation. Hence, as Gregory explains, the threat that metaphysical naturalism entails to human dignity and human rights: if we are, after all, mere biology, a combination of molecules and energy, we are ultimately no different from algae or amoebae, and dignity and rights cannot be but fictions,[29] devoid of any solid foundation. As Max Scheler wrote, if man is no longer clear to man, one could hardly know what human dignity means. If we are just the last result of the evolution of our planet, if man is just the peak of vertebrate mammals, he is not, after all, more than a mammal vertebrate, because the peak continues to belong to the same as the rest of the pyramid. According to Spaemann, although there has always been violations of dignity of individuals or groups, after the scientific objectification has reduced the human being to a natural being (Spaemann 1991, 81–110, 106),[30] an object of research, our dignity has been conceptually threatened as never before. The disenchantment of the world identified by Max Weber in the early twentieth century (Weber 1992, 86 ss., 107 ss.) cannot tolerate notions like dignity unless it breaks and analyses it and finds it able to support a 'scientific' analysis.

This mistake – to understand man as a combination of molecules and energy – underlies the recognition of rights for animals. We do not object to recognising our duties to animals, that we do have, as to nature generally (Ballesteros 1992, 128–129),[31] but object to considering that animals can have genuine rights: the trouble lies in the recognition that after all man does not differ radically from animals, and therefore it is possible to consider that both animals and men are rights holders, and even dignity holders.[32]

[29] Cf. Gregory 2012, 224–230 and elsewhere.

[30] "[B]iological anthropology, psychology, and sociology can explain art, morality, religion, and even science itself, only from the point of view of survival strategies. For them, as noted by the celebrated psychologist Skinner, an archaic idea such as dignity is a hindrance".

[31] Relations between a man and an animal can never be of a legal nature because they lack the "ontological parity" mentioned by Ballesteros when he forwards the universality of unconditional respect to others as the foundation of law. Law adjudicates disputes between two human persons, not between men and animals. Even without ontological parity we have duties to animals, because it is good to behave in a certain way to animals, for example, by avoiding gratuitous cruelty. However, one can kill an animal to eat, or can have it for pleasure or for sport, which one could never do with a man.

[32] See Animals Protection Act enacted in the Federal District of México, February 26, 2002. The wording lavished here and there throughout the text is "dignified and respectful treatment of animals" *("trato digno y respetuoso a los animales";* see arts. 3, 4.xvii, xix and xxxviii, 6, 9.i and ii, 12.i and vii, 14, as well as the long Chapter VII, dealing with "The Dignified and Respectful treatment of Animals", comprising arts. 23 to 55). The Act does not say explicitly that animals have dignity, but it can be inferred from the above, since no one can be entitled to dignified treatment if he has no dignity. The art. 4, para. xxxviii, clarifies what is meant by dignity and respect: "[t] he measures this Act [...], the zoological rules for Mexico City, and the Mexican official norms establish to avoid unnecessary pain or distress during the time of possession or ownership, breeding, capture, transfer, display, quarantine, marketing, [etc.] of the animal", all of which sounds reasonable at first sight but hardly justifies the recourse to such a notion as (human) dignity.

6. What can we understand, then, when we speak of human dignity or when we read it in a legal text? To begin with: what did the drafters of the *Universal Declaration of Human Rights* have in mind when they recognised in its Preamble "the inherent dignity [...] of all members of the human species", or the framers of the German Constitution when they solemnly carved in the constitutional marble that "human dignity is inviolable"? Did they include it in the Declaration and in the Basic Law as a smokescreen to provisionally hide other deeper disagreements, as Habermas wonders? (Habermas 2010a, 467).[33] It may not seem so but for them human dignity simply did not require further explanation: everyone knew, more or less vaguely, what it meant, although they could not give a satisfactory philosophical account of it – and small wonder: there are quite a few things we abide by without being able to render a proper scientific description. Zachary Calo thinks that the general consensus at the time should not in retrospect be considered a smokescreen (Calo 2012, 473 ff., 475). Neither did our ancestors a century ago spend their time asking each other what a human being is, at least not the man in middle of the road in his daily life. According to the Norwegian philosopher Janne Haaland Matláry, in the West a remarkable fundamental ethical agreement was alive and visible until the sixties:

> For many centuries European democracies have shared approximately the same moral norms, derived from the ancient and Christian legacy. The Ten Commandments were more or less acceptable to all. These moral rules were also reflected in law and politics. There was no essential contestation of what should be taught in school or punished in the criminal code. The family was a given and natural institution; the right to life was not an issue in politics, and there was a basic agreement on what belonged to the private and the public sphere. True, different political ideologies had different views on the latter, and also on the role of the family in the economic and societal structure, but these were debates about the role of the state, of the relationship between economics and politics, and when it comes down to the anthropological issues, it was a debate over the existence of the soul – of whether man was simply material or not. (Matláry 2007, 20–21).[34]

Two basic formulations of dignity are frequently found: one of Judeo-Christian descent, which appeals to the *imago Dei* inscribed in man, and the other of Kantian roots, based on the autonomy of man. Now, in the age of Pico della Mirandola, Cromwell or Calderón de la Barca, Kant was not yet born, and even in the nineteenth century an American poorly educated novelist such as Melville surely knew little of the great philosopher of Koenigsberg, not to mention Dostoievsky, in whose works little Kantianism can be found.

To get an idea of what dignity means we can briefly recall the sense of dignity in each of these formulations and to what extent they are compatible with each other. We did not know modern-minded, articulated defences of dignity until the controversial speech by Giovanni Pico della Mirandola in 1486,[35] although this does not

[33] Habermas does not believe it was a smokescreen.

[34] Taylor 2007, *passim,* also thinks that until the sixties there existed in the West a great deal of a basic moral consensus.

[35] Pico della Mirandola's *Oration on the Dignity of Man* was a public speech challenging doctors of traditional schools – hence its antagonising style. Rather than defending human dignity as we

mean dignity was unknown before: in fact, Pico did not examine so much human dignity in itself as the dignity of the philosophical profession and the possibilities of human knowledge, as well as the liberal arts, which suggests that the former was not so controversial. Later on, the most important philosophical development is undoubtedly that of Kant in the *Groundwork of the Metaphysics of Morals* in 1785, which makes human dignity lie in man's autonomy or his ability to give himself a law that binds him. Kantian dignity would thus come to express the requirement that everyone respects the sphere of free will of each person. Over time, the European way of understanding dignity experienced a decisive change that, as Habermas writes, lies in the moralisation of individual freedom, in the wakeof Hugo Grotius and Samuel Pufendorf.[36] For Kant, human dignity requires us to deal with every man or woman as an end, never as a means, and so dignity lies in man's autonomy, that is, in the constitution of the will by which it comes to be a law to itself. However, why does this autonomy require absolute respect? Actually, human dignity and its requirement of absolute respect cannot be justified only on the properties that can be discovered in the human being: these properties can be signs of dignity, but not its cause ('no one can rise himself up by pulling the straps of his own boots', as the American dictum goes). That would explain the superiority of the human species over all other creatures, but not necessarily the dignity of every human being,[37] not to mention the absolute and permanent character of his or her dignity. The only possible way to understand the aspect of the human condition referred to by Kant and consisting of being an end in oneself, which could substantiate the requirement of absolute respect, is to have the human being understood as wanted for himself or herself.

If no one can rise up by pulling his own bootstraps, if nobody can get out of a lake by pulling his own ears up, the ultimate possible serious, solid, cause of human dignity would be in one way or another transcendent. Such a dignity would be conferred by something or someone that logically could never be equal or less than me: dignity would then be bestowed or derived, as in the argument of Pico della Mirandola, often considered as the prototype of the Renaissance philosopher.[38] Now

are concerned with in this research, Pico della Mirandola's point was the defence of the capacity of the human intellect as well as the dignity of philosophers (a fact that included him, incidentally) and displayed a handful of theses, typical of Renaissance syncretism. Human dignity as such is not the sole or principal topic of his presentation. He built dignity upon the Greek classics and the already traditional Judeo-Christian trend: man, created by God in his image and slightly inferior to angels. (This version: *Oration on the Dignity of Man*, translated from the Latin by Caponigri with an Introduction by Russell Kirk, Chicago, Henry Regnery, 1956.) Some of the works of Pico della Mirandola would be later translated by Thomas More.

[36] Cf. Habermas 2010a, 474.

[37] Cf. Spaemann 1991, 91–92 and Habermas 2010a, 473–4.

[38] Kirk thinks that "Pico [...] knew that no being can dignify himself: dignity is a quality with which one is invested; it must be conferred. For human dignity to exist, there must be a Master who can raise Man above the brute creation. If that Master is denied, then dignity for Man is unattainable. For despite all the cant concerning the dignity of man in our time, the real tendency of recent intellectual currents has been to sweep true human dignity down to a morass of mechanistic indig-

we must stop here for a while: have we said 'bestowed' or 'received' from some sort of on high, will European reader wonder? Our answer is that, rationally speaking this is likely to be the case. However, according to Habermas, mature secularist citizens who have left behind the teenager acne of a derailed secularism, should not renounce the sources of that Judeo-Christian concept, but rather translate them into secular language[39] without rejecting the religious understanding – such a rejection would imply giving up many aspects of our culture which experience suggests not to give away.

As concerns the everyday life of the law, and in so far as no particularly hard cases arise, to have the dignity of other citizens respected, admitting the basic traces of human dignity is enough, even if ordinary people cannot fully explain their ultimate reasons. Anyway, to explain that ultimate cause and why dignity is not at our disposal, no specific revealed religion is strictly required, but simply an awareness that dignity cannot be bestowed upon me by myself or by another like me, because *nemo dat quod non habet*. It is a natural way of reasoning that may afterwards benefit from Christianity, as it was the case in our historic experience: what Christianity really made with dignity was simply to build upon natural, previous layers. This could be seen when Christianity and pagan ius naturalism first met in Athens circa A.D. 51. Paul of Tarsus introduced to the intellectual élite of the time, gathered in the Areopagus, the new religion. To this end, he built upon Aratus's verses precisely on a point related to dignity: "For we are also [God's] offspring".[40]

We have mentioned the belief in man in relation to dignity and the origins of constitutionalism, and rightly so, but we cannot ignore that now those days are over in many countries. Agreement on fundamentals is gone. The disenchanted world, the recent consideration of man as an object of scientific research, legislation and even everyday public administration, the risks Scheler warned of in 1928, the loss of the fundamental agreement since the sixties, as well as a variety of other factors have led to a situation in which the belief in man and his dignity cannot be taken for granted (Negro 2009).[41] If Kantian or post-Kantian ideas of dignity, still common currency among European élites today, depended on the famous 'philosophical turn' that led to modernity, it could be compelled to give way when a new philosophical

---

nity. [...] Without God, Man cannot aspire to rank with Cherubim and Seraphim" (Russell Kirk, "Introduction" to Pico della Mirandola, pp. xvii–xviii).

[39] The constitutional, liberal, secular state should not neglect dignity sources coming from the Judeo-Christian tradition (debate with the then Cardinal Ratzinger at the Akademie Katholische Bayern, Munich, 2004, accessible on the Internet).

[40] See *Acts of the Apostles*, 17:19 and ff.; Aratus was a stoic poet of centuries 4th–3rd B.C. Interestingly, the audience did not seem to overtly reject the new message till Paul told them of the resurrection of the dead.

[41] The place of man in the political cosmos and the place of politics in today dominant vision seem to have changed. Negro argues that old, 'cratological', power-oriented politics no longer craves for colonising territories but the human person. Political ideologies have given way to 'bioideologies' that instead of dealing with political freedom or forms of government, tend rather to deal with man, the self, life, or sex. Interestingly, 'bioideologies' show less concern with the *res publica* or *agora* and are not altruist.

turn, the postmodernity turn, spreads throughout public opinion, as it is doing at a very quick pace. If so, the first thing that comes to mind is that, whatever the foundation of dignity, if we want it to be solid, *in re,* it should not depend too much on the turns that drive or have driven the various philosophical currents that over time came and went. Otherwise nobody could prevent that post-Kantian dignity may at some point be overtaken by another vision that, say, places the root of dignity elsewhere, or does not attribute much significance to it. The possibility of leaving Kantian ground seems to cause little concern to contemporary writers such as Sloterdijk or Žižek (2003). Charles Taylor is not misguided in arguing that strong standards of moral behaviour ask for proportionately strong nourishing sources, and for him the strongest ones came and still come from the Judeo-Christian *acquis* (Taylor 1989, 516).[42]

Challenges

7. Given the speed at which philosophical changes occur today, a new paradigm shift could happen in a relatively short time. In 2013, it matters not just whether our vision is Judeo-Christian, Kantian or post-Kantian, – all this could be left behind soon. As of today we cannot ignore that the new philosophical and anthropological trends of Posthumanism and Transhumanism create serious problems for dignity (Sandel 2007).[43] Some authors overtly reject the concept of human dignity, such as Steven Pinker (2008, 28)[44] and Ruth Macklin (2003, 1419–1421).[45] Posthumanism is based on premises that would sweep away everything upon which the Renaissance

[42] Taylor, not finding strength enough in our naturalistic humanism, heir of the Enlightenment, prefers to trust Judeo-Christian theism (p. 521). "I do think naturalist humanism defective in these respects-or, perhaps better put, that great as the power of naturalist sources might be, the potential of a certain theistic perspective is incomparably greater", as Dostoievsky showed insurmountably (p. 518). Just a point on Dostoievsky: his defence of theism is convincing, but he seems not to defend similarly the value of the human being, as if between divine law and human law an intermediate layer of natural law accessible to all were missing. He should have a more positive, favourable view of human nature and human reason because, having both been created by God, as he constantly reminds us, he should not seem so hopeless.

[43] Sandel refers to the 'perfection' that can produce biotechnology and contrasts 'gift' and 'domain'" (pp. 29 ff., 92 ff.), arguing that there is more freedom when we accept the gift for what it is, something given, untouchable. See his ideas on human dignity and giftedness in pp. 85 ss.

[44] He sees it as a religious concept and a conservative barrier to progress and freedom, against which fires an immoderate artillery that will not stop even at *ad hominem* arguments. Pinker gives importance to respect for the person, which sounds convincing but, on closer inspection, comes to result in treating everyone as he or she wants to be treated, which would not exclude the voluntary pact of slavery. Excessive emphasis on dignity as just 'autonomy' – which takes place when it is thought of in terms of 'capacity' or 'self-direction' rather than 'gift' – could give substance to Pinker's claim that in having autonomy, dignity becomes redundant.

[45] To Macklin, as to Pinker, rhetorical excesses and abuses of dignity provide ammunition for her attacks. She writes that it is a useless concept that can be removed without any loss of actual content (p. 1419). Note that the article of Macklin is not legal but medical.

humanism was built on, Pico della Mirandola and Kant included. Transhumanism, in turn, would establish strong inequalities between normal men and 'enhanced' ones. We come thus to a problem of disbelief in mankind rather than one of choice among several (for the most part far from new) understandings of man. When man's understanding gives way to disbelief in man, any democratic-minded constitutionalist will feel uncomfortable. In his *Rules for the Human Park* (Sloterdijk 2000; Habermas 2003), a provocative book that sends shivers down one's spine, where men are seen as beings to be tamed and grazed, not sufficiently different from animals, Peter Sloterdijk endorses the posthumanism that denies a fixed, immutable human nature, which seems to him to be malleable and politicisable.

We have said before that in everyday legal life a person with a reasonable dose of common sense, in so far as he or she does not have to face very hard cases, would not need a particularly deep study to respect the dignity of his or her fellow men and women. Nowadays this is also changing, first – at least in Spain – because of the difficulty of finding a reasonable dose of common sense alive and operating in our social life. To our mind, the decline of common sense would have consequences which are no less serious than the diffusion of certain minor immoral behaviour. Scientism, legalism, disuse of reasoning by analogy and its replacement by reasoning by evidence, the loss of the habit of reading by oneself in the book of nature and life, and the lack of confidence in our own judgement[46] undermine common sense, which seems to have given way to reports of experts (no matter how little reliability and common sense they are showing in the present economic crisis). Second, those serious problems, unknown to the man in the middle of the road till recently, are already before us every day: the terrible terrorism of our time and the War on Terror that justifies ignoring dignity, the possibility of patenting embryos and trading with them, the possibility of 'enhancing' the human species, and so on (Calo 2012, 473ff).[47]

Habermas is right in the desirability of respecting the original, religious sources of dignity, and shows both commendable mental flexibility and intellectual honesty, but, as the saying goes, things of this kind are 'easier said than done.' If the secularist projects of which there is no shortage in Europe go ahead, it will be difficult for religions to continue producing material to keep the fires alive, because those projects involve restricting religion to the strictly private sphere – a point of which our secularists seem to make a matter of honour. If religion-inspired visions and argumentations cannot play their full-blown roles in the public conversation, if they disappear from the forum and the *agora* where the tree of the *res publica* grows, little sap could be brought to it.

[46] "Well, who are you going to believe, me or your own eyes?" asks Chico Marx in the film *Duck Soup* (1933).

[47] According to Calo the notion of human dignity has shaped and been shaped by recent bioethical debates, particularly concerning the issue of genetic engineering and enhancement.

Is Dignity Legally Enforceable?

8. The number of international instruments, as well as national and sub-national constitutions, that have laid down dignity is now so large that we could not go into great detail even if we had twice the space we have, and all the more can be said of the case law of those countries. Besides space limitations, it should be noted that not all those constitutions would be worth the effort since rhetorical proclamations of scarce actual content abound, not to mention formulations that simply repeat others with little consideration for real circumstances. As for case law, although there is also plenty of it, relatively few verdicts delve into the roots of the problem, and an even smaller number use it as *ratio decidendi*. As stated before, Spanish constitutional case law contributes little and generally fails the test of using dignity as *ratio decidendi* in a minimum substantial number of rulings. Slight is the difference, therefore, between dignity being present or absent from the wording of the Spanish Constitution, even when it comes to sensitive issues like abortion, which the Constitutional Court in practice ends up leaving to the legislature, almost *etsi dignitas non daretur* or as if it were not in the Magna Carta but in secondary legislation or in any kind of an inferior statute not binding on the legislature.

It is with all such precautionary attitudes, and with that scenario taken into account, that we must look out for dignity in the legal reality of the European Union. We know that the fact of its not being mentioned in the U.S. Constitution does not negatively affect how dignity fares in that country, and we know that its presence in the Spanish Constitution is not noticed too much. Yet, we also know that its presence in the German one is. Does dignity play an important role in the jurisprudence of the European Union and the countries that have proclaimed it in their constitutions? Today, the countries that proclaim human dignity in their constitutions are many, inside and outside the Old Continent. More than once, one can see that the presence of dignity in the Constitution does not make much difference, as deduced from the fact that many of the judgments mentioning it could easily come to the same conclusion without doing so. If we let ourselves be carried along by this train of thought, we would be tempted to agree with Macklin when she considers dignity a useless concept; although for a reason contrary to hers: the useless thing would not be dignity – too great to be captured by any legal written norm – but the belief that just laying it down in a legal article or provision without guaranteeing its actual content, or rhetorically alleging it in a timely and untimely manner, will make any serious difference.

'Damages', instead – to name but one example tin contrast is a legal concept much more specific and suitable for litigation. Can we hence assume that 'damages' should be preferred to 'dignity' in the legal world? In a case in which damages are at stake, can judges do without it in their reasoning? Obviously not. Instead, they can do without 'dignity' with far less harm to their argumentation. The cause is not dignity being unimportant but its being far too profound and embracing, so that it bases, justifies and in a way encompasses law. In the German legal world, dignity has possibly served more than in others; at least, it has served to prevent treating human beings as things on occasion (see, a bit later, reference to the judgement of Karlsruhe on the German Aviation Security Law).

We will thus come to a close by devoting our attention to four judgements, although they are not the only relevant ones nor do they include all important positions on the issue. All four originated in Germany and each of them shows one (or more) relevant aspect.

(A) In the widely-known judgement of the ECJ in *Omega,*[48] originated in Germany, the judges could perhaps have reached the same conclusion without resorting to dignity. In this case the free circulation of goods conflicted with the protection of dignity, so dear to the *Grundgesetz,* and the Luxembourg judges, instead of directly protecting the dignity by themselves, chose as their course of action to endorse the German protection. The reasoning of Advocate General Christine Stix-Hackl was brilliant. She posed the case as one of a clash between that freedom and the fundamental right to dignity, to be resolved by balancing interests but without incurring excessive restriction of the fundamental rights involved. For our purposes, she considered that human dignity "undoubtedly forms one of the fundamental interests of any society committed to protecting and respecting fundamental rights. The finding that a fundamental interest of society has been affected is determined in the light of national value judgments" (Stix-Hackl 2004, paragraph 104).[49] Stix-Hackl defended a discretion to respect the understanding of human dignity according to the respective national and 'constitutional identities', since it is not understood exactly the same way in all member states (Stix-Hackl 2004, paragraph 100–102). (Making my dignity a matter of 'balancing' is another question that may make me feel uneasy, but this would take us beyond the province of our present topic).

(B) The recent European ruling on patentability and commercial use of frozen embryos[50] also originated in Germany. It is characterised by the Luxembourg Court openly wielding dignity, referring to it half a dozen times in a not a very long judgement: in this case dignity can be considered the *ratio decidendi*, for it is the main substantive argument. The case has several procedural aspects (what margin of manoeuvre is left to national courts), but as for its material part, (what a 'human embryo' is) the Court reaches the conclusion of excluding the patentability of embryos on the basis of dignity. The decision on embryos is an example of how the new challenges we referred to above (bioethics, genetic engineering) end up bringing dignity to the fore. This litigation originated in Germany and not by chance but because of the specific weight of dignity in its Fundamental Law, its 'constitutional identity' and its political culture. Reading the arguments of the judges one wonders

[48] See *Omega Spielhallen- und Automatenaufstellungs-GmbH v Oberbürgermeisterin der Bundesstadt Bonn,* case C-36/02 (ECR I-9609,14 October 2004). It was a game room in Bonn where a machine was installed with games that involved simulated homicides. In whole or in part, these machines came from another EU country, which added the dimension of free movement of goods.

[49] Opinion of Advocate General.

[50] See *Brüstle against Greenpeace*, case C-34/10, 18 October 2011.

whether they could reach the same result, were dignity absent from the *Grundgesetz*: the answer is probably not, or not that easily. Thus in this case dignity has proven some efficacy; a somewhat *negative* efficacy – preventing the treatment of human embryos as patentable and marketable material – which is entirely correct, from our point of view, since dignity should not be promoted, much less produced, but respected and defended against those who do not respect or in some way undermine it. The basic attitude regarding dignity should be respect, which, as Stith explains, is mainly negative in nature and always refers to each individual, since dignity is not collective (Habermas 2010a, 473–474),[51] except in an analogical sense.

(C) The German Federal Constitutional Court (BVG), in the judgement on the *LuftSiG*[52] uses dignity correctly, and *en passant* the judges do not fail to seize the opportunity to give us a lesson, albeit brief, in the philosophy of dignity *more kantiano*. Again, dignity is brought on stage as a result of the brutal current challenges: in this case, the response to terrorism after the attack on the Twin Towers in New York in September 11, 2001. The Court considered incompatible with the Basic Law article 14.3 of the Act, which authorised the German federal army to shoot down commercial aircrafts occupied by civilians, were they hijacked and used as projectiles, as had happened in New York. According to the judges, that would be contrary to the right to life (art. 2.2 of the Basic Law) and the guarantee of human dignity (art. 1.1) because the use of force against those planes would affect people not involved in the crime, and the State, by using their deaths as a means to save other people, would turn them into objects, denying the respect due to every human being for itself. The passengers and crew in such a case would no longer be the masters of their own lives, a fact that would render them into mere objects not only tof criminals but also of the State, which in such a situation would treat them as the equivalent of mere objects of a rescue operation aimed to protect other persons. Under dignity of article 1.1 of the Basic Law, to intentionally kill people in such a desperate situation under cover of a legal authorisation is entirely unacceptable.

Karlsruhe rejects the opinion held by some people that in a hypothetical case similar to September 11, people on the hijacked aircraft are in any case doomed to die, and says that life and human dignity enjoy the same constitutional protection irrespective of the duration of the physical existence of the individual concerned.

All in all, this decision makes another good product from the German judicial factory. In this case dignity is quite the opposite of a rhetorical *flatus vocis*. As usual,

---

[51] "The attitude and act called 'respect' brings forth much more adequately than 'value' the distinctively individual priority of persons, allowing our common humanity to be a reason for each person's separate significance" (Stith 2004, 167). According to Stith, people are respected; things are valued, are expendable. While respect is negative and individual, valuation is active, sets goals, and could in the end lead to an optimisation program. According to Habermas, too, dignity is individual.

[52] *Luftsicherheitsgesetz (LuftSiG)* judgement of 15 February 2006, BVerfG, 1 BvR 357/05. The claim had been filed, among others, by an aviation commander. The ruling has another interesting aspect not affecting us now, the competence for taking such action. The Court denied the *Bund* its alleged exclusive legislative competence because it is a matter in which the *Länder* have a shared competence.

we must ask: would the judges have reached the same conclusion, were dignity absent from the Basic Law? Using other arguments – such as the right to life, art. 2.2, the principle 'ends do not justify means' or the absolute prohibition of killing an innocent – it could perhaps be so, but there is no denying that dignity in this case made things easier for the Karlsruhe judges. Interestingly, the constitutional judges indirectly give two partial but plausible responses to the question about what dignity consists of: the prohibition of dealing with another human being as an object, and the characterisation of dignity as one being loved or appreciated for oneself. Furthermore, and with a specifically Kantian mind, the Court, when it came to form its opinion, did not forget to refer to the autonomy of the people in the hijacked plane. Finally, another remarkable aspect of this judgement is the 'negative' efficacy of dignity. Summing it all up, this is another decision that serves to undermine Pinker's and Macklin's claims that dignity is useless or stupid.

(D) In the BVG's recent judgement on welfare and minimum living,[53] dignity would not be strictly necessary, because the constitutional principle of the Social State (art. 20.1 of the Basic Law) would probably suffice to reach the same decision. The constitutional judges often speak of the subsistence minimum in line with human dignity, but prudently refuse to give specific quantities (they merely say that the benefits granted by the law in question cannot be *a priori* considered as insufficient to guarantee the subsistence minimum according to dignity). The fundamental right to the guarantee of a subsistence minimum comes from connecting dignity with the principle of the Social State and ensures for every person in need the material conditions necessary for physical survival and minimal participation in political, social and cultural life, all of which is no longer at the disposal of the legislature, although the specific quantities and details will from time to time have to be updated by the legislator.

Not for the first time, the problem of social assistance and minimum subsistence jump to the highest litigation,[54] but if we apply the same test of asking what conclusion would the judges have arrived at if had it not been for dignity being formally proclaimed in the Constitution, the effectiveness of dignity seems questionable in this case. Several totalitarian or at least authoritarian political regimes, provided abundant welfare benefits to the lower classes of their countries. If, however, the German Constitution lacked the principle of Social State, this issue probably would have not been brought before the Federal Constitutional Court.

By Way of a Conclusion

9. Human dignity has at least three aspects that are relevant to law to some degree – let us leave aside for now the fact that on closer inspection it might come to have more. First, it creates an obligation to respect; second, it forbids treating others as

[53] BVerfG, 1 BvL 1/09 of February 9, 2010.

[54] Remember the ECJ ruling *Stauder*, cit.

objects, and third, it prohibits relationships of very disproportionate dominance between humans, because of the aforementioned requirement of ontological parity. History shows that there have been millions of slaves not treated as things, and in Rome many of them became *liberti,* but still slavery is radically incompatible with dignity. The same could be said of transhuman enhancement and Sloterdijk's shepherding of some humans by other humans.

We think that dignity, as with other major notions – life, love, beauty, the good, conscience, solidarity and a moderately long list – overflows law. It cannot capture them properly, and there is nothing wrong with this. Now, even though the law cannot produce or promote dignity, maybe it can protect it or reprimand those who violate it. Historical experience shows that whenever serious rights have existed, stronger than acts of statute, fundamental or equivalent,[55] human dignity was at work behind the scenes, working as a background, or as a foundation, be it mentioned or not in legal texts.

Our practice of human dignity depends heavily on our understanding of man, which explains how the disappearance of the basic consensus and the new challenges of the twentieth century have brought dignity to the forefront, where it had never been before because it was taken for granted.

If agreement on the fundamentals fails or disappears, no legislator will be able to produce it *ex novo* by an Act of Parliament. Yet – half a loaf is better than none – we may take agreement on procedurals seriously; an attitude that would probably put us on the right track towards a more substantial agreement. Let us imagine humanity is a freshly created club – *The Humankind Club* – and that its members, the human beings, share nothing and have no agreement at all. For obvious reasons they have to make afresh a set of rules. Imagine they have common sense and a natural desire to survive, thrive, and be left in peace like the Hobbits in the Shire. Imagine Rule 1 states that 'all human beings are equal.' If they take it seriously and elaborate upon it, over time they will be likely to develop an agreement of a more fundamental nature, and then, if the 'slippery slope' theory works, eventually they will find themselves accepting something like human nature, human rights, a minimum mutual respect for all their fellow club members, and the rule of law.

Like many a basic notion that work well only when taken for granted, dignity is comfortable when backed by an agreement on fundamentals and by strong sources of basic meaning. Before joining battle in Trafalgar, Nelson just harangued his men: "England expects that every man will do his duty." Had the sailors decided to hold meetings to discuss the ideas of 'England', 'man' and 'duty', the battle would have been won by the French-Spanish fleet, which outnumbered Nelson's. Dignity thrives and feels more comfortable when it lives on solid soil made up of those 'underlying' emotions (*The Economist* 2006, 11),[56] moods and trained, quasi

[55] Or, for that matter, the equivalent to 'fundamental'. We cannot discuss herein rights denominations and visions, as these are beyond the scope of this essay, although the topic is not without relevance.

[56] According to historian Sir Lewis Namier, what matters most about political ideas is the 'underlying emotions' the 'music' to which ideas are a mere 'libretto' – perhaps of a very inferior quality.

instinctive mental dispositions, that Plato thought to be on the chest of men – hence the importance of common sense.

Constitutions cannot work miracles, but the sum of the constitution, the political culture, 'constitutional identities', and traditions, although performing no miracle, will at least be able to do the kind of things which fall within its reach: solving conflicts, limiting power, enforcing some degree of rule of law, and protecting rights, at least to a certain degree.

Bibliography

Ballesteros, J. 1992. *Sobre el Sentido del Derecho*, 2nd ed. Madrid: Puento.

Bustos, G. 2006. La función jurisdiccional en escenarios de pluralismo constitucional. Sáiz Arnáiz, A. (Dir.). *Integración Europea y Poder judicial*. Oñate: IVAP.

BVerfG, 1 BvL 1/09 of February 9, 2010.

Calderón De la Barca, P. 1642. *The Mayor of Zalamea*.

Calo, Z. 2012. Human dignity and health law: Personhood in recent bioethical debates. *Notre Dame Journal of Law, Ethics & Public Policy* 26(2): 473–499.

Cardinal Ratzinger. 2004. Debate at the Akademie Katholische Bayern. Munich.

Constitution of Belgium. 1994.

Constitution of the Czech Republic. 1992.

Constitution of Finland. 2000.

Constitution of Greece. 1975.

Constitution of Ireland. 1999.

Constitution of Italy. 1947.

Constitution of Lithuania. 1992.

Constitution of Portugal. 1976.

Court of Justice of the European Communities (ECJ) *Stauder v. City of Ulm* (case 29/69 ECR 419), 1969.

Court of Justice of the European Communities (ECJ) judgment *Nold, Kohlen-und Baustoffsgrosshandlung v. Commission* (case 4/73 ECR 491), 1974.

De Miguel, C. 2013. Eficacia interna de las sentencias del Tribunal Europeo de Derechos Humanos. *Revista Quincena Fiscal* 19: 61–83.

Dostoievsky, F. 1862. *The house of the dead*.

Dostoievsky, F. 1880. *The Brothers Karamazov*.

Duck Soup. 1933.

ECJ, Judgment of 9 October 2001, (case C-377/98 ECR I-7079).

ECR, Omega Spielhallen- und Automatenaufstellungs-GmbH v Oberbürgermeisterin der Bundesstadt Bonn, case C-36/02 (ECR I-9609,14 October 2004).

Gregory, B. *The unintended reformation*. Cambridge, MA/London: Belknap Press of Harvard University Press.

Habermas, Jürgen. 2003. *The future of human nature*. Wiesbaden: Polity Press.

Habermas, Jürgen. 2010a. The concept of human dignity and the realistic utopia of human rights. *Metaphilosophy* 41(4): 464–480.

Habermas, Jürgen. 2010b. Das Konzept der Menschenwürde und die realistische Utopie der Menschenrechte. *Deutsche Zeitschrift für Philosophie* 58(3): 343–357.

Hartley, T. 1998. *The foundations of EEC law*. Oxford: Oxford University Press.

Macklin, R. 2003. Dignity is a useless concept. *British Medical Journal* 327: 1419–1421.

Matláry, J. 2007. *When might becomes human right*. Leominster: Gracewing.

Melville, H. 1851. *Moby Dick*.

Negro, D. 2009. *El Mito del Hombre Nuevo*. Madrid: Ediciones Encuentro Año.
Rawls, J. 1999. *The law of peoples with the idea of public reason revisited*. Cambridge, MA/ London: Harvard University Press.
Pinker, S. 2008. The stupidity of dignity. *The New Republic*, 2008, May 28.
Sandel, M. 2007. *The case against perfection*. Harvard/London: Harvard University Press.
Serna, P. 1995. La dignidad de la persona como principio del Derecho público. *Derechos y Libertades* 4.
Serna, P. 1998. El derecho a la vida en el horizonte cultural europeo de fin de siglo. In *El Derecho a la Vida*, ed. Massini, C. y Serna, P. Pamplona: Eunsa.
Sloterdijk, P. 2000. *Rules for the human park*. London: Belknap Press.
Spaemann, R. 1991. La naturaleza como instancia moral de apelación. In *El Hombre: Inmanencia y Transcendencia. Actas de las XXV Reuniones Filosóficas*. Pamplona: Eunsa.
Stith, R. 2004. The priority of respect. *International Philosophical Quarterly* 44(2): 165–184.
Stix-Hackl, C. 2004. *Opinion of Advocate General on Omega (case 36/02, ECR I-9609, 14 October 2004)*. Delivered on 18 March 2004.
Taylor, C. 1989. *Sources of the self*. Cambridge: Cambridge University Press.
Taylor, C. 2007. *A secular age*. Cambridge: Harvard University Press.
The Economist. 2006. June 24.
Tridimas, T. 2006. *The general principles of EU law*. Oxford: Oxford University Press.
Weber, M. 1992. Wissenschaft als Beruf, 1919. In: Mommsen-Schluchter-Morgenbrod (eds). 2006. *Gesamtausgabe*, Tübingen.
Žižek, S. 2003. Bring me my Philips Mental Jacket. *London Review of Books* 25(10): 3–5.

Erratum to: The Convergence of the Fundamental Rights Protection in Europe

Rainer Arnold

R. Arnold (ed.), *The Convergence of the Fundamental Rights Protection in Europe*, Ius Gentium: Comparative Perspectives on Law and Justice 52,
DOI 10.1007/978-94-017-7465-9

DOI 10.1007/978-94-017-7465-9_13

The chapter "**Human Dignity and European Constitutionalism: Flatus Vocis or Ratio Decidendi?**" was unfortunately omitted from the original version of this book. Now the chapter is added as chapter 12 at the end of the book after the chapter 11 "**Access to Services of General Economic Interest Under Article 36 of the Charter of Fundamental Rights EU and the National Law**."

The online version of the updated book can be found at
http://dx.doi.org/10.1007/978-94-017-7465-9

R. Arnold (ed.), *The Convergence of the Fundamental Rights Protection in Europe*, Ius Gentium: Comparative Perspectives on Law and Justice 52,
DOI 10.1007/978-94-017-7465-9_13

Printed by Printforce, the Netherlands